JESSE LIBERTY'S
from scratch
PROGRAMMING SERIES

Visual Basic® 6

from scratch

Robert P. Donald

Gabriel Oancea

201 West 103rd Street,
Indianapolis, Indiana 46290

Visual Basic® 6 from Scratch

Copyright © 1999 by Que Corporation

International Standard Book Number: 0-7897-2119-8

Library of Congress Catalog Card Number: 99-62606

Printed in the United States of America

First Printing: September, 1999

01   00   99   4   3   2   1

Trademarks

Warning and Disclaimer

Executive Editor
Tracy Dunkelberger

Acquisitions Editor
Michelle Newcomb

Development Editor
Bryan Morgan

Managing Editor
Lisa Wilson

Project Editor
Tonya Simpson

Copy Editor
Linda Seifert

Indexer
Cheryl Landes

Proofreader
Andy Beaster

Technical Editor
Stuart Snaith

Novice Reviewer
Robert Bickford

Media Developer
Andrea Duvall

Interior Design
Sandra Schroeder

Cover Design
Maureen McCarty

Copy Writer
Eric Borgert

Layout Technicians
Susan Geiselman
Mark Walchle

Contents at a Glance

Introduction   1

Part I   Lay Out the Foundations   **9**

Chapter 1   Introduction to Visual Basic   11

2   Brief Language Overview   27

3   Starting the Project   39

4   Validating the User Through a Login Form   53

5   Enhancing the Login Dialog   71

6   Creating a First Executable   83

Part II   Develop the User Interface: Adding UI Elements and Base Functionality   **91**

Chapter 7   Extending the Project with a New Form   93

8   Adding Controls to the Main Form   111

9   Implementing a Data-Entry Form   133

10   More About Forms and Controls: Properties, Methods, and Events   145

11   Creating an Explorer-Style Form Using TreeView and ListView Controls   165

12   Designing a Master-Detail Style Form   187

Part III   Add Functionality: Creating Persistent Objects   **201**

Chapter 13   Elementary Object-Oriented Concepts   203

14   Defining the Interface: Properties and Methods   227

15   Elementary Database Concepts: Persisting the State of Our Objects   247

16   Adding Class Persistence   269

17   Finalizing the Classes in the Project   293

Part IV   Integrate the Subsystems: Finalizing the Application   **305**

Chapter 18   Saving and Retrieving Data   307

19   Retrieving and Editing Objects from the Database   335

20   Error Handling and Reporting   347

21   Printing   363

Part V Final Touches: Debugging and Testing the System 381

Chapter 22   Finalizing the Project   383

     23   Application and Project Settings   397

     24   Debugging and Testing the Application   407

     25   Revisiting the Process   423

     26   Distributed Components: The Way of the Future   429

Part VI Appendixes 445

Appendix A   COM, ActiveX, and Automation   447

     B   Visual Basic Controls   451

          Index   459

Table of Contents

Introduction   **1**

Part I Lay Out the Foundations   **9**

Chapter 1 Introduction to Visual Basic   **11**

Introduction 11
A Tour of the Visual Basic Environment 12
    The Title Bar 14
    The Menu Bar and Menus..14
    The Toolbar 17
    The Project Explorer Window 17
    The Properties Window 18
    The Forms Window..18
    The Form Layout Window 19
    The Toolbox 19
    The Code Window..19
Saving Your Work 21
    Saving to a New Directory 21
Types of Visual Basic Projects...23
Types of Visual Basic Files 23
Customizing Your Environment..24
Next Steps 25

Chapter 2 Brief Language Overview   **27**

Variables...28
Datatypes 29
    Can I Define My Own Datatypes? 30
Arrays 31
Constants 33
Operators 34
Forms 35
Subroutines 35
Functions 35
Modules 36
Classes 37
Naming Conventions 37
Next Steps 38

Chapter 3 Starting the Project   **39**

Introduction 39
Defining the Project Used Throughout the Book.............................39
Project Requirements 40
    Administrative Services 41
    Customer Services 42
Creating a Visual Basic Project from Scratch 43
Creating the Login Form 45
    Adding a Label to a Form 47
    Setting Tab Stops on a Form 50
    Setting Shortcut Keys...51
Running the Login Form 51
Next Steps 52

Chapter 4 Validating the User Through a Login Form   **53**

Introduction..53
Adding Procedures and Functions 53
What Are Modules?..54
Contents of a Standard Module 55
Adding a Standard Module and Creating the `CheckLogin` Function 57
Adding Code to the Form...61
A Closer Look at the `If...Then` Statement 64
A Closer Look at Using `MsgBox`..65
Next Steps 69

Chapter 5 Enhancing the Login Dialog   **71**

Introduction..71
Set Command Button Properties on the Login Form.......................71
Command Button Properties 73
Add Code to the Cancel Button 76
Events and Event-Driven Programming 77
    Event Handlers..78
    Command Button Events...78
Next Steps 81

Chapter 6 Creating a First Executable   **83**

Introduction..83
Interpreted Languages...83
Making a Visual Basic Executable..85
Next Steps 90

Part II Develop the User Interface: Adding UI Elements and Base Functionality 91

Chapter 7 Extending the Project with a New Form 93

Add a Form to the Project 93
Add a Menu Bar to the Main Form 95
    Creating Child Menus 97
    Creating a Control Array to Store Menu Items 100
Implementing the Menu Click Event...101
Adding a New MDI Child Form 102
    Creating and Working with Objects 103
Adding Custom Properties and Methods to the Form 105
    Implementing Property Procedures 106
Next Steps 110

Chapter 8 Adding Controls to the Main Form 111

Introduction...111
Adding the Windows Common Controls Reference....................................112
Adding a StatusBar Control to the Main Form 113
    Properties of the StatusBar Control 114
    Adding Panels to the StatusBar Control 115
    Extending StatusBar Functionality Using Code 118
Adding an ImageList Control to the Main Form 119
    Properties of the ImageControl...119
    Adding Images to the Control 122
Add a ToolBar Control to the Main Form..123
    Properties of the ToolBar Control 123
    Adding ToolBar Buttons..125
    Adding Drop-Down Buttons 126
    Adding Code for the ToolBar Control 129
    Implementing the `ButtonMenuClick` Event 130
Next Steps 132

Chapter 9 Implementing a Data-Entry Form 133

Adding Controls to the Customer Form 133
    Changing the Font Property of a Control 135
    Adding a MaskedEdit Control..136
Other Properties for the Built-In Controls 138
Handling Events from the Controls on the Customer Form 141
    `GotFocus` and `LostFocus` 141
    The `Click` Event..142
Next Steps 143

Chapter 10 More About Forms and Controls: Properties, Methods, and Events   145

Adding a New Form for Products 145
    Adding Controls to the Form 146
    Adding a ComboBox Control 146
    Adding a Common Dialog Box Control 148
Adding Code for the Product Form 148
    Opening a File Using the Common Dialog Control 149
    Handling Errors in Code 152
    Handling the Save and Cancel Click Events..153
Form Interaction—The `Activate` and `Deactivate` Events..............................155
Adding a New Form to Display an Image—The Image Control 156
    Adding Code to Show the Form 159
Adding a New Form to View a Document—The RichTextBox Control 160
    Adding Code to Handle Form Resizing 160
Next Steps 162

Chapter 11 Creating an Explorer-Style Form Using TreeView and ListView Controls   165

Adding a New Customer Orders View Form 165
Adding the TreeView Control...166
    Properties of the TreeView Control 168
Adding the ListView Control 169
    General Properties of the ListView Control..170
    Other Properties of the ListView Control 172
Adding the ImageList Controls 172
Adding a Custom Resources File to the Project 173
Adding Code to Resize the Splitter Form 174
    Resizing the Controls..175
    Changing the Mouse Shape Depending on the Mouse Position 176
    Executing the Resize—Handling Mouse Events 178
Adding a Right-Click Pop-Up Menu 182
    Activating the Pop-Up Menu from Code 182
Next Steps 185

Chapter 12 Designing a Master-Detail Style Form   187

Adding the Order Entry Form 187
    Adding a Grid to the Form 189
    FlexGrid Properties 189
    Completing the Order Form 191
Adding the Order Item Dialog Box 193
Adding Code to the Order and Order Item Forms 196
Next Steps 199

Part III Add Functionality: Creating Persistent Objects   **201**

Chapter 13 Elementary Object-Oriented Concepts   **203**

Object-Oriented Concepts 204
  Classes, Objects, and Properties 204
  Methods 206
  Encapsulation 207
  Inheritance 207
  Polymorphism...208
Classes in Visual Basic 208
  Properties 209
  Property Procedures..210
  Methods 211
  Class Initialize and Class Terminate 211
Adding a Customer Class to the Project 212
  Property Get Procedure...214
  Property Let Procedure...215
  Property Set Procedure...216
Adding the Product Class and the Order Class to the Project......................218
Using Enumerations for Order Status Properties 221
Next Steps 225

Chapter 14 Defining the Interface: Properties and Methods   **227**

Validating Property Values 228
Implementing Calculated Property Values...232
Verifying Required Properties 233
Expanding the Order Class to Contain a Collection of Order Items 234
  Modeling the Order 234
  Creating the OrderItem Class..236
  Creating the OrderItemColl Class 238
  Adding Order Items to the Order Class...242
Next Steps 245

Chapter 15 Elementary Database Concepts: Persisting the State of Our Objects   **247**

What Is a Database? 247
Database Concepts 249
  Tables 249
  Columns 250
  Rows 250
  Primary Keys 251
  Foreign Keys...252
  Indexes 253

SQL Primer 253

    INSERT 253

    UPDATE 254

    DELETE 255

    SELECT 255

Setting Up a Data Source Name (DSN) 256

Defining the Project Schema 259

    TCustomers 259

    TProducts..260

    TUsers 260

    TOrders 261

    TOrderItems 261

Using ActiveX Data Objects (ADO) for Database Access.............................262

    Opening a Database Connection...263

    Inserting Records 263

    Updating Records..264

    Deleting Records 264

    Selecting Records 264

ADO, OLE DB, ODBC—Help! 265

Next Steps 267

Chapter 16   Adding Class Persistence   **269**

Encapsulating the Database 269

    Creating the DbSession Class...270

    Connection.Open in More Detail 273

    Creating a Global DbSession Object 273

Adding Persistence to the Customer Class 273

    Saving a Customer 274

    Finding a Customer 277

    Deleting a Customer 279

Adding Persistence to the Product Class 280

    Saving a Product..280

    Finding a Product..281

    Deleting a Product 281

Adding Persistence to the Order, OrderItemColl, and OrderItem Classes 282

    Helper Methods in the OrderItem Class 282

    Saving and Deleting the Collection of OrderItem Objects 284

    Retrieving the Collection of OrderItem Objects 285

    Saving an Order 287

    Finding an Order 290

Next Steps 291

Chapter 17 Finalizing the Classes in the Project   **293**

Add Database Support to Validate the User..293
Adding Class Events 295
Next Steps 304

Part IV Integrate the Subsystems: Finalizing the Application   **305**

Chapter 18 Saving and Retrieving Data   **307**

Adding Persistence to the Customer Form 307
  Introduction to Three-Tiered Software Topology 308
  Modify the Customer Form to Make It Persistent....................................309
Adding Persistence to the Product Form 312
Adding Persistence to the Order Item Form 314
  Retrieving a List of Products from the Database 315
  Populating the Products Combo Box 317
  Refreshing the Controls on the Form..319
  Saving Changes and Returning a Flag..320
  Handling the Form Close User Action 323
Adding Persistence to the Order Form 324
  Populating the Customer List 324
  Integrating with the Persistent Order Object...326
Next Steps 334

Chapter 19 Retrieving and Editing Objects from the Database   **335**

Adding a Search Form for the Customer...335
  Designing the Form 335
Implementing Code for the Customer Find Form 338
Next Steps 346

Chapter 20 Error Handling and Reporting   **347**

Adding a Tabular Data Form for the Customer..347
  Designing the Form 347
Adding Code to the Customer List Form 349
Error Handling and Reporting in Detail 357
Next Steps 361

Chapter 21 Printing   **363**

Adding a Custom Printer Selection Dialog Box 363
  Designing the Form 364
  Adding Code to the Select Printer Dialog Box..365
  Setting Printer Properties 366
Printing an Order 369
Next Steps 379

Part V   Final Touches: Debugging and Testing the System   **381**

Chapter 22   Finalizing the Project   **383**

Finalizing the Customer Orders Form...383
Adding an About Form 390
Adding Help to the Application 394
Next Steps 395

Chapter 23   Application and Project Settings   **397**

Application Settings...397
Project Settings 400
Conditional Compilation and Preprocessor Usage 403
Next Steps 405

Chapter 24   Debugging and Testing the Application   **407**

Introduction to Debugging..407
  Compile-Time Errors 407
  Exceptions...408
  Runtime Errors...409
Debugging Techniques 409
  Monitoring Variable and Expression Values at Runtime 410
  Changing the Value of Variables While Debugging.......................415
  Changing the Code While Debugging 415
  Changing the Next Statement to Be Executed 416
  Error Handling Considerations When Debugging 417
  Using Breakpoints and Stepping Through Code 418
  Using Conditional Breakpoints 419
Testing the Application 420
Next Steps 421

Chapter 25   Revisiting the Process   **423**

Analysis...423
Design 424
Implementation 425
  Graphical Design of the UI 425
  Adding Objects 426
  Integrating the System 427
Documentation and Testing 428
Next Steps 428

Chapter 26 Distributed Components: The Way of the Future   **429**

Introduction 429
Advantages of Distributed Components...430
Splitting the Projects 433
Project Settings 437
Next Steps 443

Part VI Appendixes   **445**

Appendix A COM, ActiveX, and Automation   **447**

Implementing COM Interfaces...448
Microsoft COM-Based Technologies 449

Appendix B Visual Basic Controls   **451**

Standard Properties, Methods, and Events 451
Intrinsic VB Controls 453
    CheckBox 453
    ComboBox 454
    CommandButton 454
    Data..454
    DirListBox, DriveListBox, and FileListBox 454
    Frame 455
    HScrollBar and VScrollBar 455
    Image..455
    Label 455
    Line 455
    ListBox 456
    Menu..456
    OptionButton 456
    PictureBox...456
    Shape..457
    TextBox 457
    Timer 457

Index   **459**

Foreword

Welcome to *Jesse Liberty's Programming From Scratch series*. I created this series because I believe that traditional primers do not meet the needs of every student. A typical introductory computer programming book teaches a series of skills in logical order and then, when you have mastered a topic, the book endeavors to show how the skills might be applied. This approach works very well for many people, but not for everyone.

I've taught programming to over 10,000 students: in small groups, large groups, and through the Internet. Many students have told me that they wish they could just sit down at the computer with an expert and work on a program together. Rather than being taught each skill step by step in a vacuum, they'd like to create a product and learn the necessary skills as they go.

From this idea was born the Programming From Scratch series. In each of these books, an industry expert will guide you through the design and implementation of a complex program, starting from scratch and teaching you the necessary skills as you go.

You may want to make a From Scratch book the first book you read on a subject, or you may prefer to read a more traditional primer first and then use one of these books as supplemental reading. Either approach can work: which is better depends on your personal learning style.

All of the From Scratch series books share a common commitment to showing you the entire development process, from the initial concept through implementation. We do not assume you know anything about programming: From Scratch means from the very beginning, with no prior assumptions.

Although I didn't write every book in the series, as Series Editor I have a powerful sense of personal responsibility for each one. I provide supporting material and a discussion group on my Web site (www.libertyassociates.com), and I encourage you to write to me at jliberty@libertyassociates.com if you have questions or concerns.

Thank you for considering this book.

Jesse Liberty

Jesse Liberty
From Scratch Series Editor

About the Authors

Bob Donald has been working professionally in the software industry for 11 years. In that time, Bob has designed and built software using C++, Visual Basic, and Java. He has gained valuable experience on a variety of operating systems including Microsoft Windows (3.1, 95, and 98), Windows NT (3.51 and NT 4.0), Macintosh, and UNIX.

Bob has also been a guest speaker to various organizations including the Boston Area COM Users' Group and the Connecticut Object-Oriented Users Group (COOUG). He also has published material in *Distributed Computing Magazine*.

Currently at ONTOS Inc., Bob contributes to the design and implementation of their E-Commerce Web-enabling technology and constantly evaluates new technologies as they apply to future products.

Gabriel Oancea has been writing code since he was 13. Fortran was the language *du jour*, and the future—according to sci fi novels—did not include personal computers. In the last 15 years, he has developed software in C, C++, Visual Basic (since version 1.0), and Java, on a variety of platforms, including major flavors of UNIX, Windows, and Windows NT.

He has worked for both large and small companies in North America and Europe. He specializes in design and architecture of large-scale distributed systems using COM and/or CORBA.

Currently Gabriel is a principal software architect for ONTOS, Inc. He is involved in the design and development of their revolutionary E-Commerce Web framework.

Dedication

Thank you to Patty, Bobby, and Alex for your patience.

And to those of you who embark on a journey beyond self-imposed limits, don't look back.

—Bob Donald

To John Galt.

—Gabriel Oancea

Acknowledgments

We want to thank ONTOS, Inc. and Macmillan Computer Publishing for their help and support. Thanks also to Jesse Liberty and Steve Zag for the opportunity to write this book.

Introduction

The Audience for This Book

This book is aimed toward novice programmers, programmers experienced using another language, and students or weekend hobbyists interested in learning a new programming language. Throughout the book, we walk through the development of a complete application using Visual Basic 6.0. Along the way, specific Visual Basic topics are introduced and explained.

If you have programming experience in another language but don't know where to begin to develop a Visual Basic application, this book is for you. We start from scratch by defining a problem to be solved and then continue throughout the book building a complete application. In doing so, we cover the development environment, common controls, and the Visual Basic language. This process allows you to get a jump start in developing applications in Visual Basic without having to read an entire book on the subject first.

If you are a student learning programming skills and don't know Visual Basic, this book is for you. In addition to presenting the Visual Basic Development environment and the language, we cover programming concepts as part of building the application. Hopefully in this process, your programming skills become elevated as you progress through the book.

Last but not least, if you are a weekend hobbyist and just love learning new stuff about developing software, this book is also for you. This is your chance to build an application in Visual Basic and gain an insight into the process of software development.

Conventions Used in This Book

The following are some of the unique features in the *From Scratch* series.

 An icon in the margin indicates the use of a new term. New terms will appear in the paragraph in *italics*.

EXCURSION

What Are Excursions?

Excursions are short diversions from the main topic being discussed, and they offer an opportunity to flesh out your understanding of a topic.

With a book of this type, a topic might be discussed in multiple places as a result of when and where we add functionality during application development. To help make this all clear, we've included a Concept Web that provides a graphical representation of how all the programming concepts relate to one another. You'll find it on the inside cover of this book.

 Notes offer comments and asides about the topic at hand, as well as full explanations of certain concepts.

 Tips provide great shortcuts and hints on how to program in Visual Basic more effectively.

Warnings help you avoid the pitfalls of programming, thus preventing you from making mistakes that will make your life miserable.

Also, code listings are provided throughout the book. Each code listing has a heading that includes the name of the Visual Basic module and the filename in which the module is stored. For example, a form module named Form1 and saved in the file Form1.frm will have the following code listing heading:

Form1(Form1.frm)

The Approach This Book Uses to Teach Visual Basic

Rather than presenting Visual Basic as a logical grouping of topics centered around the Visual Basic language, this book takes you through the development of an application from start to finish. You learn how to program in Visual Basic as you go. You begin by learning a quick introduction to Visual Basic in order to establish a base level of knowledge. This includes a tour of the Visual Basic development environent and a very high-level overview of the language. The introductory information is then revealed in more detail throughout the rest of the book.

After the introduction, the project used throughout the book is defined. In each chapter, you are taken through the development of a specific part of the application. The project starts out simple and expands throughout the remaining chapters. This allows basic topics to be discussed up front and then allows us to migrate to more complex topics as the chapters move on. By the end of the book, you will complete a working application that demonstrates the capabilities of Visual Basic. Most importantly, you have developed an understanding of Visual Basic and the skills required to be a Visual Basic developer.

The Concept Web gives you a roadmap of the structure of this book. A legend accompanies the Concept Web to illustrate the elements in the web. The web starts from the VBFS project, which is the application you build in this book. From the main project, you develop forms and classes in a series of steps. Each step involves learning new concepts. The development of each form teaches the properties and methods of the most-used ActiveX controls.

Building the application deals with many Visual Basic programming concepts. The numbers within the web elements represent the chapter numbers where the element is presented.

The Application

We wanted to pick an application that is conceptually familiar to most people. Hopefully it is also interesting and complex enough to cover a broad depth of Visual Basic topics and still be able to completely develop it in one book. To that end, the application you build in this book is a virtual store that involves customers, projects, and orders.

When the application is complete, you will be able to enter customers and products into a database through the application. You can then browse the products and create new orders for a customer. This order status is then tracked through the application based on whether the order is brand new, the products on the order have been shipped, the customer has been billed for the order, or the customer has paid. Building an application to support this involves many facets of Visual Basic programming, as you will see.

The application does not pretend to be a commercial application. It is only intended to be a vehicle for learning Visual Basic. Therefore, if you come across anything in the application that you believe could be done better, you are challenged to do just that. In a learning environment, striving to make things better improves the learning experience as you gain more insight.

Chapter Highlights

Chapter 1 presents the Visual Basic development environment. This environment provides everything you need to develop an application for somebody to use. It provides the means by which you can design some of the user interface (the part of the application the user sees), enter the code (which is the set of commands run by the computer), debug the application, and observe exactly how the application is running.

Chapter 2 presents a quick overview of the Visual Basic programming language to give you a head start in understanding the language before you get into writing some code. Don't let this chapter worry you. The information in this chapter is covered in more detail in the remaining chapters.

In Chapter 3, we define the application in more detail. This gives you a better understanding of what you are going to build.

Then, in Chapter 4, you start the development of the application by creating your first form, which validates a user. This involves creating a form for the user to enter his or her name and a password. This information is used to verify the user and grant him or her access to the use of the application.

Chapter 5 involves creating command buttons and handling events. This covers the concept of an event and how to trap an event in your code. Additionally, this adds more functionality to your login form by addressing such issues as tab order and key commands.

You create your first executable in Chapter 6. This chapter applies only if you are not using the Visual Basic Working Model Edition. An executable can be generated from your Visual Basic project and then distributed to those people you choose.

In Chapter 7, you create the main form for your application and start adding menus. After you have logged in to the application, the main form is the central point for providing access to the application features such as browsing customer and product information and creating orders. The menus available from the main form provide the navigation to these features.

In Chapter 8, you add additional functionality to the main form by adding support for a toolbar and a status bar. The toolbar provides quick access to menu commands by providing a set of buttons, each representing a menu command. The status bar is a control that displays text to the user about the status of the activity the user is currently engaged in. This status bar is generally found near the bottom of an application window.

In Chapter 9, you create the customer form for displaying and editing customer information. In building the customer form, you add controls and write code that responds to events from the controls.

In Chapter 10, you create a product form that builds on the work you did in Chapter 9. In building the product form, you also deal with new controls such as the Image control, ComboBox control, and RichTextBox control.

Chapter 11 involves creating a browser of customers and orders. This browser is implemented as a form that enables you to list your customers and view the orders associated with each customer. This chapter covers the TreeView control, the ListView control, and the ImageList control.

You then create a more complex form in Chapter 12 for creating new orders. This form supports creating multiple order items as part of the order. Here you use the Microsoft FlexGrid control in support of displaying the order items.

In Chapter 13, you jump into the concept of classes. Some object-oriented concepts are presented in order to gain conceptual insight into the meaning of classes. After that, you create a customer, product, and order class that you build upon in the next few chapters.

You add complexity to the classes in Chapter 14 to support the concept of required properties, calculated properties, and some data validation. Support for order items is added to the Order class. This deals with creating classes that contain lists of objects.

The next step with the classes is to add database persistence. Database persistence is the capability of the class instances to save themselves to a database. Additionally, class instances must be able to be re-created based on the data stored in a database. Before adding this database persistence, Chapter 15 presents a database primer for those readers not familiar with relational databases. This chapter covers database constructs (databases, tables, columns, rows), the Structured Query Language (SQL), data source names, the database schema used by the application, and the use of ActiveX Data Objects (ADO) for communicating with the database.

You then add class persistence in Chapter 16. This chapter takes the material covered in Chapter 15 and applies it to the implementation of your customer, product, and order classes.

In Chapter 17, you expand your use of the database. Because you are on the topic of database interaction at this point in the book, you add support for validating the user based on user information present in the database. Also, the relationship between the Order class and the OrderItem class presents an interesting issue with regard to automatically updating an order total when a new order item is added to the order. This issue can be addressed using events in Visual Basic. To illustrate this, you add event support to the classes that collectively represent an order.

Chapter 18 deals with adding support to your forms to use the classes you completed in Chapter 17. When this is complete, the forms can create the appropriate objects based on information in the database. The forms will also be capable of creating new objects that result in creating new records in the database.

Chapter 19 involves creating a customer find form. This form is then used to allow the user to enter some customer information to search the database to find a particular customer.

In Chapter 20, you add a tabular data form that will allow the user to see a list of customers. We also deal with the issue of error handling and reporting.

Chapter 21 demonstrates how to add printing support to your application. Printing an order will be used to illustrate miscellaneous printing techniques.

In Chapter 22, you add some final touches to your Explorer-like form. We also present issues related to adding help to the application.

Chapter 23 presents an overview of the project and application settings.

Chapter 24 deals with the process of debugging your application and presents some debugging techniques.

Chapter 25 is a summary of the process you went through in this book.

Now that the project is complete, Chapter 26 presents an alternative approach to partitioning your application. This involves taking the current project and splitting it into two projects. One project is for the part of the application that deals with the user interface features. The second project contains the code that can be used by more than one application and entails creating a dynamic link library. This is a very common approach and is discussed in more detail in this chapter.

What You Need to Get the Most Out of This Book

It is possible for you to pick up this book and just read it. However, if you really want to get the most out of it, we suggest you work along with us in programming the application. To do this, you need a computer capable of running Visual Basic 6.0. If you have not purchased Visual Basic 6.0 on your own, the Visual Basic Working Model Edition is provided on the CD-ROM as part of this book. This version of Visual Basic is limited, however, and cannot be used to produce applications for you to distribute to other people to use.

Most importantly, you must set aside some of your free time to devote to reading this book and the development of the application. I assume that because you picked up this book and started reading it, Visual Basic is intriguing to you and you want to have a better understanding of the product. Now is the time to take action and transform your goal of learning Visual Basic into a reality.

Next Steps

If you have not already installed Visual Basic, install the version of Visual Basic you purchased or install the Visual Basic Working Model Edition from the CD-ROM that came with the book. After Visual Basic is installed, begin with Chapter 1.

Part I

Lay Out the Foundations

In this chapter

- *Introduction*
- *A Tour of the Visual Basic Environment*
- *Saving Your Work*
- *Types of Visual Basic Projects*
- *Types of Visual Basic Files*
- *Customizing Your Environment*

Chapter 1

Introduction to Visual Basic

Introduction

If you are interested in developing professional software applications that run on a Windows platform, Visual Basic is for you. Visual Basic (VB) is simple, quick, and easy to master. You and I are going to start from scratch and build a complete application in Visual Basic. Prior programming experience is not required to gain an understanding of Visual Basic when reading this book. This book is also targeted to users who have written code in another programming language such as C++. By the time you finish reading this book, you will have written a complete Visual Basic application.

In this book we are going to develop an application, and in the process explore Visual Basic topics as we encounter them. This is different than other books on software languages that present the language and leave you to apply it in building an application on your own. This way we can discuss Visual Basic features and capabilities in the context of what we are building.

Part I of this book tours the Visual Basic environment. The tour of the VB environment introduces the different parts of the environment and familiarizes you with it. During the initial introduction of the Visual Basic development environment, we will not go into depth on what all the different parts do. We will go into details when we build the application as necessary.

Next, we cover some introductory VB topics, and then define in more detail the application we are going to build. The application is a virtual store. There are two classes of users for the application: store employees and store customers. The user designated as a store employee has the ability to maintain products. The user designated as a customer can browse and purchase products.

After defining the application, we start by creating a VB project and build the first form. We end Part I by creating and running our first Visual Basic executable.

Let's get started on our journey to learn Visual Basic. At this point, it is assumed you have already installed Visual Basic on your computer. If you have not, you might want to do so now. This enables you to follow along with the book in building the Visual Basic application.

A Tour of the Visual Basic Environment

Let's begin by touring the Visual Basic environment. Start Visual Basic by selecting it from the Start menu on the taskbar. When Visual Basic starts up, you are presented with a New Project dialog box similar to the one in Figure 1.1.

Figure 1.1

The Microsoft Visual Basic New Project dialog box.

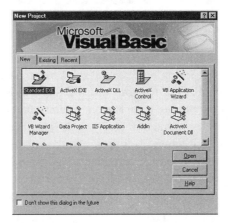

This box has three tabs across the top that enable you to create new projects, open existing projects, and quickly open a recently used project. This dialog box will become familiar to you as you continue to work with Visual Basic. Select each tab window by clicking on the tab name. If there are more items in the window than can be displayed, you will notice a scrollbar on the right side of the window. Use this scrollbar to move the items up and down to view them. After the desired icon is in view, you can open it by clicking the icon to select it, and then clicking the mouse on the Open button. You also can double-click the icon in the window to select it and automatically open it. We will revisit this dialog box later when we get into the development of our project.

A *project* in Visual Basic is the collection of several different types of source files that make up your program. After you open the project, you are able to edit the source files through the Visual Basic environment.

An *application* is the final program that is used by people. An application can be made up of one or more Visual Basic projects. You focus on one project for your application through most of the book, and then learn how to create an application with more than one project in Chapter 26, "Distributed Components: The Way of the Future."

For now, click the Standard EXE icon on the New tab. You are presented with the default Visual Basic development environment shown in Figure 1.2.

Figure 1.2

The Microsoft Visual Basic development environment.

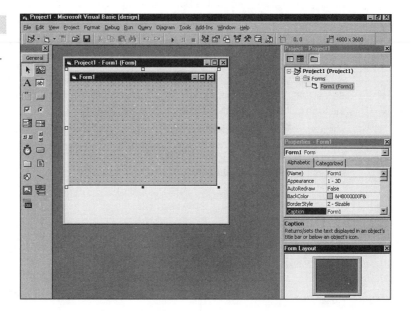

Familiarize yourself with the workspace that is currently open. Depending on the version of Visual Basic you have installed, you might see differences between what is on your screen and what you see in this book. If you see a difference, don't worry about it; you still can use your version of Visual Basic for the project in this book. The differences you'll see are mostly the components that are installed for each version (we discuss more about components later). The version of Visual Basic that we have installed on our computer is the Enterprise version. This is the full-blown version of VB that has all the options available to a developer. You also can purchase the Learning Edition and Professional Edition depending on your needs. There exists another version of VB that you can't purchase—Visual Basic Working Model Edition is usually provided free. We have included this version on the CD for you to install and use.

EXCURSION

The Different Versions of Visual Basic

The Visual Basic Learning Edition includes all the intrinsic controls, the grid control, the tab control, and the data bound controls. This version also includes Learn VB Now (a multimedia CD-ROM title) and full online documentation.

The Visual Basic Professional Edition includes all the features from the Learning Edition and additional ActiveX controls. This version also includes the Internet Information Server Application Designer, Integrated Data Tools and Data Environment, Active Data Objects (ADO), and the Dynamic HTML Page Designer. Additional documentation is provided in the form of the Visual Studio Professional Features book.

The Visual Basic Enterprise Edition is the most comprehensive version for creating distributed applications. It includes all the features of the Professional Version. It also comes with other tools, including SQL Server, Microsoft Transaction Server (MTS), Internet Information Server (IIS), Visual SourceSafe, and SNA Server. Additional documentation is provided in the form of the Visual Studio Enterprise Features book.

The Visual Basic Working Model Edition is very limited but can be used as a Visual Basic learning tool. It cannot create an executable file for the purpose of distributing applications. Also, the only type of project you can create is an application. For example, you cannot create Dynamic Link Libraries with this version.

The Title Bar

Across the top of the Visual Basic application you see Project1 - Microsoft Visual Basic [design] as shown in Figure 1.2 and Figure 1.3.

Figure 1.3

*The Visual basic
title bar.*

Title bar

The first part of the title is the name of your project. Whenever you start a new project in Visual Basic, your default project name is Project1. Later, we will explain how to rename the project (and all other objects for that matter). The next part of the title is the name of the application. In this case, it is Microsoft Visual Basic. The last part of the title is [design]. This tells you that you are in design mode. You are in the mode of developing an application.

The Menu Bar and Menus

The menu bar is just below the title bar. In general, menu bars consist of one or many menus. Each menu normally has a logical grouping of menu items that correspond to the name of the menu. Figure 1.4 shows the top-level menu bar within Visual Basic.

Figure 1.4

The top-level menu bar in Visual Basic.

Menu bar

As you can see, there are many menus within Visual Basic. Don't worry if it seems overwhelming at this point. You will become familiar with the menu bar as we progress through the book. As a start, take a closer look at a menu. Click on the File in the menu bar. The menu appears below the mouse cursor as in Figure 1.5. After the menu appears, you can move the cursor down over the menu. Each available menu item is highlighted as you move over it. After the desired menu item is highlighted, use the mouse to left-click or press the Enter key on the keyboard to activate the menu item and perform its intended action. You can move the cursor off the menu then left-click to cancel the menu at any time.

Figure 1.5

The Visual Basic development environment File menu.

The following items are included on the File menu:

- Icons
- Normal text
- Grayed text
- Underlined characters
- Key sequences (such as Ctrl+N)
- … (ellipses)
- →(right arrow)

Each of these items has a specific meaning and is discussed in the following sections.

Icons

The icons on menus are a visual representation of the action with which the menu item is associated. The icon on the menu may also show up elsewhere on a toolbar (we will discuss this later in the chapter). The idea is that once you associate an icon with a task, you can be assured the next time you see the same icon that it represents the same task. For example, a picture of a printer is on the Print menu item of the File menu. Clicking the Print menu item with the mouse prints the contents of the window. If you come across the same picture of a printer elsewhere in the application, it most likely has the same meaning, and in this example prints the contents of the window.

Normal Text

The normal text (not grayed) on a menu item is the name of the task the menu item performs.

Grayed Text

Grayed text has the same meaning as normal text. However, it also means that the menu item is unselectable, or disabled, at this time. Some menu items are only available depending on the context of the application. In Figure 1.5, for example, notice the menu item Save Selection on the File menu is grayed. This is a result of not having anything selected.

Underlined Characters

The underlined characters in a menu are used to indicate accelerator keys, also known as mnemonics. You can press the Alt key to focus the application on the menu. You then have the option to press any key that corresponds to an underlined character on the menu bar. Try Alt+F. This enables you to select and show the File menu. When the File menu is up, you can type a key to select a menu item. Again, you want to type a key that corresponds to an underlined character on the desired menu item. At this time, you can press the O key to open the File Open dialog box.

Shortcut Keys

Shortcut keys are key sequences that show up to the right of the menu item text. They represent the key combination that invokes the menu item. As an example, if you press Ctrl+O the File Open dialog box appears.

... (Ellipses)

Ellipses on a menu item indicate that selecting it will bring up a dialog box for the purpose of presenting or gathering more information.

→ (Right Arrow)

The right arrow indicates a submenu. After you briefly highlight the menu item, the submenu appears. You can then move the cursor over the submenu and make a choice.

Take the time to scan the submenus by clicking File and moving the mouse across the menu bar. Another way to do this is to click the first item on the menu bar, such as File, and then use the keyboard's right and left arrow keys to move from one menu to another. The up and down arrow keys enable you to move up and down the selection on a menu. As you look at an individual menu, you will notice a few things that make up the menu. When you are finished scanning the menus, move the cursor off the menu and click to cancel.

The Toolbar

The toolbar is just below the menu bar. The toolbar contains a row of icons that when pressed, cause an action to be taken. If the icons on the toolbar are not familiar to you, move the cursor over the icons (do not click on the icon). After a second or two, a ToolTip appears. The ToolTip tells you what the icon does if you click it.

In Figure 1.6, you can see the Standard toolbar displayed within Visual Basic. Notice the two vertical lines at the beginning of the toolbar. If you press the left mouse button and hold it on these lines, you can move the toolbar. Move the toolbar right and left (as you are holding down the left mouse button). Now, press the left mouse button on the vertical lines and move the toolbar down. This enables you to undock the toolbar and make it a floating window. After the toolbar is floating, press the left mouse button and hold on the title bar of the floating toolbar. Now, move the toolbar back to its original position below the menu bar and release the mouse button.

Figure 1.6

The Standard toolbar in Visual Basic.

The Project Explorer Window

The Project Explorer window is a structured view of the major parts of your project. This window uses a tree control to display the contents of your project. A *tree control* is another user interface control that displays a hierarchy of items. In this case, at the top of the tree is the project itself. Under the project are folders that contain groups of similar items. For example, in Figure 1.7 you can see the Forms folder. Under the Forms folder is a list of forms. Currently, there is only one form in your project.

Figure 1.7

The Project Explorer window.

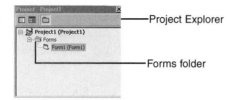

Project Explorer

Forms folder

The Properties Window

The Properties window enables you to see and modify properties of Visual Basic objects. Examine an object by clicking Form1 in the Project Explorer. The Properties window now displays all the properties of the form. There are two tabs in the Properties window that enable you to see the properties alphabetically or by category. Use the scrollbar to look at all the properties. The Properties window is shown in Figure 1.8.

Figure 1.8

The Properties window.

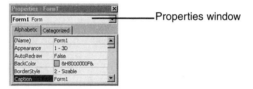

Properties window

The Forms Window

The Forms window enables you to graphically design a form. In Visual Basic, forms are windows that you design to display data and gather data from users. Several types of controls are available to assist you in the development of a form. These controls include labels (to display data), text boxes (to enter data), and command buttons (to perform a defined action). You can use the toolbox to choose which controls you want to put on the form. After the controls are on the form, you can move them around, resize them, and modify their properties. We will start playing around with this form after we start the project. The Form window is shown in Figure 1.9.

Figure 1.9

The Form window.

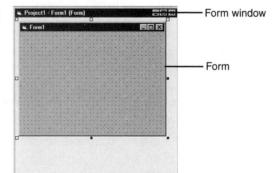

Form window

Form

The Form Layout Window

The Form Layout window shows how big a form is in relation to the screen. It also displays the position of the form when it is displayed after the project is built and running. Use the Form Layout window to set the form position. Press and hold the left mouse button over the form in the Form Layout window. Without letting go of the mouse button, move the form anywhere on the screen and let go of the mouse button. This position is the relative position of the form on the screen when the application is running. The Form Layout window is shown in Figure 1.10.

Figure 1.10

The Form Layout window.

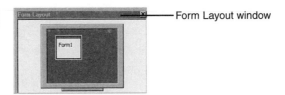
Form Layout window

You also have the option of right-clicking the mouse to display a pop-up menu. This pop-up menu has additional settings that can be set, including the window startup position. For example, the window startup position can be set to Center Screen to automatically center the window onscreen when it is first displayed.

The Toolbox

The Toolbox is made up of a set of controls that are available to you to place on forms. For example, you have Label controls that enable you to place text on a form. You can place a TextBox control on a form for a user to type in some information. And, you can add a command button for which you can write code in response to a user click. We will discuss these controls later in our project. It is easier to explain and understand what these controls do and how to use them in terms of a real application. For now, the Toolbox is where you go to get controls to place on a form. The Toolbox is shown in Figure 1.11.

The Code Window

There are a few different ways to open the Code window. You can select a form from the Project Explorer window by clicking on a form item. When the form is open and displayed you can double-click the form to open the Code window containing the code associated with the form. Instead of double-clicking, you can click the View menu and select the Code menu item. Or, you can right-click a form or module in the Project Explorer window and select the View Code option.

Figure 1.11

The Toolbox.

If you've been involved with programming in any other language, the Code window will be the most familiar to you. This window is where you write the actual code within your Visual Basic project. It is an editing window where you type the statements and commands that are executed as part of the running application. Notice the two drop-down boxes at the top of the Code window (see Figure 1.12). The one on the left tells you which object you are editing. You can also use this drop-down list to select another object to edit. The drop-down box on the right is the name of the procedure or function you are currently editing. This drop-down list also enables you to select another procedure or function, which is part of the object you are editing.

Figure 1.12

The Code window.

Saving Your Work

It is important to save your work every now and then just so you don't lose it if the computer inadvertently shuts off. When you exit Visual Basic, it automatically prompts you to save your work if you have not already done so. Let's save the project we opened at the beginning of the chapter. Click the File menu on the menu bar. Move the cursor down to the Save Project menu item and click it. Because you have not previously saved the project, Visual Basic prompts you for the location and file-names of the objects within your project. You see a dialog box like the one shown in Figure 1.13.

Figure 1.13

The Save File As dialog box.

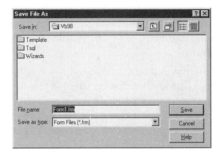

Visual Basic saves your files to the default location of the installation directory of VB. Although you can choose to save your projects here, it is recommended that you save to another location. Let's walk through the steps required to save a project to a new directory.

Saving to a New Directory

Use the combo box at the top of the Save File As dialog box (as shown in Figure 1.13) to choose a drive. Pick The C: drive by clicking the down arrow on the combo box, highlighting the Drive (C:) element in the list, and then left-clicking the item.

You should now be at the root of C: drive. Click the Create New Folder icon. This creates a new folder and requires you to name it. Type VBFS, and then press Enter. Double-click the VBFS folder you just created. You should now be in the VBFS folder and you are finished setting the location for the project.

The next thing you want to do is name the files. The filenames default to the name of the object and have the file extension based on the type of object being saved. We discuss more about file types later. The name currently in the dialog box is Form1.frm. For now, use the name given to you by Visual Basic and click the Save button. After the form is saved, you are prompted for the name of the file to save the project information. This defaults to <*the name of the project*>.vbp. Your project name is currently Project1, which translates into Project1.vbp. Accept this and save the project by clicking the Save button.

Now, you might have Visual SourceSafe installed. If you do not, things are simpler. If you do, you will see a dialog box like the one shown in Figure 1.14.

EXCURSION
Visual SourceSafe and Source Code Control

Visual SourceSafe is a software product sold by Microsoft. This product integrates with Visual Basic to provide source code control directly into your Visual Basic development environment. If you have Visual SourceSafe installed on your computer, it is automatically set up to be used by Visual Basic (which is why you may see this dialog box while using Visual Basic on your computer).

Source code control is useful in developing software products. It gives you the capability to check in your code when you are finished making changes to it. This puts the code into a secure place to prevent accidental changes. If you need to make changes, you check out the code, make the changes, and then check it back in. You also have the added benefit of specifying comments each time you check in your code. This enables you to specify a description of the change.

You also can create a label for the current state of the code that is checked in. This enables you to retrieve the complete set of code using the label, even if you continue to make changes to the code. Over a period of time, you will most likely have several labels. You can get the state of the code for each label if you need to and compare versions to identify which code changed from one version to the next.

If you plan to develop software to sell, you should consider using a source code control product to help you manage your code.

Figure 1.14

The Source Code Control dialog box.

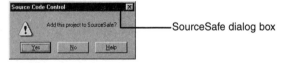

SourceSafe dialog box

For the rest of this book, click the No button when this dialog box appears. If you click the Yes button, it is assumed you are familiar with and know how to use the source code control system.

Your project is now saved. In the development of any project, you want to make sure you periodically save so that you minimize the possibility of losing your work.

Types of Visual Basic Projects

You might have noticed there are several types of projects you can create when you start Visual Basic. Table 1.1 describes each to give you an idea of the breadth of applications you can create with Visual Basic.

Table 1.1   Visual Basic Project Types

Project Type	Description
Standard EXE	A normal application with a user interface
ActiveX EXE	A COM control standalone server
ActiveX DLL	A COM control in-process server
ActiveX Control	An ActiveX graphical UI control
VB App Wizard	Creates an application by prompting you with options
VB Wizard Manager	Creates a wizard with several pages
ActiveX Document DLL	Creates an OLE document in-process server
ActiveX Document EXE	Creates an OLE document out-of-process server
AddIn	Creates a Visual Basic add-in
Data Project	An application with additional data access support
DHTML Application	Creates a Web-based application
IIS Application	Creates an IIS-based application
VB Enterprise Edition Controls	Creates an application that has an extensive set of controls in the Toolbox

Types of Visual Basic Files

We have just taken a brief tour of the Visual Basic development environment and have come across several new items such as projects, forms, controls, and VB code. Each of these saves information to your hard disk when you save the project. Additionally, each of these has a corresponding file type designated by a three-letter file extension. Table 1.2 lists the file types used by Visual Basic.

Table 1.2   Visual Basic File Types

Extension	Type of File
.frm	Form file
.bas	Basic file
.cls	Class file
.res	Resource file

continues

Table 1.2   continued

Extension	Type of File
.ctl	User-defined control file
.pag	Property page file
.dsr	Designer file
.vbp	Visual Basic project
.vbg	Visual Basic group

Knowing these file extensions comes in handy if you are using the File Explorer as part of Windows 95/98 or Windows NT. When browsing the directory in which your project is saved, you can quickly explore the parts of your project by visually scanning the names of the files and their extensions. For example, a file named Main.frm is a form that the developer named Main. Most likely this is the main form of the application.

Customizing Your Environment

You can customize many options from within Visual Basic. Here are a few you should set to help you get started.

Select the Tools option on the main menu, and then select the Options menu item. This brings up the Options dialog box, which contains several tabs. Each tab contains a logical grouping of options based on the name of the tab. This dialog box is shown in Figure 1.15.

Figure 1.15

The Visual Basic Options dialog box.

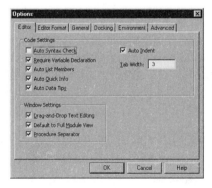

The Editor tab window is visible by default. In the Code Settings section, click Auto Syntax Check so that it is unchecked. This option can be helpful if you don't know the syntax of a statement. However, the more you use Visual Basic, the more of a nuisance Auto Syntax Check becomes. Auto Syntax executes when you move off the line of code you are editing. Sometimes you might want to copy some text from another line of code before finishing the current line. If you have this option checked, you will be prompted about a syntax error in the middle of your editing.

Also in the Code Settings section of the Editor tab window, click Require Variable Declaration so that it is checked. This forces you to declare variables before using them. This helps if you have misspelled a variable without knowing it. If you have this option checked, the Visual Basic compiler lets you know if you have this type of error.

Also in the Code Settings section of the Editor tab window, change the default Tab Width to 3. Everyone has his own opinion of what this value should be, but 3 seems to be more of the standard, especially when dealing with other languages, such as Visual C++.

After you make your changes, make sure you click the OK button to accept and apply the changes.

Next Steps

In this chapter we took a tour of the Visual Basic development environment and introduced the main windows. The focus was not on a detailed explanation of the windows, but rather to show you your way around before we start developing an application. We will get into more detail as we start programming, so don't worry if you still have questions about the development environment. Consider this your first day on a new project.

Chapter 2, "Brief Language Overview," focuses on a brief introduction of the programming language. We are not going to go into too much detail because we want to explore Visual Basic programming in-depth as part of the development of an application. We focus on data types, variables, operators, functions, subroutines, and forms. Armed with this knowledge, you should be in a great position to start the project.

In this chapter

- *Variables*
- *Datatypes*
- *Arrays*
- *Constants*
- *Operators*
- *Subroutines*
- *Functions*
- *Classes*
- *Naming Conventions*

Chapter 2

Brief Language Overview

Visual Basic is the simplest and easiest programming language and environment used to create applications that run in Windows 95/98, Windows NT, and the new Windows 2000 operating systems. Visual Basic started out as a simple scripting language with a short list of features. Despite limitations of the earlier versions, it has grown into a rich development environment with an impressive list of features that now rivals other programming languages such as C++. The speed at which you can create Windows applications using Visual Basic has contributed to its success. You do not have to understand the lower-level programming calls used by other languages such as C++ to create an impressive application that is enjoyed by many users.

Visual Basic enables you to create forms for displaying data and getting input from the user. Forms can contain different types of controls such as text boxes. Text boxes are used on forms to enable users to enter data. You also have other types of controls, such as buttons for performing an action, labels for displaying data, list boxes for displaying lists, and image boxes for showing images. These are just a few of the types of controls available to developers using Visual Basic.

Visual Basic also integrates seamlessly with COM components. COM is a language-independent standard for building and deploying independent units of executable code. Because it is language independent, you have the option of writing COM component in C++, Visual Basic, and even Java. From Visual Basic's standpoint, you can write VB code and use components as though they were VB objects. The components can be implemented in any language that supports implementing COM components (such as C++, Java, and Visual Basic). When using components, VB does not care in which language the components themselves were written. This opens VB up to a whole new world of possibilities.

Besides forms and user-interface controls, Visual Basic has a comprehensive language for writing code. If you have programmed before, Visual Basic has most, if not all, of the types of statements you would normally see in a programming language. If you have not programmed before, do not worry because we will explore the language as we go through this book.

Visual Basic 6.0 contains new features such as data access controls, enhancements to existing data access controls, Internet application support, a new set of controls, control creation support, language additions, and new wizards for use by existing applications and creating new applications.

The goal of this chapter is to introduce some of the basics of Visual Basic programming. Here we discuss some of the fundamental programming issues such as variables, datatypes, subroutines, and functions without going into too much depth. If you have programming experience in another language, you might want to skim this chapter paying attention to the syntax. If this is your first language, this chapter is an important primer, although this material is covered in more detail throughout the rest of the book. Therefore, don't worry if you are not completely clear on these topics by the end of the chapter.

Variables

After you start writing a program, no matter what language you are in, you usually come across a situation in which you want to store a piece of data so that you can use it somewhere else in your program. For example, you might want to write a program that enables the user to type in his name. How would you store his name somewhere in your program so that you can print it somewhere onscreen or even in a report? The answer is in a variable.

A *variable* is a location in the computer's memory where your program can store data. A variable can store many different types of data, such as numbers or text. For example, you can declare a number variable to store the user's age and a text variable to store the user's name.

Use the Dim statement to declare a variable in your program. The word after the Dim is used to name the variable. Here is an example of declaring a variable using the datatype String to store a text value representative of a name (more on String later):

```
Dim name As String
```

Variable names must follow several rules:

- The variable name must begin with a letter
- The variable name can contain only A–Z, a–z, 0–9, and the underscore character
- The variable name cannot exceed 255 characters in length
- The variable must be unique in the same scope

Later in this chapter we discuss variable scope and how this affects your programming.

After the name of the variable comes the keyword As and then the datatype of the variable. In the previous example, we declare a variable As String, which allows the variable to contain text such as "Fred".

Datatypes

There are undoubtedly many types of variables you can and will want to create within an application. You will want to create variables that contain text, numbers, dates, and even currency. Table 2.1 lists the built-in datatypes supported by Visual Basic.

Table 2.1 Visual Basic's Built-In Datatypes

Datatype	*Supported Values*
Boolean	16-bit (2-byte) number that can be only True or False
Byte	8-bit (1-byte) number ranging from 0–255
Currency	64-bit (8-byte) integer number ranging from –922,337,203,685,477.5808 to 922,337,203,685,477.5807
Date	64-bit (8-byte) floating-point numbers that represent dates ranging from 1 January 100 to 31 December 9999 and times from 0:00:00 to 23:59:59
Double	64-bit (8-byte) floating-point numbers ranging in value from –1.79769313486232E308 to –4.94065645841247E-324 for negative values and from 4.94065645841247E-324 to 1.79769313486232E308 for positive values
Integer	16-bit (2-byte) numbers ranging in value from –32,768 to 32,767
Long	32-bit (4-byte) numbers ranging in value from –2,147,483,648 to 2,147,483,647
Object	32-bit (4-byte) memory address that references an object
Single	32-bit (4-byte) floating-point numbers, ranging in value from –3.402823E38 to –1.401298E-45 for negative values and from 1.401298E-45 to 3.402823E38 for positive values
String	A variable-length string can contain approximately two billion characters and a fixed-length string can contain one to approximately 64K characters
Variant	A variant datatype can contain a value of any other datatype except user-defined types and fixed-length strings

As you can see, Visual Basic has several datatypes that are part of the language. The term *built-in* datatype is used to refer to the datatypes that are part of the Visual Basic language and are common to all programmers using Visual Basic.

Visual Basic also supports additional datatypes that are not part of the language. These additional datatypes are defined by you or come from component libraries that are referenced by your project.

What is a variant? The *variant* datatype is useful when you might not know ahead of time what the datatype of variable is. A variable of type `Variant` can contain any value—no matter if it is a string, number, date, currency, object, and so on.

Can I Define My Own Datatypes?

You can define your own datatypes. One way of doing this is by using the `Public Type...End Type` statement. These datatypes are more commonly called user-defined types (UDTs). Suppose you want to create a datatype to store someone's full name composed of their first name and last name. You do not want to declare the full name as a string because you still want to refer to his or her first and last name individually. Let's declare a new type called `FullName`. The following code does this:

Module1(Module1.bas)

```
Public Type FullName
    firstName As String
    lastName As String
End Type
```

Now let's use the new datatype to set the name and then print it. To set the `firstName` and `lastName` of a variable based on the `FullName` datatype, you must understand a concept called dot notation. *Dot notation* is used to access properties and methods of a datatype or class. In the following code example we create a `name` variable based on the `FullName` datatype. After the variable is created we use dot notation to access the `firstName` property. You normally start with the variable then use a dot and then the name of the property that you want to access.

When you type the dot (`.`) after the variable name, VB helps you by prompting you with a list of available properties and methods for the class. You must have the Auto-list Members enabled (from the Tools, Options menu) to get this prompt.

Module1(Module1.bas)

```
Dim name As FullName

' set the first name
```

```
name.firstName = "Bob"

' set the last name
name.lastName = "Donald"

' print the name to the debug window
Debug.Print name.firstName, name.lastName
```

That's all there is to it. You can create as complex of a datatype as you like.

Arrays

 Visual Basic supports arrays. An *array* is an indexed list of values. Arrays are useful for storing a list of values in memory that you can use within your application. Arrays are indexed, which means you have access to each element in the array using an index number. A simple example would be to have an array store a list of three names. Figure 2.1 shows this example as a one-dimensional array. A one-dimensional array is essentially a table of data with one column (the one dimension) and a number of rows.

Figure 2.1

A one-dimensional array.

names(0)	"Fred"
names(1)	"Sally"
names(2)	"Joe"

In Visual Basic you can create a variable for holding the array of names shown in Figure 2.1 like this:

Module1(Module1.bas)

```
Dim names(2) As String
```

The Dim keyword is used to start the declaration of a variable. Next comes the variable name. In this example, the variable name is names. In parentheses next to the variable name is the size of the array. The size of the array tells Visual Basic the upper bound of the array (the lower bound defaults to 0).

 Note   The Option Base statement defines the default lower bound of an array. By default, Visual Basic has the lower bound of an array set to 0. Your options for setting the default lower bound are 0 or 1. If you prefer 1 as a default lower bound, use the Option Base 1 statement at the top of a module before declaring any arrays in the module.

This example creates an array of three items (indexed 0–2). Finally, you specify the datatype of the elements in the array. The datatype you specify is for all elements of the array. This requires that all elements in the array be of the same type.

 Note   If, for some reason, you must have an array that contains elements of different types, you can declare an array of type `Variant`. Because a variant can hold any datatype, the array elements can contain different types of values. Each element is still of the same type, but the data within each element is dependent on the value within the element itself. As an example, you can store a `String` value in the first element of a variant array, a `Long` value in the second, a `Date` value in the third, and so on.

The index used to access elements of the array is between 0 and the upper bound of the array, by default. You would access a specific element in the array using the index value. The following code sets the first element in the array to `Fred`:

Module1(Module1.bas)

```
names(0) = "Fred"
```

Another way to declare an array in VB is to explicitly specify the lower and upper bound of the array (the minimum and maximum legal value of an array index), as in the following example:

```
Dim names(0 to 2) As String
```

Note the use of the keyword `to`, which is used to separate the two limits. The lower bound is 0, the upper bound is 2.

You can also create multidimensional arrays within Visual Basic. With multidimensional arrays, you can create as many dimensions as you want, separated by commas. You might want a multidimensional array to hold first names and last names such as the one in Figure 2.2.

Figure 2.2

A multidimensional array.

names(0,0)	"Fred"	"Flintstone"	names(0,1)
names(1,0)	"Sally"	"Smith"	names(1,1)
names(2,0)	"Joe"	"Waters"	names(2,1)

To have a two-dimensional array contain a list of three first names and three last names, you would declare a variable in VB like this:

Module1(Module1.bas)

```
Dim names(3, 3) As String
```

Instead of just having a list of three names, this declaration creates a variable with three rows and three columns. You can access the rows and columns using the following code:

Module1(Module1.bas)

```
names(0, 0) = "Fred"
names(0, 1) = "Flintstone"
```

 The arrays we have declared so far are *static arrays* because their sizes do not change. You also can declare *dynamic arrays* that are capable of dynamically changing their sizes at runtime. You declare a dynamic array the same way as a static array except you do not specify a lower bound or upper bound. To create a dynamic array to hold names, you could declare it like this:

```
Dim names() As String
```

This tells Visual Basic the array is dynamic and the size will change at runtime. At this point, the array has no size and is not usable. You would use the ReDim keyword to resize the array at runtime. Here is an example to resize the names array to three elements:

```
ReDim names(2)
```

You can call ReDim as many times as you want on an array. However, each time you do this, the array contents are destroyed. If you want to grow the array and also keep the original contents of the array, you should use the Preserve option in the ReDim statement. Here's how to grow the names array and keep the contents of the array, before growing it, intact:

```
ReDim Preserve names(6)
```

Constants

 A *constant* is a variable you define in your Visual Basic program whose values cannot be changed while your application is running. It is excellent programming practice to use constants rather than placing numbers or strings throughout all your source code. Suppose you have an application where you need to use π (3.14). Rather than putting the actual number everywhere in your code, you should define it in a global area as a constant, and then use the constant variable name in your code.

Here is an example of declaring a constant variable:

Module1(Module1.bas)

```
Const pi = 3.14
```

Defining a constant does two things: First, you have less memory overhead because you have declared the variable in one place. Second, if you ever need to change the value (to increase precision to 3.141592, for example), you must go to only one spot in your code to make the change.

Operators

Operators are commands that act on values or variables as part of an expression. Suppose you want to concatenate two strings and assign the resulting string to a variable. You would use the & operator to concatenate the strings and then assign the result to a variable. Here's an example:

Form1(Form1.bas)

```
Dim s As String
s = "My" & " string"
```

Visual Basic supports many different operators. Table 2.2 briefly describes them. After you get into the project, we will discuss operators in more detail in the context of real code. For now, this table gives you an idea of the list of operators provided with VB.

Table 2.2   Visual Basic Operators

Operator	Description
&	Concatenates two strings
*	Multiplies two numbers
+	Adds two numbers
-	Subtracts one number from another
/	Divides two numbers and returns a floating-point result
\	Divides two numbers and returns an integer result
^	Raises a number to the power of an exponent
AddressOf	Gets the address of a procedure
And	Evaluates to True if both expressions are true
Comparison	Used to compare two expressions (<, <=, >, >=, =, <>, Is, Like)
Eqv	Returns True if both expressions are equivalent, False otherwise
Imp	Performs logical implication on two expressions
Is	Used to compare two objects' references
Like	Used for pattern matching with strings
Mod	Returns the remainder of dividing two numbers
Not	Negates the value of an expression
Or	Evaluates to True if at least one expression is true
Xor	Returns True if only one expression is true, False otherwise

Forms

Forms are an integral part of any Visual Basic application that has a graphical user interface (GUI). Forms are comprised of a visual representation and supporting code. Forms are what the users sees and interacts with. From the developer's perspective, they are graphical objects that have properties and methods. As a developer, you can design a form within Visual Basic and add controls using the Toolbox. You can then add code to respond to events on the form such as clicking a button. The methods, which are part of a form, can be either a subroutine or a function (see the next sections).

Subroutines

A *subroutine* is a named group of statements that can be invoked by using the subprocedure name. For example:

Module1(Module1.bas)

```
Public Sub Test_Message ()
   MsgBox "The button was pressed!"
End Sub
```

This sample code declares a subroutine with the name `Test_Message`. The `Public` keyword is used to define the subroutine so that it can be called from anywhere within the application. The `Sub` keyword declares the segment of code as a subroutine. The `End Sub` keywords are used to end the subroutine. Everything between the `Public Sub` line and the `End Sub` line is considered the body of the subroutine.

The body of this subroutine makes a call to `MsgBox`. This displays a message in a dialog and OK button (the default display of a MsgBox is to include an OK button). After the user presses the OK button, the next line is executed, which ends the subroutine.

This subroutine can now be called from somewhere else in your program just by using its name, like this:

Form1(Form1.bas)

```
Test_Message
```

Functions

Functions are similar to subroutines except they return a value. Functions generally take some parameters (although they are not required to), do some sort of computation, and then return a value. Here is an example of a function to add two numbers and return the result:

Module1(Module1.bas)

```
Public Function Test_Add(a As Integer, b As Integer) As Integer
   Test_Add = a + b
End Function
```

This sample code declares a function with the name `Test_Add`. The `Public` keyword is used to define the function so that it can be called from anywhere within the application. The `Function` keyword declares the segment of code as a function. Like most functions, this example has parameters that are passed to the function. We have defined two parameters of type `integer`. The function receives these integers, adds them together, and returns the result. Notice the `As Integer` at the end of the first line. This declares the datatype of the return value from the function.

The `End Function` keywords are used to end the function. Everything between the `Public Function` line and the `End Function` line is considered the body of the function. Also, notice the use of the `Test_Add` function name in the body of the function. Within the body of the function, use the name of the function when setting the value that gets returned by the function. In this case, `Test_Add` is set to the result of adding the two values passed in.

You can call this function from anywhere in your application to add two numbers together. Here is an example:

Form1(Form1.bas)

```
Dim value As Integer
value = Test_Add(1, 2)
```

The result of this sample code sets the value variable to 3.

Modules

Modules are a place where you can put your commonly used subroutines, functions, user-defined types, constants, and enumerations. It is good practice to create reusable functions and subroutines and place them in a module so that you can use them in other projects if you need to. After a module has been added to a Visual Basic project, any other forms, classes, or modules within that project can access all public members of the added module.

Classes

A *class* is a variation of a user-defined datatype that groups together data members and methods that operate on these data members. The data members and methods are saved together in a separate module called a *class module*. Each class has a name, which shows in the Properties window. The public properties and methods of a class are known as the *public interface* of the class. The public interface properties and methods are the only ones that you can use outside the class. This example defines a Size class that has two properties (height and width) and a method (the function GetArea):

Size(Size.bas)

```
Option Explicit

Public height As Single
Public width As Single

Public Function GetArea() As Single
   GetArea = height * width
End Function
```

Now you can declare variables of this type and use them. Variables of a class type are known as *object references* or just *references*. Instances of a class are called *objects*. For example:

Form1(Form1.bas)

```
Dim sz As New Size
Dim area As Single

sz.height =
sz.width =
area = sz.GetArea()
```

There are some differences between the way object references and normal variables are handled. The most important thing to remember is that a normal (nonobject) variable holds (owns) the data, whereas an object variable is just a reference to an object. The same object can be referred to by many variables.

Naming Conventions

Naming conventions are guidelines for naming your variables. The reason for naming conventions is to make code easier to read. By having and following naming conventions, you should be able to read code produced by different developers, and the code should look similar, making it easier to read. Also when you read your own code, the naming conventions help you quickly understand the datatype of a variable. This is useful information because variables can be used different ways depending on their datatypes.

When you name variables, you should add a prefix to the variable's name to denote the datatype. You can use prefixes for any variable you choose. However, in this book we use prefixes for variables of object type (forms and controls).

Besides adding a prefix to a variable name, avoid creating variable names that are too long. Try to limit yourself to creating variables with a maximum of 32 characters. Variable names should correspond to a noun, whereas function and procedure names should correspond to a verb. If you create a variable by combining more that one word, you should capitalize the first letter of each word.

Next Steps

In this chapter, we briefly introduced some terminology and language features of Visual Basic. Once again, the goal was to introduce these things to give you some common understanding before starting the project. We will explore what was introduced here in more detail as the book progresses. So let's get moving. In the next chapter, we start the project by defining what it is we are going to build.

In this chapter

- *Introduction*
- *Defining the Project Used Throughout the Book*
- *Project Requirements*
- *Creating a Visual Basic Project from Scratch*
- *Creating the Login Form*
- *Running the Login Form*

Chapter 3

Starting the Project

Introduction

In Chapter 1, "Introduction to Visual Basic," you toured Visual Basic to familiarize yourself with the development environment. In Chapter 2, "Brief Language Overview," you learned the Visual Basic language. Armed with this knowledge, you are ready to start the project that you will build on throughout the rest of the book. By working toward building an application using Visual Basic, you can learn Visual Basic in the context of a real coding situation. Like any successful software project, let's start by understanding the requirements and formulating a design.

Defining the Project Used Throughout the Book

The best approach to designing a software application is to first understand what the requirements are. Do this by interviewing some representatives of the targeted user base or by collaborating with someone with domain knowledge of the business problem. By domain knowledge, we mean someone that understands the business and the expected benefits that would be provided by the software application after it is built.

Because you are now reading a book about Visual Basic and not a book on software requirements and analysis, we do not expect you to go through the process of collecting requirements. To get to the coding part as quickly as possible, we are going to provide some basic requirements for the project. The requirements we came up with are intended to spawn the development of an application that exercises most of the features of Visual Basic. This is a daunting task considering the breadth of features provided by Visual Basic. The point we want to make is that these requirements might not exactly match the real-world requirements of a similar application;

that is not the purpose of the requirements presented in this chapter. The purpose is to have a base set of requirements (no matter what they are) so that you can start designing and developing an application.

In an effort to come up with an interesting application that you would enjoy working with, we chose to build an application that supports purchasing products from a store. This project is obviously written in Visual Basic but has the same type of functionality that you would see when browsing or ordering products over the Internet. These types of applications are intended to provide access to the warehouse of product information as well as provide the capability to purchase products.

It is possible that an application of this nature would require many different types of information with which to deal. To keep our application manageable we will be focusing on the following types of information:

- Store information
- Products
- Customers
- Orders

The overall application is a virtual store and requires the capability to minimally specify the store name and possible location. Of course, you also need products to sell. You must add products to the store and specify the prices. It also would be nice to see what the product looks like. In addition, you could really use some customers, and it would be great if they bought some products that result in purchase orders. So, now you have a basic idea of what the project is! Now, let's define some requirements.

Project Requirements

The application needs the capability to specify store information, maintain products, add and maintain customer information, and enable customers to create orders. To be more specific, here is a list of requirements we came up with. The capability to

- Edit store information
- Add products
- Edit products
- Browse products
- Add customers
- Edit customers
- Browse customers

- Create orders
- Browse orders

This requirements list should get you thinking in terms of what it is we are going to build (not what we think a real application of this type is required to do because that would be a larger list). Along the way, we will be adding more features to the project that do more than meet these requirements.

These requirements fall into two categories:

- What are the things the store worker needs to do?
- What are the things the customer needs to do?

You do not want these two categories to be part of the same user interface because you do not want to let customers change the prices of products before they buy them—you would quickly be out of business. So, you are going to build two user interfaces as part of the overall application. You will call the user interfaces Administrative Services and Customer Services. Administrative Services contains all necessary functionality for the store worker to do her job. The Customer Services provides the necessary functionality for customers to purchase products.

Administrative Services

Based on this minimal set of requirements, you must build the Administrative Services user interface to support the following:

- Maintain products
- Maintain customers
- View all orders
- Edit store information
- Create reports

Maintain Products

Obviously, you need products to sell. The user of your application must browse the products that are sold by the store. The user may be someone wanting to buy products or a worker who is performing inventory. A worker would need the capability to edit things like the price and quantity of a product. Because some products become discontinued, the worker needs to be able to delete products.

Maintain Customers

For the purposes of your store, you want to track the customers and enable them to register with your store. The customer can create a profile to save her address and credit card information. This information is used for any orders that are created within the application by the customer.

View All Orders

The store owner wants to view all the orders currently in the application. The owner might need to see all currently open orders, orders that have not had credit approval, and orders that have been shipped.

Edit Store Information

The store information includes the name and address of the store. This information is used to personalize the application, reports, and orders.

Create Reports

The store owner wants an inventory report and an order summary report. Any remaining reports are left to your discretion.

Customer Services

The customer who purchases products from the store uses the Customer Services user interface. This is the interface she would use to browse products and create orders. In support of this, the customer must be able to do the following:

- Add customer information
- Edit customer information
- View order status
- Browse products
- Add products to an order
- Finalize order and check out

Add Customer Information

Anyone is allowed to register as a new customer. She chooses a customer user ID and password to create her customer profile. The customer stores her billing and shipping address as well as her credit card information within the profile.

Edit Customer Information

A registered customer must be able to edit her profile at any time.

View Order Status

A registered customer might want to check on an order status to verify a purchase and the order's shipment. Occasionally, a customer might want to cancel an order.

Browse Products

Anyone must be able to browse the products before choosing to become a customer or before placing an order.

Add Products to an Order

While viewing the products, a registered customer must be able to collect a list of products that will eventually become part of one order. By choosing to add to a shopping cart, these products are added to the list of products for purchase.

Finalize Order and Check Out

After adding one or many products to a shopping cart, the user must be able to finalize the order.

We are going to stop here with the requirements definition so that we don't get too deep into analysis paralysis. This is the state where software projects don't move forward because of some techno-religious belief that everything must be defined before you write some code. If you feel you are in this situation, build something to validate the requirements you have defined. You can always revisit the requirements and design later. You will not be able to revisit anything if you have not developed anything. Treat software development as a continuous cycle.

The intention is to familiarize you with what we are going to build. We do not need to cover all the details of what we are going to build because we will explore these details as we build the application. Throughout this book, we are going to add functionality as we see fit for the purpose of maximizing our use of Visual Basic in this learning process.

You now have a good idea of what you are going to build. Let's start by creating a Visual Basic application with an initial logon screen.

Creating a Visual Basic Project from Scratch

Open Visual Basic and, at the initial dialog box, choose Standard EXE on the New tab to create a new standard application project. The Standard EXE option should be highlighted by default. If it is not, click it. After the option is selected, click the Open button in the dialog box to create the new project. After you have created a new Standard EXE project, you are presented with a workspace that looks like the one in Figure 3.1.

Notice that new Visual Basic projects start with a default name of Project1. The project also contains one form that has a default name of Form1. The first thing you want to do is change the name of the project and the form to a more descriptive name, and then save the project.

Figure 3.1

A new Visual Basic application workspace.

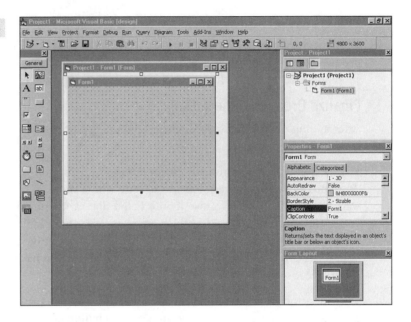

Click the element named Project1 at the top of the tree in the Project Explorer. The content of the Properties window (just below the Project Explorer window) now contains the properties of the project. The Properties window always displays the properties of whatever is selected in the Project Explorer window. Double-click the Project1 text in Name property within the Properties window. This selects the entire text. Now type a new name for the project. Enter **VBFS** for the project name. Figure 3.2 shows the Properties window containing the new name of the project.

Figure 3.2

Change the name of the project.

Project Name property

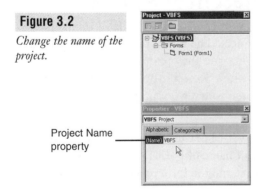

Creating the Login Form

The initial form you are going to develop is the login form. This form is used to get the user's name and password before starting the application. Let's start this form by renaming it. Just like you did for the project, click the Form1 form in the Project Explorer. Again, the contents of the Properties window reflect the selection in the Project Explorer. This time you will notice many more properties for forms as opposed to projects. You can view the properties using the scrollbar to the right of the Properties window. Also, clicking the value of a particular property puts you into an edit mode for that property. We will explore the form properties later; for now, double-click the Form1 text in the Name property within the Properties window. Now type **frmLoginDlg** as the new name.

Standard Visual Basic naming conventions include prepending frm to form names to distinguish them from other objects within the code. This is not a requirement of the Visual Basic language. It is just good practice for you to follow naming conventions to make your code more understandable to yourself and others. As you read through the code it really helps to be able to identify the datatype of a variable when naming conventions are followed. Other people will be able to read and understand your code more readily, and it will help you when you are debugging your application.

Before adding any controls to the form, let's change the form title to give it a friendlier name for the user. Change the form title by clicking the Caption property, and then setting the text to Login to VBFS. Also, change the form icon by clicking the value of the Icon property. Then, click the button with the ellipses in it. This causes a Load Icon dialog box to come up, which enables you to choose an icon for the form. Choose any icon you want, or cancel the dialog box.

 Do you notice all the dots on the form (refer to Figure 3.2)? The dots are the visual representation of the *alignment grid*. This grid is used to align controls on a form. When you place controls on a form, they will automatically line up to the nearest horizontal and vertical line designated by the dots. This simplifies lining up your controls because they snap to the grid. There might come a time when you don't want the controls to align to the grid. To disable this, you must turn off the grid so you can get a finer grain of alignment. To turn off the grid, Choose Tools, and then Options. Click the General tab to view the grid options (see Figure 3.3). You can turn on and off the grid display by clicking the Show Grid check box. Also, you can turn on and off the automatic alignment of controls by clicking the Align Controls to Grid check box.

Figure 3.3

The Visual Basic Options dialog box.

Show Grid check box

Align Controls to Grid check box

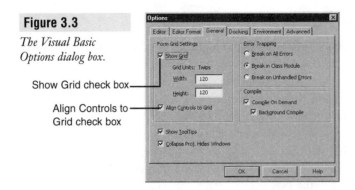

 The next step is to add support to the form for gathering the information you need—specifically, the user's name and password. You are going to add support for this data gathering by adding controls to the form. *Controls* are graphical components that have specific visual appearances and behavior designed for gathering data from the user or displaying data to the user. You are going to use the Toolbox to add controls to your form. Place the mouse cursor over the icons on the Toolbox and wait for a second until a text message appears. The text is the name of the control that the mouse cursor is over.

Click the Label control to select which control to add to the form. Now go to the form to add the control. You do this by clicking and holding down the mouse button on the position to which you want to add the label. Then drag the mouse cursor slightly to the right. As you move the mouse cursor, a rectangle shape appears on the form. The top left of the rectangle is where you clicked on the form. The bottom right of the rectangle is the current mouse cursor position. At this point, you are choosing the size of the label. When the size of the label looks good to you, release the mouse button. That's it, you just added a control to a form. The process is the same for any additional controls you need to add to the form. If the size or position is not exactly as you want, you can always use the Properties window to adjust it (or use the mouse to move and resize it). To move a control on a form, click and hold down the mouse button, move the mouse cursor to the desired location, and then release the mouse button. To resize the control, move the mouse to the lower-right corner of the control. When you see the mouse cursor change, click the mouse and hold down the mouse button. Then, as you move the mouse, you will see the control change size. When the desired size is reached, release the mouse button. Figure 3.4 shows the label added to the form.

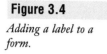

Figure 3.4

Adding a label to a form.

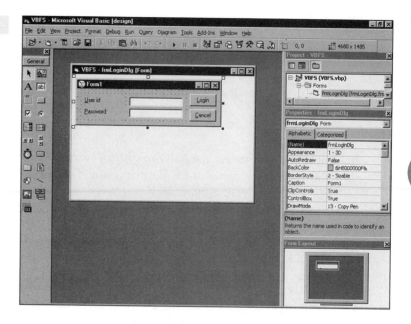

There is no need to change the name of the label because you do not need to refer to it anywhere in code. You do need to change the Caption property, however. Change it to `&User id:` by clicking the Caption property and editing the text.

Adding a Label to a Form

Let's add a second label just below the first label and give it a caption of `&Password:`. Again, there is no reason to change the name of the second label.

Note

The & in the Caption property is used to define an access key for the label. By pressing the Alt key and the access key simultaneously, the focus is set to the control on the form that follows the label in the tab order.

If you are like me, the two labels you just added are not the same size and do not line up with one another. Fortunately, Visual Basic provides some help in fixing this. Press and hold the left Ctrl key to select both labels on the form. With the left Ctrl key pressed, click each label. Using both the Ctrl key and the mouse enables you to select many controls at once. Let's make sure both labels are the same size. With both labels selected, select the Format main menu. There are several options on this menu for sizing and positioning controls. If you click the Make Same Size menu item you will see a submenu appear to the right. This submenu contains options for making the selected controls the same height, same width, or both the same height and width. This is shown in Figure 3.5. Select the Both option.

Figure 3.5

Making controls the same size.

It is important to note that the order in which you select the controls affects the behavior of the menu items on the Format menu. The last control you select is the main control used for the command. If you have three controls that are all different sizes on a form and you want to make them the same size, you would select each control (simultaneously using the Ctrl key and the left mouse click), and then select the Format, Make Same Size, Both menu item. The resulting size of all the controls is based on the size of the last control selected.

Now that the controls are the same size, let's make sure they are lined up the same. With both labels selected, select the Format main menu again. Select the Align menu item to bring up the submenu to the right of it (see Figure 3.6). This submenu has many options for aligning controls relative to each other. Select the Lefts option so that the left sides of the controls line up. Each alignment option is described in Table 3.1.

Figure 3.6

Aligning controls.

Table 3.1 Control Alignment Options

Alignment	Description
Lefts	Horizontally aligns left sides of controls
Centers	Horizontally aligns centers of controls
Rights	Horizontally aligns right sides of controls
Tops	Vertically aligns top sides of controls
Middles	Vertically aligns middles of controls
Bottoms	Vertically aligns bottom sides of controls
To Grid	Performs Lefts and Tops alignment

If you have Align to Grid turned off (which you should not at this point), you can create controls at any size. You are not confined to the alignment grid for sizing. If you create a control under this scenario and you want to size the control to the grid, you can quickly do this by selecting the control then selecting the Format menu then the Size To Grid menu item. This is not an issue for you right now because you have Align to Grid on.

An issue that you might encounter is spacing between controls. On the form you have built so far, if there is too much or too little space between the labels, you could manually move them. Or, you could use the Horizontal Spacing and Vertical Spacing on the Format menu to adjust the spacing between controls. There are four options for each of these: Make Equal, Increase, Decrease, and Remove (see Figure 3.7).

 Note   The Make Equal option on the Horizontal Spacing and Vertical Spacing sub-menus requires at least three controls selected. The remaining options on these submenus require at least two controls selected.

Figure 3.7

The horizontal spacing and vertical spacing menus.

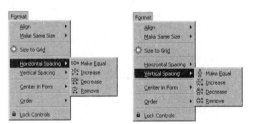

We now need to add the text boxes to the form for the user to enter the user name and password. Select the text box from the Toolbox, and then add it to the form to the right of the first label. Adding a text box is identical to the process we used in adding labels to the form. Change the name of the text box to txtUserId. The standard naming conventions for text boxes in Visual Basic includes prepending the name of the text box with txt. This enables you to quickly identify text box variables when reading your code. Select the text box from the Toolbox then add another one to the right of the second label. Change the name of the text box to txtPassword. You now have two text boxes into which the user can enter data.

Notice that the two text boxes contain text that defaults to the actual name of the control when it was added to the form. The first text box added to a form contains Text1, and the second text box contains Text2. In each text box, the text you see in the control is the value of the Text property of the text box. Let's clear out the contents of these TextBox controls by clicking the Text property on each of the TextBox controls and clearing the value. To clear the property value, double-click the value so that it is highlighted. After it is highlighted, use the Delete key to remove the value.

The user must be able to cancel the login form, as well as start the login process after the user data has been entered. Add a command button to the right of the txtUserId text box and name it cmdLogin. You add command buttons to a form by selecting the CommandButton control on the Toolbox and placing it on the form in the same manner we added labels and text boxes. Also, set the caption to &Login. Add another command button to the right of the txtPassword text box and name it cmdCancel. Set the caption to &Cancel.

At this point, you have all your controls on the form. You can lay out the controls on the form like you want by moving and resizing them. You can also resize the form however you like. Click the form to select it, and then put the mouse cursor at the bottom right of the form until you see the cursor change. After this happens, click and hold, and you can resize the form as you desire. This process is identical for resizing controls on forms.

After all controls have been laid out and the form is the desired size, you can lock the controls to avoid accidentally moving them when you click on them. To lock the controls, select the controls individually by pressing and holding the left-Ctrl key and then use the mouse to click on each of the controls. Because you want to lock all the controls, you could also use Ctrl+A to select everything on the form. After the controls are selected, select the Format menu then select the Lock Controls menu item (see Figure 3.8). Notice the picture of the lock on the menu. The picture of the lock changes to appear as though it is depressed into the menu. This changed appearance of the lock denotes a locked control.

Figure 3.8

Locking controls.

Setting Tab Stops on a Form

One important aspect of developing forms is setting the tab stops. Tab stops are used to define the order in which controls get focus if the user is using a keyboard. If the user is using a keyboard and he wants to select the next field on a form to enter data, he would press the Tab key (or Shift+Tab to move backward). This movement of the focus is dependent on the order of the tab stops.

The tab order is controlled by the two properties TabIndex and TabStop. The TabIndex property specifies the position in the list of controls. The TabStop property contains the value True or False. If the TabStop property is set to True on a control, this means the focus will stop here as the user cycles through the tab stops. If the value is False, focus will not stop on the control. On your logon screen you want the user to be able to use the Tab key to cycle through the username, password, Login button, and Cancel button. Use the values in Table 3.2 to set the tab stops.

Table 3.2   Login Form Tab Stops

Control	*TabIndex*
Label1	0
txtUserId	1
Label2	2
txtPassword	3
cmdLogin	4
cmdCancel	5

Setting Shortcut Keys

Another important aspect of developing a user interface is setting shortcut keys to activate the most important controls on each form. For example, the cmdLogin command button has a shortcut key Alt+L. The shortcut keys are also known as mnemonic keys, or mnemonics. To activate a TextBox control, you would place a label in front of it and add a mnemonic to the label, then set the label's TabIndex property to be one less than the same property of the text box. For example, Label1 in Table 3.2 has TabIndex 0, while the text box following it has TabIndex 1. Because the label cannot be a tab stop, when the user presses the mnemonic the system will activate the next tab stop in order. In this case, it will activate the text box, which is exactly the result you wanted to achieve. The same procedure can be used to activate lists and combo boxes, and in general any control that cannot have a mnemonic (that is, does not have a Caption property).

Running the Login Form

Figure 3.9 shows the final version of frmLoginDlg.

You are now ready to run the project for the first time. It is a good idea to save the project at this point. Click the Run menu and select the Start menu item (or press F5) to run the project. The output should look like Figure 3.10.

Figure 3.9

The final frmLoginDlg.

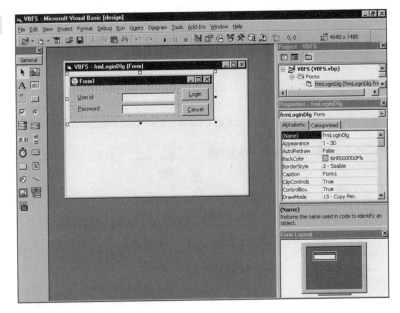

Figure 3.10

*Running the first
iteration of the project.*

Next Steps

In this chapter we defined the project that you are going to build throughout the rest of the book. The requirements on which we base our design have been identified.

Next you started your project and learned the first notions of user interface development in Visual Basic. Among the concepts introduced were forms and controls and some of their properties and methods. You jumped into developing the first form as part of your application to implement the login functionality. At the end of the chapter, you ran your first application. Chapter 4, "Validating a User Through a Login Form," involves adding code to extend the functionality of the login form. This includes adding a module and global function and exploring some new Visual Basic statements.

In this chapter

- *Introduction*
- *Adding Procedures and Functions*
- *What Are Modules?*
- *Contents of a Standard Module*
- *Adding a Standard Module and Creating the* CheckLogin *Function*
- *Adding Code to the Form*
- *A Closer Look at the* If...Then *Statement*
- *A Closer Look at Using* MsgBox

Chapter 4

Validating the User Through a Login Form

Introduction

Chapter 3, "Starting the Project," ended with the development and execution of the initial login form. As it stands now, this form has some controls on it but does not actually validate the user. You must write some code for this purpose so that unauthorized users cannot gain access to the application's data. Adding security features to the application involves maintaining a list of users and passwords in a secure place. The application uses this secure information and compares it with the information presented on a login screen that you built in the previous chapter. The end result of validating a user will involve writing code to look up user information in a database where the secure information is stored. Your goal in this chapter, however, is to start adding structure to your Visual Basic project and not database programming. Therefore, you will focus on adding some structure to your project using modules. Chapter 15, "Elementary Database Concepts," discusses database programming in Visual Basic. And in Chapter 17, " Finalizing Classes in the Project," you will insert the code to look up and compare the user information against the information stored in the database.

Adding Procedures and Functions

You could start by adding the security code directly to the form code for validating the user if you wanted to. Normally, the code you add as part of a form is in support of the form's functionality and specific to the form. If you add code to the form and you want to use it from somewhere else in the application other than within the form's code, you are required to use the form's name before the procedure name. For example, if you wanted to call the DoSomething procedure defined in Form1 you would use the following code:

```
Form1.DoSomething
```

Generally, when you call a procedure of an object in this manner, you would expect that the procedure is doing something in respect to the form. If the DoSomething procedure contains code that has nothing to do with the form, it is conceivable that the DoSomething procedure could have been written as a Public procedure. This way it can be invoked by using only the name itself. It is not very intuitive to call Form1.DoSomething if DoSomething is a generic procedure.

Visual Basic uses modules to address this exact issue. If you want to write some code that must be callable by the rest of your application, you should consider placing the code in a module. Because you are building a complete application, you already know that you are going to create several functions and procedures for use by the entire application. If you know you are going to create at least one global function or procedure, you should create a standard module. As you design and build applications, try to think ahead and create building blocks on which you can expand. To that end, you are going to add a standard code module to your VB project and write a validation function to be used by the login form. Let's get some more details about modules first.

What Are Modules?

There are three kinds of modules in Visual Basic: form, standard, and class. Each of these modules can contain procedures and declarations of variables, constants, and types.

Standard modules are used mostly to define a library of commonly used global variables, constants, types, procedures and functions. Files of this type end with the .BAS file extension.

Form modules contain information about the visual controls placed on the form, any other forms it references, and the form's event procedures. Files of this type end with the .FRM file extension. You have already seen this type of module when you created the login form.

Class modules are used to define objects. We will get into object-based features of VB later in this book. Files of this type end with the .CLS file extension.

Visual Basic supports adding multiple modules within a project. This way you can package your code based on categories of functionality. Standard modules were not supported in earlier versions of Visual Basic. This required programmers to place supporting code directly within the form module. This caused lots of code to be duplicated and non-reusable because the code within a form module is accessible only within the form module in which it is defined. If two forms needed the same set of code, the code had to be copied to the other form. Now, reusable code can be added to a standard module to minimize the coding and maximize the reusability of your work.

Contents of a Standard Module

A standard module is comprised of the Declarations section plus functions or procedures. Simply put, the Declarations section is the top of the module where variables, types, and constants are declared. After the Declarations section, you define all your functions and procedures.

You can access the Declarations section by scrolling to the top of the Code window or by using the drop-down lists at the top of the Code window. Using the drop-down lists, select the General item in the drop-down list at the top left of the Code window. Then select the Declarations item in the drop-down list at the top-right of the Code window.

You have the option of declaring variables in the Declarations section for use by all functions and procedures only within the module or additionally for use by the entire application. By declaring a variable using the `Dim` or `Private` statement, the variable can be seen and used only by the functions and procedures within the module. The variable is created when the application starts and maintains its value until the application ends.

Scope refers to the visibility of a variable within your code. A variable can be referred to only as long as it is in scope. Any code outside the scope of a variable cannot refer to the variable. The following are some examples:

- A variable declared using `Dim` or `Private` at the top of a form is visible within any code in the form.
- A variable declared using `Dim` or `Private` at the top of a module is visible within any code in the module.
- A variable declared using `Dim` in a function or procedure is visible only within the function or procedure.
- A variable declared using `Public` at the top of a form is visible anywhere in the project. However, you must prefix the name of the variable with the name of the form.
- A variable declared using `Public` at the top of a module is visible anywhere in the project.

When you declare a variable using the `Public` or `Global` statement, the variable can be seen by the entire application. The variable is created when the application starts and maintains its value until the application ends.

```
Public name as String
```

 Note Variables default to `Private` if you do not specify `Private` or `Public`.

You also can define your own datatypes within the declarations section of a module. The same scoping rules apply for your own datatypes. If you want to use the datatype only within the module, use the `Private` statement. The following code shows how to create your own datatype private to a module:

```
Private Type FullName
   First as String
   Middle as String
   Last as String
End Type
```

If you want to use the same datatype beyond just the module, you use the `Public` statement like this:

```
Public Type FullName
   First as String
   Middle as String
   Last as String
End Type
```

 Note User-defined datatypes default to `Public` if you do not specify `Private` or `Public`.

The Declarations section also is used to declare constant values. Variables that contain constant values are defined along with their initial values. They differ from regular variables in that their values cannot be changed while the program is running.

 Note You should consider using constants when you find yourself placing specific strings or numbers within the body of your code. If you do not use constants, you might run into problems when you have to maintain your code and change a string or number. It can sometimes be difficult to find all the places in your code that you have to update. By using constants, you can just go to the Declarations section and update the constant values appropriately.

Here is an example of defining a private constant string:

```
Const Hello = "Hello"
```

To make the constant `Public` and usable by the entire application, define it this way:

```
Public Const Hello = "Hello"
```

 Note Constants default to `Private` if you do not specify `Private` or `Public`.

Individual functions and procedures are defined after the Declarations section. You can define functions and procedures as `Private` so that they can be used only within the module or as `Public` for use everywhere. The following code defines a simple `Private` procedure that does nothing:

```
Private Sub MyProc()
End Sub
```

To make the procedure `Public` you would define it this way:

```
Public Sub MyProc()
End Sub
```

You should now be ready to create a new standard module as part of your application.

Adding a Standard Module and Creating the `CheckLogin` Function

Rather than adding the validation logic to the login form, let's add a new module and create a new function to perform the validation. Add a new module to your project by using the Project, Add Module menu item. Click the Open button to create a new module. If you are developing a project of your own and you already have a VB module that you want to incorporate into your new project, you can click the Existing tab to locate and select the module to add (see Figure 4.1). For this project you want to create a new module.

The first task is to rename the module after it has been created. If it is the first module in your project, the name defaults to Module1. In the Properties window, double-click the value of the Name property. Now type **Modmain** to set the new name for the module. This module contains all the utility code for your project.

4

Figure 4.1

*The Add Module
dialog box.*

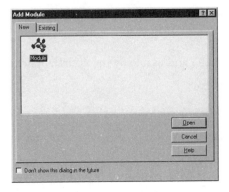

You now must write some code that checks a user's name and password and determines whether the user is valid. You are going to write this code as a function because functions generally take arguments and always return a value. If you do not want a value returned to you, you could write a procedure instead. This function accepts the user's name and password, performs some validation, and returns an answer. The login form then checks the returned value and performs some conditional logic.

Select the Tools, Add Procedure menu item to create the new function. A dialog box displays asking for the function name, type, and scope. Enter **CheckLogin** for the name, check the Function radio button, and select Public as scope. Figure 4.2 shows this dialog box. Click OK now to generate the function.

Figure 4.2

*The Add Procedure
dialog box.*

Now you must add two arguments for the new function: the user name and password. Both arguments are of type `String`. You also need to add a return type for the function, in this case it is `Boolean`. If the return value is True, the user is validated; otherwise, the validation failed. Additionally, the function must be declared as `Public` so that it can be called by code outside the module.

Enter the code as shown here:

modMain(Main.bas)

```
Public Function CheckLogin(ByVal userId As String, _
                           ByVal password As String) As Boolean
 CheckLogin = True
End Function
```

Again, `Public` is used to define the scope of the function. This allows the function to be called from any other code in your VB project. If the function is defined as `Private`, it can only be called from code within the module itself. This is useful if you need to create a private function to support code within the module but don't want to grant access to it outside the module.

Another important observation here is the use of the keyword `ByVal` in front of both string arguments. An argument passed to a function can be passed in one of two ways: by value or by reference. By value means that a copy of the value of the argument is passed to the function and any changes made to this copy are discarded when the function returns. `ByRef` means that the function receives a reference to the original value of the argument; any changes to it affect the value itself, and the changes are not discarded when the function returns. It is generally safer to pass arguments by value in order to avoid some potentially difficult to find problems.

EXCURSION

ByRef

Arguments in Visual Basic default to `ByRef` if you do not specify it. The effect of this is that the contents of the variable passed to the argument of a function or procedure can be changed directly. When the function or procedure exits, the changes made to the argument are retained in the variable passed to the function or procedure.

Here is a sample procedure created with a parameter that defaults to `ByRef`:

```
Public Sub MyProc(s As String)
s = "Gabriel"
End Sub
```

Now assume the following code:

```
Dim myStr As String
myStr = "Bob"
MyProc myStr
```

In this code, because the parameter is `ByRef`, the value of `myStr` is `"Bob"`. After exiting the procedure `MyProc`, the value of `myStr` is `"Gabriel"`. This is because the procedure was passed a string variable by reference, which allows the procedure to modify the variable directly.

Here is a sample procedure created with a parameter that defaults to `ByVal`:

```
Public Sub MyProc(ByVal s As String)
s = "Gabriel"
End Sub
```

Now assume the following code:

```
Dim myStr As String
myStr = "Bob"
MyProc myStr
```

In this example, the value of myStr remains "Bob" after the procedure exits. This is because the procedure was given a copy of the variable myStr to work with, not the actual variable.

Because Visual Basic defaults variables to ByRef, it may lead to unexpected behavior. Be careful to specify ByVal (or ByRef when necessary) to minimize this potential problem.

Also notice the line continuation character in the declaration of the CheckLogin function, which in VB is the underscore (_). This character enables you to break longer lines of code on multiple lines of text.

For now, your function returns True by setting the name of the function to the value True. This is how you set the return value of a function. You will add code to do the real validation later. The reason for this is that the validation you want to have will use a database to look up the user information and compare it to what the user entered on the Login form. Writing that code now would immediately jump you into some database concepts and programming. We are going to hold off on this for now.

 Note A function without a specified return type returns a Variant.

Visual Basic also supports defining optional arguments. By using the keyword Optional, the code that makes a call to the function or procedure does not need to provide values for the arguments defined as optional. Any or all arguments can be designated as optional. However, if an argument is designated as optional, the remaining arguments to the right must be declared as optional also. Here is an example of declaring an argument as optional:

```
Public Sub MyProc(ByVal x As Integer, Optional ByVal y As Integer)
End Sub
```

Here are two valid examples of calling the procedure:

```
MyProc
MyProc 1,
```

The first example calls the procedure MyProc and passes a value to the first argument and does not pass anything to the second argument. The second example calls the procedure and passes values for both arguments.

You may also specify default values for optional arguments. You do this by setting the argument equal to a value in the declaration of the function or procedure. Here is an example:

```
Public Sub MyProc(ByVal x As Integer, Optional ByVal y As Integer = 2)
End Sub
```

This sets the optional argument y to the value 2 if a value is not passed to it by the calling code.

If you choose to declare a parameter as Optional you might run into a situation in which you need to know whether the optional parameter value was passed to the procedure. The function IsMissing() is provided by Visual Basic for this purpose. This enables you to programmatically find out whether an optional parameter was passed a value. After we discuss statements such as If...Then, the conditional logic you can do based on whether an optional argument has a value or is missing will become more apparent.

```
Public Sub MyProc(ByVal x As Integer, Optional ByVal y As Integer)
Dim yMissing As Boolean
yMissing = IsMissing(y)
' check value of yMissing and perform appropriate actions
End Sub
```

Now take a look at the drop-down list at the top right of the Code window (see Figure 4.3). This list assists you in navigating directly to the declarations section or any function or procedure in the module.

Figure 4.3

Code navigation.

Code navigation

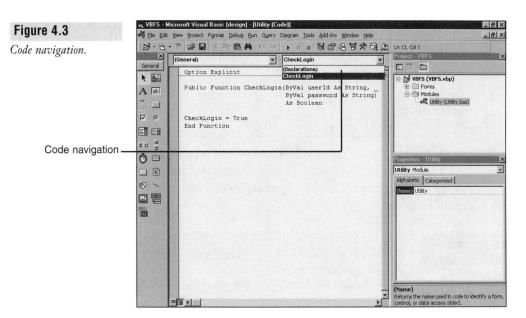

Adding Code to the Form

Within the login form you must add code to respond to the user clicking the Login command button. The simplest way to do this is to double-click on the command button. VB generates an empty event procedure for you and opens the Code window positioned in the procedure. The name of the procedure is cmdLogin_Click, which is the concatenation of the control name and the event name (mouse click). The scope of the procedure is private. Figure 4.4 shows the empty procedure created by VB.

Figure 4.4

The cmdLogin_Click event procedure.

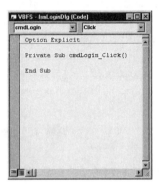

In this procedure, you want to validate the user's name and password. You use the function you just created in the ModMain module for this purpose. Enter the following code to the cmdLogin_Click procedure:

frmLoginDlg(frmLoginDlg.bas)

```
Private Sub cmdLogin_Click()
 If Not CheckLogin(txtUserId.Text, txtPassword.Text) Then
  MsgBox "Invalid user ID or password", vbCritical, "Login failed"
  Exit Sub
 End If
 Unload Me
End Sub
```

There are several new things introduced with this code. Let's start with the If...Then statement. The If...Then statement enables you to control the flow of your application logic. You can test an expression and perform some logic if the expression is true.

 Note An evaluated expression in Visual Basic must result in a Boolean value (True or False). Expressions could be as simple as a single variable or very complex involving variables, functions, and Boolean logic operators (And, Or, Not). If an expression results in something other than a Boolean, such as a number or string, you will get an error when running the program.

The first line of this procedure uses an `If...Then` statement to check if the user is valid. The expression used in the `If...Then` statement is

```
Not CheckLogin(txtUserId.Text, txtPassword.Text)
```

The expression is evaluated by calling the function `CheckLogin` passing `txtUserId.Text` and `txtPassword.Text` as arguments. `Text` is a property of the TextBox controls. The value of this property is the text currently displayed.

The function returns a Boolean value, which is a result of checking the authenticity of the user information. The `Not` operator then negates the result of the function. If the function returns True, it is negated and the resulting value of the expression is False. If the function returns False, it is negated and the resulting value of the expression is True. If the expression evaluates to True, the statements after the `Then` are executed. If the expression evaluates to False, the statements after the `End If` are executed. The code you have just entered tests whether the user is valid. If the user is not valid, you must display a message to the user. This is the next line of code after the `Then`.

The next line of code after the `If...Then` statement calls the `MsgBox` function. The syntax for this Visual Basic function is as follows:

```
MsgBox(prompt[, buttons] [, title] [, helpfile, context])
```

We take a closer look at using `MsgBox` later in this chapter. However, in the `CheckLogin` function we specified the first three parameters to the `MsgBox` function. The first parameter is the message the user sees onscreen. The second parameter is the type of icon displayed to the left of the string indicating the severity of the message. Here we are specifying a critical error message to the user. The third parameter represents the textual string displayed on the title bar of the message box window.

This alerts the user that the login process failed. In the call to `MsgBox`, you set the message the user sees within the box, the style of the message box (`vbCritical` shows a red circle with an X), and the title on the message box (see Figure 4.5).

Figure 4.5

A Login Failed error message.

The `Exit Sub` statement does exactly what its name implies. When this statement is executed, the procedure is exited and control returns to the caller.

The `End If` line completes the `If...Then` statement.

The last line in the procedure (`Unload Me`) unloads (that is, discards from memory) the current form. The keyword `Me` is used to designate the current object. A form is an object and, in this case, `Me` refers to the form you are in. The `Unload` in this case concludes the execution of the program.

A Closer Look at the `If...Then` Statement

Let's take a closer look at `If...Then` statements. In the code you just entered, you used a simple version of the statement. This version is in the following format:

```
If value = True Then
  MsgBox "value is True"
End If
```

This is an even simpler version:

```
If value = True Then MsgBox "value is True"
```

Notice that you do not need the `End If` if you put a statement immediately after the `Then`. If you mistakenly add the `End If`, you will get a compile error. You also can use this format to execute multiple statements on the same line after the `Then` by using a colon. Here is an example:

```
If value = True Then MsgBox "value is": MsgBox "True"
```

The previous two examples do not require using `End If`; however, it is good practice not to use these formats so that you can have structured, readable, and easy-to-maintain code.

These examples enable you to run code if an expression is True. What if you wanted to run some code if the expression is True and different code if the expression is False? You can accomplish this by using this format:

```
If value = True Then
  MsgBox "value is True"
Else
  MsgBox "value is False"
End If
```

What about when the expression is False and you want to evaluate another expression before deciding what statements to execute? You can do this using the format:

```
If value = True Then
  MsgBox "value is True"
ElseIf anothervalue = True Then
  MsgBox "anothervalue is True"
Else
  MsgBox "Nothing is True"
End If
```

It is generally better to use the `Select...Case` statement for doing this type of conditional logic where we are testing multiple logical expressions. This statement is covered in Chapter 8.

A Closer Look at Using MsgBox

`MsgBox` is widely used by Visual Basic programmers to display messages to users. `MsgBox` can be used in many different situations and has several options that control the look of the resulting message box to the user. First, there are five parameters to `MsgBox`. Table 4.1 lists the parameters and a description of each.

Table 4.1   MsgBox Parameters

Parameter	Description
prompt	String expression containing the message displayed in the dialog box. This parameter is required.
buttons	Numeric expression specifying the buttons on the dialog box and the display style. This parameter is optional.
title	String expression containing the title displayed in the title bar of the dialog box. This parameter is optional.
helpfile	Name of the help file to use. This parameter is optional.
context	Numeric expression specifying the help context ID defined in the help file. This parameter is required only if the helpfile parameter is specified.

The `prompt` parameter is the message displayed in the dialog box. This message can be as long as 1,024 characters. The actual maximum length depends on the display width of the characters used in the message string. When using a proportional font, the *W* character is wider than the *i* character. You can separate the message into multiple lines using the carriage return character (`Chr(13)`)and linefeed character (`Chr(10)`).

 Note

The carriage return character and linefeed character are special nonprinted characters that cannot be typed using the keyboard. The ASCII code table contains a list of characters along with an associated code. If you know the code, you can create the character using the `Chr()` function. The carriage return character has an ASCII code of 13. The linefeed character has an ASCII code of 10. In addition, the `Asc()` function can be used to get the ASCII code of a character.

The following code is an example of creating a message that can be used to display two lines in a message box:

```
Dim msg As String
msg = "First line" & Chr(13) & Chr(10) & "Second line"
MsgBox msg
```

The Buttons parameter is a numeric expression that controls the look of the message box. Here is where you specify what buttons to use and the style. Combining zero or one value from five groups of values creates the number expression. Each number value has a corresponding VB constant defined. It is preferable to use the constants when dealing with a message box. Also, the constants are automatically displayed for you when you are typing in code that calls a MsgBox. Tables 4.1 through Table 4.5 represent each of the five groups of values for the Buttons parameter.

Table 4.1   Group 1 Values for MsgBox Buttons Parameter

Constant	Value	Description
vbOKOnly	0	Shows OK button only (Default)
vbOKCancel	1	Shows OK and Cancel buttons
vbAbortRetryIgnore	2	Shows Abort, Retry, and Ignore buttons
vbYesNoCancel	3	Shows Yes, No, and Cancel buttons
vbYesNo	4	Shows Yes and No buttons
vbRetryCancel	5	Shows Retry and Cancel buttons

Table 4.2   Group 2 Values for MsgBox Buttons Parameter

Constant	Value	Description
vbCritical	16	Defines critical messages and displays an icon showing a red circle with an X in the middle of it. Use this option when you need to report a major problem to the user.
vbQuestion	32	Defines a query and displays an icon showing a callout with a question mark in the middle of it. Use this option when you need to ask the user a question.
vbExclamation	48	Defines critical messages and displays an icon showing a yield sign with an exclamation point in the middle of it. Use this option when you must tell the user something important, but not necessarily a problem.
vbInformation	64	Defines a query and displays an icon showing a callout with an "I" (stands for Information) in the middle of it. Use this option when you want to give the user some informational feedback.

Table 4.3   Group 3 Values for MsgBox Buttons Parameter

Constant	Value	Description
vbDefaultButton1	0	Sets first button to be the default (default)
vbDefaultButton2	256	Sets second button to be the default
vbDefaultButton3	512	Sets third button to be the default
vbDefaultButton4	768	Sets fourth button to be the default

Table 4.4   Group 4 Values for MsgBox Buttons Parameter

Constant	Value	Description
vbApplicationModal	0	Sets the message box to be application modal (default)
vbSystemModal	4096	Sets the message box to be system modal

What is a modal window? A *modal window* does not allow input to any other window besides itself. When a modal window appears, the user is forced to deal with it before interacting with any other window. These types of windows are used by applications when necessary information must be entered or displayed before continuing with the use of the application. Specifically, application modal windows do not allow input to other windows that are part of the application. Application modal windows do allow users to interact with the other applications, however. Only one application modal window can be visible per application at a time. A system modal window does not allow input to any other window on the computer. Only one system modal window can be visible at a time. Modal windows are opposites of modeless windows. Modeless windows have no effect on other windows. Many modeless windows can be visible at any time. Most windows are modeless.

Table 4.5   Group 5 Values for MsgBox Buttons Parameter

Constant	Value	Description
vbMsgBoxHelpButton	16384	Adds a Help button
vbMsgBoxSetForeground	65536	Sets the message box window as the foreground window
vbMsgBoxRight	524288	Right justifies the text in the message box
vbMsgBoxRtlReading	1048576	Specifies text should appear as right-to-left reading on Hebrew and Arabic systems

Values from each group are combined using the + character to add the values. The following code example combines a value from each group for the `Buttons` parameter:

```
MsgBox "Are you sure?", vbYesNo + vbQuestion + vbDefaultButton1 + _
    vbApplicationModal + vbMsgBoxHelpButton
```

This code generates a message box like the one in Figure 4.6.

Figure 4.6

*An example of a
message box.*

The next parameter is the `Title`. This parameter specifies the string expression that is displayed in the title bar of the message box. If this string is not specified, the title bar text defaults to the name of the application.

The `Buttons` parameter and the `Title` parameter are help related. If you have a Help button on the message box, you can specify the name of the help file in the `Helpfile` parameter and the help context number in the `context` parameter. If both of these are specified to the message box, this implies the message box has context-sensitive help. When the user clicks on the Help button, the text for the help is retrieved from the specified help file, and the help context number is used to search for the correct help topic. When it's found, the help is displayed onscreen. Unlike the other buttons on the message box, clicking the Help button does not close the message box.

`MsgBox` can be used as a procedure or a function. If you call `MsgBox` as a procedure, you must not use parentheses. If you call `MsgBox` as a function, you must use parentheses and you have the extra capability of getting a return value from the `MsgBox` function (all functions return values). Table 4.6 lists the possible return values from calling the `MsgBox` function.

Table 4.6 `MsgBox` **Function Return Values**

Constant	Value	Description
vbOK	1	The OK button was clicked.
vbCancel	2	The Cancel button was clicked.
vbAbort	3	The Abort button was clicked.
vbRetry	4	The Retry button was clicked.
vbIgnore	5	The Ignore button was clicked.
vbYes	6	The Yes button was clicked.

The return value of MsgBox indicates the button that was clicked by the user. This is useful if you need to know how the user responded to your message. You could combine an If...Then statement with a MsgBox function call to test which button the user pressed. This enables you to write code in response to a specific button, which is clicked. Here is an example of this:

```
If MsgBox("Are you OK so far?", vbYesNo) = vbYes Then
    ' user pressed Yes button, do something here
End If
```

Getting back to your project, notice in the cmdLogin_Click procedure that you called the MsgBox procedure and not the MsgBox function. This is because you are informing the user the login failed and presenting only an OK button. You don't care what button the user presses given this situation. The OK button is the only option for this message box anyway.

You are now ready to run the project for the first time. It is a good idea to save the project at this point. Click the Start menu item on the Run menu (or press F5) to run the project. The output should look like Figure 4.7.

Figure 4.7

Run the first iteration of the project.

Next Steps

In this chapter, you added a module to your project where you can place any global utility functions and procedures. This gives you the flexibility to define generalized functions and procedures for the application. Without this flexibility, you would have to write all the necessary code as part of the form itself. Also, after you have defined a library of functions and procedures, you can use it as part of another VB project by adding the module to it.

We covered the structure and contents of modules, including the scope of variables, types, constants, functions, and procedures in relation to modules.

After creating a module, we defined the login validation function that accepts a user name and password then verifies the information. The function returns True if the validation check passes and False otherwise. The code to call the function was then added to the login form. This is where we covered the use of the If...Then statement and the MsgBox function and procedure.

By the end of this chapter, the login form is visually complete and calls a function to validate the user. In the next chapter, we finish the login form by setting some special command button properties. Also, we add the code to support the Cancel command button. In doing this, we explore command button properties, form properties, procedure events, and event handlers.

In this chapter

- *Introduction*
- *Set Command Button Properties on the Login Form*
- *Command Button Properties*
- *Add Code to the Cancel Button*
- *Events and Event-Driven Programming*

Chapter 5

Enhancing the Login Dialog

Introduction

The appearance of the login form is now complete. This enables the user to enter a name and a password for the purpose of logging into the application. You added a module that contains your utility function for validating the user. You also have added code in response to the Login button for calling this function to do the validation check. You are almost finished with the first form. The remaining tasks are to set some properties on the command buttons and add some code in response to the Cancel button.

Set Command Button Properties on the Login Form

For any dialog box that you write in Visual Basic, you should designate which command button on the form is the Default button. There can be only one Default command button on a form. When you set one of the command buttons to be the Default, all other buttons on the form are set to not be the Default. The reason you want to set a button to be the default is to allow the user to press Enter and, no matter where they are on the form, the Default command button is invoked. This makes your application easier to use with the keyboard. The user is already using the keyboard because he is required to type information into fields and can use Tab and Shift+Tab to move between fields. You want to avoid requiring the user to constantly switch between using the keyboard and the mouse. By setting the Default command button, you give the user the option to press the Enter key or use the mouse to click on the button.

On the same topic, you should designate which command button is the Cancel button. By doing this, the user has the option of pressing the Escape key to invoke the command button, which presumably cancels the form (you decide what the Cancel button does). When you designate a command button as the Cancel button, all other command buttons on the same form are designated as not the Cancel button. Only one command button can be designated as the Cancel button.

You designate the Default and Cancel command buttons through the command button properties. Let's first set the Default command button. Open the frmLoginDlg form using the Project Explorer. With the form displayed onscreen, click the cmdLogin button, which has the caption Login. Notice that the Properties window changes to reflect the properties of the button you just clicked. You must change the Default property from False to True. Click on the combo box to display a list of possible values for the property, as shown in Figure 5.1. Then click the value in the list you want to change it to. In this case, it is the value True. Instead of clicking to see the list of values, you could also double-click to toggle the values.

Figure 5.1

Change the Default property of command button.

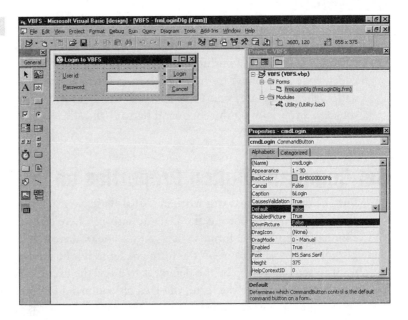

Now let's change the Cancel property of the cmdCancel button. This button has the caption Cancel. Click on this button to display the properties associated with it. Locate the Cancel property and this time double-click the value to toggle it from False to True. The end result should be that the cmdCancel button has the Cancel property set to True (see Figure 5.2).

Figure 5.2

Change the Cancel property of the command button.

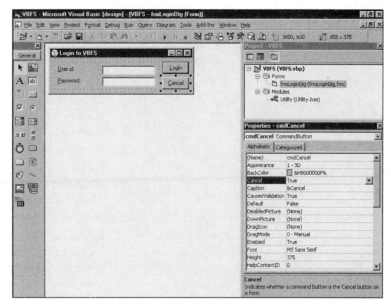

That completes the property changes you must do for this form. However, you might have noticed that command buttons have several properties. In the next section, we discuss each of the properties to introduce you to the range of control you have with command buttons.

Command Button Properties

Command buttons, like many controls, have several properties you can inspect and change. Table 5.1 lists the properties of command buttons along with a description of each.

Table 5.1   Properties of a Command Button

Property	Type	Description
Name	String	The Name property defines the actual name of the button. This name becomes the name by which the button is referred to in the actual code. Most notably, the name is used when defining procedure event handlers, which we discuss later in this chapter.
Appearance	Enumeration	This property defines either a 3D look or an old-style flat look. Developers rarely change this value to Flat.

continues

Table 5.1 continued

Property	Type	Description
BackColor	Enumeration	The background color of the command button.
Caption	String	The string displayed on a command button.
DisabledPicture	File	Set this property if you want to change the look of a disabled command button. The picture you specify is displayed on the command button when Enabled is set to False.
DownPicture	File	Set this property if you want to change the look of a clicked command button. The picture you specify is displayed on the command button when it is clicked or is in the down position.
MaskColor	Color	Defines the color in the button's picture that is the mask color. The mask color becomes transparent if UseMaskColor is set to True and Style is set to 1.
Picture	File	Sets the picture displayed in the command button if the Style property is set to 1.
Style	Enumeration	Sets the style of the button to either Standard (0) or Graphical (1). If the button is graphical, you can select a picture to be displayed in the button.
UseMaskColor	Boolean	True causes the mask color to become transparent in the picture within the button. False displays the picture as is. This takes effect only if Style is set to 1.
Cancel	Boolean	True causes this button to be invoked if the Escape key is pressed on the form. False is the default.
CausesValidation	Boolean	A True value causes a Validate event to be sent to the command button when focus is moved off the button. This enables the developer to respond by writing validation code. A False value does not cause a valid event to be generated.
Default	Boolean	A True value causes this button to be invoked when the user presses the Enter key.
DragIcon	Icon	The icon that is used during a drag-and-drop operation.

Property	Type	Description
DragMode	Enumeration	The mode of dragging is 0 (Manual) or 1 (Automatic). Automatic mode automatically starts a drag-drop operation when the command button is clicked. Manual requires the use of the `Drag` method on the command button to start the drag-drop operation.
Enabled	Boolean	A True value for this property enables users to click on the button. A False value grays it out and disables the button from being clicked on.
OLEDropMode	Enumeration	Defines whether this button can be a target for an OLE drop operation.
RightToLeft	Boolean	Ignore this property if you are not using the Middle Eastern version of Microsoft Windows.
TabIndex	Integer	The index within the tab order of all the controls on a parent form.
TabStop	Boolean	This property is used when the user presses the Tab or Shift+Tab key while on a form. A True value stops the focus on this button when the tab order reaches the TabIndex of this button. A False value causes the focus to skip over this command button.
Visible	Boolean	A True value causes the button to be visible on the form. If you want to hide a button, set this property to False.
Font	Font	The font used by this button.
HelpContextID	Long	Set the help file context ID for the command button.
Index	Integer	This property is used to create control arrays. A value of 0 means it is not a control array but rather a single command button. A value greater than 0 creates a control array (this value being the upper bound).
MouseIcon	Icon	Defines the custom mouse icon.
MousePointer	Enumeration	Specifies a custom mouse pointer that is displayed when the mouse cursor is over the command button. When this property is set to 99, the value in the MouseIcon is used to create the mouse pointer.

continues

Table 5.1   continued

Property	Type	Description
Tag	String	Stores any extra data you might need as part of your program.
ToolTipText	String	Defines the text displayed when the cursor is paused over the command button.
WhatsThisHelpID	Long	Defines the context sensitive help ID used in searching a help file for a help topic.
Height	Single	The height of the command button.
Left	Single	The distance between the left edge of the command button and its parent container.
Top	Single	The distance between the top edge of the command button and its parent container.
Width	Single	The width of the command button.

As you might have already noticed, command buttons are more than visual controls on which you click. You have the flexibility to change the behavior and look of command buttons by setting the appropriate combination of properties. The last remaining task you need to accomplish for the login form is to add code in response to the user's click on the Cancel button.

Add Code to the Cancel Button

When the user clicks the Cancel button, the application should end. You must write an event procedure for the Cancel button that responds to the mouse click event. The simplest way to create this type of event procedure is to open the form and double-click the button. This automatically creates an event procedure for the mouse click button. (I bet you did not expect it to be that easy.) Let's walk through this on our login form.

Open the Login form and double-click the Cancel command button. You should now be in the code window with the cursor in a newly created procedure (see Figure 5.3).

This procedure is named cmdCancel_Click. Visual Basic created the event procedure using the name of the button (cmdCancel) and the event to which the procedure responds (Click). Now add the following code to the body of the procedure:

frmLoginDlg(frmLoginDlg.bas)

```
Unload Me
```

Figure 5.3

Create an event procedure for the command button.

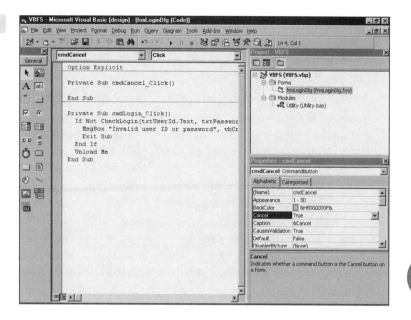

This code unloads the current form (which is designated by the keyword Me). The application ends at this point because the Login form is the startup form. If the Login form is not the startup form, this code would unload the form and return the control back to the code that brought up the login form. You are now finished with the Login form. However, you must understand more about events and how to handle them. The rest of this chapter discusses events in more detail.

Events and Event-Driven Programming

The term *event* is used to define something specific that happened. Events normally result in a message being sent to signal that an event has occurred. Objects can listen for a particular event message and respond to them when they happen. If there are no listeners for an event, the event is ignored. Such things as the operating system, a mouse, a keyboard, and even your application can generate events.

Events introduce a different way of thinking when you are designing an application in Visual Basic. You must consider what events your forms should respond to in addition to the tasks the form must accomplish. Here is an example. A person gets dressed by putting on clothes in a sequential set of steps. The exact steps are not relevant. The fact that a person starts getting dressed, puts on clothes, and then is completely dressed is a procedural process. There is no event, so far, just a process. However, a person may get dressed in response to an event. Now let's say it starts raining and the person puts on a rain coat. The event is that it started raining. The person's response to the event was to put on a rain coat. The act of putting on the rain coat until it was completely on is a procedural process. This process was triggered by the event.

When you are developing an application and you write code that responds to events, you are doing event-driven programming; that is, programming that is driven by the response to the creation of events. Visual Basic is both a procedural and an event-driven programming language. As such, you should take advantage of responding to events when writing your application. This should simplify your task by enabling you to write code that is in response to a specific event and not a general procedure that runs a lot of tests. For example, when a person gets dressed, they mentally run through a check of the current weather and maybe the expected weather later in the day. The check involves whether it is sunny, raining, snowing, cold, or hot. But, when the rain event happens, the person puts on their rain coat. The task of putting on the rain coat is specific, and it is a targeted response to the rain event. The initial procedure of getting dressed is not specific, but rather a general process with many tests that are executed before meeting the result.

Visual Basic enables you to respond to events using event handlers.

Event Handlers

As a developer you have the option of responding to events in addition to setting and inspecting properties. In Visual Basic, you do this by writing event handlers. The events are ignored if you do not write a corresponding event handler.

Event handlers are special procedures in Visual Basic that respond to particular events. The name of an event procedure follows a specific syntax. It starts with the name of the object that is receiving the event followed by an underscore character (_) and ends with the name of the event. An example is the `cmdCancel_Click` event procedure you added earlier in this chapter.

Event handlers are like any other procedure. The only difference is the syntax of the name. As such, you can make the event handler as sophisticated as you like.

Command Button Events

You now have a basic understanding of events. You know what command buttons are because you have added two to your Login form. You have created an event handler for the command buttons that have code in them. We have not discussed what other events are generated by command buttons. The best way to view the list of available events for an object is from the code window. Open frmLoginDlg from the Project Explorer. Double-click the Cancel button. You should now see the code window like the one shown in Figure 5.4.

Figure 5.4

The code window.

Code window—

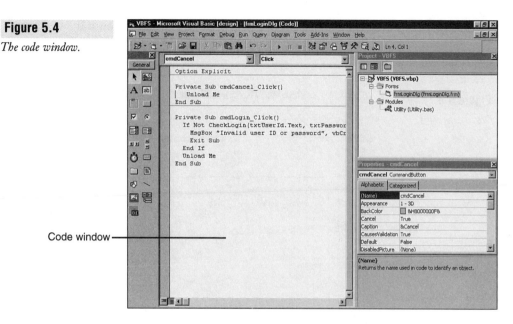

Notice the two drop-down combo boxes at the top of the code window. The one on the top left contains a list of objects that are available on the Login form. The list is shown in Figure 5.5.

Figure 5.5

A list of objects.

List of objects—

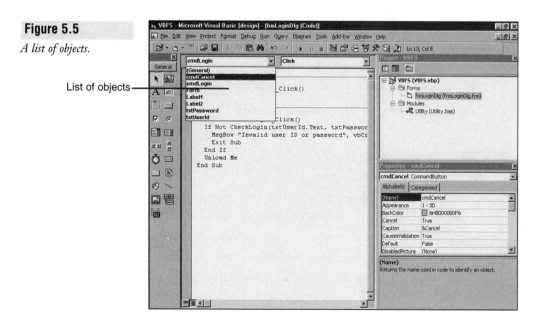

Select the cmdCancel object from the list. The list at the top right of the code window now contains the events that can be generated for the object. This is shown in Figure 5.6.

Figure 5.6

The list of events.

List of events ——

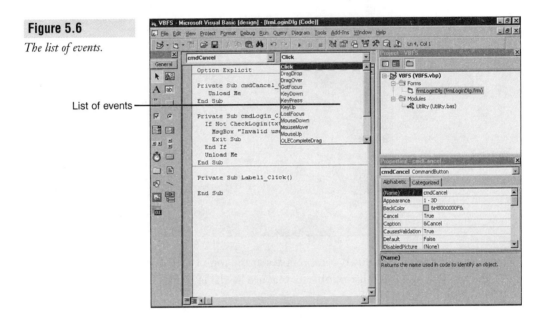

Each bold item in the list means an event handler is already defined for the event. Selecting a bold item brings you to the event handler within the code window. Selecting a nonbold item creates a new event handler and places the cursor in the body of the procedure for you to start entering code.

Table 5.2 lists some of the events for command buttons along with a brief description of each.

Table 5.2 Command Button Events

Event	Description
Click	Generated by mouse click on command button
DragDrop	Generated by OLE drop on target command button
DragOver	Generated by dragging OLE source over command button using the mouse
GotFocus	Generated when command button gets focus
KeyDown	Generated when user presses a key down
KeyPress	Generated when user presses and releases a key
KeyUp	Generated when user releases the key after a KeyDown event
LostFocus	Generated when focus leaves the command button

Event	Description
MouseDown	Generated when mouse is pressed down over command button
MouseMove	Generated when mouse is moved over command button
MouseUp	Generated when mouse button is released over command button

Any additional events are created as part of OLE drag and drop.

 OLE *drag and drop* is a phrase associated with the process of dragging an item from one place onscreen and dropping it onto another location. The user clicks and holds the button down on an item, moves the item to another location onscreen, and then releases the button when the mouse is over the desired location. This process creates several events that are trapped and responded to in order to implement drag-and-drop capability.

When Visual Basic detects an event, it automatically calls the appropriate event handler if one exists. It does this by matching the name of the object and the event to find the event handler with the same combination of object name and event name.

You can always look at the list of events at the top right of the code window to see what events are available for which write event handlers. This applies for command buttons, forms, and other controls.

Next Steps

In this chapter, we set the Default command button and the Cancel command button. This allows your form to perform the login when the user presses the Enter key and to cancel the form when the user presses the Escape key. We covered the command button properties to present the many types of uses for command buttons. You completed the Login form by adding the code in response to the user's click of the Cancel button. The last part of the chapter involved events and event procedures. We covered the concept of events and showed what is involved in writing a procedure that responds to a particular event.

The next chapter takes you through building the application you have developed so far. You will build the application and create an executable file that can be distributed.

In this chapter

- *Introduction*
- *Interpreted Languages*
- *Making a Visual Basic Executable*

Chapter 6

Creating a First Executable

Introduction

Up to this point, you have developed the first complete form for your application. This first form is the Login form, which provides security, a requirement of your application. Let's take a look at creating your first executable application based on the work you have done so far.

 Note If you are using the Visual Basic Working Model Edition that came with this book, you cannot create an executable file, and some of the tabs in the project properties dialog box are not visible. Regardless, this chapter remains important to the Visual Basic developer who needs to create executable files. This applies to any developer who wants to create an application and distribute it to customers. If you are using any other version of Visual Basic besides the Working Model Edition, you should have no problem working along with this chapter.

Interpreted Languages

Software development languages fall into two categories: compiled and interpreted. A compiled language takes your source code, checks the syntax for correctness, and then converts your source code into low-level machine language, which is executed directly by the computer's processor. An interpreted language is checked and converted to machine language at runtime. Visual Basic is both an interpreted and compiled language. When you create an executable from your project, you have the option of generating P-Code or Native code.

You create *compiled code* by taking the source code you write and running it through a compiler. The compiler checks the code for correct syntax as defined by the specific language of the compiler. If there are no errors, the compiler creates a separate set of code for using by the computer directly or into an intermediary step called P-Code.

P-Code is an intermediate step between source code and Native code. P-Code is interpreted and compiled at runtime into native code. *Native code* is the lowest-level code and is executed directly by the computer's processor. Native code is not interpreted at runtime; it is executed exactly as is.

Interpreted code is checked for correctness at the point the program is running. Typically, interpreted code is checked line by line as the program runs. When a line of code is reached, it is checked for syntax. If it passes, the code is executed. If the code does not pass, the program reports an error. Interpreted code is slower than compiled code.

The Visual Basic compiler uses the same compiler that comes with Visual C++. This addresses some of the speed issues that existed in earlier versions of Visual Basic.

In relation to Visual Basic, an application compiled to P-Code is not necessarily slower than an application compiled to Native code. This is because a Visual Basic application spends about 5% of its time within the source code you write. Most of the time is spent within forms, calling functions in DLLs (Dynamic Link Libraries), Visual Basic runtime services, and components. This means that if you want to optimize your code by compiling to Native code you may only be optimizing 5% of your application. This is not to say you shouldn't compile to Native code. If you have algorithms in VB that are computationally intensive, for example, compiling to Native code should provide a significant performance boost.

When you create an executable, Visual Basic compiles and links your application into an EXE file. The application does not require the use of the Visual Basic development environment to run after you have created an executable. However, the executable does require the use of the Visual Basic runtime services, which exist in MSVBVM60.DLL.

You do need to ship some VB runtime files with your application in case your customer does not have them on his system. The customer does not need to have purchased Visual Basic to run your application.

After you have built your application and are ready to distribute it, you must have a way of getting the application installed on your customer's computers. You have a few options available to help you in this process. You can use the Package and Deployment Wizard that comes with Visual Basic (except the Working Model Edition). The Package and Deployment Wizard walks you through packaging your application for deployment. This tool quickly and easily creates installation programs based on your answers to some options presented by the wizard.

If you are looking for a more robust installation program, you can buy other professional tools. Two common examples are InstallShield and Wise Installation. Both are quality, extensible, products that enable you to tailor your installation programs to suit your needs.

Remember, your customer's first look at your product is when the installation program runs. If you want to make a good first impression, spend the effort required to create an installation program to accomplish this.

Let's build an executable for your application to get comfortable with creating a VB executable early in the development of our application. It is a good idea to build your application in stages so that you don't have to wait until the end to see your results. This way you also can react to issues earlier. If you are involved in the development of a larger project, it is customary to build the application at defined milestones—to test the work periodically and identify what works and what doesn't. (This is a good idea in smaller projects as well.) Also, never send a customer something that has not been thoroughly tested. If you do, it will most likely come back to you (no matter how good you are). The earlier you start testing, the more quality you put into your work.

An *executable* is a file that contains compiled code. After you have successfully built an executable, it can be distributed to other computers for use.

In this light, let's compile the code and create an executable.

Making a Visual Basic Executable

The first step is to verify the project settings for compiling your application. Open the Project Properties dialog box by clicking the VBFS Properties menu item from the Project menu (see Figure 6.1).

This dialog box has five tabs for different categories of settings within the project. The first tab is for setting general information. There is no need to change any of the information on this tab at this time. However, notice that the application type is set to Standard EXE, which creates a standalone application. Also notice that the startup object is frmLoginDlg, which is your Login form. The startup object is the place where you specify which form in your project is the first window that comes up when your application runs. You also have the option of selecting Sub Main as the startup object if you want to execute a procedure instead of a form as the first thing when the application runs. Leave the option set to frmLoginDlg. Figure 6.2 shows the General tab.

Figure 6.1

The Project Properties menu item.

Figure 6.2

The General tab in Project Properties.

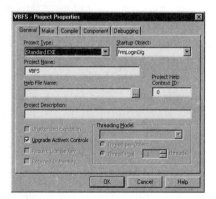

Next is the Make tab. Here you will set the information about the executable that you are now creating.

In the Version Number section, click the Auto Increment check box. This setting causes the version number to be automatically incremented each time the executable file is created so you don't have to set it manually each time. In the Version Information section, you enter information pertaining to the company building the application. There is no need to change this, but you are welcome to add information now if you like. Figure 6.3 shows the Make tab.

Figure 6.3

The Make tab in the Project Properties dialog box.

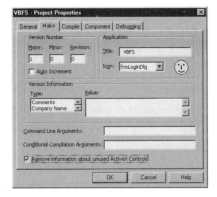

 Note

The version number is a number that is stamped on the executable file and can be viewed in the file's properties window. The file properties window can be displayed on any file by right-clicking on the file in the File Explorer in Windows. The version number is helpful if you need to identify which version of the file is currently installed on a computer.

The next tab is the Compile tab. This is where you choose to generate P-code or Native code. The settings default to fast Native code. Figure 6.4 shows the Compile tab.

Figure 6.4

The Compile tab in the Project Properties dialog box.

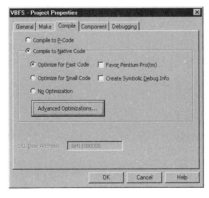

Table 6.1 lists the most common settings on the Make tab.

Table 6.1   Make Tab Common Settings

Setting	Description
Compile to P-Code	Generates intermediate code that is interpreted at runtime.
Compile to Native Code	Generates machine-level code that is not interpreted and is executed directly by the computer's processor at runtime.
Optimize for Fast Code	Optimizes code in favor of speed without regard for the size of the executable. Option available only with compiled Native code.
Optimize for Small Code	Optimizes code in favor of a small executable size without regard for speed. Option available only with compiled Native code.
No Optimization	No optimizations performed.

There is no need to change the settings on this tab. The remaining two tabs (Component and Debugging) are not configurable within a standard application project. For this reason we do not cover them here.

At this point, click the OK button on the Project Properties dialog box to save any changes.

You are now finished changing the project settings for the application and are ready to make the executable. Select the Make VBFS.Exe option from the File menu (see Figure 6.5).

Figure 6.5

Select Make VBFS.Exe from the File menu.

This opens a Project dialog box that enables you to specify where the executable file is going to be placed. You also can name the executable file by typing the name in the File Name field on the dialog box. Click the OK button to create the executable (see Figure 6.6).

Figure 6.6

The Make Project dialog box.

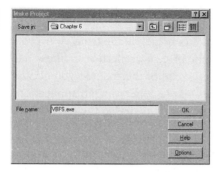

Assuming your code was written perfectly, Visual Basic compiles the code and then writes the resulting executable to the location you just specified. If for some reason you made a mistake, you will see a message box notifying you of a compile error. I purposely created an error in my version of the code to show you what this message box looks like (see Figure 6.7).

Figure 6.7

A compile error message box.

Click the OK button to immediately go to the line that contains the code that the compiler is having trouble with. After you are on the line, you can modify the code to resolve the error and try to build the application again. For this error, you would click on the OK button of the compile error message box. This places the cursor in the code window where the error occurred. The error I created was placing a space between M and e. Here is the code with the error in it:

frmLoginDlg(frmLoginDlg.bas)

```
Unload M e
```

The fix involves changing the code to

frmLoginDlg(frmLoginDlg.bas)

```
Unload Me
```

After all of the compile errors are gone, the application's executable is generated as a result of choosing the Make VBFS.Exe menu item.

6

Next Steps

In this chapter, you created an executable file from your project. In this process, you learned the importance of the project properties and how they relate to generating P-code or Native code. By the end of the chapter, you became comfortable with defining the project settings before generating an application. After you choose to generate an application, you quickly reviewed the process of fixing any compiler errors before regenerating.

In the next chapter, you add the main application to your project and continue to explore new areas of VB programming.

Part II

Develop the User Interface: Adding UI Elements and Base Functionality

Chapter 7

Extending the Project with a New Form

In Part I, "Lay Out the Foundations," we implemented the Login dialog box and learned a few basic concepts pertaining to forms and controls. In this chapter, you will continue to build your project by adding the main form of your application. In doing this, you will also explore a few new areas of Visual Basic programming.

The complete code for this chapter can be found in the Chapter07 folder of the main VBFS folder on the CD-ROM that accompanies this book.

Add a Form to the Project

You want your users to be able to view and edit multiple objects (customers, orders, or products) at the same time; therefore, the logical choice for the main window of your program is an MDI window. MDI stands for Multiple Document Interface and represents a style for user interfaces (UI). MDI enables the user to open multiple documents, each in its own window, or to open multiple instances of the same document. The MDI form normally has menus, toolbars, and a status bar. Most of the document-based applications are implemented as MDI—word processors, image editors, and so on. Other user interface styles include Single Document Interface (one document open at any given time; Notepad is an example) and Explorer-like user interface (most Web browsers and Windows Explorer).

Use an MDI form if your application is displaying multiple views of the same document or multiple documents at the same time. The term *document* in this context is a collection of data items, such as a text file, spreadsheet, or image.

In a VB program, MDI is implemented as a main form (the MDI form) that acts as a container for a set of MDI child forms. There can be only one MDI form per project. The MDI form is slightly different than the regular VB forms—some properties and methods are not available, and there are a few new methods and properties. We will explore the most important ones throughout this chapter.

Let's start by adding an MDI form to the project. This can be done in one of three ways. You can use the following:

- The menus by selecting Project, Add MDI Form
- The drop-down toolbar button
- The pop-up menu of the project by right-clicking, and then selecting Add/Add MDI Form

Notice that the new added form has a different background color from the normal forms, making the distinction easier.

If you try to insert another MDI form in the project, you will notice that the menu item is now disabled—VB is enforcing the "one MDI form per project" rule.

The next step is to set a few properties of the form. Change the default name (MDIForm1) to frmMain and the caption to VBFS Main Form, in the properties for the MDI form. The name of any VB object (forms included) represents a datatype; that is, you can have variables of that type and through the variables you can access properties and call methods of the type. For example, you can create an instance of the frmLoginDlg using the New keyword, assign it to a variable and access any properties of the form through that variable, as in the this code:

```
Dim f As frmLoginDlg, s As String
Set f = New frmLoginDlg
s = f.Caption
```

The MDI form is an exception. You cannot create new instances of it using the New operator; there is only one instance of the MDI form in the project.

This is a good time to save your work by clicking the Save toolbar button. VB prompts you to save the new form, so be sure you save it in the same folder as the rest of the project. The result so far should look similar to Figure 7.1.

Figure 7.1

Adding an MDI form to the project.

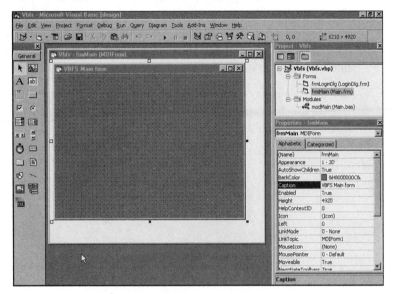

Add a Menu Bar to the Main Form

Next, you will add a menu bar to your main form. Almost every Windows application has menus. The menu bar is one of the most common user interface features. The menu system in Windows consists of a menu bar containing the top-level menu items. Each top-level menu item contains child menu items that appear when the user clicks on the top-level menu (or presses Alt and the underlined letter in the menu text). For example, Alt+F opens the File menu on most applications.

The first step in defining a menu bar, as well as in all aspects of programming, is to think of how you want the final result to look; that is, the design phase. For this project you need the following menu items: an item to create new customers and products, one to open and edit existing ones, and a menu item to view customer and product lists. You also need order-specific menu items: one item to enter a new order, one to change the order status, and one menu item to view a list of orders. It is also customary in an MDI application to provide Window and Help top-level menu items. Other popular menu item choices (depending on the application) are Edit, Tools, and Insert. For this project, use a File, View, Orders, Window, and Help top-level menu, each with a few child menu items.

In VB, you edit all menu items through the Menu Editor. Open the Menu Editor by right-clicking on frmMain and selecting Menu Editor. Alternatively, you can click on the toolbar button that opens the Menu Editor. The Menu Editor is one of the least intuitive editors in VB, and it also is one of the oldest. It has not changed much since VB 1.0. Figure 7.2 depicts the component parts. The editor has two main areas: The lower part is a list of all the menu items defined so far for this form, and the upper half shows the properties of the currently selected menu item in the list. You will find out more on each part as you progress through the rest of this task.

In a development environment like Visual Basic, an *editor* is a specialized tool that enables the developer to modify a specific part of the application. For example, the Menu Editor enables you to modify the menu items for a form.

Figure 7.2

The VB Menu Editor.

When the Menu Editor is opened for the first time for a form without menus, a new, empty, top-level menu item is added to the list. Let's set some properties for this menu item. First, set the caption to **&File**. You will notice that the text &File is now shown in the list too. As you probably have guessed, the ampersand (&) is used to define the letter used (in combination with Alt) to activate the menu from the keyboard and is usually called a mnemonic. The same convention also applies to some other built-in and custom controls (most notably the label, we will see later in this section).

The next step is to give your menu item a name. All menu items (as well as any other object in VB) must have a name. The convention for menu names is to start the name with mnu followed by the actual menu name. Let's call this menu item mnuFile. Names should conform to the VB naming rules for types (that is, it must begin with a letter and must contain only letters, digits, and underscores). You will take the defaults in the Menu Editor for all other properties of this item. At this point the contents of your Menu Editor should look similar to Figure 7.2.

Now continue by adding all the top-level menu items. You need View, Orders, Window, and Help menu items. Click the Next button in the Menu Editor and notice that a new empty line has been added to the list of menu items in the lower part of the dialog box. At the same time, the upper part has been reset to the default properties of an empty menu item. Enter **&View** and **mnuView** for the caption and name, respectively. Repeat the procedure for Orders (**&Orders** and **mnuOrders**), Window (**&Window** and **mnuWindow**), and Help (**&Help** and **mnuHelp**). Figure 7.3 illustrates the how the editor looks after entering these menu items.

Figure 7.3

The top-level menus.

Creating Child Menus

Now you can add child items to each of the top-level menus. For the File menu, we need a New item (which will be used to create new customers and products), an Open item (to open existing menu items), and an Exit item. The Exit menu is there mostly due to tradition—not many users use File, Exit when they can simply click the Close (X) button in the upper-right corner of any window. The User Interface design guidelines recommend that any action that can be accomplished with a mouse also should be accomplished using only the keyboard. Therefore, to be compliant with the guidelines, you should add a File, Exit menu item.

Click on the View menu in the list, then on the Insert button: a new item is inserted between File and View. To tell VB that you want this new item to be a child item of the File menu, you must indent it by clicking on the right-pointing arrow button. Four dots are now displayed in the empty line, indicating that this is a child item of the File menu. Name it **mnuFileNew** and **&New** for the caption. Using the previous procedure, now insert the next child menu of File, which is Open. Click the Insert button—a new item is inserted above New, with the same indent as New (that is, a child of File). You want to have the menus in the order New, Open, Exit, so you must move it down below New. You can do this by clicking on the down-pointing arrow button. Now enter the menu caption and name: **&Open** and **mnuFileOpen**.

Repeat the procedure for the Exit menu (**E&xit**, **mnuFileExit**), and place it below
Open. Because New and Open are related, it would be nice to show that by grouping
them together. You can do this by inserting a separator menu item (the separator
appears as a line on the drop-down menu).

Click the Exit menu item in the list and then on the Insert button. You now have an
empty menu item, and to make it a separator you must set its caption to – (a minus
sign) and give it a valid name. The name for separators is unimportant. Because you
will never get a click event for a separator, our approach is to name them with the
parent name (mnuFile, in this case), and then add the string Sep plus an ordinal. In
this example, that would yield mnuFileSep1. The results of your work at this point
should be similar to Figure 7.4.

Figure 7.4

Adding child menus.

You must specify what to create when New is clicked, and you also must specify what
to open when the Open menu option is selected. You need to add a few child menus
to both New and Open. Click on the Open item in the list and then click on the
Insert button—an empty item is inserted before Open. To show that it is a child of
New, indent it once by clicking the right-pointing arrow button (the same way you
did with the children of File). Now enter a caption **&Customer** and a name
mnuFileNewCustomer. You can expect your users to use this a lot, so define a
shortcut key for this menu item. Select Ctrl+C from the drop-down list labeled
Shortcut. Repeat the operation for a menu item called Product (**&Product**,
mnuFileNewProduct, shortcut Ctrl+P). You must do the same for the Open menu,
so repeat the preceding two steps and create two submenus of Open: Customer
(**&Customer**, **mnuFileOpenCustomer**) and Product (**&Product**,
mnuFileOpenProduct). At this point your menu bar should look like the one in
Figure 7.5.

Figure 7.5

Adding submenus.

You have probably noted the repeated mnemonic (the letter preceded by &) for the Customer and Product menus, in both submenus of New and Open. You can have the same mnemonic in different submenus, and even in the same submenu more than once, but you will always get the first item that matches it. However, it is illegal to have the same shortcut key assigned to more than one menu item at a time (VB does not allow you to save the changes to the menu bar if you do). You do not have to have a mnemonic for each menu item, although it is recommended.

Tip   It is a good idea to provide easy-to-remember shortcut keys for the menus you expect the user to use most often.

7

If you have made any mistakes when designing the menus you will find out when you try to save by clicking the OK button. VB lets you know what the problem is. One of the most common mistakes is to forget to name a menu item or separators.

It is a good idea at this point to save your work and run it to see whether it looks good. Click on OK, and notice that the menus are now shown on the main form. Click on File, New, Customer, and the code editor opens in the Click event of mnuFileNewCustomer. Close the code window for now and let's finish all the menus for the main form.

Open the Menu Editor again and add the following menu items as submenus of View: **&Customers list, mnuViewCustList** and **&Product list, mnuViewProdList**.

Under Orders add three child items: **&New Order, mnuOrdersNew, &Order list, mnuOrdersList** and **&Customers and orders, mnuOrdersCust**.

Creating a Control Array to Store Menu Items

Under the Window menu item you will add the usual window positioning menu items, but you will do it in a slightly different fashion. You will add the standard items—Cascade, Tile Horizontally, Tile Vertically, and Arrange Icons—as a control array.

 A *control array* is a dynamic array of controls of the same type declared at design time. A control array behaves the same as any regular array; the difference is that it contains control references, not data of some sort. For example, you can have four menu items declared as an array if they are contiguous (that is no other items, including separators, are interposed between the items in the array). To do this define the four items **&Cascade**, **Tile &horizontally**, **Tile &vertically**, and **Arrange &icons**, and give all of them the same name: **mnuWindowPos**. Then, set the Index property of each of them to an integer from 0 to 3 (in order). All control array items must have a valid and unique index—very much like any ordinary array. The reason for using a control array in this case will be revealed shortly.

It would be nice to offer the users a way to quickly jump to any open child of the MDI frame. That is, have a list of all open windows so that the user can click on the one of choice and activate it (bring it to the front). You can do this by adding a menu item of type WindowsList—the check box on the right of the dialog. First, add a separator menu item (-, **mnuWindowSep1**) after the &Arrange icons item. Then insert a menu item after the separator and call it **&Windows**, **mnuWindowsList**, and then check the box labeled WindowsList. This is all you need to do, VB supplies the implementation code for this item.

Finally under the Help item, add a child item called **&About**, **mnuHelpAbout**.

There are a few properties of the menus that we did not discuss here, some we will encounter later (like the `Visible` property), and some we are not using in this project. Among the latter, we will only mention briefly the Enabled and Checked properties. Setting Enabled to False for a menu item causes the item to appear disabled (grayed). Setting Checked to True causes a check mark to appear before the menu item. This is used normally to show an on/off style option, or as part of an array to show a group of options of which only one can be selected at any one time. Both those properties can be set in code at runtime, as well as at design time in the Menu Editor.

You have now finished with the design of the menu items. Now save and test the changes. To see the form, you must write code to show it at runtime. To do this, change the code in `cmdLogin_Click` to show the main form (if the login was successful). Add the bold line to the `cmdLogin_Click` in `frmLoginDlg`.

frmLoginDlg(LoginDlg.frm)

```
Private Sub cmdLogin_Click()
  If Not CheckLogin(txtUserId, txtPassword) Then
    MsgBox "Invalid user ID or password", _
          vbCritical, "Login failed"
    Exit Sub
  End If

  frmMain.Show
  Unload Me
End Sub
```

The Show method is an intrinsic (built-in) method of all the forms that loads the form and makes it visible and active. It has two optional arguments: a modal flag and an owner reference. The first argument indicates whether the form is to be shown modal or modeless (default). Modal means the form is shown as a dialog box; that is, the user does not have access to other forms in the same application as long as this form is visible. Modeless means that the user can switch freely to and from this form and other forms in the application. The second argument of the Show method is of type form and is a reference to the owner of the form to be shown. The default value of the owner is Nothing (for example, no form).

Now you can save the project and run it. Try opening the menus and using the mnemonic keys.

Implementing the Menu Click Event

As you have seen in the previous chapters, the programming model for VB (and in general, for most modern UI-oriented languages) is event driven. That means you write code to respond to user actions, actions of which you are notified through events. In VB, the events are handled in event procedures: private procedures associated with each object (control, form, and others).

  Note   Events can also be triggered by the code you write. For example, calling the Show method of a form will trigger some of the Form class events (Load, Activate).

In the case of the Menu class, the only event that can occur is Click. It occurs (as the name suggests) when the user clicks on the menu item or presses the shortcut key associated with it. At this point, the VB runtime is calling the handler procedure for that menu item, if one exists. If no event handler exists, the default action for this class and event is executed (normally no action).

When you click on a menu item in design mode, VB opens the code editor and creates an event handler for the menu item selected. Click on the File, New, Customer. You will be positioned in the code editor, in the empty body of the sub `mnuFileNewCustomer_Click`, as illustrated in Figure 7.6.

Figure 7.6

Adding code for a menu event handler procedure.

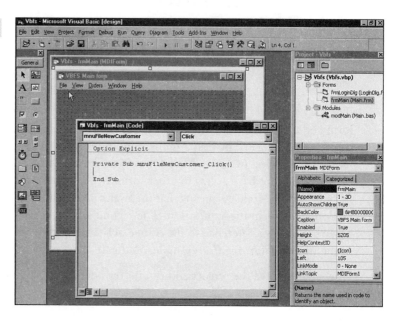

Note the two drop-down lists at the top of the code editor window. The one on the left contains a list of all the controls on the form, the form itself, and a section labeled (General) that contains general declarations and procedures for this form. The drop-down list on the right contains all the possible events for the object selected in the list on the left. In this case, the only item in the list is Click.

Adding a New MDI Child Form

In this procedure, you will open the form that will be used to create a new customer. This means you must add a new blank form to the project. Select Project, Add Form. The Add Form dialog box opens. The first item labeled Form is already selected; just click on the Open button. A new blank form is added to the project. Set the name of this new form to **frmCustomer**, the caption to **Customer**, and the MDIChild property to **True**. This last setting tells VB that this form is always shown as a child of the MDI form (remember there can be only one MDI form in a project, known as a parent). Leave the rest of the properties alone for now. It is a good idea to save your work. Name the file Customer.frm. VB by default uses the form name, but because the file has an .frm extension, the prefix is superfluous.

Now you can continue your implementation of the event handler. Close frmCustomer and switch to the code editor for frmMain. Enter the following code:

frmMain(Main.frm)

```
Private Sub mnuFileNewCustomer_Click()
  Dim f As frmCustomer
  Set f = New frmCustomer
  f.Show
End Sub
```

This code declares a variable of type frmCustomer (the form you just added to the project), and then creates a new instance of the form and sets the variable to refer to it. Finally, it calls the Show method of the new object.

Creating and Working with Objects

Let's explore a little deeper the preceding snippet of code. The first line declares a variable—so far nothing new; all variables must be declared because you have Option Explicit turned on. The only difference from what you have already seen is the variable type, which in this case is one created by you: a form of type frmCustomer. A variable of object type (any object, including an intrinsic one) is a reference to that object, not the object itself. This is an important distinction between object types and regular types (Integer, String, and so on). It means that you can have multiple variables referring to the same object, which is not true of the non-object types. Hence, the use of Set as assignment (in the second line of code) to indicate that it is an object type you are assigning and to distinguish it from a non-object assignment that uses just the = operator.

Also notable is the New operator, which is used to create a new instance of an object and return a reference to that instance. As an alternative to the first two lines of code in this procedure, you can use

```
Dim f As New frmCustomer
```

The end result is identical: a new instance of the frmCustomer form is created and a reference to it is assigned to the variable f. The last line of code calls a method of the object you have created; that is, it shows the form.

 Note   The Show method normally takes two arguments, as mentioned previously. However, neither of these arguments has meaning in the case of MDI-child forms, and neither should be used.

You can now test your code. Press F5 to run and click on File, New, Customer or just press Ctrl+C. A new form is created and shown every time. Your running program should be similar to the one shown in Figure 7.7.

Figure 7.7

Testing the menu handler code.

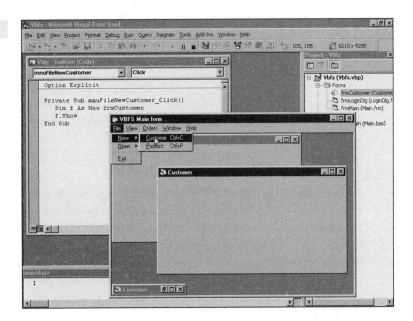

The next step is to add code that handles the Window menu items; that is, arranging the child windows and icons. Click on the frmMain Window, Cascade menu item. Notice that there is a difference between the two event handlers: the mnuWindowPos_Click has an argument named Index of type Integer. This argument represents the index of the menu that has been clicked from the control array. Recall from earlier that you have declared the four menu items that deal with child window positioning as a control array with indexes from 0 (Cascade) to 3 (Arrange icons). The reason for this decision is illustrated by this code:

frmMain(Main.frm)

```
Private Sub mnuWindowPos_Click(Index As Integer)
  Me.Arrange Index
End Sub
```

Note the use of the keyword Me, representing a reference to the current form, frmMain. Me is an object reference to the current object (class or form). It can be used as any other object variable, with one exception: one cannot assign anything to Me, it is read-only.

This example uses the `Arrange` method of the MDI form that does all the work for you. Depending on the value of the argument, a different action is taken, as illustrated in Table 7.1. You can use the enumerated values or the numeric values.

Table 7.1 `Arrange` **Method Argument Values**

Value	Action
`vbCascade` (0)	Arrange all non-iconized child windows in cascade style
`vbTileHorizontal` (1)	Horizontal tiling of all non-iconized child windows
`vbTileVertical` (2)	Vertical tiling of all non-iconized child windows
`vbArrangeIcons` (3)	Arrange the icons of all iconized child windows

When designing the menus, we have intentionally given index values corresponding to the enumerated values (shown in Table 7.1) to the control array items. That allows us to use the `Index` argument as shown in the `Click` event procedure code shown earlier (instead of writing four event handlers, one for each menu item). This is an example that shows that carefully planning ahead in the design phase can help save a lot of work in the coding stage.

You can run the code now, create a few `frmCustomer` instances, and then arrange them in different ways using the Window menus. At this point, you can also use the Window, Windows menu to see a list of all the open windows (all of them named Customer). You can use the list to activate any of them. This functionality is supplied by VB because you have set the `WindowsList` property of the menu item to True.

7

Adding Custom Properties and Methods to the Form

The last item we want to achieve in this chapter is to provide the means to store the name and password of the user for the duration of the session—the time in which the user runs the application. Because frmMain is your container for all the other parts of the application, it looks like a good candidate. You will add the user name and password as custom properties of frmMain.

To do this, you will add two private variables of type String at class level, provide read access to them, and provide a method to initialize them from the frmLoginDlg.

Open the code window for frmMain by right-clicking on the form and selecting Edit Code. Move the cursor to the top of the file and insert the following code just below `Option Explicit`:

frmMain(Main.frm)

```
Private m_userName As String
Private m_userPwd As String
```

This code declares the two string data members as being private; that is, no one from outside this class (form) can access them directly. It is a good practice to protect the class data members in this way and provide access to them through public properties. This is one of the basic principles of object-oriented design and programming and is known as *encapsulation*. In simple terms, this principle requires that the implementation should be kept separate from the interface of the class. In this case, the data members (class variables) should be declared as private, and access to them should be exposed through public property procedures. In this way, no one outside this class can depend on the particular representation of the data members.

Note

If you implemented the two properties as public data members of the class and in a future release of the product, a request comes to use a new object of type UserProfile to get the name and password instead of the strings, you would have to change all classes that directly access the string data members.

Please note the m_ prefix used for the names of the two variables. It is a coding convention that recommends that all variable names for the class level variables begin with m_ (for data member).

Implementing Property Procedures

You will implement two property procedures—one Get and one Let property for each string. A *property procedure* is a variation of a subroutine that allows defined access to a property of an object (to get it or to set it). Hence, there are three types of property procedures: Get (read), Let (write, nonobjects) and Set (write, objects). It is not required to have both a Get and a Set/Let. One can have read-only properties (implementing only the Get) or write-only properties (implementing only the Let/Set).

Enter the code as shown here:

frmMain(Main.frm)

```
Public Property Get userName() As String
  userName = m_userName
End Property
```

The first thing to notice is the property Public, which means that anybody has access to it. You can also have Private properties, which are visible only within that class. These aren't used much in real life because you can access the data member directly within the class. You can also have Friend properties for COM components. We will discuss them later on.

The structure of the property procedure is similar to a function returning a value: it has a type (the As String) and its value is returned by assigning it to the property name (userName = ...). Within the body of a property you can declare variables, call other functions, trap errors, and generally do anything you can do in a function. If you omit the assignment to the property name, the default value for the type of the procedure is returned (0 for numeric values, empty string for strings, Null for Variants, and Nothing for objects).

A client of the object can invoke the property by using the normal dot notation:

```
myString = frmMain.userName
```

The complementary property Let looks similar:

frmMain(Main.frm)

```
Public Property Let userName(v As String)
  m_userName = v
End Property
```

The Get and Let properties can each have a different scope (for example, one can be Public the other one Friend), but they must have the same signature, which means the datatype of the property (Get or Set) must be the same. Having different signatures for the same property—for example, having a property Get as String and the same property Let as Long—is a compile-time error.

The same dot notation is used for the Let and Set properties as for the Get properties:

```
frmMain.userName = myString
```

Notice that the property name now appears in the Autolist of members (that shows when you type the "." after frmMain).

Now implement the similar properties for the user password, as shown here:

frmMain(Main.frm)

```
Public Property Get userPwd() As String
  userPwd = m_userPwd
End Property
Public Property Let userPwd(v As String)
  m_userPwd = v
End Property
```

7

> **Tip** A quick way to achieve this is by copying the two userName properties and pasting them below. Then highlight the pasted code and replace (Edit/Replace) in the selection the word userName with userPwd.

Now change the code in frmLoginDlg.cmdLogin_Click to store the user name and password in frmMain. Open the code editor for frmLoginDlg and add the two lines of code in bold type:

frmLoginDlg(LoginDlg.frm)

```
Private Sub cmdLogin_Click()
  If Not CheckLogin(txtUserId, txtPassword) Then
    MsgBox "Invalid user ID or password", _
           vbCritical, "Login failed"
    Exit Sub
  End If

  frmMain.userName = txtUserId
  frmMain.userPwd = txtPassword
  frmMain.Show
  Unload Me
End Sub
```

You have used the Let properties to store the two strings in frmMain. Now you will use one of the values inside frmMain. You must add some code in the Load event handler of frmMain. The Load event occurs when a form or MDIForm is first opened, before it is actually displayed. It is normally used to set values for controls and properties (for example, populate a list, set the caption of the form, and so on). Table 7.2 lists the order in which some of the most important form events (related to opening and closing of the form) take place.

Table 7.2 Event Order in the Form Life Time

Event	Occurs When
Initialize	The form (object) is created
Load	The form is loaded (prepared for display)
Activate	The form becomes the active form
Deactivate	The form ceases to be the active form
QueryUnload	The form is requested to unload
Unload	The form is unloaded from memory
Terminate	The form (object) is deleted

Show the user name in the caption of your main form, formatted as VBFS - <UserName>. That means you need to use the Load event of the MDIForm. In the code window of frmMain, select MDIForm from the left drop-down list. VB creates an empty procedure for the Load event. Enter this code:

frmMain(Main.frm)

```
Private Sub MDIForm_Load()
  Me.Caption = "VBFS - " & Me.userName
End Sub
```

In this procedure, you set the caption of the form (represented by Me) to be the literal string "VBFS - " concatenated with the return value of the property Get userName of the form (again referenced through Me). The & is the string concatenation operator in VB.

Note

Alternatively, you can use the data member (m_userName) directly, which is more efficient (saving a function call). We used the property for the purpose of illustrating the use of a Get property.

You can also use +. For clarity reasons, in this book, we will use & when dealing with strings.

Now run the program again, enter a name in the text box labeled User Name on the login form, and click the Login button. Notice that the name is now shown in the caption of the main form, as shown in Figure 7.8.

Figure 7.8

Running the application as implemented in Chapter 7.

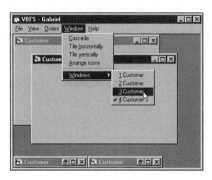

Next Steps

In this chapter, we have added an MDI form to the project, learned to use the Menu Editor to add a menu bar to the form, wrote code to handle the click event for menu items, added class-level data members, added property procedures to access the data members, and implemented code to alter the caption of the form in the Load event.

In the next chapter, we add a toolbar and status bar to the main form, write code to link the toolbar events to the menu item events, and learn some properties, methods, and events for a few of the most-used Windows common controls (Toolbar, StatusBar, and ImageList).

In this chapter

- *Introduction*
- *Adding the Windows Common Controls Reference*
- *Adding a StatusBar Control to the Main Form*
- *Adding an ImageList Control to the Main Form*
- *Add a ToolBar Control to the Main Form*

Chapter 8

Adding Controls to the Main Form

Introduction

Your next step is to improve the functionality of the user interface for the main form of your project. You will add a status bar and a toolbar control. You will then write some code utilizing the capabilities of these controls.

 Note The complete code for this chapter is found in the Chapter08 folder of the main VBFS folder on the CD-ROM that came with this book.

First, you will add a toolbar and a status bar to the main form to offer the users quick access to the menu commands (through the toolbar) and informational messages (through the status bar). You will start by adding the status bar, an image list, and then the toolbar control. Next, you will add code to handle events from these controls and to provide the main form with more functionality.

As you have briefly seen before, custom controls are also known as ActiveX controls. They are add-on components that provide additional functionality, not present in the built-in controls (like the label, list, text box, and so on). ActiveX controls can have custom properties, methods, and events. These properties, methods, and events are the ones used to add new functionality. The capability to extend the development environment with custom controls is an important part of Visual Basic's success: It allows developers to add functionality beyond that provided by the environment and easily integrate this functionality into the VB programming model. This is achieved by using binary components; that is, compiled code. That means the developers of the controls are not required to provide code or header files. It also means that the users of the controls do not need to maintain complicated dependencies in their projects.

Adding the Windows Common Controls Reference

The status bar, toolbar, and image list controls are all members of a group of controls named the Windows Common controls because they are used by many Windows applications. In the same group are the ListView control, the TreeView control, the TabStrip control, the ProgressBar control, the Slider control, and the ImageCombo control (in version 6 of the Windows Common controls).

To use any custom controls, you must first select the control from the list of available components on your computer. Open the Project menu and select Components (or right-click on the toolbox and select Components or press Ctrl+T). A list like the one shown in Figure 8.1 displays. Scroll down to the component named Microsoft Windows Common Controls 6.0 (as shown) and check the box adjacent to it, then click OK.

Figure 8.1

Adding a component to your project.

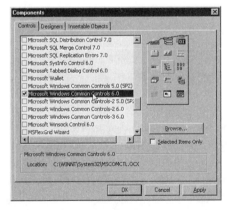

 Note   Your list might look different, depending on what controls are registered on your machine.

Nine new icons appear in the toolbox (see Figure 8.2). They were added when you selected the component. You can determine the name of each new control by moving the cursor on each and letting it rest for a few seconds so that the ToolTip for that control appears.

Adding a StatusBar Control to the Main Form

The first control you will use is the StatusBar control. Open the main form from the Project window (frmMain). Now select the StatusBar control in the Toolbox. Notice that the shape of the cursor has changed to a crosshair. Using the mouse, draw a rectangle anywhere on frmMain with a height roughly the size of normal text height. When you lift the mouse, you will see the new control aligned to the bottom of the form. The result should be similar to the one in Figure 8.2.

 A StatusBar control usually is displayed at the bottom of an MDI form. It is used to display useful information, such as the status of the Ins and CapsLock keys and the date and time.

Figure 8.2

Adding the StatusBar custom control to the form.

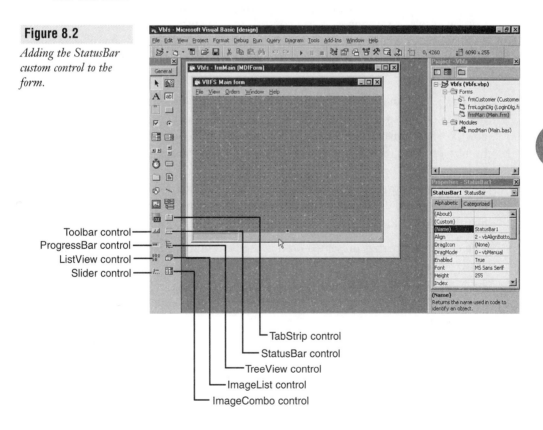

Toolbar control

ProgressBar control

ListView control

Slider control

TabStrip control

StatusBar control

TreeView control

ImageList control

ImageCombo control

In the Properties window, change the name of the control to sbr. Note that the Properties window for the new control has some new properties that none of the VB regular controls have. First (in alphabetical order, from top) is an entry in the properties list labeled (Custom). This is not really a property, it is used to activate a dialog box containing all the custom properties for the control. All custom controls have this entry in the list.

Properties of the StatusBar Control

Another important property to notice is the Align enumerated property, by default set to 2 - Align Bottom for this control. Align indicates how the control is aligned within its container. Bottom means it is displayed at the bottom of the container and its width is automatically resized. Left means that the control is aligned to the left of the container and its height is automatically adjusted with the container. On an MDI form you only can place custom controls (visible at runtime) that have an Align property set to a valid setting other than VbAlignNone (VbAlignTop, VbAlignBottom, VbAlignLeft, or VbAlignRight). Also, please note that the only standard controls (visible at runtime) that can be placed on an MDI form are PictureBox and Data control. By visible at runtime we mean controls that the user can potentially see (that is all the controls you have encountered so far). Examples of controls invisible at runtime are the Timer control and the Common Dialog control, as you will see later in this chapter.

To see the custom properties of the StatusBar control (and of any other custom control) you can use the ellipsis button in the (Custom) property (in the Properties window), or alternatively right-click on the control (on the form) and select Properties from the pop-up menu. Either of these actions causes Visual Basic to display that control's custom properties dialog box, also known as a Property Pages dialog box. This dialog box presents the custom properties implemented by the control, traditionally classified under a few tabs (known as pages). In Figure 8.3 you can see the first page of the Property Pages dialog box for the inserted status bar.

The custom properties presented on this page are summarized in Table 8.1. The rest of the properties on this page are standard VB properties (MousePointer, OLEDropMode, Enabled, and Visible).

Table 8.1   Custom Properties of the StatusBar Control: The General Tab

Property	Type	Description
Style	Enumerated	sbrNormal (default)—Normal status bar with panels
		sbrSimple—Simple (text only) status bar
SimpleText	String	The text to be displayed for the sbrSimple style

Figure 8.3

The StatusBar custom properties dialog box.

Adding Panels to the StatusBar Control

You can leave this page unchanged and go to the Panels page (click on the tab labeled Panels). This page requires a little clarification on the functionality of the control. The StatusBar control is normally divided into a few panels used to display information to the user. The panels look like small inset labels on the status bar. Each panel is an object in itself, and the status bar control contains an ordered collection of panels. Each panel has its own properties, such as Style, Alignment, Bevel, AutoSize, and others. Table 8.2 lists all custom properties of a panel.

Table 8.2   Custom Properties of the StatusBar Control: The Panels Tab

Property	Type	Description
Index	Integer	Panel index (sequential number) in the collection.
Text	String	The default text displayed for the text style panels.
ToolTipText	String	The ToolTip that is shown to the user for this panel.

continues

Table 8.2 continued

Key	String	A unique key used to identify the panel in the collection (can be Null).
Tag	Variant	A Variant version of the standard VB tag property.
MinWidth	Single	Minimum width of the panel.
Alignment	Enumerated	sbrLeft/sbrCenter/sbrRight—Alignment of the text within the panel.
Style	Enumerated	sbrText (default)—User-defined text.
		sbrCaps—Show status of CapsLock key.
		sbrNum—Show status of NumLock key.
		sbrIns—Show status of Ins key.
		sbrScrl—Show status of ScrollLock key.
		sbrDate—Show system date.
		sbrTime—Show system time.
		sbrKana—Show the text KANA when the scroll lock is enabled.
Bevel	Enumerated	sbrInset (default)—Panel appears inset.
		sbrRaised—Panel appears raised.
		sbrNoBevel—No bevel (3-D effects) for this panel.
AutoSize	Enumerated	sbrNoAutosize (default)—No automatic resizing is performed.
		sbrContents—Resize panel to the minimum of the contained text and the MinWidth property.
		sbrSpring—Resize panel so that the whole empty space on the bar is filled by pushing all the panels to the right of this one to the right margin of the bar, and automatically resizing it. Normally you have only one panel of this type and it is the left most one (index 1).
Picture	Picture	The picture for the panel, if one is provided (can be any bitmap, icon, or metafile).

The scope of the Panels tab of the Property Pages dialog box is to present this collection of panels one at a time. You can insert new panels, change properties of existing ones, or remove existing panels. To navigate in the collection, you can use the left and right arrow buttons, placed near the Index panel. See Figure 8.4 for an illustration of the Panels tab of the properties dialog.

Figure 8.4

The Panels tab in the StatusBar custom properties dialog box.

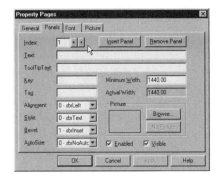

First, set the AutoSize property of the panel that was inserted by default (and has an index of 1) to be of type sbrSpring, the Text to be Status bar message, and the ToolTipText also to Status bar message. Next, insert a new panel (click on the Insert Panel button) and click on the right-arrow button to move to this second panel. Set the Style of this one to be of type sbrTime (to show the system time), and its AutoSize property to sbrContents and the MinWidth property to 120 (any small number greater than 0 will do). The control will set the panel width as required to fit the width of the text (time) displayed.

Click OK to save your changes. The results should be similar to the ones illustrated in Figure 8.5.

Figure 8.5

The StatusBar control.

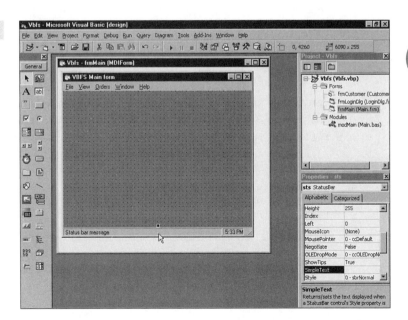

Extending StatusBar Functionality Using Code

You are finished configuring the status bar control, now you need to add a procedure that will enable you to display a message in the first panel of the status bar. You add this procedure to the main form and set its scope to Public so that you can access it from other parts of your application.

Right-click frmMain and select the menu item View Code. From the Visual Basic menu bar, select Tools, Add Procedure. The Add Procedure dialog box is displayed. Enter the procedure name, let's call it SbrMessage. Click OK to generate the procedure body. Now add an argument to the procedure: add an argument named msg of type String and passed by value, as shown in this code:

frmMain(Main.frm)

```
Public Sub SbrMessage(ByVal msg As String)
    sbr.Panels(1).Text = msg
End Sub
```

The line of code entered assigns the string argument passed in to the Text property of the first panel (index 1) of the status bar (sbr) control. Note the use of the property Panels of the status bar control to get a reference to the first panel using the index value (1 in this case).

 Tip   In a similar fashion, you can retrieve a reference to any panel from the status bar collection. It is important to remember this procedure to retrieve an item reference from a collection because you will use it frequently.

Now test this procedure by calling it from the MDIForm_Load event handler. Set the status bar text to Ready, to show your users that the application is now loaded. Add to the MDIForm_Load sub the line of code in bold type shown here:

frmMain(Main.frm)

```
Private Sub MDIForm_Load()
    Me.Caption = "VBFS - " & m_userName
    SbrMessage "Ready"
End Sub
```

Run the application and you will notice that the text displayed in the status bar is now Ready, when the main form is displayed.

Adding an ImageList Control to the Main Form

To have a nice-looking toolbar for your application you need some images for the toolbar buttons. The standard way to handle this task for any Windows Common control is to have the images stored in an ImageList control. The ImageList control is a container for a set of images that you use in other controls. Each image stored in the control has an index associated with it. The control itself is not visible at runtime. It is what is known as an invisible control. It merely serves images to other controls, known as client controls. Because it is invisible at runtime, it is one of the subset of controls that can reside on an MDI form.

To add an image list to your main form, first close the code window for the main form (if it is open). Select the ImageList control from the Toolbox by clicking on it. To identify the ImageList control, place the mouse on each control and let it rest for a few seconds. VB displays the name of the control in the ToolTip window. Move the mouse around until you find the ImageList control, and then click on it. Using the mouse, draw a rectangle anywhere on frmMain. The ImageList control should appear on the MDI form, as illustrated in Figure 8.6.

Figure 8.6

The ImageList control.

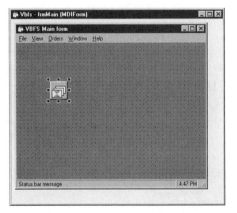

Properties of the ImageControl

Now change the name of this control to iml. As you can see, it does not have too many properties. The most notable property is the MaskColor. This represents a color that is filtered out of all the images in the list when they are displayed by any client control of the image list. *Filtered out* means that the portions of the image that are of that color become transparent, creating the 3D effects that most Windows

Common controls have. Another property (of type Boolean) is the `UseMaskColor`, which tells the control whether the `MaskColor` will be used. The `UseMaskColor` property has the value True by default. Changing it to False instructs the ImageList control to serve the images to its clients as they are, with no filtering.

The `MaskColor` property is of type `color`. In Windows, the colors are represented by a weighted combination of three basic colors: red, green, and blue (known as the RGB combination). The weight (intensity) of any of the basic colors is between 0 (minimum = total absence of the color) to 255 (maximum). For example, the brightest pure red is obtained by combining 255 Red + 0 Green + 0 Blue. A dark shade of red is obtained by combining 127 Red + 0 Green + 0 Blue. Bright yellow is obtained by combining 255 Red + 255 Green + 0 Blue. Pure white is obtained by combining 255 Red + 255 Green + 255 Blue. Pure black is obtained by combining 0 Red + 0 Green + 0 Blue—that is the total absence of all colors.

The value for any color in Windows is represented by a 4-byte number. The least significant 3 bytes contain the values of the intensities of the three basic colors, in this order: Red is the least significant byte, followed by green, and then blue. The most significant flag is used to indicate the system colors (as set by the color scheme for each PC; that is, the one you set in the control panel). In VB the 4-byte value of any color is equivalent to a Long value, represented as a hexadecimal long value.

For example, the default value for the `MaskColor` property for the ImageList control is `&H00C0C0C0&`, which is actually light gray. Because it can become a tedious task to define colors using hexadecimal (hex) numbers, VB helps by providing a color selection dialog box for all the properties of type `color`. To activate the dialog box, click on the arrow button to the left of the value in the `MaskColor` property. Figure 8.7 shows this dialog box.

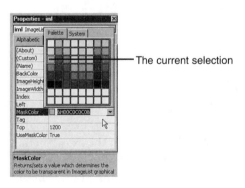

The current selection

The first thing to notice is the presence of two tabs at the top of the dialog labeled Palette and System. The Palette tab (the one shown in Figure 8.7) enables you to select or create a color based on the RGB values. The System tab, as illustrated in Figure 8.8, enables you to pick any of the system colors from the list displayed.

Figure 8.8

The System tab of the color selection dialog box.

In the Palette tab, you have the choice to pick one of the predefined colors. Visual Basic has a selection of the most commonly used colors. The current selection (light gray in this case) is highlighted by a rectangle (see Figure 8.7). You can pick a color by clicking on it. The dialog box closes and the hex value for the selected color is shown as the value for the property. However, if the color you are looking for is not shown in the palette, you can create it. Right-click on any of the white empty rectangles at the bottom of the palette to create a custom color. The Define Color dialog is displayed, as shown in Figure 8.9. You can pick a color by clicking in the desired area of the color box, and you can adjust the intensity of the color using the bar on the right of the dialog box. When you are finished, select the Add Color command button to add your color to the palette.

8

Figure 8.9

The Define Color dialog box used to create a custom color.

Select white from the palette to change the MaskColor property for the ImageList control to white. The value should be &H00FFFFFF&.

Adding Images to the Control

You are now ready to add images to your control.

 Note   Visual Basic comes with an assorted set of images (icons, bitmaps, and metafiles). You might want to use some of these images rather than create them from scratch.

You will need to open the Property Pages dialog box of the control. To do this, right-click on the control and select Properties. The first page of the properties (General) is not used much for this type of control because most of the values on this page are automatically set from the images stored in the list. Click on the tab labeled Images. This tab shows the actual images (sized to fit) in the order you have added them. By default, the page is empty, so let's add a few images. Click the Insert Picture command button. The Select Picture dialog box appears. Go to the Res folder residing in the Vbfs/Program folder, on the CD that accompanies this book. Select NewObj12.bmp and click Add. The image has been added to the list. In Figure 8.10 you can see an illustration of the Property Pages dialog box, with the first image inserted in the list.

Figure 8.10

Adding images to the ImageList control.

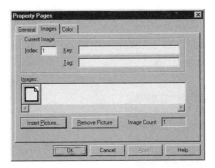

Note that each image has an index, key, and tag (similar to the panel properties you have seen previously). Repeat the operation for the following files: OpenObj12.bmp, Clist12.bmp, Olist12.bmp, and Plist12.bmp. If you make a mistake, you can remove an image by clicking it to select it, and then clicking the Remove Picture command button.

Click OK to save your changes. You are finished with the image list control.

Add a ToolBar Control to the Main Form

You are now ready to add a toolbar to your main form. Select the ToolBar control from the toolbox by clicking on it, and then place it on the main form by drawing a rectangle anywhere on frmMain with the mouse. The result should be similar to the one shown in Figure 8.11.

Figure 8.11

Adding a toolbar to the main form.

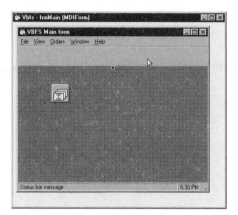

A toolbar is a control that acts as a container for buttons and other controls. It has an `Align` property, similar to the status bar control. The default value for the `Align` property of the toolbar is 1 - vbAlignTop, because normally the toolbars reside at the top of the parent form, beneath the menu bar. The ToolBar control has a sorted collection of Button objects, which can be accessed through the `Buttons` property. This also is similar to the StatusBar control's Panels collection. Each Button object has its own properties, as you will see shortly.

Properties of the ToolBar Control

First, change the name of your control from the default ToolBar1 to `tbr`. Next look at some custom properties of this control. Display the Property Pages for this control by right-clicking on the control and selecting Properties. On the first page, the notable properties are ImageList, DisabledImageList, and HotImageList. All these properties are of type `ImageList`, and have default values <None>.

The `ImageList` property contains a reference to the ImageList control that will be used to retrieve the images required by the buttons on the toolbar. From the drop-down combo to the right of the `ImageList` property, pick the ImageList control you created above: iml. The DisabledImageList contains a reference to an ImageList of images that the buttons will display when their Enabled property is set to False.

 Note Note that each button's Enabled property must be set to False to display a disabled image, and not the toolbar control's Enabled property.

The HotImageList property contains a reference to an ImageList control that contains the "hot" images. These are used by the buttons to indicate a clickable spot when the mouse is positioned over that button. To use this property, the Style property of the toolbar must be set to tbrTransparent. This style gives your toolbar the look and feel of the toolbars in Microsoft's Internet Explorer.

Keep the default values for both the DisabledImageList and the HotImageList (<None>).

The Style, Appearance, and BorderStyle enumerated properties define the aspect of the toolbar. The TextAlignment enumerated property indicates how the string in the Text property is going to be aligned within the toolbar. It refers to the text of the toolbar and not to the text of each individual button.

The AllowCustomize Boolean property enables (if checked) the users of your application to customize this toolbar, by right-clicking on it.

The Wrappable Boolean property enables the control to "wrap" its buttons if the width of the form that contains the control is too small. That is, it will display the buttons on more than one row by increasing its height.

Use the defaults for the other properties on this page. Figure 8.12 illustrates the General tab of the ToolBar control Property Pages dialog box.

Figure 8.12

The General tab of the ToolBar property pages dialog box.

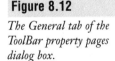

Adding ToolBar Buttons

The Buttons tab is used to edit the properties of the buttons in the Buttons collection of the control. You use the Insert Button and Remove Button command buttons to add new buttons to the list and remove unwanted buttons from the list. Use the arrow buttons to navigate the list. The Index property of each button indicates its position in the list.

To add a button, click on Insert Button. A new button with index 1 is inserted, and most of the button properties become editable.

At this point you should look at the styles of buttons that can exist on a toolbar. The `Style` property of each button indicates how the button looks and behaves. You will see shortly some of the possible values for this enumerated property, as you insert more buttons.

Now let's change the style of this first button to `tbrSeparator` (select it from the Style drop-down list of values). The separators are not really buttons; they represent empty space between buttons, or in this case between the left margin of the control and the next button.

Let's insert another button. Note the index is now 2. Accept the default style for this one, `tbrDefault`. This style indicates a normal button, similar to the built-in CommandButton control. It can have a caption, an image, or both. It has a ToolTipText property and a Key property, which must be unique in this collection. You can select an image for it by entering a value in the Image property that points to a valid image in the associated ImageList control.

You want to set this button to open the list of customers—the same action as the menu item with the same name. Set the Key property to be CList and the Image value to 3. Set the ToolTipText property to Open List of Customers. Now click the Apply command button at the bottom of the dialog box, and you will notice the changes applied to the toolbar. The result should look similar to Figure 8.13.

Continue by adding two more buttons: one for the list of products and one for the list of orders. Insert a new button by clicking on Insert Button. Note that the index is automatically incremented to 3. Set the Key for this button to Plist, its Image to 5, and the ToolTipText to Open list of Products.

Repeat the same procedure for the list of orders button. Click on the Insert Button. Set the properties of this new button: Key to Olist, Image to 4 and ToolTipText to Open list of orders. If you click the Apply command button at the bottom of the dialog box, you should see your changes applied to the main form, behind the dialog.

8

Figure 8.13

Add a tbrDefault *button to the ToolBar control.*

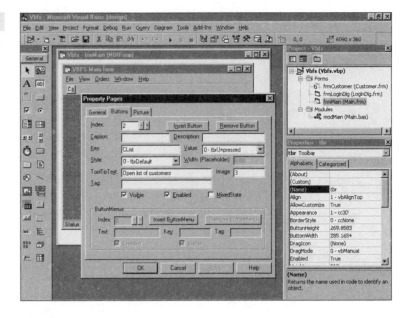

Adding Drop-Down Buttons

You also need three buttons to allow your users to create a new customer, product, and order. Because these actions are related, you should group these buttons somehow. The answer is to add a different style of button: a drop-down button. A button with the Style property set to tbrDropdown is similar to a top-level menu item: when clicked it displays a drop-down list of subitems, named ButtonMenu objects. It also features an arrow button attached to the button to indicate its style. It is similar to the two left-most buttons on the main Visual Basic toolbar and looks like Figure 8.14.

This new button should be the first button on the toolbar (after the separator). Use the arrow buttons at the top of the dialog box to navigate to the first button, the one with Index 1 - a separator. Then insert a new button. Note that the new button is inserted after the current position in the list of buttons, it has index 2. Set the Style of this button to be tbrDropdown. Set the Key to New, the Image to 1 and the ToolTipText to New.... Click on Apply to save the changes done so far.

Now you can add the ButtonMenu objects that will be displayed in the drop-down list. Click the Insert ButtonMenu command button situated in the lower part of the dialog box. A new ButtonMenu object is added to the current button. The Button object has a sorted collection of ButtonMenu objects, similar to the way the ToolBar object has a list of Button objects. A ButtonMenu is similar to a regular menu item;

it has a Text property (the text that will show in the drop-down list), a Key property (a unique key identifying the object in the collection), and the regular Tag, Enabled, and Visible properties. The Index property is used to sort the items in the collection. We will use the Key to identify individual ButtonMenus.

Figure 8.14

A drop-down toolbar button.

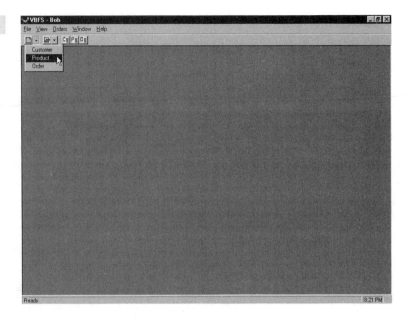

Set the Text property to Customer and the Key property to NewC. We now repeat the steps above for two more ButtonMenus. Click on the Insert ButtonMenu. A new ButtonMenu with Index 2 is added. Set the Text to Product and the Key to NewP. Insert another one (Index will be 3) and set the Text to Order and the Key to NewO.

At this point your dialog should be similar to the one in Figure 8.15.

Now you can add another drop-down button for the open customer and open product actions. But first you should add a separator button, to leave some space between the current button and the next one.

Insert a new button by clicking on the Insert Button command button at the top of the dialog box. Set its Style to `tbrSeparator`.

Now insert a new button. The Index value should be 4. Set the Style property to tbrDropdown, the Key to Open, the Image to 2, and the ToolTipText to Open.... Click on Apply to apply the changes to the form.

8

Now you can add the ButtonMenus for this new drop-down button. Insert a new ButtonMenu. Set the Text property to Customer and the Key property to OpenC. Insert a second ButtonMenu, with Index 2. Set the Text to Product and the Key to OpenP.

Figure 8.15

Add a drop-down button to the ToolBar control.

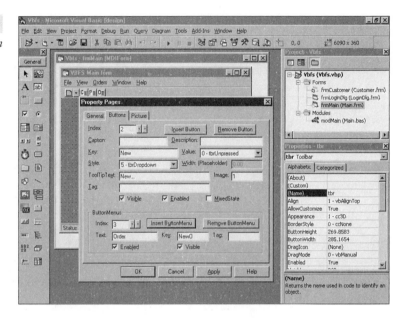

The last step in designing your toolbar is to insert a new separator after this drop-down button. Insert a new button. Index should be 5. Set the Style to tbrSeparator.

You are now finished with the design of your toolbar control. Click OK to save your changes, and then save the project. You can now see how the toolbar looks by running the project. Press F5 to run. When the main form is displayed, you can try the buttons and the drop-down buttons. Also check the ToolTips for each button to make sure they are correct. Figure 8.16 illustrates the running application.

Figure 8.16

Running the application using the toolbar.

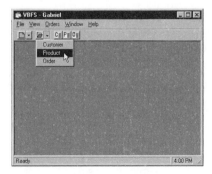

You have not used all the button styles available. The following styles are not used in this project, although they might prove useful in other occasions: `tbrCheck` (acts as a check box; for example, On/Off), `tbrButtonGroup` (acts as a group of radio buttons: only one of the group can be down at any time), `tbrPlaceholder` (a variation of the `tbrSeparator` with a variable width).

Adding Code for the ToolBar Control

Now add some code to handle ToolBar control events. The most important event for a ToolBar control is the `ButtonClick` event. This event occurs when the user clicks a button on the toolbar. To write code to handle this event, double-click the `tbr` control in `frmMain`.

Implementing the `ButtonClick` Event

The code editor is open and you are placed in the empty body of the `ButtonClick` event. As you can see, the event has one argument, the `Button` object that was clicked, of type `MSComctlLib.Button`. The type of the argument is given using the fully qualified notation.

 Note

> The fully qualified notation consists of the name of the library (COM library) that contains the implementation for this class (`MSComctlLib`), followed by a dot and the actual class name (`Button`). This notation allows your project to use classes with the same name from different libraries. For example, if you had your own `Button` class, using the nonqualified notation (`As Button`) would result in an ambiguous declaration.

8

To identify which particular button was clicked, you can use the Index or the Key properties. The Index has the disadvantage that it changes if you change the structure of the toolbar (by inserting new buttons or removing existing ones). For this reason, use the Key property of the buttons to identify them. The Key is a property you set and does not depend on the button's position in the collection.

To identify the button that was clicked, use a `Select Case` statement. This statement is used to select one group of statements to be executed from several groups, based on the value of an expression. In your case, write

```
Private Sub tbr_ButtonClick(ByVal Button As MSComctlLib.Button)
  Select Case Button.Key
    Case "CList"
      ' mnuViewCustomerList_Click
    Case "PList"
      ' mnuViewProductList_Click
    Case "OList"
```

```
        ' mnuOrdersList_Click
  End Select
End Sub
```

The first thing to observe are the keywords Select Case, followed by the expression to test—in this case Button.Key, which is the value of the Key property of the Button object that was clicked. This test value is used by VB to determine which Case statement to execute. Each Case statement is followed by a value, which is compared with the test value, to determine whether this branch of the Select Case is executed. For example, if your Product List button is clicked, the value of the test expression is the value of the Key property of this button, PList. VB takes this value and compares it with all values following the Case keyword until a match is found. In this example, the second Case is matched—the string "Plist" is the same as the value of the test expression.

This means that the application will execute the statements following the "PList" Case, and up to the next Case or the end of the Select Case statement (End Select). In this example. there is only one line of code, which invokes the handler for the Click event of the menu item mnuViewProductList. It is logical to do this because in both cases you want to do the same thing: display a list of all the products you are selling. However, because you have not defined the menu handler yet, you should comment out the code by adding a single quote in front of the line. That prevents the compiler from calling a procedure that does not exist (and generating an error). We will return to this code after defining the procedure mnuViewProductList_Click to uncomment the code.

A similar Click event occurs when the user selects one of the ButtonMenu objects and is named ButtonMenuClick. We will write code similar to the previous code example, again using a Select Case statement to identify the ButtonMenu that was clicked and take appropriate action.

Implementing the `ButtonMenuClick` Event

In the code window, from the drop-down list at the top-right of the editor, select the ButtonMenuClick event. An empty procedure is created. Enter the following code:

```
Private Sub tbr_ButtonMenuClick(ByVal ButtonMenu As MSComctlLib.ButtonMenu)
  Select Case ButtonMenu.Key
    Case "NewC"
      mnuFileNewCustomer_Click
    Case "NewP"
      'mnuFileNewProduct_Click
```

```
    Case "NewO"
      'mnuOrdersNewOrder_Click
    Case "OpenC"
      'mnuFileOpenCustomer_Click
    Case "OpenP"
      'mnuFileOpenProduct_Click
  End Select
End Sub
```

As you can see, the code is similar to the one you entered for the `ButtonClick` event. For the same considerations you use the Key property of the objects to identify the one that was clicked. The only difference is that the `mnuFileNewCustomer_Click` procedure is implemented, which means you can call it. The rest of the calls you are commenting out for now.

The `Select Case` statements can have a default `Case` statement (`Case Else`) that, if present, will be executed if no match on the previous `Case` statements is found. This one is normally the last in the `Select Case`, just before the `End Select`.

EXCURSION

The Expression of the `Case` *Statements*

The expression of the `Case` statements can be of any type that matches the type of the test expression. For example, it can be any numeric type or `Variant`. This expression also can be a range of values (expressed as `startVal To endVal`), a relational expression (`Is comparison-operator value`), or a comma-delimited list of any of the previous. For example:

```
Select Case I
  Case 1 To
    ' statements
  Case Is >= 6, Is <=
    ' statements
  Case Else
    ' statements
End Select
```

Also it is important to know that if a value is matched by more that one Case statement, only the first one is executed and no error is raised.

You are now ready to test this iteration of your project. Save the changes to the project and press F5 to run the project. You now can open the Customer form by either selecting the menu item or by pressing the New toolbar button and selecting Customer from the drop-down list.

8

Next Steps

In this chapter, you have improved the user interface of your main form by adding a few custom ActiveX controls from the Windows Common control group. You have learned to configure a StatusBar control by adding panels and setting their properties. Also, you now know how to configure and add images to an ImageList control. You also are familiar with the ToolBar control, you can add different styles of buttons and button menus, and you can and set their properties.

In terms of coding, you have learned how to handle events from various controls and how to link button-click events to menu-item click events. You also have used some of the properties of the controls inserted to improve the look and feel of your application.

In the next chapter, you continue to add UI elements to your project. You design and implement the Customer edit form. You learn to use the MaskedEdit control, and learn more about child MDI forms and about the properties and events of the built-in VB controls.

In this chapter

- *Adding Controls to the Customer Form*
- *Other Properties for the Built-In Controls*
- *Handling Events from the Controls on the Customer Form*

Chapter 9

Implementing a Data-Entry Form

In this chapter, you will design and implement the frmCustomer form used to edit the data for one customer. You will also explore issues regarding the navigation on the form and add more functionality using the built-in VB controls. You will also use the MaskedEdit ActiveX control.

You can find the complete code for this chapter in the Chapter09 folder of the main VBFS folder on the CD-ROM that accompanies this book.

Adding Controls to the Customer Form

In the previous chapters, you added the frmCustomer child MDI form to your project. Start by opening this form. From the Project window double-click on the frmCustomer form.

You want to allow your users to edit the data items that define a customer. These data items are divided into two categories: required (that the user must supply to have a valid customer) and optional (that might be present in some cases, but not in all cases).

You have identified the following data items required for a customer: the first and last name and the telephone number. You have as optional data items middle initial, street address, city, state, zip code, and email address.

 The BorderStyle property is used to specify how the form will look at runtime. The most common styles used are dialog, sizable, and non-sizable.

Start by changing the BorderStyle of the form from Sizable to Fixed Single. Select from the BorderStyle property drop-down list 1 - Fixed Single. The reason for this change is so the form has a fixed size. It does not make much sense to allow it to be resized by the user. Note that changing the border style of the form made the maximize and minimize window control buttons in the top-right corner of frmCustomer invisible. You do not need the maximize button but it would be nice to have the minimize button. Scroll down in the Properties window to the MinButton property (which is set to False) and change it to True by double-clicking on it. Now both minimize and maximize are shown on the form, but maximize is disabled.

Now you can start adding controls to the form. The first cut of the form with some of the controls on it is presented in Figure 9.1.

Now add first a Label control for the customer name: click on the Label control in the VB Toolbox, then draw the label close to the upper-left corner of the form. Set the Caption property of the control to Name:. If necessary, use the handles on the control to resize it to the desired size and width. Also, you can drag it to a different position by clicking on it and with the left button pressed, move the control to the new position.

Let's add another label control to the form to identify the text box that will be placed under it as the first name. The easiest way to do that is to right-click on the existing label and select Copy. Then right-click anywhere on the form and select Paste. VB will display a message box stating that we already have a Label1 control, and asking if we would like to create a control array.

 **Note**   As you have briefly seen before, a control array is an indexed array of controls of the same type. The Index property of the members of the array starts normally at 0. If the control is not indexed, the Index property is empty (Null).

Select Yes to create a control array. The new label (with the same caption as the existing one) is placed in the upper-left corner of the form. Move it to the right and above the Name label (see Figure 9.1). Set the Caption property of the new label to &First. Note the &, which has the same meaning here as in the menu items: it marks the letter following it as the mnemonic for that control. More on the importance of this shortly.

Now add a TextBox control to contain the first name of the customer: select the TextBox toolbox button and draw the control under the label &First. See Figure 9.1 for a graphical representation of the form with the first few controls loaded.

In the Properties window, you are positioned on the Text property of this new control. You want to set this property to an empty string (""). Click on the property
value and erase the default Text1 string added there by VB. Now scroll up in the
Properties window to the Name property and change it from the default Text1 to the
more descriptive `txtFirstName`.

Now you can add (in order) the rest of the controls depicted in Figure 9.1. First, add
a new label control by using the copy/paste method illustrated previously. Notice
that this time Visual Basic does not ask for confirmation for a control array because
you have already created one. Set the Caption of this label to Initials. Add a new
TextBox for the middle initial of the customer, under the Initials label. Set the Name
of this control to be `txtMiddleInitial` and the Text property to an empty string.
Again, paste a new label control and set the caption to &Last name, and place it as in
Figure 9.1. Now add a new TextBox for the last name, place it under the label with
the same name, change the Name to `txtLastName` and the Text property to an empty
string. If necessary you can resize the form to fit the controls, using the same technique as with the controls (drag the handles in the lower-right corner or on the left
or right of the form). At this point your form should look similar to the one in
Figure 9.1.

Figure 9.1

*The frmCustomer with
the first controls.*

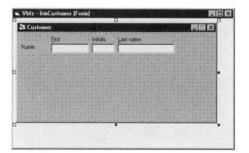

Changing the Font Property of a Control

Now set the Font property to bold for the labels that precede required text box controls. This indicates that the text box labeled by these controls has required entries.
Select the label for the first name by clicking on the control. From the Properties
window select the Font property, and then click on the ellipsis button to the right of
the value for this property. The Font dialog box is displayed, allowing you to select a
font and set some properties for the selected font. The only property you want to
change is the Font Style: select the Bold style. The dialog box is illustrated in
Figure 9.2.

Figure 9.2

The Font dialog box.

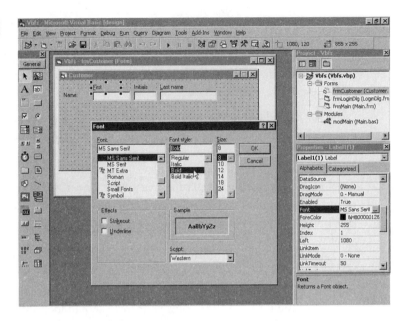

Repeat the operation for the label for the last name.

Now add the rest of the data fields for the customer form in pairs, one label to one text box. The final look when you have added all the controls is illustrated in Figure 9.3.

Figure 9.3

The frmCustomer with all the controls.

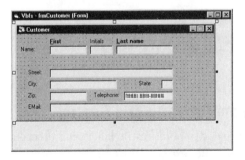

Start by adding a label/text box pair for the street address. Name the text box `txtStreetAddress`. Next add a label and text box for the city and name the text box `txtCity`. Repeat for state (name it `txtState`) and zip (name it `txtZip`).

Adding a MaskedEdit Control

For the telephone number, you use a special variation of the text box control that enables you to specify the format of the text displayed, as well as an input mask to simplify the data input for your users. First add the label &Telephone: and make the font bold. Now add the component that contains this control to your project: right-click on the Toolbox and select the menu item Components.... Then from the dialog box presented scroll down to the item Microsoft Masked Edit Control 6.0, and check the box to the left of it to include it in the project. Click OK when you're finished. Figure 9.4 illustrates this dialog box.

Figure 9.4

Add the MaskedEdit component to the project.

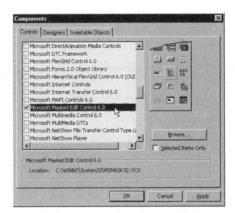

Notice the new icon added to the bottom of the Toolbox, representing the new component you inserted (refer to Figure 9.3). Select the icon and draw the control after the label &Telephone:. In the Properties window, change the name of this control to txtTelephone. The MaskedEdit control is an extended version of the regular TextBox control. Extended functionality is implemented through a few custom properties. The first one to note is the Format, which is a String property that indicates how the Text value of the control is displayed. The format string is similar to the intrinsic VB function Format, and it does offer a lot of different options, depending on the type of data that is stored in the Text property. A few examples are given in Table 9.1.

Table 9.1   Format Examples

Value	Description
#,##0	Use commas to delimit thousands, millions, and so on (numbers)
$#,##0.00;($#,##0.00)	Currency, show negatives in parentheses.
dd-mmm-yyyy	Show dates as 04-Jul-2000 (date)
hh:mm AM/PM	Time in short format 09:12 PM (time)
(###) ###-####	Typical telephone number representation

You will use the last one because you are displaying telephone numbers. Click on the Format property in the Properties window and set it to (###) ###-####.

Another important property is the Mask string. It contains a string that is used when the user enters data into the Masked Edit control. It uses a set of characters as place-holders (masks) for the data that the user will enter. For example the # is a place-holder for an optional digit, 0 is a placeholder for a required digit, while the A is a mask for an alphanumeric value (a–z, A–Z, and 0–9). If the user tries to enter an invalid character (for example, a letter where a digit is required), a `ValidationError` event is fired, and the event handling procedure is called (if any is implemented). The default action if no `ValidationError` event handler is present is to reject the invalid entry. We will use the same string as for the Format property, select the Mask property of the control and set it to (###) ###-####.

Another important property is the ClipMode property, which indicates whether the literals in the Mask property are included in the string when doing a copy and paste command on the control.

The ClipText property returns the Text string value without the mask literals. For example, if the user enters (800) 123-4567, the Text property of the control returns (800) 123-4567, while the ClipText property returns 8001234567. You will use this property in code, when saving the customer to the persistent storage (database).

Insert another label/text box pair for the email address. Name the text box `txtEmail`.

The final controls that you add to the form at this point are two CommandButton controls that are used to save the changes and to cancel changes to the customer data.

Add one CommandButton to the right of the form. Change the caption to &Save and the name to cmdSave. Set the Default property to True.

Add another button just under the cmdSave. Change the caption to &Cancel and the name to cmdCancel. You will write code for these buttons later.

Other Properties for the Built-In Controls

A useful property for the TextBox controls is MaxLength, which, as the name suggests, is the maximum length of the text that can be entered in that control. The data your users will enter in the text boxes on the form will be stored in a database table, each data field into a table column. But table columns of type text have a fixed size, so if you attempt to store a string that exceeds the size of the column an error might be generated, and the data will be truncated. To avoid this, set the MaxLength property for some of the TextBox controls on the customer form to reflect the size of the columns in the database table.

 Note   We will look in detail at the way the data is stored in the database later in this book.

Click on the txtFirstName. In the Properties window, scroll down to the MaxLength property. It is now set to 0, meaning that the user can enter as many characters as desired. Change this to 32. That allows the user to enter as many as 32 characters, including spaces.

Set the MaxLength for the rest of the controls to reflect the contents of Table 9.2.

Table 9.2   MaxLength Values for the Controls on the frmCustomer Form

TextBox Control Name	*MaxLength*
txtMiddleInitial	6
txtLastName	32
txtStreetAddress	64
txtCity	32
txtState	2
txtZip	16
txtEmail	64
txtTelephone	14 (should be set)

Another important property for the controls on a data entry type form is the TabIndex property. The TabIndex is an ordinal number from 0 to the number of controls on the form. Together with the TabStop property it controls the focus order on each form. The TabStop property is a Boolean property of the focus-capable controls, indicating whether the control should receive focus with the Tab/Shift+Tab. Focus-capable controls are defined as controls that can have focus (for example TextBox, ComboBox, CommandButton, and so on). All controls (regardless of the capability to receive focus) have a TabIndex property.

 Note   If a control has a TabStop property it means it can receive focus.

9

On each form, at any given time, only one control receives input from the keyboard. By input from the keyboard, we mean any key pressed that is not a shortcut for another control and also is not one of the system key combinations. This control is known as the active control—or the control that has focus.

You can think of all the controls on the form as being in a list, ordered by the TabIndex property. Some controls in the list can receive focus, some cannot. If the user presses the Tab key, VB will attempt to move the focus to the next control in the TabIndex order (the next item in the list). If the end of the list has been reached, it restarts at TabIndex 0. If the next item in the list is able to receive focus, it will be given focus, otherwise the next control in the list is queried. A control can receive focus if it is visible (its Visible property is True), is enabled (its Enabled property is True), can receive focus (depends on the control type), and has the TabStop property set to True.

If you set the TabStop property to False, the control will be skipped in the Tab and Shift+Tab navigation of the TabIndex list. However, it can still receive focus through other means (mouse action, shortcut key combination, or programmatically—from code).

The TabIndex property is set by VB in the order you have added the controls to the form. The first control has a TabIndex value of 0, the next one has a value of 1, and so on. It might seem peculiar that controls that cannot receive focus have a TabIndex property, but it is actually quite useful, as described later.

The Label controls cannot receive focus (and as such they have no TabStop property). But they can be used as bookmarks to set focus to the control (TextBox or similar) that follows after them in the TabIndex order. For example, you set the mnemonic of the label that precedes `txtFirstName` TextBox to F. That means that when the user presses Alt+F, the focus moves to the TextBox control following after the label in TabIndex order: in this case the `txtFirstName`. In this way (combining several properties of both controls), you have achieved your goal to have a mnemonic for a text box.

A quick way to check and set the TabIndex order on a form is to click on the first control on the form, then in the Properties window, scroll down to the TabIndex property. If the TabIndex property is not zero, type a 0 on the keyboard. Now click on the control that you would like to be next. The TabIndex shows the value for this control. Change it as required, using only the keyboard. VB shifts the values around so that no two items have the same TabIndex value.

Now you can test your form. Save your work, then press F5 to run the application. Open a Customer form (from the menu or from the toolbar). Try to enter the controls. Try to navigate with the Tab/Shift+Tab and with the mnemonics. Try to enter a text string longer than the control's MaxLength.

Handling Events from the Controls on the Customer Form

The first task for this form is to change the behavior of the TextBox controls so that when they receive focus the whole text in the control is selected. This improves the usability of your UI, allowing the users to overwrite the contents of a text field easier. This behavior is also becoming the *de facto* standard for data entry text boxes.

GotFocus and LostFocus

First you need to know when the control becomes active. VB helps you in this case by providing two events for the controls that can have focus: `GotFocus` and `LostFocus`. These events are fired every time the control gets focus and loses focus. A control can get focus as a result of the user moving the focus to the control (using the mouse or the keyboard), or programmatically, using a method called `SetFocus`.

 Note When moving focus from one control to another, the `LostFocus` event of the control with focus occurs before the `GotFocus` event of the control that will receive focus next. This order of events might prove important in some instances.

For your purpose, `GotFocus` is the ideal place to mark the entire text in the control selected. Edit the event handler for the `txtFirstName` control. If you double-click on the control, the code window for the frmCustomer is displayed. The cursor is positioned in the `Change` event handler for the `txtFirstName`. Because you are not interested in the `Change` event, select from the list of events the `GotFocus` event. Now enter the code as listed here:

```
Private Sub txtFirstName_GotFocus()
  txtFirstName.SelStart =
  txtFirstName.SelLength = Len(txtFirstName.Text)
End Sub
```

The code is using the `SelStart` and `SelLength` properties of the standard TextBox control to mark the contents of the control as selected. Both properties are not available at design time, which means you cannot see them in the properties window. The `SelStart` property represents the beginning of the selection, and it is 0-based. The `SelLength` is the number of characters from the text string that are selected,

9

starting at SelStart. Both properties are changing as the user selects text, or can be set from code, having the same effect: the text in the control appears selected. Note the use of the intrinsic Len function to determine the length of the text string displayed by the control.

Let's try the code you just entered. Save your work and run the project. After login, open a new Customer form and type some text in txtFirstName. If you move to the next text box and then come back, the text will show as selected. To replace it just start typing.

Now repeat the above procedure for all the text boxes on the form, including the MaskedEdit txtTelephone. When you are finished, save the project and test the changes.

The Click Event

Now you can add code to handle the Click events for the two command buttons. On the frmCustomer, double-click on the Cancel command button. The code window appears, positioned in the cmdCancel_Click procedure. The action you want to take in this case is simple: you do not want to save any changes made by the user to the customer being edited. That is, you must unload this form, as shown here:

```
Private Sub cmdCancel_Click()
  Unload Me
End Sub
```

If the user clicks the cmdSave button, you must validate the data on the form and then save it to the database. Then you can close the form. You will write code to validate that the required fields have been entered, but you will skip (for now) the saving to the database. Enter the code as shown here:

frmCustomer(Customer.frm)

```
Private Sub cmdSave_Click()
  If Len(txtFirstName) <= 0 Then
    MsgBox "First name is required to save changes!", vbExclamation
    txtFirstName.SetFocus
    Exit Sub
  End If
  If Len(txtLastName) <= 0 Then
    MsgBox "Last name is required to save changes!", vbExclamation
    txtLastName.SetFocus
    Exit Sub
  End If

  ' code to save the data will be added here
  Unload Me
End Sub
```

Be sure that both the first and last name are not empty. If either of them is empty, the Len function will return 0 and the If block will be executed. A message box will be displayed to alert the user of the omission. Then the focus is set to the appropriate text control, using the SetFocus method. Finally the current procedure is exited, using the Exit Sub statement.

 Note   The SetFocus method is available on all controls that can have focus. This method will fail (an error will be raised) if the control on which we invoke the method is not visible and enabled.

And now, if everything is all right, this form can be closed using the Unload statement.

Save your changes and run the project. Log in, then open a new customer form and enter a first name but no last name. Click on Save. You should get a message box warning of the error. Figure 9.5 illustrates the dialog box. Note the vbExclamation style used.

Figure 9.5

The final version of frmCustomer running.

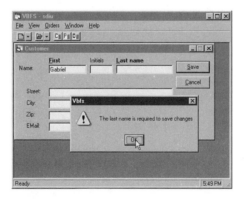

This concludes the chapter. You will return to the code in this form to add the actual functionality—editing and saving data for a customer.

Next Steps

In this chapter, you have created a data entry form for your customers. You have explored more properties, methods, and events for some of the built-in controls. You also have used a new ActiveX control—the MaskedEdit control. You have learned about form navigation and focus issues, in both design time and runtime. You have learned how to select text in a TextBox control from your code.

In the next chapter, you add a few new forms to your project and use some new controls. You learn some of their properties, methods, and events. Specifically, you learn how to display images and view documents in Rich Text format. More properties and events of the Form class are also used.

In this chapter

- *Adding a New Form for Products*
- *Adding Code for the Product Form*
- *Form Interaction—The Activate and Deactivate Events*
- *Adding a New Form to Display an Image—The Image Control*
- *IAdding a New Form to View a Document—The RichTextBox Control*

Chapter 10

More About Forms and Controls: Properties, Methods, and Events

You will add a new form to your project that will enable the users to add and modify products sold in your virtual store. You also will create two auxiliary forms that display the image and the documentation for a product.

The complete code for this chapter is found in the Chapter10 folder of the main VBFS folder on the CD-ROM that accompanies this book.

You have determined that the products sold in your store (books, music CDs, videotapes, DVDs, and software) have the following attributes: name, author, description, product type, image, attached documentation, supplier, and price. You know that the product name and price are required. You will design the form based on this information.

Adding a New Form for Products

First, add a new form to the project. From the Project menu, select Add Form. In the dialog box that opens, click on the Open button. A new form, named Form1, is added to the project. Change the Name of the form to frmProduct, the BorderStyle property to 1 - Fixed Single, the Caption to Product, the MinButton property to True, and the MDIChild property to True.

Tip

You can toggle a Boolean property from True to False, or the opposite, by double-clicking on the property in the Properties window.

Save your project. Make sure you save the new form in the same folder as the rest of the project.

Adding Controls to the Form

We can start adding controls to the form. First add a Label control for the name of the product. Use the final form depicted in Figure 10.1, later in this chapter, as a guide to the position and size of the controls. Set the label's caption to &Name: and the Index property to 0. Setting the index to 0 declares the label as part of an array, avoiding the VB dialog box that is displayed when you copy and paste the label.

Now add a TextBox control to the right of the label, set the Text property to "" (empty), the name to txtName, and the MaxLength to 32.

You can now copy and paste the label control right underneath the first one. Change the caption to &Author:. Add a text box to the right of the label. Set the name to txtAuthor, MaxLength to 32, and Text to "".

Paste another copy of the label underneath the one labeled &Author: and change the Caption to &Description:. Add a text box to the right of the label. Resize it to about two to three lines of text height. Name it txtDescription. Set the Text to "" and the MultiLine property to True. If the MultiLine property is True, the users can enter text on multiple lines in the control. Also set the ScrollBars property to 2 - Vertical by selecting from the drop-down list. A vertical scrollbar is now displayed in the control, enabling the users to navigate up and down in the control using the mouse. Set the MaxLength property to 128.

Paste another copy of the label underneath the description label and change the Caption to &Product type:. The product type is a selection type of value: the user provides input by selecting a value from a list. The most commonly used controls for this type of task are the ListBox and the ComboBox with the Style set to Dropdown List. A ListBox is a control that offers the user a choice from a list of possible options, presented as text lines in a box. A ComboBox is a combination between a ListBox and a TextBox, hence the name. You will use the ComboBox because it takes less space on the form.

Adding a ComboBox Control

Add a ComboBox control by selecting it from the Toolbox and drawing it to the right of the label. By default, it is named Combo1. Change the name to cmbProductType. You also need to change the Style property to 2 - Dropdown List. The Style property indicates how the control behaves at runtime. See Table 10.1 for details.

Table 10.1   Format Examples

Value	Description
0 - Dropdown Combo	(Default) The user can either enter text in the text part of the control or make a selection from the list part. Useful when a set of common values is used but the user can enter new values.
1 - Simple Combo	Both the text and list part are visible at all times. Not used much.
2 - Dropdown List	The user must select an item from the list. Useful when the selection must be made from a set of existing options.

Add another copy of the label underneath the one for the product type. Set the Caption to Image file:. Add a new text box to the right of it. Name it txtImageFile, set the Text to "" and the MaxLength to 128.

Add a CommandButton control adjacent to the right of the txtImageFile. Change its name to cmdBrowse, its Caption to "..." and its Index to 0. Now size the control so that it fits at the end of the txtImageFile (if necessary). Look at Figure 10.1, later in this chapter, for an illustration.

Tip   You can fine tune the position and size of a control by setting its Top, Left, Height, and Width properties in the Properties window. This sometimes might be necessary if the grid settings you are using are too coarse.

Repeat the previous steps for the Document file: label and for the txtDocFile text box. The MaxLength for the txtDocFile is also 128. Now copy and paste the cmdBrowse button and place it at the end of the text box.

Add the Supplier: label and the txtSupplier text box. Set the MaxLength of the txtSupplier to 64.

Add the &Price: label. Use a MaskedEdit control for the price text box. Set the name to txtPrice, the ClipMode to 1 - mskExcludeLiterals and the Format to $#,##0.00;($#,##0.00)—select it from the drop-down list.

Next add a few command buttons for saving the product or canceling the changes and for viewing the image or document file.

Open the frmCustomer form. Select both cmdSave and cmdCancel by either clicking on each of them while keeping the Shift key down or by drawing with the left mouse button a rectangle that intersects them. Right-click on them and select Copy. Close the frmCustomer form. Right-click on frmProduct and select Paste. Move the newly

10

added buttons to their place. Note that the copy and paste operation does not copy the code for the event procedures you have implemented for the two buttons. You will have to copy the code by hand or re-implement the event handlers.

Add a new command button to the right of the first `cmdBrowse` button. Set the Name to `cmdShowImage` and the Caption to Show image. Repeat for `cmdShowDocFile`, with a Caption Show doc.

The last thing you must add to the form is a Common Dialog ActiveX control. This control provides easy access to some of the commonly used dialog boxes used in the Windows UI: open a file, save a file, select a printer, select a font, or select a color. It provides the users with a standard interface, the same between applications, for opening a file, for example. The control itself is not visible at runtime and cannot be resized (as most of the controls invisible at runtime).

Adding a Common Dialog Box Control

From the Project/Components menu scroll down to Microsoft Common Dialog Control 6.0 and select it (check the check box to the left of it). Its icon is now added to the Toolbox. Select it and add it to the form. You can place it anywhere because it is invisible at runtime. Change the name to `dlg`. Also set the CancelError to True. This tells the control that you want an error if the user selects the Cancel button on any of the dialog boxes.

At this point you are finished with the graphical aspects of the form. Figure 10.1 illustrates the final form, including all the controls.

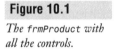

Figure 10.1

The `frmProduct` *with all the controls.*

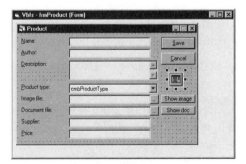

Adding Code for the Product Form

You have added a ComboBox control that enables the user to select a product type. Now let's add code to populate the list—providing the options from which the user can choose. Double-click on `frmProduct`. The code editor is now open and the cursor is placed in the empty body of the Form_Load procedure. Add the following lines of code:

frmProduct(Product.frm)

```
Private Sub Form_Load()
  cmbProductType.AddItem "Books/publications"
  cmbProductType.AddItem "Music tapes/CDs"
  cmbProductType.AddItem "Video tapes/DVDs"
  cmbProductType.AddItem "Software"
  cmbProductType.AddItem "Miscellaneous"
End Sub
```

Use the AddItem method of the ComboBox class to add an item (a string) to your drop-down list. This method takes an optional argument (Index), which specifies the position in the list where the new item is inserted. If this argument is omitted (as you have done), the new item is added to the end of the list.

Note You can also add items to the list in the Properties window, by editing the List property of the control. However, this method is less used, mainly because it makes the code less readable and can create problems when supporting multiple languages.

Opening a File Using the Common Dialog Control

Next, you can add code to enable the user to select an image or dialog file by browsing the file system. You will use the cmdBrowse and the dlg controls defined previously. Remember that you defined a control array of two command buttons (named cmdBrowse) for the two types of files you need to open: image (with the Index 0) and document (with the Index 1).

Double-click on any of the cmdBrowse command buttons. The code editor window is activated, with the cursor in the empty procedure handler for the Click event. Note the Index argument passed in: it will tell us which of the two controls has been clicked. Now enter the following code:

10

frmProduct(Product.frm)

```
Private Sub cmdBrowse_Click(Index As Integer)
  dlg.DialogTitle = "Select " & _
                    IIf(Index = 0, "image", "document") & _
                    " file to open"
```

Note the use of the underscore (_)as a line continuation character. This symbol, if it occurs by itself at the end of a line, tells VB that the statement continues on the next line. When we refer to a line of code in the rest of this book, we mean the entire statement—a logical line, not only the physical line.

This line of code sets the DialogTitle property of the dialog control to a string. Because you use the same procedure for both image and document files, you need to set the property to a different string depending on which button has been clicked. If the user intends to select an image file (Index will be 0), the string will be "Select image file to open". If the user intends to select a document file, then the text will be "Select document file to open". You achieve this by using the IIf or Instant If function. This function takes three arguments: the first one is named *expression* and is Boolean (can be either True or False), and two variant arguments named truePart and falsePart. If the expression evaluates to True, it returns the truePart as a return value; otherwise, it returns the third argument (falsePart). In this case, if the Index is 0, it will return the string image, otherwise will return the string "document". The return value will be concatenated (using the string concatenation operator &) with the literal strings before and after it (the return value) to form the final string. This string becomes the value of the property DialogTitle of the control; that is, the title of the dialog box.

Let's continue in the same procedure. Add the following code:

frmProduct(Product.frm)

```
If Index = 0 Then
  dlg.FileName = txtImageFile
  dlg.Filter = "Windows bitmap files (*.bmp)¦*.bmp¦" & _
               "GIF files (*.gif)¦*.gif¦" & _
               "JPEG files (*.jpg)¦*.jpg¦" & _
               "Icon files (*.ico)¦*.ico¦" & _
               "All files (*.*)¦*.*"
  dlg.FilterIndex =
Else
  dlg.FileName = txtDocFile
  dlg.DefaultExt = ".rtf"
  dlg.Filter = "Rich text files (*.rtf)¦*.rtf¦" & _
               "Text files (*.txt)¦*.txt¦" & _
               "All files (*.*)¦*.*"
  dlg.FilterIndex =
End If
```

In this snippet of code, we are setting three other properties of the dialog control: FileName, Filter, and FilterIndex. These properties are set differently, depending on the button that was clicked: image or document files.

The `FileName` property is used to set or get the fully qualified filename (that is, path included) selected by the user. Normally, it is set to the filename before opening the dialog box, so that a previously selected file is preserved. After the dialog box is closed, it contains the new selection made by the user (if any). You set it to the text string contained in the appropriate text box control.

The `Filter` property is a custom property of the `CommonDialog` class, used to display (at the bottom of the dialog box) a drop-down list of possible file types that can be handled by the dialog box. If the user selects a type from the drop-down list, the dialog box will display a filtered list containing only the files that match that type. Each file type consists of a description and an associated extension, delimited by a vertical bar character (¦). For example, `Text files (*.txt)¦*.txt` is a file filter for files of type text, having an extension .txt.

If you have more than one type of file, use the ¦ to delimit the types. It is customary to add a filter at the end that includes all file types; for example, `All files (*.*)¦*.*`. See Figure 10.2 for an illustration of the Select Image File to Open dialog box, and note the file types shown in the drop-down list labeled Files of Type:.

Figure 10.2

An example of a File Open common dialog box.

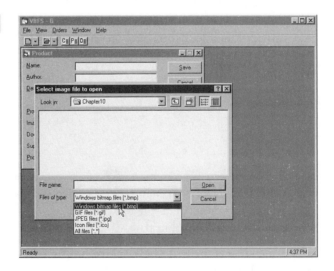

The `FilterIndex` property is used to set the default filter from the list of available filters. It is a 0-based number. Setting it to a non-existent index will cause an error.

Let's continue to add code to the `cmdBrowse_Click` event procedure:

frmProduct(Product.frm)

```
dlg.Flags = cdlOFNFileMustExist
```

The next step in refining the dialog box control is to set the `Flags` property. This property can be set to a combination of flags (constant values) specific to each type of dialog box that can be displayed. If more than one flag is required, it must be added together using the + arithmetic operator. Table 10.2 lists a few of the most common flags used for Open and Save dialog boxes. For a detailed description, check the online VB reference.

Table 10.2   Common Values for the `Flags` Property of the Common Dialog Box

Value	Description
cdlOFNAllowMultiselect	Allows the user to select more than one file in the dialog box. The `FileName` contains all files selected, separated by spaces.
cdlOFNFileMustExist	The file must exist (cannot enter a new filename).
cdlOFNPathMustExist	The folder containing the file must exist.
cdlOFNReadOnly	If this is set after return, the file is read-only.
cdlOFNHideReadOnly	Hides the read-only check box on the dialog box.
cdlOFNOverwritePrompt	The user is prompted for confirmation if attempting to overwrite an existing file (in Save As dialog boxes).

In this case, you need the file to exist, and therefore require the flags to be set to the constant value `cdlOFNFileMustExist`. Next you open the dialog box and allow the user to select the file:

frmProduct(Product.frm)

```
On Error Resume Next
dlg.Action =
If Err.Number = cdlCancel Then Exit Sub
On Error GoTo
```

The first line of code tells VB that if an error occurs in the code that follows this statement, it should be ignored, and the following statement on the line after the one with the error should be executed next.

The next line of code sets the write-only `Action` property of the dialog to 1, which stands for Open File dialog box. This opens the dialog box and does not return until the user has either selected a file or canceled the operation. Expect a potential error here. If the user cancels the dialog box, you will get a `cdlCancel` error, as mentioned previously. That is the reason for using the `On Error Resume Next` error handler.

Handling Errors in Code

An error is a condition that a piece of code did not expect. For example, attempting to divide a number by 0 is an error. Errors can be built-in errors like the ones mentioned previously or custom errors (defined by a custom component, as it is in this case). An error has a number, a description, and a source associated with it. VB stores the information for the last error in the global unique object named `Err`. This object can be accessed from anywhere in your code. If an error occurs (is raised either by attempting to execute an illegal operation or by using the `Raise` method of the `Err` object) and no code handles the error, VB deals with it by displaying a message box stating the error and then terminates your application. Because this is not acceptable from the user's point of view, the developer must provide an error-handling mechanism.

In this case, we just resume to the next statement, which is checking to see whether the dialog box generated the error because the user has selected the Cancel button. If this is true (that is, the Number property of the global `Err` object is `cdlCancel`), we honor the request to ignore the operation by exiting the procedure. Otherwise we continue by disabling the error handling using the statement `On Error GoTo 0`. This statement comes from the days when Basic was not Visual, and it had line numbers. The effect is that it disables the effects of the `On Error Resume Next`, or any other error handler active. We will return to error handling later and in more detail in Chapter 20.

Let's conclude the event procedure. Continue with the code:

frmProduct(Product.frm)

```
    If Index = 0 Then
      txtImageFile = dlg.FileName
    Else
      txtDocFile = dlg.FileName
    End If
End Sub
```

At this point the dialog box has returned and the `FileName` property contains the file selected by the user. Set the appropriate text box control to the string returned by the `FileName` property of the common dialog control. Note that again you distinguish between image and document files, using the Index argument value. The event procedure `cmdBrowse_Click` is now completed.

Handling the Save and Cancel Click Events

Let's add code for the `cmdCancel_Click`: you simply unload this object:

frmProduct(Product.frm)

```
Private Sub cmdCancel_Click()
  Unload Me
End Sub
```

In a similar fashion to the `frmCustomer`, in the `cmdSave_Click` you check that the required fields (name and price) have been set, then you unload the form (for now):

frmProduct(Product.frm)

```
Private Sub cmdSave_Click()
  If Len(txtName) <= 0 Then
    MsgBox "Product name is required to save changes!", vbExclamation
    txtName.SetFocus
    Exit Sub
  End If
  If Val(txtPrice) <= 0 Then
    MsgBox "Product price is required to save changes!", vbExclamation
    txtPrice.SetFocus
    Exit Sub
  End If

  ' code to save the data will be added here
  Unload Me
End Sub
```

Note the use of the intrinsic function `Val` to convert a string to a numeric value. If the string is empty, the value returned will be 0.

Now add code to show the form when the menu item and toolbar buttons are clicked. Open `frmMain` and select the menu item File, New, Product. The code editor for `frmMain` is opened and the event procedure `mnuFileNewProduct_Click` is displayed. Enter the code as follows, to create and display a new form for editing the product:

frmMain(Main.frm)

```
Private Sub mnuFileNewProduct_Click()
  Dim f As New frmProduct
  f.Show
End Sub
```

Now you need to call the menu event procedure when the toolbar button is clicked. Scroll the code window to the `tbr_ButtonMenuClick` procedure and uncomment the line in bold type, as shown here:

frmMain(Main.frm)

```
Private Sub tbr_ButtonMenuClick(ByVal ButtonMenu As MSComctlLib.ButtonMenu)
  Select Case ButtonMenu.Key
    Case "NewC"
      mnuFileNewCustomer_Click
    Case "NewP"
      mnuFileNewProduct_Click
    Case "NewO"
```

```
        'mnuOrdersNewOrder_Click
    Case "OpenC"
        'mnuFileOpenCustomer_Click
    Case "OpenP"
        'mnuFileOpenProduct_Click
  End Select
End Sub
```

Now you can test your work. Save your project and press Ctrl+F5 to do a full compile and run. If you have made any errors in code, the compiler will let you know. Otherwise the program will run. Open a new Product form and try some features. Try the dialog boxes and make sure the filenames are set properly. Figure 10.3 shows the program running.

Figure 10.3

Entering a new product.

Form Interaction—The `Activate` and `Deactivate` Events

We would like to show what type of form is currently active in the status bar of the main form, and eventually some tips for the users, related to the currently active object.

You can achieve this by using the `SbrMessage` method you have added to the main form. You can do that in the `Activate` event of both `frmCustomer` and `frmProduct`.

Open the code for `frmProduct` and select the item labeled Form from the left dropdown list at the top of the code editor. Then select the `Activate` event from the right drop-down list. VB creates an empty event procedure and places the cursor in there. Enter the following code:

frmProduct(Product.frm)

```
Private Sub Form_Activate()
  frmMain.SbrMessage "You are now editing a Product"
End Sub
```

The Activate event occurs every time the form receives focus (normally one of the controls on the form receives focus). The Deactivate event occurs when the form loses focus (another form or a control on another form receives focus).

Repeat the operation for frmCustomer. Enter the code as follows:

frmCustomer(Customer.frm)

```
Private Sub Form_Activate()
  frmMain.SbrMessage "You are now editing a Customer"
End Sub
```

Now you can run the project, and by opening one form of each type and then switching focus from one to the other, you will notice the appropriate message being displayed in the status bar of the main form.

Notice that when you close the last child form the message does not get erased, it is still reading "You are now editing." This is incorrect, and you must fix this by setting the message to nothing ("") when the form is unloaded. In a similar fashion, you add code for the Unload event for both frmCustomer and frmProduct forms:

frmProduct(Product.frm) and frmCustomer(Customer.frm)

```
Private Sub Form_Unload()
  frmMain.SbrMessage ""
End Sub
```

That corrects the problem. Run the project now and verify that it fixes it. You might wonder: Why not use the Deactivate event to clear the message in the status bar? The reason is that the deactivate event does not occur when an MDI child form is closed.

Adding a New Form to Display an Image—The Image Control

The next task is to add a global utility function that checks the existence of a file and returns True if the file exists, and False otherwise. Open the modMain module, and enter this code:

modMain(Main.bas)

```
Public Function FileExists(ByVal sName As String) As Boolean
  Dim a As VbFileAttribute
  On Error Resume Next
  a = GetAttr(sName)
  If Err.Number <> 0 Then
    On Error GoTo
    Exit Function
  End If
  FileExists = Not (a And vbDirectory)
End Function
```

Use the intrinsic `GetAttr()` function to get the attributes for the given file. If the file does not exist, the error number will be different than 0, and the only thing you need to do is to clear the error using the `On Error GoTo 0` statement and exit the function. Because you did not set the return value, the default value is used—False for the Boolean type. So the function in this case returns False. If the file exists and it is a folder (directory) name, the attribute returned by the `GetAttr` function will be a combination of the `vbDirectory` flag and possibly other flags (for example, `vbArchive`). Use the bitwise `And` operator to check whether the file is a directory. The return value of the function is the negated result of the expression that checks for the directory flag. It is True if it is a file, False if it is a directory.

Now continue the project by adding a new utility form, which is used to show an image. Begin by inserting a new form into the project. Set the form name to be `frmImageView` and the MDIChild property to True. The only control on this new form is a built-in Image control.

 Note

The Image control is used (as the name suggests) to display an image. The image can come from a bitmap, icon, metafile, JPEG, or GIF file. The image can be stretched to fit the control size, or the control size can be resized to fit the image.

10

Draw an Image control on the form. Set the Name to `img` and set the Top and Left properties to 0.

Now add code to load and display an image from a file into the control. The method to add is a public procedure of the form. Add this code:

frmImageView(ImageView.frm)

```
Public Sub SetImage(ByVal imgFile As String)
  If Not FileExists(imgFile) Then Exit Sub
```

continues

frmImageView(ImageView.frm) continued

```
    img.Picture = LoadPicture(imgFile)
    Me.Width = img.Width + (Me.Width - Me.ScaleWidth)
    Me.Height = img.Height + (Me.Height - Me.ScaleHeight)
End Sub
```

First, you must check whether the file exists. If it does not, exit the sub without any change. If it does exist, load the image into the image control by using the intrinsic function LoadPicture (which takes a filename and returns a Picture object) and by setting the Picture property of the image control. Thus the image control displays the picture and is resized to fit the size of the picture.

   Note   You can have a fixed size image and have the picture stretched or compressed to fit the size by setting the Stretch property of the Image control to True.

The next two lines of code are required to resize the form so that it fits the img control nicely. Note the use of the Width and ScaleWidth, Height, and ScaleHeight properties of the form.

The Width and Height properties of a form indicate the external size of the form (including the borders and the caption bar). They are always measured in twips. A twip is a screen-independent measure unit equal to 1/1440 of an inch. The default VB unit of measure for graphics is the twip, although it can be changed.

The Width and Height properties of each control are expressed in the units defined by the ScaleMode of their container (normally the form or another control).

The ScaleWidth and ScaleHeight are the sizes of the internal area of the form or control (excluding the borders and the caption bar). By default, they are also measured in twips, but changing the ScaleMode property of the form to the desired setting can alter this. The most commonly used value, other than twip, is pixel.

To change the size of a control or form, you must set the Width and Height properties. In this case, you want the image control to completely fill the form. So set the form width to the image width plus the difference between the Width and the ScaleWidth of the form, which is the size of the nonpaintable area of the form (borders and caption bar). Do the same for the Height.

Adding Code to Show the Form

Now add code to display the form. Open the frmProduct form. Double-click the Show Image button. The code editor is loaded and you are positioned in the Click event procedure for the command button. Enter the following code:

frmProduct(Product.frm)

```
Private Sub cmdShowImage_Click()
  Dim f As New frmImageView
  Load f
  f.SetImage txtImageFile
End Sub
```

When the button is clicked, a new instance of frmImageView will be created and loaded, and then the public method you have implemented previously will be called to display the image file from the txtImageFile text box.

You can now save the project and run your code to select, and then load, an image file. This iteration of the application is illustrated in Figure 10.4.

Figure 10.4

View an image for a product.

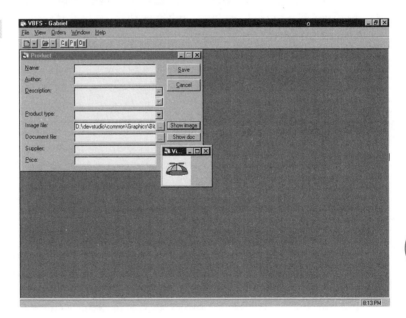

Adding a New Form to View a Document—The RichTextBox Control

Now add a new utility form that enables the users to see the document attached to a given product—if any was provided. Add a new form to the project. Set the form name to frmDocView, the Caption to View documentation, and the MDIChild property to True.

To view document files, use the ActiveX custom control named RichTextBox. This control enables viewing (and editing) of normal text files, as well as documents in Rich Text Format (RTF). From the main menu of VB select Project, Components. Scroll down to the component named Microsoft Rich Textbox Control 6.0, and check the box to include this component in your project. Click OK. The new control icon appears in the Toolbox.

Select the new control and draw it on the new frmDocView to cover the whole area of the form. Change the control name from RichTextBox1 to rtb, and the Text property to "". In the Properties window, scroll down to the Locked property and set it to True. The Locked property indicates that the user is prohibited from making changes to the text in the control. It is a property that applies to most built-in controls and to some custom controls. If the control is locked, the user can still scroll up and down and select text (for example, to copy a portion of text), but no changes can be made to the text. This is different from a control that is disabled (that is, has the Enabled property set to False). A disabled control cannot have focus, and therefore the user cannot scroll or select/copy text from the control.

Also set the ScrollBars property to 3 - rtfBoth; you want the user to scroll the text as required. The ScrollBars enumerated property is used to select the type of scrollbars used by the control.

Adding Code to Handle Form Resizing

Now you must enter code to resize the control to fill the whole form when the user resizes the form. Double-click on the form to open the code editor. You are positioned in the empty body of the Form_Load event procedure. You will not use this procedure for this form. Select the Resize event from the events drop-down list (top-right of the editor window). The Resize event occurs when the size of the form changes as a result of an user action (resizing the form with the mouse, maximizing or minimizing the form), or as a result of an action executed from code (for example setting the Width or Height properties of the form). This event can occur several times in sequence, as the user resizes the form using the mouse, for example. Enter the following code:

frmDocView(DocView.frm)

```
Private Sub Form_Resize()
  If Me.WindowState = vbMinimized Then Exit Sub

  Dim w As Single, h As Single

  w = Me.ScaleWidth - 2 * rtb.Left
  h = Me.ScaleHeight - 2 * rtb.Top
  If w > 0 Then rtb.Width = w
  If h > 0 Then rtb.Height = h
End Sub
```

The first line of code checks to see if the window is minimized (is an icon). If it is, the procedure is exited because no resizing will be required (the control is not even visible). The check for minimized state is done using the WindowState property of the form, which can have one of the three value: vbNormal (normal form), vbMaximized (the form is maximized to fill the whole screen), and vbMinimized (if it is an icon). This property also can be set to one of the constant values above, to cause the form to change the window state to the one requested. For example, to maximize a window one could set the WindowState property to vbMaximized.

Next compute the width and the height that the rtb control requires to be centered within the form. Dimension two variables of type single precision to hold the computed values. Use single precision because this is the type used for all calculations involving graphical sizes and positions in VB.

Calculate the width by subtracting two times the Left value of the rtb control from the value of the ScaleWidth property of the form. The ScaleWidth value is the current size of the internal (client) area of the form. This is the area excluding the borders and the caption bar. The w variable contains the width value of the rtb so that it is centered horizontally within the form. Note that if the ScaleWidth is less than two times the value of the Left value for the rtb, w will be negative. Because it would be an error to set the Width property of a control to a negative number, make sure that only a positive w is assigned to the Width property. You can achieve this by using the one-line If statement.

The same type of calculation is done for the Height of the rtb control, and the same precaution is taken to avoid assigning a negative number to the Height property of the rtb.

Now you need to enter some code to load the document file into the control. Add the SetDoc public method—similar to the SetImage() method of the frmImageView. Enter this code in the code editor:

10

frmDocView(DocView.frm)

```
Public Sub SetDoc(ByVal docName As String)
  If Not FileExists(docName) Then Exit Sub
  rtb.FileName = docName
End Sub
```

Make sure the file passed in exists, using the utility function defined previously. If it does not exist, exit the procedure. If it does exist, load the file into the control by setting the FileName property of the control to the value passed in the docName argument.

You have finished the design and coding for this form. You now add code in the frmProduct to open the form for a document selected by the user. Open the frmProduct and double-click on the command button labeled Show doc. The code editor opens for the Click event procedure. Enter the following code:

frmProduct(Product.frm)

```
Private Sub cmdShowDocFile_Click()
  Dim f As New frmDocView
  Load f
  f.SetDoc txtDocFile
End Sub
```

The code creates a new form of type frmDocView, and then loads it and calls the SetDoc method passing in the name of the document file (contained in the text box txtDocFile). This opens the form and displays the document.

Save the project. Make sure you save the new form in the same folder as the rest of your project. Now you can run the project and test the new form. Figure 10.5 shows the running project, with the frmDocView open.

Next Steps

In this chapter, you added three new forms to your project and learned about the properties and methods of new controls, both built-in (like the ComboBox) and custom (like the CommonDialog and the RichTextBox). You also have used new properties of the Form class and of the controls you have encountered before.

In the next chapter, we will introduce two new important ActiveX controls: the TreeView and ListView controls. You also will learn more about mouse-related events and properties and how to design a simple splitter window using VB. We will also take a look at pop-up menus.

Figure 10.5

View a document file for a product.

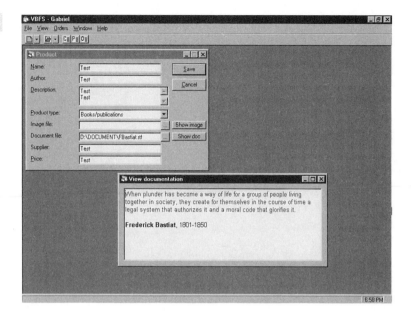

10

In this chapter

- *Adding a New Customer Orders View Form*
- *Adding the TreeView Control*
- *Adding the ListView Control*
- *Adding the ImageList Controls*
- *Adding a Custom Resources File to the Project*
- *Adding Code to Resize the Splitter Form*
- *Adding a Right-Click Pop-Up Menu*

Chapter 11

Creating an Explorer-Style Form Using TreeView and ListView Controls

In this chapter, we will expand your project by adding a new form to it. We will design this form in Windows Explorer style. It will have two resizable panes: a tree view in the left pane and a list view (or detail view) in the right pane. You also will add a pop-up menu, activated by the right-click of the mouse. We will write code to handle the resizing of the two panes and also some mouse events. Later on in the book we will complete the form by writing code to populate the lists.

The complete code for this chapter can be found in the Chapter11 folder of the main VBFS folder on the CD that accompanies this book.

Adding a New Customer Orders View Form

The form you are going to create in this chapter will be used to display a list of all customers and the orders for each customer within an Explorer-like window. When an item is selected in the tree pane of the form, the details for that item are displayed in the right pane (the list pane). This is similar to the way Windows Explorer shows a hierarchical tree of drives and folders in the left pane and the files in the selected folder in the right pane. If you are not familiar with the Windows Explorer interface, it would be a good idea for you to open it and look at how it works, from the user interface perspective.

Insert a new form in the project. Change the Name property of the form to frmCustOrders. Set the Caption property to View Customer Order. Set the ScaleMode property to 3 - Pixel. As you have seen in the previous chapters, the ScaleMode is a property of forms and control containers (that is, controls that can "hold" inside other controls, like the Frame or PictureBox controls). This property indicates the units used to measure the size or position of the controls in the container (the form in your case). The ScaleMode property is an enumerated value, so you need to select one value from the drop-down list in the Properties window. If you select pixels, the sizes and positions of all controls on this form will be measured in pixels.

Note   The ScaleMode property of a control is not automatically inherited from the container. For example, if you have a form that has the ScaleMode set to pixels and on the form a PicturePox control, the ScaleMode of the PictureBox is not set to pixels. You must manually set it to pixels, if this is required.

The ScaleMode property also indicates what units are used to measure the ScaleTop, ScaleLeft, ScaleWidth, and ScaleLeft properties of the container itself. In our case all these properties will be measured in pixels.

Please note that this form is not an MDI child form (that is, the MDIChild property is set to False). We will elaborate on this shortly.

Adding the TreeView Control

From the VB Toolbox, select the TreeView control by clicking on it. As we have mentioned before, the TreeView control is part of a group of controls named Windows Common controls. These controls are grouped in what is known as a component DLL or ActiveX DLL. Draw the control on the form. Use the form illustrated in Figure 11.1 as a guide to the position and size of the control.

Change the name of the control to tvw. The TreeView control is used to display a hierarchical view of some data items. An example of a hierarchical data structure is a file system, where each folder can contain files and other folders, very much like a tree that has branches and each branch can have leaves or other branches. The items represented in the tree are named *nodes*. Each node can have child nodes. By default, each node has a label and an image preceding the label. Items that have child items normally have a plus (+) sign in front of them, to indicate this fact. Clicking on the + opens the child items and the + sign becomes a – sign, indicating that the child items are visible. The Windows Explorer left view of the folders is an example of a TreeView control.

Figure 11.1

frmCustOrders with the TreeView and ListView controls.

Open the Property Pages dialog box by right-clicking on the control and selecting Properties. The first page of the dialog box (illustrated in Figure 11.2) contains some of the properties that apply to the control as a whole. Let us explore some of the properties specific to the TreeView control. We will skip the properties that are common to all VB controls.

Figure 11.2

Property Pages dialog box of the TreeView control.

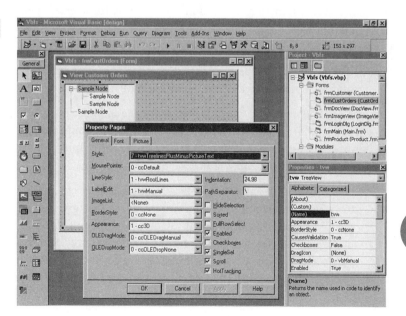

11

Properties of the TreeView Control

The Style property is an enumerated property that indicates how the nodes are represented in the tree. The possible values for this property consist of all the possible combinations of the following:

- Tree lines (the dotted lines from a node to its child nodes)
- Node labels
- + and – signs for the non-leaves nodes
- The picture for each node

One can choose to show only the labels, or the labels and the + and – signs, and so on. In this case, we take the default, which is to show everything.

The LineStyle property indicates how the root nodes are shown. The enumerated value can be either `tvwTreeLines` (default) or `tvwRootLines` (all root nodes are shown as starting from one root). Change the LineStyle property from the default `tvwTreeLines` to `tvwRootLines`. Click on Apply to see the changes.

The enumerated LabelEdit property indicates how the label editing is handled. The label editing occurs when the user clicks on the label of a node, for example, when renaming a file or folder in the Windows Explorer. If it is set to `tvwAutomatic`, the user can change the label of each node. The control fires the BeforeLabelEdit and AfterLabelEdit to notify you of the changes. In this case, you do not want this behavior, so change the LabelEdit to `tvwManual`. This setting enables you to control which labels can be edited, using a method of the control named StartLabelEdit.

The ImageList property points to a valid ImageList control that will be used as a source of pictures for all the nodes. You can add an ImageList later.

The Indentation property is the size of the indentation that occurs between a parent node and its child nodes, measured in twips. You might want to reduce it a bit. You can experiment with different values and use the Apply button to see the results without closing the dialog box.

The String PathSeparator property indicates what character will be used as a separator when constructing the FullPath property for a given node. The FullPath is a String property that consists of the concatenation of the Text properties of all the nodes between the given one and the root of the tree, separated by the PathSeparator character. The FullPath is similar to the path in a file system, which contains the names of all folders between the current position and the root (the drive or server name). It is, in effect, the unique address of the node in question. We will use the default for this property, which is the \ character.

The HideSelection Boolean property indicates whether the selected items are "hidden" (that is, not shown as selected) when the control does not have focus. You do not want this behavior, so uncheck the check box. Now the selected items display as selected even if the control does not have focus.

The Sorted property tells the TreeView control to automatically sort all the children of each node. Leave the property to the default value of False (unchecked).

The FullRowSelect property indicates whether an entire row is selected when the user selects one item. It applies mostly to ListView controls.

The Checkboxes property indicates whether a check box is displayed in front of each node in the list, allowing selection to occur by checking the box in front of the node. You do not need this behavior, so leave it unchecked.

The SingleSel property specifies that only one node can be selected at any given time. Normally, multiple nodes can be selected (for example, multiple files in Windows Explorer). You do not need this behavior, so check the box to set the SingleSel property to True.

The Scroll property indicates whether the tree scrolls up or down when a drag-and-drop operation is in effect and the user moves the mouse drop cursor to the upper or lower part of the control. Use the default of True for this property.

Finally, the HotTracking property indicates whether the control will highlight the node when the mouse cursor is above it, to give feedback to the user of the current position. The default feedback is given by changing the node label font to an underlined font. Set this property to True.

The Font tab of the Property Pages dialog box is used to set the font properties for the control, similar to the standard Font dialog box. The Picture tab is used to set a custom mouse cursor for the control.

Click OK to save your changes and save the project. Select a name for your form, and save it in the same folder as the rest of your project.

Adding the ListView Control

From the VB Toolbox, select the ListView control. Draw the control on the form using the mouse. Use the form illustrated in Figure 11.1 as a guide to the position and size of the control.

Change the name of the control to lvw. The ListView control is used to present a list of items to the user in different formats, as shown in Figure 11.3. The item objects are known as ListItems. Each one of them has two images associated with it—one large and one small. The ListItems also have a Text property—the label that is shown in the list. Additional text items may be attached to each ListItem; they are named subitems or detail items. These subitems become visible in report view. An example of a ListView control is the right pane of the Windows Explorer that shows the files in any given folder. Now we will explore some of the most important properties of the ListView control.

General Properties of the ListView Control

Open the Property Pages for the control by right-clicking on it and selecting Properties. On the first page, you find general properties that affect the control as a whole, as shown in Figure 11.3.

Figure 11.3

The Property Pages dialog box of the ListView control.

The View enumerated property is used to get or set the type of view the list control displays currently. It can be one of the four enumerated values listed here:

Value	Description
lvwIcon	Large icons
lvwSmallIcon	Small icons
lvwList	List of items
lvwReport	Details for each item

You must set the View to start in detail mode, therefore select lvwReport.

The enumerated Arrange property is used in the first two views (icons and small icons) to arrange the icons. It can be set to the following:

Value	Description
lvwNone	Icons are not arranged
lvwAutoLeft	Icons are arranged from the left
lvwAutoTop	Icons are arranged from the top

The LabelEdit property is similar to the property with the same name of the TreeView control. You do not want the user to change the labels, so set it to manual.

The HideColumnHeaders property determines whether, in the lvwReport view, the column headers are visible. The column headers are shown by default. For example, in the Windows Explorer detail view for each file the name, extension, size, date/time, and attributes appear. The column headers enable the users to resize the column widths and sort by a specific column. You want the column headers to be visible, so leave the check box unchecked.

The HideSelection property is the same as the TreeView control HideSelection property. Leave it checked for this control.

The LabelWrap Boolean property indicates whether the text for each ListItem will be wrapped if it is too long to fit in one line. This applies to the lvwIcon view only.

The MultiSelect property indicates whether the user can select multiple items from the list. It is similar to the SingleSel property of the TreeView control.

AllowColumnReorder is a Boolean property that indicates whether the user can change the order of the columns in lvwReport view. Check the box to set this property to True.

The Checkboxes property is identical with the TreeView property of the same name.

The FlatScrollBar property indicates what the appearance of the scrollbars shown in the control is going to be like: flat or 3D.

The FullRowSelect property enables the user in report view to select a whole row at a time, and not only one item at a time.

The Gridlines property indicates whether in Report view the control is displaying delimiting grid lines between columns.

The HotTracking property is the same as the property with the same name in TreeView control. We will not enable this property for the List control.

11

The HoverSelection property indicates whether an item from the list will be selected when the mouse cursor is placed above it (hovers), but without clicking on it.

Other Properties of the ListView Control

The second page of properties for the ListView control enables you to select the ImageList controls that are used for the large icon image, the small icon image, and the images used by the column headers. None of these must be set; they are all optional.

The page labeled Sorting enables you to specify whether the control items are sorted, and if they are, what is the sorting key and the type of sorting (ascending or descending). The sorting key is a numeric index to one of the text properties of the ListItems in the control. For example, in Windows Explorer you can sort the contents of the file list by filename, size, or modification date and time. We are not using sorting.

The column headers are displayed in the Report view, if the HideColumnHeaders property is False. There must be one column header for each subitem text of the ListItems. For example, if each of your items has a name, size, and type, you need three column headers. The column headers are represented by a collection of ColumnHeader objects, as a property of the ListView control (similar to the Buttons collection on a toolbar). Each ColumnHeader object has an Index, a Text (the text that is shown in the column header), and a Key (a unique string identifying each object in the collection). The Width property is expressed in twips and can be set at design time or runtime. The IconIndex property refers to the ImageList control added for the column headers. You can add ColumnHeader objects at design time using this dialog, or you can do it at runtime in code. We will set the column headers in code later in this chapter.

The last three pages of the dialog are the standard Color, Font, and Picture pages.

Adding the ImageList Controls

You need (for both the TreeView and ListView controls) some images to display in front of the items. You will add two image controls: one for the large images used by the ListView controls and the other for the small images used both by the ListView and TreeView control.

Add an ImageList control to the form. Change its name to `iml24`. Open the Property Pages dialog box for the control and click on the tab labeled Images. You will insert some pictures into the control using the Insert Picture button. From the Res subfolder of the main Vbfs/Program folder on the CD, insert the following pictures in this order: Customer24.bmp, Order24.bmp, OrderItem24.bmp, and Product24.bmp. From the Color tab, select the MaskColor and set it to white.

Add another ImageList control. Name it `iml12`. Open its Property Pages dialog box and select the Images tab. From the same location, insert the following images in this order: Customer12.bmp, Order12.bm, OrderItem12.bmp, and Product12.bmp. Set the MaskColor property to white.

Now you can go back to the TreeView and ListView controls and set the image lists. Open the Property Pages dialog box for the `tvw` control. From the drop-down list of the ImageList property, select `iml12`. Save the changes. You will now notice that the sample nodes displayed have the image in front of them.

Open the Property Pages dialog box for the `lvw` control. From the ImageLists tab, select the `iml24` for the Normal image list, and the `iml12` for the Small image list. Save the changes.

You have completed the graphical design part of the form. Next you will add a resource file to the project.

Adding a Custom Resources File to the Project

A custom resources file contains compiled (binary) resources like images, cursors, and even strings. You need the custom resource file for the two custom mouse cursors used in this chapter. You can create your own resource file using a resource editor tool (like the one supplied with Visual Developer Studio) and then compile it using the Resource Compiler (RC).

We have provided the resource file already compiled. Please copy the file Res.res from the Vbfs/Program folder on the CD to the folder in which your project resides. From the VB main menu bar, select Project, Add File. From the Add File dialog box, select the file you just pasted in your project folder, and select OK. Notice that there is now a new folder in your Project window, labeled Related Documents, which contains the resource file you added.

The next step is to create two public constants for the two mouse cursors you are interested in. Each resource in the resource file has a resource ID, which is used to load the resource at runtime. Open the modMain module. Add the declarations listed here at the top of the module, below the `Option Explicit` statement:

```
Public Const IDC_SizeDragNS = 109
Public Const IDC_SizeDragWE = 106
```

11

In this case, the resource identifiers for the two cursors are 109 and 106, respectively. You could have used the numbers directly, but it is not a good practice to do so, for a number of reasons. The most important is that if you ever change the value (say to 110), you will have to change every single occurrence of 109 with 110. If you miss one occurrence, another resource will be loaded, potentially causing a crash at run-time. Another reason to use constants is readability of the code. It makes more sense to somebody reading your code (and even to yourself in six months from now) to see the symbolic constant IDC_SizeDragNS rather than the number 109. The practice of sprinkling the code with various numbers is called programming with "magic numbers."

The two cursors you need are now ready to use from your code. You will use them in the next paragraphs when you implement the resizing of the panes of this form.

Adding Code to Resize the Splitter Form

You will add code to the frmCustOrders to change the size of the two visible controls on it (TreeView and ListView) using the mouse. In effect, you want to change the widths of the two controls as indicated by the user, while dragging the mouse. The idea is to keep the ratio between the widths of the two controls in a private variable on the form, and adjust the control widths based on this ratio multiplied by the form's width. For example, if the ratio is 0.33, the width of the TreeView control (tvw) will be 1/3, while the width of the ListView (lvw) will be 2/3 of the ScaleWidth of the form (excluding the margins). When the user starts to drag the mouse with the intent of resizing the controls, you change the ratio variable, based on the mouse position, and redraw the controls on the form. This procedure can be used for any type of splitter form, horizontal, vertical, or combined.

Start by opening the code editor for the frmCustOrders form. At the top of the module, just below the Option Explicit, add the following code:

```
Const margin =
Private m_ratio As Single
Private m_resizing As Integer
```

You will need a constant for the width of the interval between the form and the controls, and between the two controls. Because the ScaleMode is pixels, set the constant value to 3 pixels. Next you have the ratio variable declared as a single precision value with values between 0 and 1. Finally, declare a variable that indicates whether a resizing is in progress or not (by holding a value of 1 or respectively 0). Please note that the names of the variables begin with an m_, which stands for data members of this class (form). This is useful for distinguishing them from local variables (declared within the body of procedures in the class).

Resizing the Controls

The next step is to set a default value for the m_ratio variable, otherwise it will be 0 (which would mean the tvw control will have a width of 0, or not visible). The Form_Load event procedure is the best place to initialize form-level variables. From the left drop-down list of the code editor, select Form. You are positioned in the empty body of the Form_Load procedure. Enter the code listed here:

frmCustOrders(CustOrders.frm)

```
Private Sub Form_Load()
  m_ratio = 0.33
End Sub
```

Now you need to write the code that sets the size and positions of the two controls in the form. From the right drop-down list of the code editor, pick the Resize event and enter the following code:

frmCustOrders(CustOrders.frm)

```
Private Sub Form_Resize()
  Dim h As Single, w As Single

  w = Me.ScaleWidth - 3 * margin
  h = Me.ScaleHeight - 2 * margin
  If w < 0 Or h < 0 Then Exit Sub
  If m_ratio < 0 Then m_ratio =
  tvw.Move margin, margin, w * m_ratio, h
  lvw.Move tvw.Width + 2 * margin, margin, w * (1 - m_ratio), h
End Sub
```

First, dimension two single-precision variables, which hold the available width and height on the form. Calculate the width as the ScaleWidth of the form less three times the margin (the constant you have declared previously). The three accounts for the left margin between the form and tvw, the middle interval between tvw and lvw and the right margin between the lvw and the form. The same calculation is done for the height. Subtract the top and bottom margin intervals from the ScaleWidth of the form. If any of the w or h variables is negative, it would be illegal to continue, so exit from the sub. This can happen if the form is too small or iconic.

Next make sure that the m_ratio is positive or 0 to avoid the same type of error (that is, setting a control's size to a negative value).

The final two lines use the Move method of the controls to change their size and position. Move takes up to four arguments, the last three being optional. The arguments are left, top, width, and height. The effect of calling Move is to reset the control's position (the upper-left corner defined by the left and top arguments) and

11

size (defined by the width and height arguments). If any argument is missing, the current value for that setting is preserved. For example, if only the position arguments are given, the control is moved at the new position but the width and height are not changed.

First call Move for the tvw control. The upper-left corner is always at margin pixels from left and margin pixels from the top of the form. The width is set to the available width (w) multiplied with the ratio (m_ratio). The height for both controls will be h.

Next do the same for the lvw control. In this case, the left coordinate is set to the left of tvw (= margin) + width of the tvw control + the margin between the two controls. That makes the width of tvw + 2 times the margin constant. The top is the same as for the tvw and is set to be the margin. The width is the result of subtracting the width of tvw from w. Finally, the height is h, the same as for the tvw.

Notice that the code in the Resize event procedure draws the two controls sized by the m_ratio variable, which is what you intended. Now add code to show this form, so that you can test your work. Add the following code snippet in frmMain, in the Click event procedure of the mnuOrdersCust menu item:

frmMain(Main.frm)

```
Private Sub mnuOrdersCust_Click()
  frmCustOrders.Show vbModeless, Me
End Sub
```

Please note that you are not creating a new form and showing it, but rather using the show method on the class name itself (frmCustomer). That means you will show the same form every time, which in this case is what you intend.

Save your project and run the application. Open the frmCustOrders and try resizing the form. Notice that the ratio between the tree and list views is constant and the size of the tree view is roughly 1/3 of the width of the form.

Now you must give the user the ability to change the value of the variable so that, at runtime, he can easily resize the controls as required.

Changing the Mouse Shape Depending on the Mouse Position

The best way to achieve this is to allow the user to drag the bar between the two controls using the mouse. You need to visually indicate to the user when resizing is possible (that is, when the mouse cursor is above the bar). The easiest way to do this is to change the shape of the mouse cursor to the double-headed arrow pointing west and east. We can do this in the MouseMove event of the form. The MouseMove event takes place every time the mouse is moved above an open area of the form (not used by a control). From the form list of events pick MouseMove and enter this code:

frmCustOrders(CustOrders.frm)

```
Private Sub Form_MouseMove(Button As Integer, Shift As Integer, _
                    x As Single, y As Single)
  If margin + tvw.Width <= x And x <= lvw.Left Then
    Me.MousePointer = vbSizeWE
  Else
    Me.MousePointer = vbDefault
  End If
End Sub
```

Notice that the MouseMove event has four arguments passed in:

Argument	Description
Button	Indicates which mouse button is pressed (if any)
Shift	Indicates which of the Shift, Ctrl, and Alt keys (or combination) is pressed
x, y	The mouse coordinates when the event is fired, in units of the form or control (that is as defined by the ScaleMode)

The only useful argument is x. You must determine whether the mouse cursor is positioned above the area separating the two controls. Do this by comparing the x coordinate with the right margin of tvw and the left margin of lvw. If it is between the two, change the mouse pointer to the predefined constant value sbSizeWE. Otherwise, set the mouse pointer to the default value. Note the use of the And logical operator. The Boolean expression will be True if both expressions related by And are True.

If the mouse moves above one of the controls on the form, you must reset its shape to the default. If you do not reset the mouse shape, it will retain its custom shape (sbSizeWE), which is not desirable. We write the following code for the MouseMove events of both tvw and lvw:

11

frmCustOrders(CustOrders.frm)

```
Private Sub tvw_MouseMove(Button As Integer, Shift As Integer, _
                         x As Single, y As Single)
  Me.MousePointer = vbDefault
End Sub
```

And:

frmCustOrders(CustOrders.frm)

```
Private Sub lvw_MouseMove(Button As Integer, Shift As Integer, _
                         x As Single, y As Single)
  Me.MousePointer = vbDefault
End Sub
```

At this point, you can try your work. Run the application and move the cursor above the bar between the two controls. You should notice the change in the shape of the mouse cursor as illustrated in Figure 11.4.

Figure 11.4

Running
frmCustOrders with
the mouse cursor
changed.

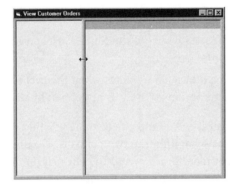

The change in the mouse shape gives the user an indication as to when it is possible to start resizing.

Executing the Resize—Handling Mouse Events

When the user decides to resize the controls, he will press the left mouse button to drag the bar to the new position (with the left button pressed). At this point, change the mouse cursor again to indicate that a drag operation is in progress, set the m_resizing variable to 1 (to indicate that resizing is taking place), adjust the m_ratio according to the mouse position, and then call the Form_Resize procedure to redraw the controls. When the resizing is completed, the user releases the mouse button. At this point, reset the m_resize variable to 0, and change the shape of the mouse to the default.

The following shows the order of the events and a summary of the actions you need to take.

Event	Actions Required
Form_MouseDown	Set m_resizing to 1 and change mouse cursor
Form_MouseMove	Recalculate m_ratio and redraw the controls
Form_MouseUp	Set the m_resizing to 0 and reset the mouse cursor to default

First let's enter the code for the MouseDown event. This event occurs when the user presses a mouse button. The MouseDown and MouseUp events occur in pairs, but not necessarily for the same control or form. For example, the user might press the left button on a control, and with the button down he might move the cursor above another control and release the button there. In this case, the first control gets one MouseDown event (and possibly some MouseMove events) and the second control potentially gets some MouseMove events and certainly one MouseUp event.

From the list of events for the frmCustOrders (in the code editor), select MouseDown and enter the following code:

frmCustOrders(CustOrders.frm)

```
Private Sub Form_MouseDown(Button As Integer, Shift As Integer, _
                           x As Single, y As Single)
  If Button <> vbLeftButton Or m_resizing <> 0 Then Exit Sub
  If margin + tvw.Width <= x And x <= lvw.Left Then
    m_resizing =
    Me.MouseIcon = LoadResPicture(IDC_SizeDragWE, vbResCursor)
    Me.MousePointer = vbCustom
  End If
End Sub
```

The first thing to notice is that the list of arguments for the event procedure is identical to the ones for the MouseMove, and as you will see shortly, identical to the ones for the MouseUp event. The list of arguments and return values of a procedure are known as the *signature* of the procedure or function. If two procedures have the same arguments (and return values for functions), it is said they have identical signatures.

The first one-line If statement checks which mouse button was pressed and what the value of the m_resizing variable is. If the mouse button is not the left button or if the resizing is already in progress, the expression evaluates to True and the Exit Sub statement is executed. Please note the Or logical operator. If both expressions are False, the result of the Or operation is False. Otherwise, if at least one of the two expressions is True the result is also True.

The next line checks to see whether the x mouse coordinate is between the right margin of the tvw and the left margin of the lvw. If it is, the m_resizing variable is

11

set to 1. Then a custom mouse cursor is loaded from the resource file and assigned to the MouseIcon property of the form. The custom cursor is used to reflect back to the user the fact that he started the resizing operation.

The LoadResPicture function retrieves a resource of type bitmap, icon, or cursor from a resource file. The arguments are the resource ID (the constant you defined previously) and an enumerated argument indicating what type of picture it is, which can be one of vbResBitmap, vbResIcon, or vbResCursor. The function returns a handle to the loaded resource picture, or an error if the ID is invalid. The MouseIcon property of the form holds a custom mouse cursor, which is displayed when the MousePointer property of the form is set to the intrinsic constant vbCustom. This is exactly what the next line of code achieves.

Next, you need to write code to respond to the MouseMove event. Notice that you already have a MouseMove event procedure. That means you must distinguish between the two cases: when the mouse move occurs without resizing and when the move occurs while resizing. Hence the need for the m_resizing variable that will tell you in which one of the two cases you are. Change the code in the MouseMove event by adding the lines shown in bold type below. You will also need to indent the existing code so that it fits inside the If/End If block.

frmCustOrders(CustOrders.frm)

```
Private Sub Form_MouseMove(Button As Integer, Shift As Integer, _
                           x As Single, y As Single)
  If m_resizing <> 0 Then
    m_ratio = (x - margin) / (Me.ScaleWidth - 3 * margin)
    If m_ratio < 0 Then m_ratio =
    If m_ratio > 1# Then m_ratio = 1#
    Form_Resize
  Else
    If margin + tvw.Width <= x And x <= lvw.Left Then
      Me.MousePointer = vbSizeWE
    Else
      Me.MousePointer = vbDefault
    End If
  End If
End Sub
```

The first thing to observe is that you have the two cases in which the MouseMove event might be fired handled by the two branches of the If statement. If you are not resizing the controls (that is, the m_resizing is 0), the Else block of statements will be executed as described previously.

If you are resizing, the Then block of statements is executed. First, the m_ratio is calculated based on the current mouse x coordinate. The next two one-line If statements prevent the m_ratio from being out of bounds (it must be between 0 and 1).

And after you calculate the `m_ratio` you simply call `Form_Resize` to redraw the controls. Please notice that the event procedures can be called as any other regular procedures (that is, the use of the `Form_Resize` procedure shown previously).

When the user is finally finished resizing the controls, you will receive a `MouseUp` event, in which you need to reset the value of `m_resizing` and set the mouse to the default. Enter the following code for the `MouseUp` event procedure:

frmCustOrders(CustOrders.frm)

```
Private Sub Form_MouseUp(Button As Integer, Shift As Integer, _
                         x As Single, y As Single)
  If m_resizing = 0 Then Exit Sub
  m_resizing =
  Me.MousePointer = vbDefault
  Me.MouseIcon = LoadPicture()
End Sub
```

The first line of code checks that you are in resizing mode. If you are not, there is nothing to do in this procedure, so exit. Otherwise set the `m_resizing` to 0, signaling in this way the end of the resize operation. Then you reset the mouse cursor to the default cursor for the form. The last thing you do is set the MouseIcon property to nothing, using the `LoadPicture()` without any arguments. The `LoadPicture` intrinsic function loads a picture from a file. If no argument is specified, it clears the property to which it was assigned. In this case, it unloads from memory the resource cursor you have loaded when the resize operation started.

Now that you are finished with the resizing, save your project and run it. Open the form `frmCustOrders` and try to resize the controls. It should look like the image presented in Figure 11.5. Please note the cursor change while you drag the bar.

Figure 11.5

Running `frmCustOrders` *while resizing the controls.*

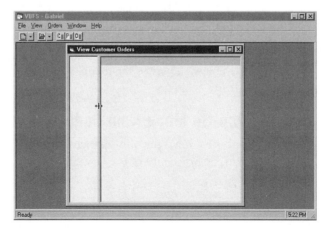

11

Adding a Right-Click Pop-Up Menu

You would like to offer your users the ability to view your ListView control in any of the four possible views presented previously. To do this, use a right-click pop-up menu box, similar to the ones used by VB and many other applications.

A pop-up menu is nothing more than a top-level menu item with some subitems. Normally it is not part of the menu bar (it is invisible) because the actions that it can execute are specialized and apply only to a subset of controls.

The first step is to design it using the menu editor. Open the frmCustOrders form, right-click on it, and select Menu Editor.

Let's add a top-level menu item. Set the Caption to Lvw and the name to mnuLvw. Uncheck the Visible check box. Now click the Next button.

This is going to be a child item of the mnuLvw. Set the Caption to &Refresh and the name to mnuLvwRefresh. Use the right arrow button to indent it so that it becomes a child of the mnuLvw. Click the Next button to insert the next menu item.

You need a separator, so set the caption to – and the name to mnuLvwSep0. Click Next again.

Set the Caption to Large &icons and the Name to mnuLvwV. Set the Index to 0, in this way you have created a control array. Click Next again.

Set the Caption to &Small icons, the Name to mnuLvwV, and index to 1. Click Next again.

Set the Caption to &List, the Name to mnuLvwV, and index to 2. Click Next again.

Set the Caption to &Details, the Name to mnuLvwV, and index to 3. Check the check box labeled Checked. This will place a check box on this menu item. We can have only one of the four view types active at a time, and we use the check mark near the mnuLvwV menu items to indicate which one of them it is.

You are finished with the design part of the menu, so close the editor and save the changes.

Activating the Pop-Up Menu from Code

Now write code to activate (show) the pop-up menu. As expected, you need to do this in the MouseDown event procedure of the ListView control.

In the code editor, select the lvw control in the left drop-down list and the MouseDown event in the right drop-down list. Enter the following code:

frmCustOrders(CustOrders.frm)

```
Private Sub lvw_MouseDown(Button As Integer, Shift As Integer, _
                          x As Single, y As Single)
  If Button <> vbRightButton Then Exit Sub
  PopupMenu mnuLvw, vbPopupMenuRightButton
End Sub
```

First, check to see whether the right mouse button was pressed. If it is not, then you have nothing further to do in this procedure, so exit. If it is, use the intrinsic PopupMenu function to load and show the menu passed in as the first argument. The next argument is a flag (or combination of flags) that affects the look and behavior of the pop-up menu. The following table lists some of the most common ones. There are also two optional arguments indicating the position where the pop-up box is displayed. If not specified, the current mouse position is used.

Event	*Actions Required*
vbPopupMenuLeftAlign	The left side of the pop-up box is located at the x coordinate
vbPopupMenuCenterAlign	The pop-up box is centered on the x coordinate
vbPopupMenuRightAlign	The right side of the pop-up box is located at the x coordinate
vbPopupMenuLeftButton	The click event on the pop-up menu occurs only when the left button is clicked
vbPopupMenuRightButton	The click event on the pop-up menu occurs when either the left or the right mouse buttons is clicked

Adding the values of the constants can combine the flags. For example, to have the pop-up menu to the right of the mouse position and have both the right and left buttons generate click events we would use:

```
PopupMenu mnuLvw, vbPopupMenuRightButton + vbPopupMenuRightAlign
```

To write code for the Click event, select the menu name from the left drop-down list of controls in the code editor for frmCustOrders. By default, the Click menu event

11

procedure is displayed. In this case, you deal with a control array, so the procedure has an Index argument of type Integer. Enter the following code:

frmCustOrders(CustOrders.frm)

```
Private Sub mnuLvwV_Click(Index As Integer)
  Dim i As Integer
  For i = 0 To
    mnuLvwV(i).Checked = False
  Next i
  mnuLvwV(Index).Checked = True
  Select Case Index
    Case 0: lvw.View = lvwIcon
    Case 1: lvw.View = lvwSmallIcon
    Case 2: lvw.View = lvwList
    Case 3: lvw.View = lvwReport
  End Select
End Sub
```

The first thing you do (aside from dimensioning i as an integer) is to clear the Checked property of each item in the control array. Use a For loop for this. Note the range of the loop counter (i) from 0 to 3. That means the loop body (between the For and Next lines) will be repeated with values of i starting at 0 and up to and including 3. In this case, set the Checked property of each item in the array to False, an action that will clear the existing check mark of the pop-up menu item.

Next, set to True the Checked property of the item that has been clicked (the one at the position identified by the value of the Index argument in the array).

Finally, use a Select Case statement to decide which value we assign to the View property of the list control (lvw). We decide this based on the value of the Index argument. Please note the use of the : to write the two statements on the same line, that is, the Case and the property assignment. It is used sometimes to save white space (empty space in code). The following code achieves the same thing, but it takes four more lines of code to do that:

```
Select Case Index
  Case
    lvw.View = lvwIcon
  Case
    lvw.View = lvwSmallIcon
  Case
    lvw.View = lvwList
  Case
    lvw.View = lvwReport
End Select
```

Save the project and run it to test the changes you made. The pop-up menu should look similar to the one shown in Figure 11.6.

Figure 11.6

The pop-up menu for the ListView control.

Next Steps

In this chapter, you have learned to use the basic functionality of the TreeView and ListView controls, their most important properties, methods, and events. You also learned how to handle mouse events and how to use them to implement a splitter form. You have designed and implemented code for a pop-up menu.

In the next chapter, you continue your journey by designing a classical Master-Detail type of form for the orders in your application. You learn about a new and very useful ActiveX control—the FlexGrid control. In the process, you also learn some more about coding in Visual Basic.

11

In this chapter

- *Adding the Order Entry Form*
- *Adding the Order Item Dialog Box*
- *Adding Code to the Order and Order Item Forms*

Chapter 12

Designing a Master-Detail Style Form

You'll continue the project by exploring a new pattern: a master-detail form. This pattern is used when the user must provide or access information about an object containing other objects; that is, an order that contains a list of order items. You will also learn about a new ActiveX control: the Microsoft FlexGrid control.

The complete code for this chapter can be found in the Chapter12 folder of the main VBFS folder on the CD that accompanies this book.

Adding the Order Entry Form

We need to add to our project a new form for entering customer orders.

An *order* is an object that represents one transaction between a customer and the store. It contains a set of ordered items (books, CDs, and so on), the shipping information, billing information, and a set of flags for the order status. Each order item is an object in itself: It has information regarding the item ordered, quantity, price, and eventually discount.

 Note

We are using a simplified version of an order entry system. We do not cover all aspects involved in a real-world order entry system, for reasons of space and complexity.

The order items cannot exist by themselves, they are part of an order, and only one order. The relationship between order and order item is known as *aggregation* in the object-oriented world. One way to model this relationship for a user interface is to use two forms: master and detail. The master form is used to edit the container data (the order, in this case). The detail form is used to edit the aggregated item (the order item in this case). The master (order) form contains the list of detail items currently owned by the master and the means to add new items, modify existing ones, and remove items. The changes to the order and the contained ordered items are saved all at once, when the user decides to save changes from the master form.

You will add two new forms to the project: one for the order entry and one for the order item entry. The order entry form (the master form) enables the user to enter data for the order as a whole, will have a list of order items, and will offer the users the capability to add new items, modify items already in the order, and remove items from the list.

Let's start by adding a new form to the project. Change the form name to `frmOrder`, the Caption to Order Entry, the BorderStyle to 1 - Fixed Single, the MDIChild to True, and the MinButton to True. Save the project.

Let's add controls to the form. Use Figure 12.1 as a guide to the size and positions of the controls.

Figure 12.1

The completed order form.

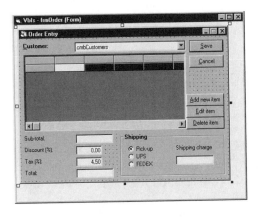

Start by adding a label. Change the Caption to &Customer:. Open the Font dialog box and set the font style to Bold to indicate to the users that this is a mandatory entry. You want the user to select a customer from a list. Add a combo box to the right of the label. Change its name to `cmbCustomers`, and the Style to 2 - Dropdown List.

Adding a Grid to the Form

Now you need to add a control that holds the list of items for this order. You could use a list box, but the list has only one text item for each row. You want to display more details for each item, including the name of the item, the quantity, price, discount, and the total price for the item. The best way to display all this information is to use a grid control. A grid control presents data in a tabular format; that is, organized in rows and columns. Each data element in the grid is called a *cell*.

Use Microsoft's FlexGrid control included with Visual Basic 6.0. As with all nonintrinsic controls, you must add a reference to the component to your project before you can use it. From the Project menu, select Components. From the Components dialog box, select Microsoft FlexGrid Control 6.0 (check the box in front of the component). Click OK. Note that the control icon is now showing in the Toolbox.

Click on the FlexGrid icon in the Toolbox and draw the control on the form as illustrated in Figure 12.1. In the Properties window, change the name of the control to grd (the default prefix for grid controls). Open the Property Pages dialog box for the new control by right-clicking on it and selecting Properties.

The General tab of the Property Pages dialog box enables you to change some of the basic properties of the control.

FlexGrid Properties

The Rows property represents the number of rows of data the control has. Setting it to a different value changes the number of rows in the control to reflect the new value (add or remove rows as required). This property can be changed both at design time and at runtime. Leave this property at the default value (2).

The Cols property represents the number of columns in the control. This property can be changed both at design time and at runtime. You need six columns to represent the order items that will be held in the grid: sequence number, product name, price per unit, discount, quantity, and total item price. Set the value for Cols to 6.

The FixedRows and FixedCols properties represent the number of fixed rows and columns, respectively. Fixed means rows and columns that are not affected by scrolling and are always visible. When the contents of the grid exceed the visible area, the user can scroll using the scrollbars. This determines the contents of the control to be shifted in the appropriate direction. The fixed rows and columns are not affected by this scrolling; they are "frozen" to the top and left of the control. Also note that they are shown in a different color, which indicates that they are fixed. Take the default values (1) for both of these properties. The first fixed row is

12

normally used for column headers, while the first fixed column is sometimes used to show the ordinal number of the row.

The AllowBigSelection Boolean property indicates that the user can select an entire row or column by clicking on the row or column headers. Keep the default value True (checked).

The ScrollBars enumerated property represents the type of scrollbars that the control uses, and it can be one of the standard enumerated values for scrollbars: none, vertical only, horizontal only, and both. Keep the default, which is 3 - Both.

The Highlight property is also an enumerated property, which represents how the selected cells in the grid are shown at runtime. It can have one of the following values:

Value	Description
flexHighlightNever	Selected cells are not highlighted
flexHighlightAlways	Selected cells are highlighted always
flexHighlightWithFocus	Selected cells are highlighted only when the control has focus

Use the default value, flexHighlightAlways.

The FocusRect enumerated property represents the style used to indicate the current cell in the grid. The current cell is the one the user clicked on last time. It can also be set from code, as you will see shortly. The styles available are

Value	Description
flexFocusNone	No focus rectangle is displayed
flexFocusLight	A light rectangle is used (default)
flexHighlightWithFocus	A heavy rectangle is used

Keep the default value, flexFocusLight.

The FillStyle property indicates whether style changes applied to one cell of the grid are repeated to all cells that are currently selected or no. Use the default, which is 0 - Single (only the current cell is affected).

The SelectionMode property indicates how you allow the user to select cells in the grid. There are three possible values for this property: select cells by row, by column, or free selection (any rectangular subset of cells). In this case, use row-based selection, so from the drop-down list for the property select 1 - By Row.

The AllowUserResizing property represents the type of resizing you want the user to perform: none, rows only, columns only, or both. Set the value to 3 - Both, which allows the user to change the width of the columns and the height of rows as required.

The second page of the Property Pages dialog box, labeled Style, enables you to further customize the appearance and behavior of the control.

The GridLines and GridLinesFixed properties are used to set the style for the lines delimiting the columns and rows, and the fixed columns and rows, respectively. It can be one of the following values: none (no lines), flat (simple lines), inset (inset lines), and raised (raised lines). Change the value to inset.

The TextStyle and TextStyleFixed properties also are enumerated properties that indicate whether any 3D effects are added to the text in every cell of the grid and in the fixed cells. Fixed cells are the cells in fixed rows and columns. The possible values include normal text, inset and lightly inset, raised and lightly raised. You can choose any style you favor.

The MergeCells property is an advanced feature used to merge cells with the same contents in larger cells that span across rows or columns. Leave the default 0 - Never, which means cells with identical contents are never merged.

The RowHeightMin property specifies the minimum height for any row of the grid. Use the default value of 0, which means there is no minimum.

The WordWrap property indicates whether the control will wrap text that is too long to fit in a cell. The default is False (unchecked). You don't need this behavior, so take the default.

The Color tab of the Property Pages enables you to set the colors for any of the colors used by the control. On the left is a list of all the color properties the control has. On the right is the standard list of system colors or the palette colors, depending on selection. You can leave all color properties at their default values.

Now you are finished setting the properties of the control. Click OK to save and apply your changes.

Many other properties of the FlexGrid control are not listed in either the Properties window or on the Property Pages dialog box. Most of those properties are available only at runtime. You will encounter some of these properties later on.

Completing the Order Form

Let's continue by adding a new label control for the subtotal field. Change the caption to Sub-total:. Use a MaskedEditBox for the subtotal field. Add a new MaskedEditBox to the right of the label. Change its name to txtSubtotal, change the ClipMode property to 1 - mskExcludeLiterals, the Enabled property to false, and

12

the Format to $#,##0.00;($#,##0.00) (you can select it from the drop-down list of the Format property). You are disabling editing for this control (by having its Enabled property set to False) because it is a calculated field. You can get the value to display in the subtotal field by adding all the prices of the order items in the grid.

Add a new label for the discount. Change its Caption to &Discount(%):. Add a TextBox control to the right of the label. Set its name to `txtDiscount`, and the Text property to 0.00. You want the default discount to be 0%.

Add a new Label-TextBox pair underneath for the tax percentage. Set the Caption of the Label to &Tax:. Set the name of the text box to `txtTax`, and the default value to 4.50. Assume that this is the sales tax for the area in which your virtual shop is located.

For the total field, copy the Label and the MaskedEditBox controls for the subtotal, and then paste them on the form. VB prompts you with a message stating that there is already a control named `txtSubtotal`, and asking if you would like to create a control array. Answer No to this question. Move the controls in place. Change the caption of the Label control to Total:. Change the name of the MaskedEditBox control to `txtTotal`.

You must add a Frame control to hold the radio buttons used to indicate the shipping type and the field for the shipping charge. A frame is a container control used to hold other controls, for example, OptionButton controls. A frame represents a way to group together controls that are somehow related, in this case, controls that refer to shipping. The advantage of grouping controls like this is that you can apply a setting to, or exercise an action on, all the controls in the frame at once. Examples include disabling the frame (which in turn will disable each control contained by the frame) or moving the frame to a new location (which will move the contents of the frame too).

Insert a Frame control to the right of the text boxes you placed on the form. Change its Caption property to Shipping and its name to `fraShipType`. The prefix used to denote Frame controls in code is `fra`.

On the frame place a control array consisting of three OptionButton controls. These controls are used to indicate the type of shipping for this order. An OptionButton control consists of a small circle and a text caption. It is used to represent a Boolean state: True or False, reflected in its Value property. If the circle is filled, the Value is True, otherwise it is False. The OptionButton controls are normally used in groups, and only one button in a group can have the Value set to True at any given time. This behavior is similar to the buttons used to change the radio frequency on the radios of some older cars: only one can be pushed in at any given time. Hence the alternative name "radio buttons" used sometimes for these controls.

Select the OptionButton control icon in the toolbox. Draw the control inside the Frame control you added previously. Change the Caption property to Pick-up, the Name to optShipType, and the Index property to 0. Recall that setting the Index property of any control creates a control array. This is exactly what you are trying to achieve: create an array of the three OptionButton controls you will be using to determine the shipping method for this order.

Now copy the OptionButton control, then click on the frame so that it is selected (the small dragging handles are displayed around the Frame control). Now paste a copy of the control. Rearrange its position to be underneath the first one. Change its Caption to UPS. Repeat the operation for the FedEx button. Do not forget to select the Frame control first, otherwise you will paste a copy of the control on the form.

Click on the OptionButton labeled Pick-up and change its Value property to True. Notice that the button appearance changes to indicate that it is "pushed."

Add a label on the frame, to the right of the option buttons. Notice that it is slightly harder to resize and position the controls because the alignment grid dots (the small dots on the form) are missing. Change the label Caption to Shipping Charge. Add a text box underneath it. Change its Name to txtShippingCharge, the Enabled property to False, and the Text to "". See Figure 12.1 for guidance.

The last task for the graphical design of this form is to add command buttons for the Save and Cancel actions, as well as for adding, modifying, and deleting order items.

Open the frmCustomer form. Select the two command buttons from the upper-right corner (Save and Cancel) and copy them. Close the frmCustomer form. Now paste the buttons from the Clipboard to the frmOrder. Change their position to the upper-right corner.

Add three new CommandButton controls for adding, modifying, and deleting order items, as shown in Figure 12.1. Change their names to cmdAdd, cmdEdit, and cmdDelete, respectively. Change their captions to Add new item, Edit item, and Delete item, respectively.

This concludes the design for your Order form. Next, you will add the form used to add and modify order detail items, that is, the items in the grid control.

Adding the Order Item Dialog Box

To add new order items and modify existing ones, you need a simple dialog form. This form enables the user to select a product, add a quantity, and determine a discount for the order item.

12

Add a new form to the project. Change the Name to `frmOrderItem`, the Caption to "Order item", the BorderStyle to 3 - Fixed Dialog, and the StartupPosition to 1 - CenterOwner. The StartupPosition enumerated property indicates how the form is positioned when it is displayed. The following table lists the options.

Value	Description
`vbStartUpManual`	Start position not specified (will be set manually)
`vbStartUpOwner`	Start position is centered on the form that owns it
`vbStartUpScreen`	Start position is centered on the screen
`vbStartUpWindowsDefault`	Start position is shown in a position decided by the operating system

The StartupPosition property is available only at design time. The StartupPosition is irrelevant for the MDIChild forms; that is, it will be ignored for these forms. The MDIChild forms are always shown inside their parent, in a position determined by their parent (the MDI form of the project). The `vbStartUpManual` setting implies that the initial position will be set from code at runtime, by setting the Top and Left properties. If it is not set, the Windows default position is used. If `vbStartUpOwner` is used, the form is shown centered on the form that owns it, as specified in the `Show` method in the second argument. If no owner is specified, the form is shown in the Windows default position. The `vbStartUpScreen` indicates that the form is shown in the center of the screen.

Next you will add controls to the order item dialog box. See Figure 12.2 for the final layout of the form.

Figure 12.2

The completed Order Item form.

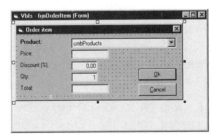

Let's start by adding a label and a combo box for the product selection list. Add a Label control. Change its Caption to &Product: and the font to bold. Add a ComboBox control. Change its name to `cmbProducts` and the Style to 2 - Dropdown List.

Open the `frmOrder` form. Select the Total Label control and the txtTotal MaskedEditBox to the right of it, then copy them to the Clipboard. Switch to the `frmOrderItem`. Paste the two controls on the frmOrderItem. Place them under the existing label and combo box. Change the Caption of the pasted label to Price: and the name of the pasted MaskedEditControl to `txtPrice`.

Repeat the operation for the Discount (%) label and corresponding text box: Copy them from the `frmOrder` and paste them on the `frmOrderItem`. Place them as illustrated in Figure 12.1. This time you keep the name and caption of the original controls.

Add a new Label underneath the Discount (%): label (or alternatively copy the existing Discount (%): label and paste it). Set the Caption to Qty:. Add a new text box. Set its name to txtQty, the Text property to 1, and the Alignment to 1 - Right Justify. The Alignment property indicates how the text is shown in the control: left, center, or right justified (aligned). Normally numbers are shown right aligned.

Switch back to the `frmOrder` form and select the txtTotal control and its corresponding label. Copy them to the Clipboard. Switch to the `frmOrderItem` form. Paste the two controls. Change their position so that they are aligned with the others, as shown in Figure 12.2.

The last two controls are the OK and Cancel buttons. Add two CommandButton controls. Set their names to cmdOk and cmdCancel, and their Captions to &Ok and &Cancel, respectively.

Select the OK button and change its Default property to True. The Default property of the command button indicates whether this control is the default button on the form. The default button receives a `Click` event if the user presses the Enter key, in addition to the normal mouse click and the mnemonic key activation. The default button is represented on the form with a black rectangle around it. There can be only one default button on any given form.

Select the Cancel button and set its Cancel property to True. The Cancel property indicates that this button receives a `Click` event if the user presses the Esc key, in addition to the regular mouse click and mnemonic key events. The Default and Cancel are useful for dialog boxes in which the user enters some data and presses Enter to accept changes or Esc to cancel the changes.

This concludes the design for your Order Item data entry form. Save your project. Next you will add code to handle some events from the controls added to this form and the Order form.

12

Adding Code to the Order and Order Item Forms

In this chapter, you will add only a part of the code for the two forms you designed previously. The rest of the code will be added after you develop the classes that will help you retrieve and save data to the database.

Select the frmOrder form. Double-click anywhere on the form to open the code editor. The cursor is placed in the Form_Load event procedure. In this procedure you will define the column headers for the grid control. Enter the following code:

frmOrder(Order.frm)

```
Private Sub Form_Load()
  grd.Rows =
  grd.ColWidth(0) = 720
  grd.ColWidth(1) = 2500
  grd.ColWidth(2) = 720
  grd.ColWidth(3) = 720
  grd.ColWidth(4) = 720
  grd.ColWidth(5) = 720
  grd.Row =
  grd.Col = 0: grd.Text = "Seq."
  grd.Col = 1: grd.Text = "Product"
  grd.Col = 2: grd.Text = "Price"
  grd.Col = 3: grd.Text = "Disc."
  grd.Col = 4: grd.Text = "Qty."
  grd.Col = 5: grd.Text = "Total"
End Sub
```

The first line of code in the procedure sets the Rows property of the grid control to 1. This action sets the number of rows displayed in the control to 1; that is, the row you will use for the column headers. As new items are added to the controls you can change the Rows property to reflect the total number of items in this order plus one row for the column headers.

The next six lines of code set the width of each column in the grid. The unit of measure is twips. The ColWidth property is an indexed (array) property. That means it holds the width values for all columns. To get or set an individual value, you must use the index of the column to which you refer. The indexed type of properties behave in a similar mode to an array. It is possible to have multidimensional properties that use more than one index.

The next line of code sets the Row property of the grid to 0. The Row and Col properties of the grid are used to set or get the current (active) cell in the grid. These properties function similar to a pair of indices in a two-dimensional array; that is, the grid itself. The Text property of the grid control refers to the current cell, so to set or retrieve the contents of any given cell in the grid you must set the Row and

Col to point to that cell. That is exactly what the preceding code does. It sets the Row property to 0 (the first and only row in the grid), then sets the Col property to point to each cell in that row (from 0 to 5), then the contents of the cell are set to the appropriate column header text for that column.

You need to do this only once because we are going to preserve the first row for the life of the form. That is why you are doing it in the `Form_Load` event procedure.

Next, write code to handle the `Click` event for the OptionButton controls used to indicate the shipping type and also for the text box that is used to enter the shipping cost. Double-click on any of the OptionButton controls on the form. Enter the following code:

frmOrder(Order.frm)

```
Private Sub optShipType_Click(Index As Integer)
  Dim i As Long
  For i = 0 To
    If Index = i Then
      optShipType(i).Value = True
    Else
      optShipType(i).Value = False
    End If
  Next i

  If Index = 0 Then
    txtShippingCharge = ""
    txtShippingCharge.Enabled = False
  Else
    txtShippingCharge.Enabled = True
    txtShippingCharge = IIf(Index = 1, "4.50", "12.50")
  End If
End Sub
```

This event procedure deals with the `Click` event for the control array you defined previously. The OptionButton controls labeled Pick-up, UPS, and FedEx have the Index 0, 1, and 2, respectively.

The first part of the procedure determines which button was clicked and sets its value to True, and at the same time sets the value of the rest of the option buttons to False. To achieve this, you iterate through the items of the control array, using a `For` loop, and if the current item is the one that was clicked (indicated by the Index argument), set its value to True or set its value to False. This ensures the correct OptionButton control is shown as "pushed."

In the second part of the procedure, determine whether the text box used to enter the shipping charge (`txtShippingCharge`) is enabled, and set its Text property to

12

reflect the default charge for particular type of shipping the user selected using the OptionButton controls.

If the user selected Pick-up (Index 0), set the Text of the `txtShippingCharge` control to `""` and disable it. This means the user is prohibited from entering a charge for pick-up.

If the shipping is done using either UPS or FedEx, there is going to be a shipping charge. Enable the TextBox control and set the Text property of the `txtShippingCharge` to be either 4.50 or 12.50 depending on the carrier. Please note the use of the instant if (`IIf`) statement to decide which value to use. Also note that `.Text` is omitted following the `txtShippingCharge`. This was done to illustrate the fact that the Text property is the default property of the TextBox controls. The default property of a control is the one used if the name of the control is used in code without using the dot notation. For example:

```
txtShippingCharge.Text = "12.50"
```

is equivalent to the shortcut version:

```
txtShippingCharge = "12.50"
```

Next add code to handle the click events for the Save and Cancel command buttons. Double-click on the Save control, then enter the code as shown:

frmOrder(Order.frm)

```
Private Sub cmdSave_Click()
  Unload Me
End Sub
```

Repeat the code for the `Cancel` event procedure:

frmOrder(Order.frm)

```
Private Sub cmdCancel_Click()
  Unload Me
End Sub
```

The code in the preceding procedures does one thing only: unloads this instance of the `frmOrder` (denoted by the `Me` keyword).

Let's add code to open the Order Item dialog box. Double-click on the command button labeled Add new item. Enter the code shown here:

frmOrder(Order.frm)

```
Private Sub cmdAdd_Click()
  Dim f As New frmOrderItem
```

```
    f.Show vbModal, frmMain
End Sub
```

The preceding code creates a new instance of the dialog box `frmOrderItem` and then displays it as a modal dialog (using the `vbModal` intrinsic constant). Note the second argument passed to the `Show` method (`frmMain`). This is the parent (owner) of the dialog box, and according to the setting for the StartupPosition (center owner), the dialog box is shown centered on the main form of the project.

You have concluded this stage of development for the two forms. The only task left is to add the code required to open the order form from the menu of the main form.

Open the main form and from the Orders menu select New Order. Then enter the following code in the code editor:

frmMain(Main.frm)

```
Private Sub mnuOrdersNew_Click()
  Dim f As New frmOrder
  f.Show
End Sub
```

This code creates a new instance of the order form (which is an MIDIChild form) and shows it.

Save your project. You can now run the project to check your work. Open a new order (from the menu select Orders/New Order) and then click on the Add New Item button. The dialog will be shown centered on the main form. Figure 12.3 illustrates the application running with both forms open.

Next Steps

In this chapter, you have designed and implemented a master-detail pattern consisting of two forms. You have explored the properties and methods of a new control class: MSFlexGrid. You have also explored new properties and methods of some intrinsic controls (option buttons and frames).

This chapter concludes the second part of the book, in which you have learned the basic concepts behind designing a user interface using components. You have also learned to control the interaction between components using their properties, methods, and events from the design environment as well as from code.

In the next part of the book, we look in-depth at custom classes and objects, elementary relational database notions, and concepts of object persistence.

12

Figure 12.3

The Order Item form at runtime.

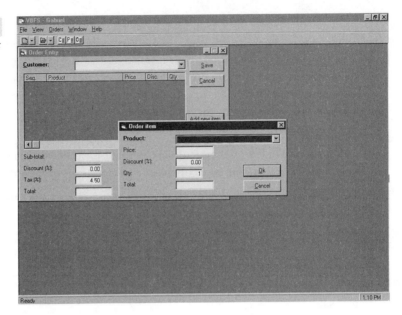

Part III

Add Functionality: Creating Persistent Objects

In this chapter

- *Object-Oriented Concepts*
- *Classes in Visual Basic*
- *Adding a Customer Class to the Project*
- *Adding the Product Class and Order Class to the Project*
- *Using Enumerations for Order Status Properties*

Chapter 13

Elementary Object-Oriented Concepts

Up to now you have dealt mostly with developing the user interface. This includes forms, dialog boxes, and controls. Because the application represents a virtual store, you need a way to save the form data somewhere for later retrieval. For example, a store employee needs to be able to put products into the store. Additionally, customers require the ability to browse the products that exist within the store and to potentially purchase them. So far, you have developed the user interface to display and modify this data but have no way to save or retrieve the data. Without this capability, you don't have a working store.

Earlier in this book, we discussed the project requirements and identified the types of information we are going to deal with in this application. These include Customers, Products, and Orders. You can develop classes in Visual Basic to support each of these types. After you develop the classes, you can create objects and interact with them in a more intuitive way. By intuitive, we mean that if you want to create an order for a customer, you can create a new order object and add the order object to a customer object. Dealing with objects that represent real-world entities is more conceptually natural than writing individual procedures containing lines of code that are not associated with an object. Hopefully, this will become more meaningful as we discuss classes and objects more.

You also want to make these objects persistent. This enables you to save the state of the objects to a database and re-create those objects at a later time if you choose to. Because this involves several concepts, we are going to devote all of Part III, "Creating Persistent Objects," to creating the persistent objects necessary for your application. In building these objects, we will cover object-oriented concepts and database concepts. Don't worry if this is unclear to you at this point. We will go into more detail on these topics, and by the end of Chapter 17 we will have completed the persistent objects. Our goal for this chapter is to create VB classes for Customer, Product, and Order. We are going to create these classes and add a set of properties that can be read and modified. Before we start creating these classes, let's start out discussing some object-oriented concepts that will help you understand what it is you are creating.

The complete code for this chapter can be found in the Chapter13 folder of the main VBFS folder on the CD that accompanies this book.

Object-Oriented Concepts

Because we are talking about creating persistent objects as part of this application, let's go over some object-oriented concepts first so that you have a basic understanding of what objects are. The following is a set of basic concepts involving some object-oriented terms and is not intended to be comprehensive coverage of the topic. If you want to gain more knowledge on object-oriented concepts beyond what is mentioned in this book, I would recommend you visit your local bookstore (or use the Web) to purchase a book on object-oriented design.

Classes, Objects, and Properties

You define objects in software languages, such as Visual Basic, C++, and Java, by creating a *class*. A class represents the abstract view of an object. It is the definition of an object and not the object itself. A class combines the capability to create complex data structures and procedures that act upon the data structure. After a class is created, you can create objects based on that class. Specifically, a class is a description of the properties and behavior of an object. It is also important to note that the terms *objects* and *instances* have the same meaning. An instance of class is the same as an object.

Object properties are defined in a class as attributes. After an object is created based on a class, each attribute defined in the class supports a specific property value of the object. For example, a name attribute defined in a class allows objects based on the class to have a property value for the name.

Object behavior is exhibited through the definition of class methods. Class methods are essentially procedures that have access to the internal property values of an object. Methods are capable of reading and modifying property values as well as performing behavior or tasks on behalf of the object.

Classes generally have attributes and methods, although it is possible to create a class with only attributes or only methods. A class with attributes and no methods is essentially a complex data structure, and nothing more. A class with methods and no attributes does not act upon or use any internal object data (because there is none). This type of class is technically equivalent to developing procedures or functions.

Let's use a flea as a real-world example of an object. A flea has *properties* that describe its size and color. A flea's size is very small and its color is black. It also has a basic behavior definition. For example, a flea does not drive a car or go to the movies. It does, however, exhibit the behavior of being attracted to animals' fur.

 An *object* is a specific instance of a class. Objects do not exist without a class to define them.

 A *property* is a named value within an object.

A class is the definition of an object. If we were to define a flea class, it would have the properties size and color. It would also have the behavior of preferring animals' fur. The exact value of the size and color of a flea is not defined by the flea class. Sure, a flea class can contain a size definition that is the range from the smallest possible flea to the largest possible flea. But, the exact size is not within the class itself. It is part of the individual flea that you and I can see. This flea would be an object, or what is referred to as an instance of a class. Figure 13.1 shows a flea class and flea instances.

Figure 13.1

Flea class and flea instances.

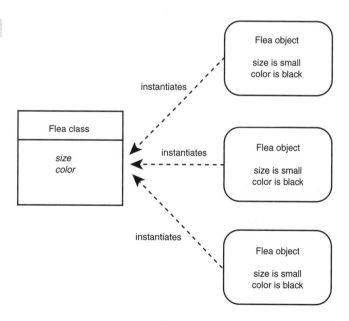

Objects contain values for properties. A flea object contains an exact size and color. It also exhibits exacting behavior that can be measured. A flea might not always go to animals' fur but you can observe and measure a real flea's properties and behavior.

Within software applications, classes are what you specify as the definition of an object, and objects are what your program interacts with. Objects contain values for the defined properties of their class. Objects cannot contain a value for a property unless the property is defined in the class. Class definitions do not contain actual values for their properties, only the definition of the properties. Using the flea example again, a flea object has an exact size and an exact color. Our flea is 1/16th-inch in height and the color is black (this is a hypothetical flea for the purpose of supporting this example). These are known quantifiable properties of the flea object. A flea does not have a hair color because hair color is not a defined property of the flea class. Fleas don't have hair. Because the class does not have a definition of this property, the flea object does not have a value for the property.

When developing a class, you define the properties of the class by specifying the property data type and the property name. Properties also have scope within the class. This means you can define the property to be visible only to code within the class or you can define the property to be visible outside the class as well.

Methods

The behavior of a class is defined by writing *methods* within that class. Methods are equivalent to functions or procedures except methods act on an object. An example of a method name in a flea class is `Fly`. When the `Fly` method is invoked on a flea object, the flea begins flying. If there are two fleas and you invoked the `Fly` method on one of the fleas, only that particular flea would begin to fly because the method you invoked is in reference to a particular flea object.

 Methods define object behavior. They are like procedures and functions except methods also have access to the internal object state which includes the object's properties.

Once again, methods are procedures or functions that act on an object. The code within the method implements the behavior of the object. The code within the method is generally referred to as the *implementation*. Suppose you have two classes, a flea class and an elephant class. Each class has an `Eat` method defined. If you create an instance of the flea class and an instance of the elephant class and then call the `Eat` method on each of these objects, the implementation of the methods defines what happens for each object. The flea object would eat and the amount would be dependant on its appetite. The elephant object would also eat but the implementation of eating for a elephant would involve a much larger amount of food (presumably).

Encapsulation

Encapsulation is the term used to describe the hiding or abstraction of properties and implementation of a class. Using a flea as an example, its color is encapsulated by the flea. You can observe the color of a flea and see that it is black. However, how the color is stored chemically within the flea is not known without looking into the internals of the flea itself. You can see the color, but you do not see the details of how the flea stores its color. A class also can define properties that are not exposed. These types of properties are encapsulated.

The implementation of methods is, by definition, encapsulated by the class because this code is not visible outside the class itself. By defining methods of a class, you can encapsulate the class's behavior within the details of the methods. This is the basic essence of object-oriented programming. You can use objects and call their methods without knowing or caring about the details of how the internals of the methods work. You should only care about what the behavior of the method is, not how it does it.

Inheritance

Class inheritance is not supported in Visual Basic, but it remains a useful topic because it is an important part of any object-oriented discussion. Inheritance is the creation of a class that inherits properties and methods from another class. Continuing with the flea and elephant examples, each of these classes has a size and color property. Rather than defining a flea class with a size and color property and a elephant class with its size and color property, let's define a creature class with a size and color property. Then, let's define the flea class as a subclass of a creature and the elephant class as a subclass of a creature. A subclass of a class is also said to inherit from that class. In this example, the flea class inherits from the creature class and the elephant class also inherits from the creature class. Figure 13.2 shows a flea class and an elephant class inheriting from a creature class.

Figure 13.2

The Flea and Elephant classes inherit from the Creature class.

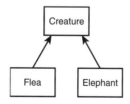

Because a flea inherits from a creature, it automatically contains the size and color properties. If the creature class had any methods defined, the flea and elephant classes would automatically inherit those methods as well. The inheriting of methods allows behavior to be reused by subclasses instead of having to rewrite the methods for each class that needs it. This reduces the need for having duplicate code within methods of more than one class. Each subclass automatically inherits the method as though the method was defined within the class itself. This reduces the necessary amount of code you must write per class. Inheritance usually involves a higher degree of design work to maximize the benefits of inherited properties and methods. Because Visual Basic does not support class inheritance, you do not need to concern yourself with it at this point.

Inheritance is the capability of one class to extend the properties and behavior of another class. One class is referred to as the *parent* class and the other as the *child* class. The child class benefits by assuming the parent class's properties and behavior. The child class can then extend the properties and behavior by defining additional properties and methods on the child class.

Polymorphism

Polymorphism describes objects that exhibit different behavior in response to the same method invocation. Using the diagram in Figure 13.2, when you call the Run method (defined in the Creature class) on each of the two objects, the objects respond differently. Polymorphism is exhibited when you interact with objects in terms of a common base class and the objects respond in a manner that is specific to the object.

Using the previous inheritance example, assume we defined a Run method on the creature class and that we defined a function that takes creature objects as its only parameter. Here is an example of this code:

```
Public Sub MyProc(c As Creature)
    c.Run
End Sub
```

Within the creature function, the Run method is invoked on the object passed to the function. The function does not care what type of object was passed to the function. The object decides what to do in response to the invoking of the Run method. The response is defined by the implementation of the method. From the function's perspective, the parameter object is polymorphic because the object behaves differently depending on the type of object that was passed to the function. Inheritance is one way to implement polymorphic behavior. Using interfaces via the Microsoft Component Object Model (COM) is another. We will discuss COM later in Chapter 26, "Distributed Components: The Way of the Future."

Classes in Visual Basic

Now that we have gone over some general object-oriented concepts, let's jump into what classes are all about in Visual Basic. Within a Visual Basic project, you can add class modules by using the Project, Add Class Module menu item as shown in Figure 13.3.

Figure 13.3

The menu item used to add a class module.

Class modules are similar to standard code modules in that you can add variable declarations, procedures, and functions. However, each of these have different meanings between standard modules and class modules. Here is a brief description of the parts of a Visual Basic class. Each of these are discussed further and in more detail when you add classes to your project later in this chapter.

Properties

As mentioned earlier, class properties define what properties an object (or instance) of this class can have. The values of the properties exist within an object of the class. The simplest way to add a property to a Visual Basic class is to declare a public variable in the declarations section of the class module. In a standard code module, a public variable in the declarations section contains one value and is accessible by the entire application. In a class module, a public variable is accessible only through an object of the class. Also, public variables in a class contain a value for each object of the class. By creating a public variable in a class, it becomes a property that can be automatically get and set within an object. For example, assume you created a Creature class and declared a name property using the following code:

```
Public name as String
```

You can refer to the name property of a Creature object using the following code:

```
Dim c as New Creature
c.name = "Horse"
```

You cannot refer to just the variable name as you could if it were defined in a standard code module. An object variable is required because the property values are specific to an object.

Sometimes you might want to declare static properties of a class. A static property contains a value that is unique and accessible to all instances of the same class. Visual Basic does not support the creation of static class properties but you can simulate them by creating a public variable in a standard code module and referring to it in your class.

Property Procedures

In most cases, you do not want to create public properties in the manner previously described because you might want to have control over getting and setting properties. The most common and best practice for defining properties and allowing access to them is to first create a private member variable. You create a private member variable using the `Private` keyword. Here is an example:

```
Private m_name as String
```

 Note   When declaring private member variables, the proper naming convention includes prepending the variable name with m_. This way when you refer to the variable in the class you can identify the variable as a member variable.

Because the property is private, you cannot automatically refer to it outside the class. Assuming we are still using the `Creature` class as an example, the following code is invalid and will not work:

```
Dim c as New Creature
c.m_name = "Horse"    ' invalid use of private member variable
```

The solution of allowing access to private member variables involves creating property procedures. Property procedures enable you to create a procedure for getting a property value and another procedure for setting a property value. Here is an example of defining a property procedure to get the name property using the m_name private member variable:

```
Public Property Get name() As String
  name = m_name
End Property
```

Here is an example of defining a property procedure to set the name property using the m_name private member variable:

```
Public Property Let name(newValue as String)
  m_name = newValue
End Property
```

Now this code works:

```
Dim c as New Creature
c.name = "Elephant"
```

The `Property Let` procedure is used to set property values that are defined using a datatype other than `Object`. If, for example, you specify a datatype of `String` and want to allow setting the property, you would define a `Property Let` procedure. If the property is defined as `Object` to contain a reference to an object, you would need to define a `Property Set` procedure. `Property Let` and `Property Set` are identical except for the distinction of whether the property is in reference to an object.

If a property procedure is not defined for getting the property, then the property is not retrievable. If a property procedure is not defined for setting the property, then the property is not settable.

Methods

Methods are defined exactly the same way as procedures and functions in standard code modules. The difference is that methods have access to the object's property values, Private (or Public) member variables, and other Private or Public methods.

Class Initialize and Class Terminate

Class Initialize and Class Terminate are two predefined events for every class. These are provided to write code that is run after an object of the class is created or destroyed. After you have created a class and you are in the code window of the class, you can create event procedures to respond to the Class Initialize and Class Terminate events. To automatically generate these event procedures, choose Class from the object list at the top left of the code window. Then, the list at the top right of the code window should now reflect the events of the class. This list includes Initialize and Terminate. If you choose either one, you will generate an event procedure and the cursor will automatically be placed in the procedure. If the event procedure already exists, the cursor will just be placed in the procedure to allow editing.

When an object is created, an initialize event is sent to the object before the creation is complete. If the `Class_Initialize()` procedure of the object is defined, the code within the `Class_Initialize()` procedure can be used to do things before the object is finally created. This includes the initialization of property values.

When an object is destroyed, a Terminate event is sent to the object before the object is destroyed. If the `Class_Terminate()` procedure is defined, the code within the `Class_Terminate()` procedure can be used to clean up any resources before the object is destroyed.

Note The most common type of clean up includes setting object variables to Nothing.

Adding a Customer Class to the Project

Now you are ready to start adding the classes to your project. Let's add the customer class and work through this class in detail. Then you will add the product class and order class. Add a customer class to your VB project using the menu item shown in Figure 13.3. After selecting this menu item, a dialog box appears enabling you to choose a type of class to create. This dialog box is similar to the one shown in Figure 13.4.

Figure 13.4

The Add Class Module dialog box.

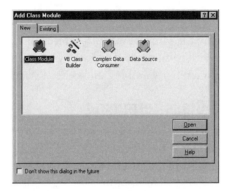

The icon named Class Module (in the upper left) is selected by default. The Class Module is used to create standard classes in Visual Basic. Click the Open button to create a new class of this type. After creating the class, you will notice a couple of things. First, a new folder has been added to the Project Explorer. This new folder is called Class Modules and contains the new class you just created. This new class has the default name Class1. Second, the code window of the class opened and the cursor is placed there for you to start writing code. Before you write any code, change the name of the class from Class1 to Customer. Click on Class1 in the Project Explorer to update the Properties window with the properties of this class. Click in the name property to change the name. This process is identical to how you changed the names of forms and standard code modules.

Next, you must add properties to the class. This is not the same as the properties that show up in the properties window. The properties in the properties window are Visual Basic class properties. The class properties are not exposed or available to an object (instance of a class) within your Visual Basic application. The properties you need to add are the ones that are available to an object within your Visual Basic application. Here are the properties you are going to add to the Customer class:

- First Name
- Middle Initial
- Last Name
- Street Address
- City
- State
- Zip
- Phone Number
- Email Address
- Identifier

Let's start with one property so that you understand the essence of implementing properties. Enter the following code in the code window corresponding to the Customer class (the code for this chapter is in the chapter13 folder on the CD that accompanies this book):

```
Option Explicit
Private m_firstName As String

Public Property Get firstName() As String
  firstName = m_firstName
End Property

Public Property Let firstName(x As String)
  m_firstName = x
End Property
```

The first line, once again, specifies that all variables in this module must be declared before using them. The next line creates a private variable for holding the value for the customer's first name. The scope of the m_firstName variable is the class module.

The variable cannot be seen or referred to directly from any code outside the class module. So how do you get and set the customer's first name from outside the class? The answer lies in the remaining lines of code in the code segment. There are two methods here—one for getting the first name and the other for setting the first name. Specifically, these are called property procedures because they are defined as part of a class and are related to a property of the class.

Property Get **Procedure**

The first property procedure allows getting the first name from a customer object. The keyword `Public` is used to allow the property procedure to be visible outside the class. If you used `Private` instead, code outside the class would not be able to get the first name from a customer object. However, a private method is callable from other methods of the class.

The keyword `Property` denotes that the name of the method is actually a property. This has value that you will see in a few minutes. Following the `Property` keyword is the `Get` keyword. This keyword further denotes the method that is called when the name property of a customer object is accessed (or retrieved).

Next is the name of the property procedure (which is the actual property name that is exposed) followed by a parameter list in parentheses. In this case, you are not defining any parameters. Finally, the return type of the property procedure is defined. The return type is the datatype of the property value that is returned to the code accessing the property.

The code following the declaration of the `Property Get` method is referred to as the body of the method. In this method, the body contains one line of code. Notice the variable name at the beginning of this line of code. This variable name must be exactly the same name that was used in the declaration of the `Property Get` procedure. The result of this line of code sets the return value to a value contained within the private member variable m_firstName. You designate the return value in exactly the same way you do with functions. Within the body of the method, set the name of the method to a value and when the method exits, that value is returned to the caller of the method.

The last line in the method is keywords `End Property`. This designates the end of the method.

A `Property Get` is a procedure defined on a class for getting a specific property value.

To understand how these property methods are invoked by code outside the class, here is an example of code that creates a new customer object and attempts to retrieve the first name property value:

```
Dim c as New Customer
Dim firstName as String
firstName = c.firstName
```

The first line of this example shows how you would create a customer object. You can create as many customer objects as you like, and each contains its own set of property values. As you can see, the first name property on the `Customer` object is referred to using the name of the method you defined. Because you have defined a `Public Property Get` procedure, you can access the first name property of the object using dot notation. Dot notation is how you reference properties or methods of an object. In this case, we refer to the variable c, then a dot, and then the name of the property. This code specifically references the first name property of the object as defined by the variable c.

Property Let Procedure

The second property procedure enables you to set the first name from a customer object. Again, the keyword `Public` is used to allow the method to be visible outside the class. If you used `Private` instead, code outside the class would not be able to set the first name from a customer object.

A `Property Let` is a procedure defined on a class for setting a specific property value. This type of procedure is used for all properties which are not defined as an object type.

The keyword `Property` denotes that the name of the property procedure is actually a property. Following the `Property` keyword is the `Let` keyword. This keyword further denotes this method that is called when an attempt is made to set the first name property of a customer object.

Next is the name of the property procedure (which is the actual property name that is exposed) followed by a parameter list in parentheses. Notice you are defining a single parameter. This parameter specifies the value to which the property will be set. In this case, you define a parameter of type `String`.

The code following the declaration of the `Property Let` method is referred to as the body of the property procedure. In this property procedure, the body contains one line of code that sets the private member variable `m_firstName` to the value contained within the parameter passed to the method. Following this line are the keywords `End Property`. This designates the end of the property procedure.

Here is an example of code that creates a new customer object and attempts to set the value of the last name property:

```
Dim c as New Customer
c.firstName = "Alex"
```

The first line of this example shows how you create a customer object just as you did in the `Property Get` example. Because you have defined a `Public Property Let` procedure, you can set the first name property of the object using dot notation. If you did not define a `Property Let` method for the `Customer` class, the second line in this example would not work and would generate a compile error when you build the application.

You have defined the `Property Get` and `Property Let` methods for the first name property of Customer. You might have noticed this accomplishes the exact same goal as defining a public variable in the class. Although this is true, you now have the ability to do more because you defined these methods. The code you entered for the `Customer` class can be expanded to include more logic, such as validation of the values before actually setting the property. You will add some validation later in the book before you complete these persistent objects.

Property Set **Procedure**

It is worth noting the third type of property procedure. When defining a property that contains a reference to an object, you cannot use the `Property Let` statement. Instead, you must use the `Property Set` statement. A `Property Set` procedure is defined on a class for setting a specific property value that is defined as an object type. Here is an example of a property of type `Object` in the `Customer` class and the corresponding property procedure for setting the property:

```
Option Explicit
Private m_object As Object

Public Property Set myObject (obj as Object)
  Set m_object = obj
End Property
```

The following code is used to set the `myObject` property of an object:

```
Dim c as New Customer
Set c.myObject = New Customer
```

Let's complete the process of adding properties to the `Customer` class. Add the following code in the declarations section to define the private data members of the class:

```
Private m_id As Long
Private m_lastName As String
Private m_firstName As String
Private m_middleInitial As String
Private m_streetAddress As String
Private m_city As String
Private m_state As String
Private m_zip As String
Private m_telephone As String
Private m_email As String
```

Now that you have defined the private data members, let's move forward by implementing the `Property Get` and `Property Let` methods for each of these properties similar to what you did with the first name property. Because none of these properties involves a datatype of an object, you can use the Property Let procedure and not the Property Set procedure to set these properties. Enter the following code after the methods you added for the firstName property:

```
Public Property Get lastName() As String
  lastName = m_lastName
End Property

Public Property Let lastName(x As String)
   m_lastName = x
End Property

Public Property Get middleInitial() As String
   middleInitial = m_middleInitial
End Property

Public Property Let middleInitial(x As String)
   m_middleInitial = x
End Property

Public Property Get streetAddress() As String
   streetAddress = m_streetAddress
End Property

Public Property Let streetAddress(x As String)
   m_streetAddress = x
End Property

Public Property Get city() As String
   city = m_city
End Property

Public Property Let city(x As String)
   m_city = x
End Property

Public Property Get state() As String
   state = m_state
End Property

Public Property Let state(x As String)
   m_state = x
End Property

Public Property Get zip() As String
   zip = m_zip
End Property

Public Property Let zip(x As String)
   m_zip = x
End Property
```

```
Public Property Get telephone() As String
   telephone = m_telephone
End Property

Public Property Let telephone(x As String)
   m_telephone = x
End Property

Public Property Get email() As String
   email = m_email
End Property

Public Property Let email(x As String)
   m_email = x
End Property
```

The ID of the Customer class is a special property because you do not want to be able to set the property from outside the class. You want the Customer class to automatically generate a new customer ID internally and at the appropriate time. To disallow the ID property from being set, define a Property Get method but not a Property Let method. This is a common technique for creating read-only properties. To define the Property Get method, enter the following code:

```
Public Property Get id() As Long
   id = m_id
End Property
```

Adding the Product Class and the Order Class to the Project

Add a new class using the Project, Add Class Module menu item. Select the Class Module icon as the type of class to create. After the class is added, change the name to Product then save it using Product.cls as the filename. Now add the properties to the class as you did with the Customer class. Here is the code for the properties of the Product class:

```
Option Explicit

Private m_id As Long
Private m_name As String
Private m_author As String
Private m_description As String
Private m_prodType As String
Private m_imgFile As String
Private m_docFile As String
Private m_supplier As String
Private m_price As Currency
```

13

```
Public Property Get id() As Long
   id = m_id
End Property

Public Property Get name() As String
   name = m_name
End Property

Public Property Let name(x As String)
   m_name = x
End Property

Public Property Get author() As String
   author = m_author
End Property

Public Property Let author(x As String)
   m_author = x
End Property

Public Property Get description() As String
   description = m_description
End Property

Public Property Let description(x As String)
   m_description = x
End Property

Public Property Get prodType() As String
   prodType = m_prodType
End Property

Public Property Let prodType(x As String)
   m_prodType = x
End Property

Public Property Get imgFile() As String
   imgFile = m_imgFile
End Property

Public Property Let imgFile(x As String)
   m_imgFile = x
End Property

Public Property Get docFile() As String
   docFile = m_docFile
End Property

Public Property Let docFile(x As String)
   m_docFile = x
End Property
```

```
Public Property Get supplier() As String
  supplier = m_supplier
End Property

Public Property Let supplier(x As String)
  m_supplier = x
End Property

Public Property Get price() As Currency
  price = m_price
End Property

Public Property Let price(x As Currency)
  m_price = x
End Property
```

Add a new class using the Project, Add Class Module menu item. Select the Class Module icon as the type of class to create. After the class is added, change the name to Order then save it using Order.cls as the filename. Now add the properties to the class as you did with the Customer and Product classes. Notice that all the properties for the Order class are read-only. Here is the code for the properties of the Order class:

```
Option Explicit

Private m_id As Long
Private m_customerId As Long
Private m_dateEntered As Date
Private m_dateShipped As Date
Private m_dateBilled As Date
Private m_datePaid As Date
Private m_subTotal As Currency
Private m_discount As Single
Private m_taxPercent As Single
Private m_shippingCharge As Currency
Private m_total As Currency
Private m_cancelled As Boolean

Public Property Get id() As Long
   id = m_id
End Property

Public Property Get customerId() As Long
   customerId = m_customerId
End Property

Public Property Get dateEntered() As Date
   dateEntered = m_dateEntered
End Property
```

```
Public Property Get dateShipped() As Date
  dateShipped = m_dateShipped
End Property

Public Property Get dateBilled() As Date
  dateBilled = m_dateBilled
End Property

Public Property Get datePaid() As Date
  datePaid = m_datePaid
End Property

Public Property Get subTotal() As Currency
  subTotal = m_subTotal
End Property

Public Property Get discount() As Single
  discount = m_discount
End Property

Public Property Get taxPercent() As Single
  taxPercent = m_taxPercent
End Property

Public Property Get shippingCharge() As Currency
  shippingCharge = m_shippingCharge
End Property

Public Property Get total() As Currency
  total = m_total
End Property

Public Property Get cancelled() As Boolean
  cancelled = m_cancelled
End Property
```

The Order class properties are almost all defined. Three additional properties would be useful: product status, billing status, and shipping status. Each property contains a defined set of values (which you will see). If you used one of the built-in datatypes, such as Long, to declare the property, you have no way of limiting the value of the property within the datatype directly. You could, of course, add some validation logic in the property methods to limit the value but there is a better way of handling this. The answer lies in the use of enumerations.

Using Enumerations for Order Status Properties

 Enumerations are another way of defining your own datatype. An *enumeration* defines a set of possible values as a named set. A sample list of enumerated values is Days of the Week, which contains the seven possible values Sunday, Monday,

Tuesday, Wednesday, Thursday, Friday, Saturday, and Sunday. After you have declared an enumeration with a set of values, you can use the enumeration name as a datatype when declaring a variable. A variable declared as an enumeration can contain only one of the values in the enumeration at a given time. Let's first run through using an enumeration for the product status. After we have gone through this we will cover the shipping status and billing status.

Enter this code in the declarations section of the Order class module:

```
Public Enum EnumProdStatus
    psInvalid = 0
    psOrderEntered = 1
    psBackordered = 2
    psShipped = 3
End Enum
```

The Public keyword is used to give the enumeration application scope. Any code within the class and outside the class can use this enumeration. If the enumeration was declared as Private, the scope would only be within the class module. Because you want to expose the status properties to any code within the application, it makes sense to declare this as Public.

The keyword Enum tells Visual Basic you are declaring an enumeration. The word following the keyword Enum is the name of the enumeration. You can name this as you choose as long as you follow the same rules as naming a variable (you can use alphanumeric characters, it must start with a character and not a number, and so on). Each line between the Public Enum and End Enum represents a valid value as part of the enumeration. Each enumeration value has two parts to it. You first name the enumerated value and then give it a value. Each of the names of the values in the enumeration starts with ps to provide some useful naming convention within this code. This is good practice, and it is recommended you do this in the enumerations you define on your own. Now that you have an enumeration defined, you can declare a private member variable to contain the product status. Enter the following code in the declarations section of the Order class module:

```
Private m_prodStatus As EnumProdStatus
```

This code declares a private data member within the Order class, and the datatype is the enumeration you just defined.

The next step is to provide a Property Get method to allow code to get the status from an Order object. At this point, you do not want to grant the ability to set the status from outside the class; therefore, you are not going to define a Property Let method.

Add the following code to the Order class to define the read-only prodStatus property:

```
Public Property Get prodStatus() As EnumProdStatus
  prodStatus = m_prodStatus
End Property
```

This code is similar to the other property methods you have previously written. The difference here is the introduction of an enumeration datatype for the property. Regarding the product status, it would be useful to also have a method to return a descriptive string about the status of the order. The client code might want a descriptive string for displaying a message to the user rather than returning a numeric code that is not apparently meaningful. Enter the following code to allow returning a descriptive string based on the product status value:

```
Public Property Get prodStatusStr() As String
  If m_prodStatus = psOrderEntered Then
    prodStatusStr = "Order entered"
  ElseIf m_prodStatus = psBackordered Then
    prodStatusStr = "Back-ordered"
  ElseIf m_prodStatus = psShipped Then
    prodStatusStr = "Shipped"
  Else
    prodStatusStr = "Invalid"
  End If
End Property
```

There is an interesting point to be made about this. There is a distinction between data members and properties. A private data member in Visual Basic does not necessarily translate directly into a property. Private data members hold data within an object as defined by the object's class. A data member does not have to be exposed through a property. If it is, a data member can be exposed through one or more properties. Using the product status to support this, notice you created a private data member (m_prodStatus) to hold the product status. You then created two properties (prodStatus and prodStatusStr) that use the private data member in support of getting the property values.

Let's now complete the status properties by defining the billing status and shipping status. Add the following code to the declarations section of the Order class. This code defines enumerations for the billing status and the shipping status.

```
Public Enum EnumBillStatus
  bsInvalid = 0
  bsOpen = 1
  bsBilled = 2
  bsPaid = 3
End Enum
```

```
Public Enum EnumShippingType
  stInvalid = 0
  stPickup = 1
  stUPS = 2
  stFedex = 3
End Enum
```

Now add the following code to the declarations section of the Order class to define the private data members to hold the status values:

```
Private m_billStatus As EnumBillStatus
Private m_shippingType As EnumShippingType
```

Finally, add this code to define read-only properties for getting the billing status and shipping status from an Order object:

```
Public Property Get billStatus() As EnumBillStatus
  billStatus = m_billStatus
End Property

Public Property Get billStatusStr() As String
  If m_billStatus = bsOpen Then
    billStatusStr = "Open"
  ElseIf m_billStatus = bsBilled Then
    billStatusStr = "Billed"
  ElseIf m_billStatus = bsPaid Then
    billStatusStr = "Paid"
  Else
    billStatusStr = "Invalid"
  End If
End Property

Public Property Get shippingType() As EnumShippingType
  shippingType = m_shippingType
End Property

Public Property Get shippingTypeStr() As String
  If m_shippingType = stPickup Then
    shippingTypeStr = "Pickup"
  ElseIf m_shippingType = stUPS Then
    shippingTypeStr = "UPS"
  ElseIf m_shippingType = stFedex Then
    shippingTypeStr = "FEDEX"
  Else
    shippingTypeStr = "Invalid"
  End If
End Property
```

The billStatus and shippingType property procedures just return the corresponding internal status value.

The billStatusStr and the shippingTypeStr property procedures use an If..ElseIf..EndIf statement to compare the internal status value against all the possible values in the enumerations. When a successful comparison is achieved, the appropriate string value is returned.

Next Steps

In this chapter, we defined three classes that will eventually become persistent. We focused on adding the classes to the project and adding the support for the properties of the classes. In the process, we covered some basic object-oriented terminology to support your understanding and project development.

In the next chapter, you are going to add some validation logic to the property procedures you created in this chapter. Additionally, you are going to expand your classes by adding more methods.

The Order class as it stands is not sufficient for your purposes. You are going to add support for the Order class to contain many order items. Each order item is associated with a single product. The sum of the order items adds up to the total order created by a customer.

In this chapter

- *Validating Property Values*
- *Implementing Calculated Property Values*
- *Verifying Required Properties*
- *Expanding the Order Class to Contain a Collection of Order Items*

Chapter 14

Defining the Interface: Properties and Methods

In the previous chapter, you added three classes (`Customer`, `Product`, and `Order`) to your project. While doing this, you implemented a set of properties for each class. You can now create objects based on these classes and use the properties that you defined. This includes the capability to get and set specific property values. At this point, however, that is all you can do. In your classes, you have not defined any methods that can act on the properties of the object and additionally give the object some behavior.

In this chapter, you are going to finish adding the properties and define methods. This involves additional concepts beyond the basic getting and setting of properties. Because you have already demonstrated how to define `Property Get` and `Property Let`/`Property Set`, you should be at the point of understanding what classes, objects, and properties are.

The next logical step regarding properties is to add logic that validates the value a property is set to. You don't want to just blindly accept any value for certain properties. In this project, we show you how to add validation logic to validate property values. Based on this concept and the code we cover, you can further expand the project and add code to validate any property to the extent you want.

It is possible to define a property that is a value and is the result of a calculation. We are going to implement two additional properties to demonstrate how you could do this.

Another common task you might want a class to do is to verify that specific properties contain values. If a property must contain a value, this is referred to as a required property. As an example, customers and products must have a name before you can use them.

You are going to revisit the classes from the previous chapter to add validation logic. Regarding the Order class, we are going to expand it to contain order items. This involves creating an OrderItem class, as well as a class to manage a collection of OrderItems. The paradigm of having an object contain a list of objects is common in the development of a software application.

By the end of this chapter, your classes should be nearly complete. After that, the remaining work is to add database support to your classes to support saving your object values to a database and to retrieve objects from a database. We cover some database concepts in Chapter 15, "Elementary Database Concepts," and will add the database support to our classes in Chapter 16, "Using Objects from Others."

The complete code for this chapter can be found in the Chapter14 folder of the main VBFS folder on the CD that accompanies this book.

Validating Property Values

Occasionally, you might want to validate a property value before it is set within the object. One approach is to document the supported values for each property of your new class and hope the users of your objects don't set the properties to improper values. This approach does not work. Developing object-oriented software helps solve this problem. By placing the validation logic within your classes, you are guaranteeing the validity of the data of the property values in your objects. Let's add some validation logic so you can see exactly what we are saying.

The first property that you are going to add some validation logic to is the firstName property of the Customer class. You have chosen to limit the length of a customer's first name to no more than 32 characters. Because you are likely to enforce the maximum character length of other properties, let's make a utility function to check the maximum length of a string.

At the bottom of the modMain module, enter the following code:

```
Public Sub EnsureMaxLength(s As String, ByVal maxLen As Long)
   If Len(s) > maxLen Then s = Left(s, maxLen)
End Sub
```

This code defines a public procedure that can be used by the entire application. The procedure name is EnsureMaxLength and has two parameters. The first parameter is the string that is checked. The second parameter is the maximum length that the string is allowed to be.

The body of the procedure consists of one line that is an `If...Then` statement. The expression `Len(s) > maxLen` is evaluated to either True or False. In evaluating the expression, the `Len` function is used to get the length of the string to compare against the value of the `maxLen` variable. The `Len` function takes a string and returns a number that is the length of the string.

The following code sets the variable l to the length of the string, which happens to be 5:

```
Dim l As Long
l = Len("Patty")
```

The logical operator >>>> logical operator is then used to compare two values. If the left side of the > is greater than the right side, the expression evaluates to True. If the left side of the > is not greater than the right side, the expression evaluates to False.

The following code sets the `result` variable to `True`:

```
Dim result As Boolean
result = Len("Patty") > 3
```

The following code sets the `result` variable to `False`:

```
Dim result As Boolean
result = Len("Patty") > 7
```

Let's get back to the `EnsureMaxLength` procedure. If the expression evaluates to `True`, the code following the `Then` is run. The code following the `Then` uses the `Left` function to extract the left part of a string up to a specified number of characters.

Using the `Left` function, you can extract the left (or first) n number of characters from a string where n represents a number you specify.

The following code extracts the first three characters from the string `"Patty"` and assigns the string `"Pat"` to the variable `str`:

```
Dim str As String
str = Left("Patty", 3)
```

If the maximum length of the string passed to the `EnsureMaxLength` procedure exceeds the number defined by the `maxLen` variable, the s variable is set to contain only the first `maxLen` characters. For this procedure to work correctly, you must notice the string parameter is defined as `s As String`. By default, Visual Basic passes variables `ByRef`. Because you are potentially modifying the value in the parameter passed to the procedure directly, you want to make sure your changes to the contents of the variable are kept after leaving the procedure. If you declared the parameter using `ByVal s As String` the changes to the variable s would not be kept because the changes would have been made to a copy of the string passed to the procedure, not the actual string itself.

Now that you have a procedure to ensure the maximum length of a string, let's add some code to a couple of the existing Property Let procedures to validate the data.

Open the code for the Customer class. The Property Let procedure for the first name should look like this:

```
Public Property Let firstName(x As String)
m_firstName = x
End Property
```

Add a call to the EnsureMaxLength procedure you just entered to guarantee that a customer's last name will not exceed 32 characters in your application. To do this, add code to call the EnsureMaxLength procedure so that the Property Let procedure looks like this:

```
Public Property Let firstName (x As String)
  EnsureMaxLength x, 32
  m_ firstName = x
End Property
```

Now, validate more customer properties, specifically middleInitial, lastName, streetAddress, city, state, zip, telephone, and email. The modified Property Let procedures should look like this:

```
Public Property Let middleInitial(x As String)
  EnsureMaxLength x, 6
  m_middleInitial = x
End Property

Public Property Let lastName(x As String)
  EnsureMaxLength x, 32
  m_lastName = x
End Property

 Public Property Let streetAddress(x As String)
  EnsureMaxLength x, 64
  m_streetAddress = x
End Property

Public Property Let city(x As String)
  EnsureMaxLength x, 32
  m_city = x
End Property

Public Property Let state(x As String)
  EnsureMaxLength x, 2
  m_state = x
End Property
```

```
Public Property Let zip(x As String)
  EnsureMaxLength x, 16
  m_zip = x
End Property

Public Property Let telephone(x As String)
  EnsureMaxLength x, 24
  m_telephone = x
End Property

Public Property Let email(x As String)
  EnsureMaxLength x, 64
  m_email = x
End Property
```

Similarly, add some validation code to the Property Let procedure of the Product class. Modify the following Property Let procedures so that they look like this:

```
Public Property Let name(x As String)
  EnsureMaxLength x, 32
  m_name = x
End Property

Public Property Let author(x As String)
  EnsureMaxLength x, 32
  m_author = x
End Property

Public Property Let description(x As String)
  EnsureMaxLength x, 128
  m_description = x
End Property

Public Property Let prodType(x As String)
  EnsureMaxLength x, 32
  m_prodType = x
End Property

Public Property Let imgFile(x As String)
  EnsureMaxLength x, 128
  m_imgFile = x
End Property

Public Property Let docFile(x As String)
  EnsureMaxLength x, 128
  m_docFile = x
End Property

Public Property Let supplier(x As String)
  EnsureMaxLength x, 64
  m_supplier = x
End Property
```

These validation changes guard against string values that are too long. Another type of validation logic includes rejecting a property change if it is being set to an illegal value. This disallows the property change if an erroneous value was detected during the setting of a property. For example, under no circumstances do you ever want to allow setting the price of the products in your application to a negative value such as –$1.00. This does not make sense for your application. So, to guard against this type of property change you must reject negative values for the price property of a product object. To do this, modify the `Property Let` procedure for `price` so that the code looks like this:

```
Public Property Let price(x As Currency)
  If x < 0 Then Exit Property
  m_price = x
End Property
```

The first line in the body of the procedure checks the value of the parameter. If the value is less than zero, the `Exit Property` statement is run, which exits the procedure before the property is set to the new value. This essentially disables setting the price property to an invalid value.

Implementing Calculated Property Values

All the properties defined so far use internal data members to get a value from and to set a value to. It is also possible to define a property of a class that is not directly related to one specific internal data member but instead is calculated from a combination of other values. To demonstrate this, let's create a `Property Let` procedure in the `Customer` class. Currently, you can get the first name, middle initial, and last name from a Customer object. However, to get each of these you must retrieve each property individually from the object. Let's create a new property called name, which is a combination of the customer's first name, middle initial, and last name. Enter the following code:

```
Public Property Get name() As String
  name = m_firstName & " " & m_middleInitial & " " & m_lastName
End Property
```

This code creates a property that can be retrieved from a customer object. A string is constructed by combining the first name, middle initial, and last name (with spaces between them) and returns the result by setting the `Property Get` procedure name to the resulting string.

A *calculated property* is derived from a combination of other object property values or through a specified calculation or algorithm. The value of the property is not typically stored as a private value of the object. It is dynamically calculated upon request of the property.

Without the `Property Let` procedure, the name property cannot be set. You could define a `Property Let` procedure that accepts a string, which must be parsed and set to each of the individual properties. Because this is not a requirement of your application, this exercise is left up to you to complete.

You also must construct a customer's full name using their last name first. To support this, create another property, which is constructed similarly except in a different order. Enter the following code:

```
Public Property Get fullName() As String
  fullName = m_lastName & ", " & m_firstName & " " & m_middleInitial
End Property
```

Notice this code works almost the same as the preceding `Property Let` procedure except the last name appears at the beginning of the resulting string.

Verifying Required Properties

After you finish creating objects in your application and finish setting some properties, you need a way to check whether all the required properties of the object have been set. The object should do the verification of the required properties itself. The knowledge of which properties are required must be shared by the object and any code using the object. This is because the application needs to know what properties are required to be set to make sure the application sets them. Additionally, the object must know what the required properties are for it to do the verification.

A *required property* is a property that must contain a value before the object is considered to have a valid identity.

In this application, the customer is required to have a last name, and a product is required to have a name. Let's write a function to check the appropriate properties and verify that the required properties have valid values. Enter the following code in the `Customer` class module:

```
Public Function IsValid() As Boolean
  IsValid = (Len(m_lastName) > 0)
End Function
```

This function is part of the `Customer` class and verifies that the last name property has a value. This function can be expanded to check more properties in the future as requirements change. The function, by itself, does not perform the verification. Later, you make a call to this function for the purpose of verifying whether the object is valid and has valid values for the required properties before saving to a database. For now, the existence of the function demonstrates verifying required properties as a method of a class. After you get into adding database support you will put this function to good use.

Likewise, in the Product class you need to verify that the name property has a valid value. Enter the following code in the Product class module:

```
Public Function IsValid() As Boolean
  IsValid = (Len(m_name) > 0)
End Function
```

This is identical to the function you added to the Customer class except, in this case, you are checking the product name.

Expanding the Order Class to Contain a Collection of Order Items

As we already mentioned, we developed an Order class that represents an actual order created by a customer for one or many products. The Order class as it stands right now only contains properties. In the real world when you purchase products from a store, your order contains a list of products and a total cost, which is the sum of the cost of all the products.

Modeling the Order

You must structure your classes in your application to support a list of products that are associated with an order for a customer. Take a moment to review Figure 14.1. This diagram uses UML (Unified Modeling Language) to define a model of the Order class and the other classes that are associated to the order. UML is a common language for presenting class diagrams that includes classes and their relationships.

Figure 14.1

Using UML to define a model of the Order class.

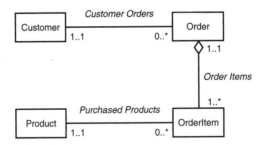

EXCURSION

Modeling Objects Using UML

UML has been gaining popularity over the past few years as a way of communicating class relationships in a diagram. Prior to the introduction of UML to the software development community, there were several other competing object modeling approaches. Because there is more than one way of expressing class diagrams, a common mechanism did not exist for this purpose. As a result, the software community needed to understand each approach to share ideas using modeling. UML attempts to be the one common modeling approach that becomes the standard for everyone to use. If you need a way to design a class diagram and express it to others, we recommend you get a book on UML and start communicating classes and their relationships via this modeling language.

In this diagram, an order is associated with one customer. Each order has a list of order items and each order item is associated with one product. The diamond shape on the association between orders and order items means that the order items are contained within the order. If the order is deleted, so are the order items. The order items do not exist without the order. However, products and customers exist without orders or order items.

Using this class diagram, you can see that an order class has a list of order items. The order class needs to add order items and calculate the total cost by adding up the cost of each of the associated order items. One approach is to have the order class contain all the code do deal with the list of order items. This approach requires the order class to contain code for dealing with the order itself and also to contain code for managing the list of order items. A simpler approach (and more object-oriented) is to create another class that manages the list of order items as part of the order. Let's call this class OrderItemColl, which stands for order item collection (see Figure 14.2).

Figure 14.2

The order diagram.

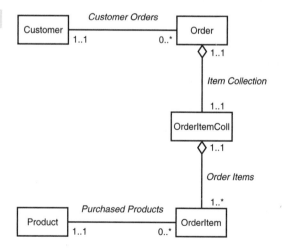

You can now add methods to the OrderItemColl class that encapsulate the list of order items. The addition of these methods essentially treats the list of order items as an object. The order class must be updated to contain one OrderItemColl object. The order class then communicates with the OrderItemColl object to manage the order items. Additionally, you can add methods to the OrderItemColl class that automatically calculate the total cost of all the order items. The order class can then call this method to get the total cost of the items in the order rather than having the order class go through the list and add up the cost itself.

Creating the `OrderItem` Class

Let's begin creating the `OrderItem` class by implementing the properties of the class. Create a new class and name it `OrderItem`. Now save the class using the Ctrl+S key combination. Within the code of the class, enter the following code:

```
Option Explicit

Private m_id As Long
Private m_productId As Long
Private m_seqNo As Integer
Private m_price As Currency
Private m_discount As Single
Private m_qty As Long
Private m_total As Currency
Private m_orderId As Long

Public Property Get id() As Long
  id = m_id
End Property

Public Property Get productId() As Long
  productId = m_productId
End Property

Public Property Get seqNo() As Integer
  seqNo = m_seqNo
End Property
Public Property Let seqNo(x As Integer)
  m_seqNo = x
End Property

Public Property Get price() As Currency
  price = m_price
End Property

Public Property Get discount() As Single
  discount = m_discount
End Property

Public Property Get qty() As Long
  qty = m_qty
End Property

Public Property Get total() As Currency
  total = m_total
End Property
```

```
Public Property Get orderId() As Long
  orderId = m_orderId
End Property
```

Table 14.1 lists the description of the properties in the OrderItem class.

Table 14.1   Properties of the OrderItem Class

Property	Description
id	Internal ID of the order item
productId	Product ID of the product associated with the order item
seqNo	Sequence number of the order item in the list
price	Price of the order item
discount	Discount associated with the order item
qty	Number of products in the order item
total	Total cost of the order item
orderId	The ID of the order

All the properties are read-only except for seqNo. Because the properties are read-only, the values of the properties are set internally. In the case of the productId and price, you want to set these the moment a product is added to an order item. Because you know that a product is associated to an order item (based on the class diagram), let's add a method for this purpose. Enter this code in the OrderItem class:

```
Public Sub SetItem(prd As Product, _
                   ByVal disc As Single, _
                   ByVal qty As Long)
  If m_id > 0 Then Exit Sub ' is not a new order item

  m_productId = prd.id
  m_price = prd.price
  m_discount = disc
  m_qty = qty
  m_total = CalcTotal(prd, m_discount, m_qty)
End Sub
```

This code declares a public procedure called SetItem as part of the OrderItem class. It takes three parameters: a Product object, the discount percentage of the product, and a product quantity. The goal of this procedure is to assign the product to the order item and set all the necessary properties in the OrderItem class based on the product being assigned.

The first line of code in the procedure is checking the value of the order item ID. If the order item ID is greater than zero, the order item must have already been created. A new order item has an ID that is zero. Later, when we show how the objects are saved to the database, you will see how the id property gets a value greater than zero.

The next few lines set the properties of the order item. Each of the properties that are set in this procedure are properties of an object of this class. Therefore, each OrderItem object has its own set of properties that can contain different values.

The product ID is set using the id property of the product passed to the procedure. The price is set to the value of the price property of the product passed to the procedure. The discount is set to the value of the disc parameter passed to the procedure. The quantity is set to the value of the qty parameter passed to the procedure. Finally, the total is set by calling a function that calculates the total price using the product, discount, and quantity. Enter the following code in the OrderItem class:

```
Public Function CalcTotal(prd As Product, _
                          ByVal disc As Single, _
                          ByVal qty As Long) As Currency
  Dim price As Currency
  price = prd.price
  CalcTotal = (price - (price * disc / 100)) * qty
End Function
```

The code declares a public function named CalcTotal. It has three parameters: a Product object, a discount as a percentage of the price, and a quantity value. This function returns a currency that is the calculated value based on the inputs.

The first line of the function creates a local variable for storing a currency value. The next line assigns the product's price to the local variable. The last line of the function assigns the result of a calculation to the return value of the function. The calculation first determines the discount by evaluating (price * disc / 100) because this is in parentheses. Next, the discounted price is evaluated by subtracting the discount price from the product price by evaluating (price - (price * disc / 100)). The discounted price is then multiplied by the quantity to determine the final total cost of the order item by evaluating (price - (price * disc / 100)) * qty.

Creating the OrderItemColl Class

You now have defined an OrderItem class that has properties and the capability to assign a product to it. The next logical step is to create the OrderItemColl class that contains a list of OrderItem objects. After the OrderItemColl class is written, you can use it within the Order class. Here is a list of the tasks the OrderItemColl class can accomplish in relation to the OrderItem objects it contains:

- Get a count of order items
- Get an individual order item from the list

- Get the total cost of all the order items
- Create a new order item
- Add an order item to the list of order items
- Remove a specific order item
- Remove all order items

Let's start by adding support to the OrderItemColl class for maintaining a list of OrderItem objects. Enter the following code in the OrderItemColl class:

```
Option Explicit

Private m_coll As Collection
Private Sub Class_Initialize()
  Set m_coll = New Collection
End Sub

Private Sub Class_Terminate()
  Set m_coll = Nothing
End Sub

Public Function Count() As Long
  Count = m_coll.Count
End Function

Public Function Item(v As Variant) As OrderItem
  Set Item = m_coll.Item(v)
End Function
)
Public Sub AddOrderItem(oi As OrderItem)
  m_coll.Add oi
End Sub
```

Notice the declaration of the private member variable named m_coll. This private data member is declared as a Collection. A Collection is a built-in object that comes with Visual Basic. It has three methods and one read-only property. Table 14.2 lists the property and methods of a Collection object:

Table 14.2   Property and Methods of a Collection Object

Method or Property	Description
Add	Method for adding an object to the collection
Remove	Method for removing an object from the collection
Item	Method for getting an object from the collection
Count	Read-only property for getting the number of objects in the collection

The syntax for the `Add` method looks like this:

```
object.Add item, key, before, after
```

The `object` is any valid variable that is declared as a Collection object. The first parameter, `item`, is any expression that evaluates to an object. The remaining parameters are optional, meaning you do not need to specify them. The `key` parameter is a string expression used to index the object in the collection. The value of the `key` parameter can be used later to retrieve the object from the collection. The `before` parameter is used to instruct the Collection object to place the object in the `item` parameter before the object specified by the index value in the `before` parameter. The value of the `before` parameter (if specified) must be between 1 and the count of the objects in the collection. The `after` parameter is used to instruct the Collection object to place the object in the `item` parameter after the object specified by the index value in the `after` parameter. The value of the `after` parameter (if specified) must be between 1 and the count of objects in the collection. The `before` parameter and the `after` parameter cannot both be specified. Neither of these parameters should be specified or only one of them should be specified.

The syntax for the `Remove` method looks like this:

```
object.Remove index
```

The `object` is any valid variable that is declared as a Collection object. The only parameter, `index`, can be either a number or a string. If it is a number, the value represents the index in the collection (1 to the count of object in the collection). If it is a string, the value is used to search for the object in the collection. If a key is found that equals the value of the `index` parameter, the corresponding object is removed. If an object is not found by using the index value (either a number or a string) an error occurs.)

The syntax for the `Item` method looks like this:

```
object.Item(index)
```

The `object` is any valid variable that is declared as a Collection object. The only parameter, `index`, can be either a number or a string. If it is a number, the value represents the index in the collection (1 to the count of object in the collection). If it is a string, the value is used to search for the object in the collection. If a key is found that equals the value of the `index` parameter, the corresponding object is returned. If an object is not found by using the index value (either a number or a string), an error occurs. Because the `Item` method is the default method of a collection, you could also use the following syntax:

```
object(index)
```

Note Collection objects contain a list of objects that are indexed by number. Like Collection objects, Dictionary objects contain a list of objects but associate a key value with an object. After an object is added to a Dictionary object and associated to a key, the object can be retrieved from the list using the key value instead of using a numbered index.

14

Getting back to the OrderItemColl class, the next two methods you added are Class_Initialize and Class_Terminate. In the Class_Initialize, you created a new Collection object and assigned it to the m_coll private data member. In the Class_Terminate, you set m_coll to Nothing, which frees the Collection object. Remember, this Class_Initialize method is called when a new OrderItemColl object is created. At that point, you want to create a Collection object that can later contain OrderItem objects. Because you are creating a new Collection object as part of an OrderItemColl object, you need to be sure the Collection object is freed when the OrderItemColl object is destroyed. Setting the m_coll variable to Nothing in the Class_Terminate method accomplishes this.

After the Class_Terminate method, you created a function that returned the count of OrderItem objects in the OrderItemColl. This function has the appropriate name of Count and returns the count of objects in the m_coll data member.)

Next, you defined a function named Item. This function takes a Variant and returns an OrderItem object. The Variant is passed to the Item method of the m_coll Collection object. By declaring the parameter as a Variant, the value could be either a number or a string. This takes advantage of the Item method of a Collection object that expects an index in the collection or a key value to search on. Because the method returns an OrderItem, which is an object, the use of Set is required when returning an object from a function.

The AddOrderItem method takes an OrderItem object and adds it to the collection represented by the m_coll data member. This code calls the Add method of m_coll without the key, before or after parameters. The result of this call simply appends the OrderItem object to the collection.

So far, you have an OrderItemColl class that manages a collection of OrderItem objects. Before you move on to update the Order class to support OrderItem objects, add a method on your OrderItemColl class to calculate the total cost of all the contained OrderItem objects. Add the following code to the OrderItemColl class:

```
Public Property Get total() As Currency
  Dim oi As OrderItem, t As Currency
```

```
  For Each oi In m_coll
    t = t + oi.total
  Next
  total = t
End Property
```

This code defines a read-only property named total. The value of the property is calculated by adding up the totals of each OrderItem object. Here we use the For Each...Next statement. This statement is used to iterate through the collection defined by m_coll. As the collection is iterated, the variable oi is assigned the current element in the collection. Then, the statements between the For Each line and the Next line are executed with respect to the current element. The result of this For Each...Next statement is that the collection is iterated and the total of each element is added to the variable t. The last line in the Property Get procedure sets the return value to the variable t ,which is the total cost of all the order items.)

Adding Order Items to the Order Class

At this point, you created an OrderItem class and an OrderItemColl class that manage OrderItem objects. Now it is time to update your Order class to take advantage of the OrderItemColl class. Add the following code to the declarations section of the Order class:

```
Private m_orderItems As OrderItemColl
```

This code creates the private data member m_orderItems. This variable is declared as an OrderItemColl object.

Now add the following code after the declarations section:

```
Private Sub Class_Initialize()
  Set m_orderItems = New OrderItemColl
End Sub

Private Sub Class_Terminate()
  Set m_orderItems = Nothing
End Sub

Public Property Get orderItems() As OrderItemColl
  Set orderItems = m_orderItems
End Property
```

The Class_Initialize method creates a new OrderItemColl object and assigns it to m_orderItems each time a new Order object is created.

Conversely, the Class_Terminate method frees the OrderItemColl object referenced by m_orderItems when the Order object is destroyed.

The orderItems read-only property also is defined as an OrderItemColl object. This Property Get procedure uses the m_orderItems private data member to return the OrderItemColl object associated with the order. This provides the capability to get an OrderItemColl object from an Order object and add OrderItem objects directly to the retrieved OrderItemColl object. This exposes the ability to manage OrderItem objects within an Order object (via the OrderItemColl object).

Right now, it is possible to get, add, and remove OrderItem objects from an Order object. Because you now have this capability, let's end the chapter by adding some more methods that help you work with an Order object. Currently, you do not have a method for creating a new order, canceling an existing order, updating the order with a shipped date, updating the order with a billed date, or updating the order with a paid date. Let's add a few methods for this purpose. Add the following code to the Order class for creating a new order:

```
Public Sub OrdEnter(cust As Customer, _
                    ByVal dateEnt As Date, _
                    ByVal shipType As EnumShippingType, _
                    ByVal discPercent As Single, _
                    ByVal taxPercent As Single, _
                    ByVal shipCharge As Currency)
  m_customerId = cust.id
  m_dateEntered = dateEnt
  m_shippingType = shipType
  m_discount = discPercent
  m_taxPercent = taxPercent
  m_shippingCharge = shipCharge
  m_prodStatus = psOrderEntered
  m_billStatus = bsOpen
  m_cancelled = False
  RecalculateTotal
End Sub

Public Sub RecalculateTotal(Optional discPercent As Single = -1, _
                            Optional taxPercent As Single = -1, _
                            Optional shipCharge As Currency = -1)
  m_subTotal = m_orderItems.total
  If discPercent >= 0 Then m_discount = discPercent
  If taxPercent >= 0 Then m_taxPercent = taxPercent
  If shipCharge >= 0 Then m_shippingCharge = shipCharge

  Dim p As Currency, d As Currency, t As Currency
  d = m_subTotal * m_discount / 100 ' discount total
  p = m_subTotal - d ' discounted sub-total
  t = p * m_taxPercent / 100 ' tax total
  m_total = p + t + m_shippingCharge
End Sub
```

The OrdEnter method takes six parameters for setting the order information. Table 14.3 lists the parameters along with a description of each. The cust parameter is a Customer object that represents the customer creating the order. The dateEnt parameter is the date on which the order was created.

Table 14.3   Parameters to Set the Order Information

Parameter	Description
cust	Customer object representing the customer that created the order
dateEnt	The date the order was created
shipType	The shipping type specified for the order
discPercent	The percentage discount for the order
taxPercent	The tax rate for the order
shipCharge	The shipping charge for the order

The OrdEnter method uses these parameter values to set individual data members as part of the order. The order bill status is set to bsOpen and the product status is set to psOrderEntered. At the end of this method, a call is made to the RecalculateTotal method.

The RecalculateTotal method calculates the total cost of the order by first getting the total cost of the order items then applying the discount, the tax rate, and the shipping charge. The final cost is then set to the private data member m_total. Notice that each of the parameters to RecalculateTotal are optional and have default values. If these parameters are not provided when calling this method, the missing parameters are defaulted to the value –1.

Now enter the following code for canceling, shipping, billing, or paying an order:

```
Public Function OrdCancel()
  If m_prodStatus = psShipped Or _
     m_billStatus = bsBilled Or _
     m_billStatus = bsPaid Then
    Exit Function
  End If

  m_cancelled = True
  'SaveOrder
  OrdCancel = True
End Function

Public Function OrdShip(ByVal dateShipped As Date)
  m_prodStatus = psShipped
  m_dateShipped = dateShipped
  'SaveOrder
```

```
  OrdShip = True
End Function

Public Function OrdBill(ByVal dateBilled As Date)
  m_billStatus = bsBilled
  m_dateBilled = dateBilled
  'SaveOrder
  OrdBill = True
End Function

Public Function OrdPaid(ByVal datePaid As Date)
  m_billStatus = bsPaid
  m_datePaid = datePaid
  'SaveOrder
  OrdPaid = True
End Function
```

The OrdCancel method first checks to see whether the order has been shipped, billed, or paid. If so, the order cannot be cancelled and the method exits. Otherwise, the order is set to cancelled by setting the data member m_cancelled. The function then sets the return value to True. Notice the SaveOrder line is commented out. We will be revisiting this line after you add database support. For now, leave it as is.

The OrdShip method has one parameter that represents the date the order was shipped. The method sets the product status to psShipped, sets the date shipped, and then returns True. Again, notice the SaveOrder line is commented out.

Just like the OrdShip method, the OrdBill method takes a date parameter, sets the bill status to bsBilled, sets the date the order was billed, and then sets the return value to True.

The OrdPaid method takes a data parameter that represents the date the order was paid. It sets the bill status to bsPaid, sets the paid date to the value passed to the method, and then sets the return value to True.

Next Steps

In this chapter, you created an OrderItem class and an OrderItemColl class. The OrderItem class represents a single line item on an order. The OrderItemColl class represents a collection of order items. This class was created to simplify the management of OrderItem objects in relation to an Order object.

We then updated the Order class to use the OrderItemColl class and OrderItem class. At this point, these classes are nearly complete.

The remaining work on these classes involves persisting the data within these objects to a database. Chapter 15, "Elementary Database Concepts: Persisting the State of Our Objects," covers elementary database concepts to assure a base level of understanding regarding databases.

Next, you will set up the database for this application on your computer and introduce a tool that enables you to view the data in the database. This also involves reviewing the database structure for your application so that you become familiar with your application specific data.

In the next chapter, we complete these classes with code that persists the object data to the database. Additionally, we create code that reconstructs the objects from the data within the database.

In this chapter

- *What Is a Database?*
- *Database Concepts*
- *SQL Primer*
- *Setting Up a Data Source Name (DSN)*
- *Defining the Project Schema*
- *Using ActiveX Data Objects for Database Access*
- *ADO, OLE DB, ODBC—Help!*

Chapter 15

Elementary Database Concepts: Persisting the State of Our Objects

In this chapter, we cover database topics in support of adding data persistence to the classes in the project. Before you can start writing the code for doing this, you must understand what a database is and how you work with it. This chapter is a database primer that covers all the necessary concepts prior to writing the code. Don't worry if some of this does not seem completely clear to you at this point. In the next chapter, it should become clearer when we start writing the code to support a database because we reiterate some of the database concepts in the context of the application.

The complete code for this chapter can be found in the Chapter15 folder of the main VBFS folder on the CD that accompanies this title.

What Is a Database?

A database stores information for an indefinite period of time in a structured format. It also provides fast reliable retrieval of the currently stored information. A person who constructs a database (typically a Database Administrator or DBA) defines the structure of how the data is stored. After the database is defined and available for use, many applications can access the database and perform searches and updates.

A *DBA* is a Database Administrator. In a project, this person defines the structure of the database and monitors its use for the purpose of identifying and resolving database issues.

Relational databases store data elements and their relationships to other data elements. Exactly how the data is stored is dependent on the structure of the database defined by the Database Administrator. Relational databases have a language that you must use to interact with the database. The most common relational databases support Structured Query Language (SQL) as a means of saving and retrieving information.

A *relational database* contains records that are related to each other. Relationships can be defined so that record X is related to record Y by defining primary keys and foreign keys. These keys can then be enforced, as an example, to require the existence of record Y in the database before adding record X to the database. Relationships are also used to retrieve groups of related records from the database by grouping records from multiple tables where the primary key of one table is equal to the foreign key of another table.

SQL stands for Structured Query Language. This language includes commands for creating new records, updating existing records, deleting records, and retrieving groups of records from a database.

Oracle, Sybase, Informix, and Microsoft SQL Server are examples of high-end SQL databases that can handle gigabytes worth of information. The application you are creating here does not require these types of databases during the development phase. Your application uses a Microsoft Access database, which is a low-end database with enough functionality to demonstrate your application. Microsoft Access supports SQL, which enables you to change to a higher-end database later, as long as it supports SQL. This enables you to develop an application on a simpler database and provides a path for your application to expand as you need a more powerful database.

Just because you are using Microsoft Access does not automatically enable you to move to Oracle or SQL Server later. If you are writing your own application and you want your application to be able to move from one database to another, you must be careful which features of the database you use. The application in this book uses basic database access, and therefore supports moving to another database. Also, we have localized (as you will see) the database access routines so that if there were a problem, you would be able to fix it quickly in a minimal number of places in the code.

We mentioned database structure as well as Structured Query Language. These topics are crucial to define and work with a database, so let's take some time to go over some of these database concepts.

Database Concepts

A database structure is commonly referred to as a *database schema* and includes the following types of objects:

- Tables
- Columns
- Rows
- Primary keys
- Foreign keys
- Indexes

 A *database schema* is the definition of the storage of data within a database. The schema includes the collection of tables, columns, and indexes and is created using Data Definition Language (DDL) or a database administration tool.

 DDL stands for Data Definition Language. This language is used to define the exact storage format of data within a database. This language includes commands for creating tables, columns, indexes, and keys.

These types of objects are created in a database using Data Definition Language (DDL) statements or an administration tool that comes with the database product you purchased. Each of these types of objects contains information and has a purpose in the operation of the database.

Let's review these objects for an internal perspective of a database.

Tables

Figure 15.1 shows a database table named TPerson with rows and columns. The TPerson table is shown to illustrate a table in a database. This table is not used by the application. Later in this chapter, all the tables used by the application are presented.

Tables contain information about specific elements of your application. Each table has a unique name and contains a set of rows and columns.

 We created a Microsoft Access database that stores our application data. In doing this, we created several tables, such as a table named TProduct for the purpose of storing product information. This table contains a set of columns that support storing the individual attributes of a product such as name and price. You will see all the tables defined in the database for this application later in this chapter.

Figure 15.1

A table with rows and columns.

Id	Name
1	Bob
2	Gabriel
3	Mark
4	Kevin
5	Jon
6	Bill
7	Gregg
8	Jonathon
9	Tom
10	Tuan

Columns

Figure 15.2 shows a table with the two columns: Id and Name.

Figure 15.2

A column in a table.

Id	Name
1	Bob
2	Gabriel
3	Mark
4	Kevin
5	Jon
6	Bill
7	Gregg
8	Jonathon
9	Tom
10	Tuan

A column is a data element or property within a table. A column is also referred to as a field. Columns are defined by a unique name within the table and a datatype. After a column is defined as part of a table, a row in the table can contain a value for that column.

Rows

Figure 15.3 highlights a row in a table.

Figure 15.3

A row in a table.

Id	Name
1	Bob
2	Gabriel
3	Mark
4	Kevin
5	Jon
6	Bill
7	Gregg
8	Jonathon
9	Tom
10	Tuan

A row is an entry within a table that contains values for each column of the table. A row is also referred to as a record.

Primary Keys

Figure 15.4 shows the table TPerson. It contains a primary key consisting of one column named Id.

Figure 15.4

A table with a primary key.

Id	Name
1	Bob
2	Gabriel
3	Mark
4	Kevin
5	Jon
6	Bill
7	Gregg
8	Jonathon
9	Tom
10	Tuan

Primary keys are a set of columns within a table that together uniquely identify a row. Primary keys are used internally by the database to uniquely identify rows in a table. This aids the database processing when searching and updating records. Because primary keys are often used, a database typically creates an index on the primary key for faster performance.

Foreign Keys

Figure 15.5 shows a table named TPerson that contains a foreign key consisting of the column AddressId, which refers to the primary key in the TAddress table. The primary key in the TAddress table consists of one column named Id.

Figure 15.5

A table with a foreign key.

The Foreign Key

TPerson

Id	Name	AddressId
1	Bob	10
2	Gabriel	20
3	Mark	30
4	Kevin	40
5	Jon	30
6	Bill	50
7	Gregg	30
8	Jonathon	30
9	Tom	60
10	Tuan	40

TAddress

Id	City	State	Zip
10	Methuen	MA	01844
20	Lawrence	MA	01840
30	Chelmsford	MA	01824
40	Lowell	MA	01854
50	Tewksbury	MA	01876
60	Tyngsboro	MA	01879

Foreign keys are a set of columns in a table that represent the primary key of another table. The presence of a foreign key in a table signifies that records in the table are related to records in the table to which the foreign key refers.

The combination of foreign keys and primary keys are used by the database to enforce referential integrity. Referential integrity exists when the value of the foreign key for every record in the database refers to a record that has the same value for its primary key. In Figure 15.5, for example, each record in the TPerson table has a value in the AddressId field that corresponds to a record in the TAddress table containing the same value in the Id field. If, for some reason, there was a value of 100 in a TPerson record for the AddressId field and there was no record in the TAddress table that contained a value of 100 in the Id field, referential integrity would be broken.

Referential integrity exists when all foreign key values in a database refer to existing records containing the corresponding primary key value. If a foreign key in a record contains a value and there is no related record containing that value as its primary key, referential integrity is broken.

Indexes

An index can be created on a set of one or more columns in a table. They are used internally by the database for faster searching and retrieval of rows from a table.

Data integrity describes the validity of the values within a record. This is not necessarily the same as referential integrity. As an example, assume a record contains two fields for storing a city and state. If the city field in the record contained the value Boston and the state field contained MA, then the data is correct. If the record contained the respective field values Boston and NH, the data is not correct because there is no city named Boston in the state of New Hampshire.

SQL Primer

SQL consists of statements for interacting with a relational database. A SQL statement starts with a SQL command. The four most common SQL commands are INSERT, UPDATE, DELETE, and SELECT. These commands are used to modify records in a database and to retrieve records from a database. Table 15.1 lists these commands and a description of each. The SQL standard consists of more than just these four commands. However, an overview of these four commands is enough for the purpose of understanding the database interaction in your application.

Table 15.1 Most Commonly Used SQL Commands

SQL Command	Description
INSERT	Inserts a record into a table
UPDATE	Updates a record (or records) in a table
DELETE	Deletes a record (or records) from a table
SELECT	Selects records from one or more tables

INSERT

The syntax of the SQL INSERT command is as follows:

```
INSERT
INTO    table  [ ( field [, field ] ... ) ]
VALUES  ( literal [, literal ] ... )  ;
```

or

```
INSERT
INTO    table  [ ( field [, field ] ... ) ]
subquery  ;
```

The first format inserts a new row into a specified table and sets the specified fields to the specified values. The second format evaluates the subquery and the resulting rows of the subquery are inserted into the specified table. The specified fields are set to the values in the resulting subquery. The first value in the resulting subquery is set to the first specified field, the second value to the second specified field, and so on. Also, the number of columns in the results of the subquery must match the number of columns specified in the SQL INSERT statement.

Here is an example that inserts a new record into the TProducts table:

```
INSERT INTO TProducts (Name, Price) VALUES ('Brush', 2.00)
```

Here is an example that inserts new records into the FREEPRODUCTS table. The inserted records are the result of checking the TProducts table for records with a price of $0.00.

```
INSERT INTO FREEPRODUCTS ( Name, Price )
SELECT Name, Price
FROM TProducts
WHERE Price = 0.00;
```

UPDATE

The syntax of the SQL UPDATE command is as follows:

```
UPDATE  table
SET     field = scalar-expression
 [, field = scalar-expression ] ...
 [ WHERE  condition ]  ;
```

This command updates records in the specified table setting each field to its new specified value. All records in the table that satisfy the condition in the WHERE clause are modified.

Here is an example that updates records in the TPRODUCTS table and sets the price of all free products to $1.00:

```
UPDATE TProducts SET Price = 1.00 WHERE Price = 0.00
```

DELETE

The syntax of the SQL DELETE command is as follows:

```
DELETE
FROM     table
 [ WHERE    condition ]   ;
```

This command deletes all records in a table that satisfy the condition in the WHERE clause.

Here is an example that deletes all free products from the TProducts table. All records that have a price of $0.00 are deleted.

```
DELETE FROM TProducts WHERE Price = 0.00
```

15

SELECT

The syntax of the SQL SELECT command is as follows:

```
SELECT      [DISTINCT] item(s)
FROM        table(s)
[ WHERE       condition ]
[ GROUP BY fields ]
[ HAVING    condition ]
[ ORDER BY fields]
[ UNION SQL_SELECT]
```

This command selects records from one or more tables. You must specify a list of fields to return or use the * character to signify the retrieval of all fields in the specified tables.

Using the DISTINCT keyword removes any duplicate rows from the list of returned records.

The FROM keyword is used to specify from which tables records are to be retrieved.

The WHERE keyword is optional and is used to specify a condition. Only records that satisfy the condition are retrieved.

The GROUP BY keywords are optional and are used to group rows together that contain the same value for the specified fields.

The HAVING keyword is optional and is used in conjunction with the GROUP BY clause. The condition in the HAVING clause is used to place a condition on each group as specified by the GROUP BY clause. For example, specifying COUNT(*) > 4 as the condition in the HAVING clause means that only groups that contain more than four records are retrieved. You cannot use the HAVING clause without the GROUP BY clause.

The ORDER BY keywords are optional and are used to order resulting rows on the specified field values.

The UNION keyword is used to return records that are in both the results of the main query and in the results of the subquery (SELECT statement).

The statement that follows selects all products that are not free from the TProducts table:

```
SELECT * FROM TProducts WHERE Price > 0.00
```

This example selects the product names that are part of any customer order:

```
SELECT TProducts.Name
FROM TProducts, TOrderItems
WHERE TProducts.id = TOrderItems.productId
```

Setting Up a Data Source Name (DSN)

ODBC stands for Open Database Connectivity. Microsoft first introduced ODBC several years ago to support developers in using a common database API when writing applications. When using ODBC, you open a connection to a database by specifying a data source name (DSN). A DSN is used to assign a logical name for your database. After a DSN is created, any application can use the database by referring to the DSN without knowing the specifics of where and what type of database it is. You must create a DSN on your computer in support of the application you are writing. Don't worry, the process of creating a DSN is presented here.

The database used for this application can be found in the Data folder of the main VBFS folder on the CD that came with this book. You can use this database rather than create a new database from scratch. Copy the file VBFS.MDB from this folder to any folder on your hard disk. After the database is copied to a hard disk on your computer, you need to set up a data source name (DSN) for it.

Let's set up a data source name for your database. Open the Control Panel on your computer by clicking the Start, Settings, Control Panel menu item as shown in Figure 15.6.

Figure 15.6

Opening the Control Panel.

In the Control Panel window, there are many icons for different purposes. The list of icons in the Control Panel varies based on what is installed on each computer. Figure 15.7 shows a sample Control Panel.

Figure 15.7

A sample Control Panel.

Find the icon labeled ODBC in your Control Panel and click on it. This opens the ODBC Data Source Administrator, which enables you to create new DSNs and modify existing ones. In the ODBC Data Source Administrator, click on the Add button to create a new DSN as shown in Figure 15.8.

Figure 15.8

The ODBC Data Source Administrator.

After you click the Add button, you are presented with a list of database drivers. Choose the database driver that is used to communicate with the database. Because you created a Microsoft Access database, select the Microsoft Access Driver option by clicking it, and then click the Finish button as shown in Figure 15.9.

Figure 15.9

The Create New Data Source window.

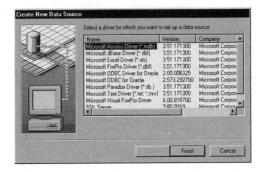

At this point, you are presented with a window specific to the database driver you selected in the previous window. Because you chose Microsoft Access, you now have a Microsoft Access Setup window for completing the process of creating a DSN for a Microsoft Access database (see Figure 15.10).

Figure 15.10

The ODBC Microsoft Access 97 Setup dialog box.

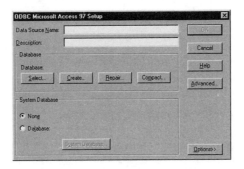

In the Data Source Name field, enter VBFS because this is the DSN your application will use. Then click Select to locate the VBFS.MDB file you copied to your hard disk. After you have located the file and clicked OK, you should now be back at the window shown in Figure 15.10. Now click OK to finish creating a DSN named VBFS. The window shown in Figure 15.8 should again be visible on the screen. Click OK on this window to end the task of creating your DSN (you also can close the Control Panel because you will not need it anymore).

Okay, that's it. You just created a DSN for your application that refers to a Microsoft Access database. So, what's in the database? As we mentioned before, we do not want to go through the process of designing and building a database as part of this book. Instead, we have provided you a database already built for your application. Let's take some time in the next section to review that database.

Defining the Project Schema

The database provided on the CD contains five tables. They are listed in Table 15.2.

Table 15.2   Tables Provided in VBFS.MDB

Table	Description
TCustomers	Table containing customers
TProducts	Table containing products for sale
TUsers	Table containing users of your application
TOrders	Table containing orders created by your application
TOrderItems	Table containing order items for each order

Each of these tables has columns and primary keys defined. Some have foreign keys and indexes defined. The following sections in this chapter discuss the columns in the tables as well as the interesting aspects of each table.

TCustomers

The TCustomers table (see Table 15.3) stores information about your customers.

Table 15.3   Columns in TCustomers

Column	Datatype	Size
id	Number (Long)	4
lastName	Text	32
firstName	Text	32
middleInitial	Text	6
streetAddress	Text	64
city	Text	32
state	Text	2
zip	Text	16
telephone	Text	24
email	Text	64

The id column is the primary key of the table. The values in the id column uniquely identify customer records in this table. The values are also used in other tables to relate records to customer records in this table. Specifically, the column customerId in the TOrders table is a foreign key to the id column in the TCustomers table. This supports relating a customer to an order.

TProducts

The TProducts table (see Table 15.4) stores product information concerning the products for sale through our application.

Table 15.4   Columns in TProducts

Column	Datatype	Size
id	Number (Long)	4
name	Text	32
author	Text	32
description	Text	128
productType	Text	32
imgFile	Text	128
docFile	Text	128
supplier	Text	64
price	Currency	8

The id column in the TProducts is the primary key of the table and uniquely identifies product records within this table.

The values in the id column are used to relate records in other tables to records in the TProduct table. Specifically, the productId column in the TOrderItems table is a foreign key to the id column in the TProducts table. This supports relating products to order items.

Also, an index is created on the name column in the TProducts table. This supports faster searching on products using a product name as the search criteria. Without the index, a search on TProducts using the product name would work, but it would be slower to return a result.

TUsers

The TUsers table (see Table 15.5) stores user information for the purpose of checking the users' access rights during login.

Table 15.5   Columns in TUsers

Column	Datatype	Size
userId	Text	32
password	Text	32
isStaff	Yes/No	1
customerId	Number (Long)	4

The userId column in the TUsers table is the primary key of the table and uniquely identifies user records within this table.

TOrders

The TOrders table (see Table 15.6) stores order information relating to a purchase of one or many products.

Table 15.6   Columns in TOrders

Column	Datatype	Size
id	Number (Long)	4
customerId	Number (Long)	4
dateEntered	Date/Time	8
dateShipped	Date/Time	8
dateBilled	Date/Time	8
datePaid	Date/Time	8
prodStatus	Number (Byte)	1
billStatus	Number (Byte)	1
shippingType	Number (Byte)	1
subTotal	Currency	8
discount	Number (Single)	4
taxPercent	Number (Single)	4
shippingCharge	Currency	8
total	Currency	8
cancelled	Yes/No	1

The id column in the TOrders table is the primary key of the table and uniquely identifies order records within this table.

The customerId column in the TOrders table is a foreign key to the id column in the TCustomers table. This relates customers to orders.

The orderId column in the TOrderItems table is a foreign key to the id column in the TOrders table. This relates order items to orders.

TOrderItems

The TOrderItems table (see Table 15.7) stores order item information relating to an order.

Table 15.7 Columns in TOrderItems

Column	Datatype	Size
id	Number (Long)	4
orderId	Number (Long)	4
productId	Number (Long)	4
seqNo	Number (Integer)	2
price	Currency	8
discount	Number (Long)	4
qty	Number (Long)	4
total	Currency	8

The id column in the TOrderItems table is the primary key of the table and uniquely identifies order item records within this table.

The orderId column in the TOrderItems table is a foreign key to the id column in the TOrders table. This relates order items to orders.

The productId column in the TOrderItems table is a foreign key to the id column in the TProducts table. This relates products to order items.

The seqNo column is used to specify the exact sequence of the order items as displayed on an order.

Using ActiveX Data Objects (ADO) for Database Access

You have defined a database, the language used by a database (SQL), and set up a database for the application. So, how do you actually communicate with the database within your program? The answer lies within ActiveX Data Objects, or the objects more commonly referred to as ADO. ADO is provided by Microsoft for programmatically accessing a SQL database server using a simple programming model.

ADO stands for ActiveX Data Objects. It provides a simple programmatic interface for communicating with a database. Most Visual Basic programs use ADO because of its ease of use within the development of a VB application.

Table 15.8 lists the objects provided with ADO.

Table 15.8   ADO Objects

Object	Description
Connection	Used to specify a connection to a database
Command	Encapsulates a SQL command
Parameter	Encapsulates a parameter to a SQL command
Recordset	Encapsulates a structured set of data. Mostly commonly represents the results of a SQL SELECT command.
Field	Encapsulates a column in a Recordset object
Error	Encapsulates an error from ADO
Property	Encapsulates a property on an ADO object

Using these objects, you have the capability to interact with a database. Rather than going into depth on each of these objects (because ADO programming is not the topic of this book), let's describe how you would issue SQL statements to a database and get results back using ADO.

In order to use ADO (or any other set of components) in a Visual Basic project, you must include a reference to it using the References menu item on the Project menu. For this application, you will define the project references to include Microsoft ActiveX Data Objects Library 2.0 in the next chapter.

Opening a Database Connection

The first step in ADO programming is to obtain a connection to the database. The connection is needed for establishing an open communication channel for sending database commands and retrieving results. To create a database connection, you must create a Connection object and then invoke the Open method. The following code creates a new Connection object then opens a database connection using the DSN defined earlier in this chapter:

```
Dim c As New ADODB.Connection
c.Open "DSN=VBFS"
```

After you have established a connection to a database, you can execute SQL statements directly to the database by invoking the Execute method on the Connection object.

Inserting Records

After you have a valid open connection to a database, you can send SQL statements directly to the database. One approach is to send a SQL INSERT statement directly to the database. Here is example code that inserts a new customer into your database:

```
c.Open "DSN=VBFS"
c.Execute "INSERT INTO TCustomers (firstName, lastName) " & _
                     "VALUES ('Jesse', 'Horne')"
```

Updating Records

Using the Execute method, you can send SQL UPDATE statements to update records in the database. Here is an example that updates an existing customer in your database:

```
c.Open "DSN=VBFS"
c.Execute "UPDATE TCustomers SET city = 'Hudson' " & _
          "WHERE firstName = 'Jesse' and lastName = 'Horne'"
```

Deleting Records

Using the Execute method, you can send SQL DELETE statements to delete records from the database. Here is an example to delete an existing customer from your database:

```
c.Open "DSN=VBFS"
c.Execute "DELETE FROM TCustomers " & _
          "WHERE firstName = 'Jesse' and lastName = 'Horne'"
```

Selecting Records

Most applications require the capability to retrieve records from the database. This is accomplished in ADO using Recordset objects. Recordset objects encapsulate results that are returned from a database. Using a SQL SELECT statement, you can describe the records you want returned from the database. Here is an example to retrieve all the customer records in the database:

```
Dim c As New ADODB.Connection
Dim rs As ADODB.Recordset
c.Open "DSN=VBFS"
Set rs = c.Execute("SELECT * FROM TCUSTOMERS")
rs.MoveFirst
While Not rs.EOF
   Debug.Print rs!lastName
   rs.MoveNext
Wend
```

After the Execute method is invoked, the list of customers is represented by rows within the Recordset object. Calling MoveFirst on the recordset moves the position to the first row in the recordset. Next is a loop that continues until the end of the recordset is reached. Inside the loop, the customer's last name is printed to the debug window, and then the position is moved to the next position by calling the MoveNext method of the Recordset object.

As far as the properties and methods of each ADO object is concerned, this book covers the aspects of ADO used in your application. Because the use of ADO is limited to Connection objects and Recordset objects, a full excursion into ADO is not warranted (especially because the excursion could cover hundreds of pages). However, there are books available devoted to this topic if you are interested.

> **Note** Using an ADO Recordset object, you can insert, update, and delete records in a database. This approach is not presented here because it completely masks all the database interaction. By presenting an approach using the `Execute` method on the Connection object, you can get a better understanding of what the exact SQL statement is being sent to the database and therefore a clearer understanding of what tables and columns are being affected. As you become more familiar with ADO, you may choose to use this approach or use recordsets for database updating. The choice is yours.

15

ADO, OLE DB, ODBC—Help!

If you have been developing for the Microsoft Windows platforms at any time during the past several years, you most assuredly have dealt with or heard someone say ADO, OLE DB, or ODBC. If you have no prior knowledge of each of these it can become confusing very quickly when you are dealing with developing a database application.

OLE DB is Microsoft's strategic low-level interface to data. OLE DB is not directly callable from Visual Basic. Because ADO uses OLE DB, a Visual Basic application that uses ADO also indirectly uses OLE DB.

ODBC stands for Open Database Connectivity. ODBC was first developed and introduced by Microsoft Corporation for standardizing SQL database access into a common set of functions.

What do these acronyms mean and how are they related? ODBC was developed before OLE DB and ADO. It is a standard developed by Microsoft that is essentially a C programming API. The push behind creating this standard was the increasing development of client/server applications where an application would run on one computer and a database server would run on another computer. The database server was available for use by potentially many client applications. Prior to the availability of ODBC, a developer was required to use an API provided by a database vendor to communicate with the vendor's database. As such, each vendor's API was different. Therefore, if you wanted to support more than one database with the same application you had to write database access routines for each database. This was and is very cost-prohibitive. Using ODBC, a developer is now able to write to one common API and support databases from different vendors.

API stands for Application Program Interface. It generally consists of a set of function calls that provide lower-level services to an application.

Next came OLE DB. OLE DB is Microsoft's strategic internal data interface to data within a corporation. OLE DB communicates to ODBC and therefore supports existing ODBC data sources. Additionally, OLE DB (with the development of OLE DB providers) supports access directly to SQL databases (bypassing ODBC), access to non-SQL data sources such as mail, video, text, and directory services, and access to mainframe data.

Next came ADO. ADO was created to simplify access to data for Visual Basic and Internet applications. ADO communicates directly with OLE DB. However, it presents a much simpler interface to the programmer. ADO provides additional features such as disconnected recordsets, client-side recordsets, and hierarchical recordsets. We do not get into details about these types of ADO features in this book. The point is that ADO adds capabilities beyond OLE DB and is worth taking a look at for inclusion in the development of database applications.

Figure 15.11 shows how ADO, OLE DB, and ODBC relate to one another. As you can see, Visual Basic uses ADO. ADO uses OLE DB for data services. OLE DB has the option of using ODBC for communication to SQL databases, communicating directly to a SQL or non-SQL data stores, and communicating with a mainframe to access legacy data. So how does OLE DB decide which method of data access to use? The answer is in the specification of the connection string used in the Open method of the ADO Connection object.

Figure 15.11

Microsoft data access architecture.

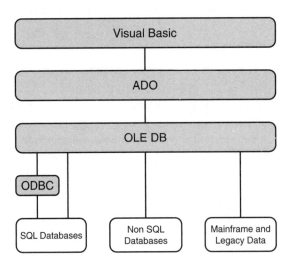

Two formats are used to define a connection string: one that uses a DSN (or File DSN) and one that does not use a DSN.

Syntax with a DSN or FileDSN:

```
"[Provider=MSDASQL;] { DSN=name ¦ FileDSN=filename } ;
 DATABASE=database;] ID=user; PWD=password"
```

Syntax without a DSN:

```
"[Provider=MSDASQL;] DRIVER=driver; SERVER=server;
 DATABASE=database; UID=user; PWD=password"
```

When specifying a connection string in ADO, ADO passes the connection string to OLE DB. If the Provider property of the connection string is specified, OLE DB attempts to use it. Omitting the Provider property tells OLE DB to use the default OLE DB provider, which is MSDASQL. This OLE DB provider automatically wraps any ODBC data source and allows access to it through OLE DB. Therefore, if you do not specify the Provider property, it is assumed OLE DB uses ODBC to connect and communicate with the database. If you do specify the OLE DB provider, OLE DB then attempts to use it and the method of communication is left to the actual implementation of the OLE DB provider. It could use ODBC, a native database API, go directly to a mainframe, or any other route so long as it implements the appropriate behavior of an OLE DB provider as defined by the standard.

If you specify the DSN property it must be defined in the ODBC Data Source Administrator in order for it to be used. You can also override the Database, User, and Password properties defined for the DSN in the ODBC Data Source Administrator by specifying them in the connection string.

If you choose not to specify the DSN property, you are required to specify the Driver, Server, Database, User, and Password properties in the connection string.

Next Steps

In this chapter, we defined database. In doing so, we discussed basic database concepts including tables, columns, rows, primary keys, foreign keys, and indexes.

Next, we covered the following SQL commands: INSERT, UPDATE, DELETE, and SELECT. These commands are the foundation of SQL database programming. These SQL commands enable you to modify records in the database and to retrieve groups of records from the database.

You then set up a data source name for the database used by your application. The database is provided on the CD and is ready to use after the DSN is created.

The database schema for the application was then presented. This included listing the five tables and their structures. Here you can see the tables and their definitions that will become important when you start adding code to your classes for data persistence.

Finally, you learned how to communicate with a database. This involves using ADO within Visual Basic. To get a better understanding of the underlying database communication, we briefly discussed OLE DB and ODBC.

With this set of knowledge, we are ready to complete our persistent classes in the next chapter by adding database logic for saving data to the database and loading data from the database.

In this chapter

- *Encapsulating the Database*
- *Adding Persistence to the* Customer *Class*
- *Adding Persistence to the* Product *Class*
- *Adding Persistence to the* Order,
  OrderItemColl, *and* OrderItem *Classes*

Chapter 16

Adding Class Persistence

In the past few chapters we created classes in Visual Basic and presented a number of database concepts. It is now time to add database persistence to these classes. This will enable you to save the data within the objects to a database and later retrieve objects from the database based on the saved data. This way, your application can use objects instead of directly communicating with the database through a database-centric API. When building an application it is more natural and easier to think in terms of objects that represent real-world entities. By adding database persistence to your Customer class, for example, you will have the capability to create Customer objects, save Customer objects, find Customer objects, and delete Customer objects. As you can probably surmise, the application is written in terms of Customer objects and not SQL statements.

Persistence is a term used to describe the saving of an object and the rematerializing of that object at a later time. After the object's data is saved, the object can be released from memory and re-created at a later point from the saved data.

The complete code for this chapter can be found in the Chapter16 folder of the main VBFS folder on the CD that accompanies this book.

Encapsulating the Database

Before you start adding database code to your application, you must add a project reference to ActiveX Data Objects 2.0. To do this, select the Project, References menu item as shown in Figure 16.1.

Figure 16.1

The Project References menu item.

This brings up the Project References dialog box where you can include different components for use within a VB application. Scroll down and click Microsoft ActiveX Data Objects 2.0 Library as shown in Figure 16.2. Then click OK.

Figure 16.2

The Add Project Reference for Microsoft ActiveX Data Objects 2.0 Library.

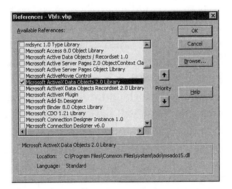

Now you have a project reference for ADO and can start programming using it. If for some reason you do not have Microsoft ActiveX Data Objects 2.0 Library in the list in the dialog box, you can try to download it from Microsoft's Web site (www.microsoft.com). Most likely it is already installed or you can download it. However, if you do not have it installed, you cannot run the final application. In that case, just follow along in the book.

Creating the DbSession Class

Now, let's start adding database code by encapsulating the database. Create a new class in the project and name it DbSession. Enter the following code, and then save the class as DbSession.cls:

DbSession(DbSession.cls)

```
Private Const csDsnName = "DSN=Vbfs"

Public Function GetConn() As ADODB.Connection
  Dim conn As New ADODB.Connection

  On Error GoTo GetConn_Fail
  conn.Open csDsnName
  Set GetConn = conn
  Exit Function

GetConn_Fail:
  MsgBox Err.description, vbCritical, Err.Source
End Function
```

16

In the first line, you create a private constant variable to hold a string that represents the connection string for connecting to the database. By declaring the connection string in the code, the application always uses the database as defined by the DSN named VBFS (defined using the ODBC Data Source Administrator).

EXCURSION

Open Database Connectivity

Open Database Connectivity (ODBC) was introduced by Microsoft several years ago to facilitate the development of applications that use a common set of functions (API) for database access. Prior to the introduction of ODBC, each database vendor supplied its own software development kit (SDK), which provided an API for writing code that communicated with the vendor's particular database. Each database vendor differentiated itself through the capabilities exposed by its proprietary API.

With the introduction of ODBC, a developer can now write an application using the API defined by ODBC to communicate with a database in a common way. The application can then communicate with a variety of databases as long as the developer uses ANSI SQL. Some databases have extensions to the SQL language. If you develop an application that uses some of these extensions, you are restricting the use of your application to that particular database. Use of the extensions might be necessary at times and is up to you. When using ODBC, you should adhere to ANSI SQL and use extensions only when absolutely necessary.

However, you probably would not use ODBC within your Visual Basic program; you would most likely use ADO. It is important to mention ODBC, however, because ADO uses OLE DB, which in turn is capable of using ODBC. You open a database connection in ADO using a data source name (DSN). A DSN must be defined on the computer before it can be used by an application. Defining a DSN internally involves specifying an ODBC driver, which is used to perform all the underlying database-specific routines. Typically, you would have an ODBC driver installed on your computer for the databases you want to communicate with. For each ODBC driver, you can create any number of DSNs that use that ODBC driver.

To set up a DSN, use the Start, Settings, Control Panel menu item. This brings up the Control Panel, which contains an icon with an associated name ODBC. This is the ODBC Administrator. You can use the ODBC Administrator to manage the DSNs defined on your computer.

Next, you created one method as part of the DbSession class. The method is used to get the database connection from a DbSession object. The first line of the method creates a new ADO connection. The next line uses the VB On Error statement. At the end of the On Error GoTo statement, you can see what is called a *label*. In this case, the label is named GetConn_Fail. Also notice the line near the end of the method that contains GetConn_Fail:. The On Error statement sets up the error handling and, in this case, tells Visual Basic that if there is an error to resume execution of the program starting at the line after the label GetConn_Fail. Using error handling in Visual Basic, you can trap errors, perform any cleanup if necessary, and notify the user of the error if you choose to. This code notifies the user using the MsgBox function. Also, notice the object variable Err. This variable is defined by Visual Basic and is a well-known object. Whenever an error is trapped by Visual Basic, you have access to the error information using the Err object. The Err object has different properties on it for retrieving error information. Here you get the description and the name of the source of the error by using the description and Source properties.

The line after the On Error statement calls the Open method of the Connection object. This attempts to open a database connection to the database as specified by the connection string (in this case "DSN=VBFS"). If the connection succeeds, program control proceeds to the next line, which sets the return value of the method to the Connection object. If the connection fails (for whatever reason), program control proceeds to the line after the GetConn_Fail label. Notice the Exit Function line. This line is necessary because, without it, program control would enter the GetConn_Fail label. The result would be a message displayed whether or not an error occurred. The Exit Function line causes the method to exit at that point, eliminating this problem. This line exits the method at this point and does not continue to call the MsgBox function.

Another interesting point about this method is that a new Connection object is created each time this method is called. When the local variable conn goes out of scope (upon exiting the method), the Connection object is released. However, the method passes back a reference to the object, and the code that receives the connection object maintains a reference to the connection object. This forces the object to be kept in memory. As long as the code maintains a reference to the object, it will not be destroyed from memory. So, this method essentially creates and passes back a new connection object while encapsulating the connection string within the DbSession object. Also, the user is notified whenever an error occurs.

Connection.Open in More Detail

The Open method of the Connection class opens a connection to a database. The method looks like this:

```
connection.Open ConnectionStr, UserId, Password, Options
```

All the parameters are optional and therefore do not need to be specified. The ConnectionStr parameter defines the connection string to the database using the format discussed in Chapter 15. If this parameter is not specified, the ConnectionString property of the Connection object is used. Either the ConnectionString property or this parameter must be specified. The UserId parameter contains the database user name used when logging in to the database. The Password parameter is used in conjunction with the UserId and represents the user's database password. The last parameter is the options used during the opening the connection. You can set this parameter to the enumerated value adAsyncConnect. This causes the connection to be performed asynchronously. This allows a database connection attempt to be started, and control moves to the next line of code before the connection is complete. After the connection is complete, a ConnectionComplete event is generated. We will cover events in Chapter 17, "Finalizing the Classes in the Project." However, this essentially means you write code that starts a database connection, and program execution continues without waiting for the connection to be complete. You can then write code that executes when the connection completion event is raised. In this application, this complexity is not necessary so we ignored the user ID, password, and asynchronous options.

Creating a Global DbSession Object

In the modMain module, enter the following code:

modMain(modMain.cls)

```
Public gSession As New DbSession
```

This declares a global variable to hold a reference to a new DbSession object. Because this is global, this DbSession object can be used throughout the entire application. This is useful for supporting a database connection. At any point in the application, a call to gSession.GetConn can be made to get a database connection.

Adding Persistence to the Customer Class

Now that you have a DbSession class to encapsulate a database and get a database connection from it, let's add persistence code to the Customer class. The goal here is to add methods for saving, finding, and deleting customers.

Saving a Customer

To save a Customer object, you are going to create a Save method within the Customer class. The Save method is responsible for saving the state of the Customer object to the database. Enter the following code in the Customer class:

Customer(Customer.cls)

```
Public Function Save() As Boolean
  If Not IsValid() Then Exit Function

  Dim sSQL As String
  If m_id <= 0 Then
    sSQL = "SELECT * FROM TCustomers"
  Else
    sSQL = "SELECT * FROM TCustomers WHERE TCustomers.id =" & Str(m_id)
  End If

  Dim conn As ADODB.Connection
  Set conn = gSession.GetConn

  Dim rs As New ADODB.Recordset
  rs.Open sSQL, conn, adOpenKeyset, adLockOptimistic
  If m_id <= 0 Then
    rs.AddNew
  End If
  ToRs rs
  rs.Update
  If m_id <= 0 Then m_id = rs!id
  Save = True
End Function

Public Sub ToRs(rs As ADODB.Recordset)
 rs!lastName = m_lastName
 rs!firstName = m_firstName
 rs!middleInitial = m_middleInitial
 rs!streetAddress = m_streetAddress
 rs!city = m_city
 rs!state = m_state
 rs!zip = m_zip
 rs!telephone = m_telephone
 rs!email = m_email
End Sub
```

Again, the Save method is responsible for saving the customer information. The first line in the method makes a call to the IsValid method to verify whether the customer information is complete before saving the data. If it is not valid, the method is exited at this point and nothing is saved.

In the next few lines of code, construct a SQL statement for use by a Recordset object later in the method. If the value in the m_id private data member is 0, this means the customer is new and has not been saved to the database yet. The value in the m_id data member is generated by the database and can have a value only if the Customer object has been previously saved. If m_id contains a value of 0, a SQL SELECT statement that selects all customer records is constructed. Otherwise, a SQL SELECT statement that selects the specific customer record is constructed.

After constructing the SQL SELECT statement, a local variable is declared to hold the Connection object that represents a connection to the database. A Connection object is retrieved by calling the GetConn method on the global DbSession variable named gSession, which you created earlier in the chapter.

After the connection object is retrieved from the global DbSession object, another local variable is declared to contain a new Recordset object. Following this, the Open method of the Recordset object is called. The Open method takes as parameters the SQL statement you constructed, the database connection, the Recordset property type, and the locking type. Notice the * character in the SELECT statement. This causes the SELECT statement to return all the columns in the TCustomers table. After the recordset is successfully opened, the resulting recordset will contain columns corresponding to each column returned from the SELECT. In this case, it is all the columns of the TCustomers table.

The Open method of the Connection class opens a connection to a database. The method looks like this:

```
rs.Open Source, ActiveConnection, CursorType, LockType, Options
```

Each parameter is optional. If you do not pass a value to a parameter, you must set the corresponding property of the Recordset object. For example, if you do not pass a value to the Source parameter, you must set the Source property on the recordset before calling the Open method.

The Source parameter accepts a valid ADO Command object, a SQL statement, a table name, a stored procedure call, or the filename of a persisted recordset. Within the application, ADO Recordset objects are limited to using SQL SELECT statements. Therefore, examples of the other types of valid values for this parameter are not covered.

The ActiveConnection parameter accepts a valid Connection object or a connection string. This application uses the Connection object retrieved from the DbSession object.

The CursorType parameter can contain values listed in Table 16.1. This application uses adOpenKeyset cursor types.

Table 16.1   Cursor Type Enumerated Values

Cursor Type	Description
adOpenForwardOnly	Performs like a static recordset except you can only move forward in the recordset.
adOpenKeyset	Performs like a dynamic recordset except you cannot see additions.
adOpenDynamic	Allows you to see additions, changes, and deletions made by other users as you scroll through the list.
adOpenStatic	Makes a static copy of the records and supports movement through the list. Additions, changes, and deletions by other users are not visible.

The LockType parameter can contain the values listed in Table 16.2. This application uses adLockOptimistic for optimal performance.

Table 16.2   LockType Enumerated Values

LockType	Description
adLockReadOnly	Specifies the records will not be changed and will only be used for read-only purposes.
adLockPessimistic	This specifies that the database provider must do whatever is necessary to lock the records for potential editing.
adLockOptimistic	This locks only the modified record when the update of the Recordset object is called.
adLockBatchOptimistic	Performs like adLockOptimistic except you can modify many records in a recordset. When you call the UpdateBatch method, all the modified records can be applied to the database as a whole.

After the recordset is opened, the m_id value is checked again. If the value is 0, you need to add a row to the recordset using the AddNew method. This adds a new row and positions the recordset to the newly added row. If the m_id variable contains a nonzero value, it is assumed you have a recordset with one row representing the customer whose ID matches the value in m_id. You can assume this for two reasons: First, the m_id cannot have a nonzero value unless the customer record was retrieved from the database. Second, the SQL SELECT statement was constructed to search for the customer record where the ID matches m_id.

Next, a call is made to the ToRs method of the Customer object. The recordset is passed to the ToRs as a parameter and used by the method for saving the Customer objects values to the recordset. Each column in the recordset can be accessed using the notation:

```
Recordset!columnName
```

Notice that in the ToRs method, each column in the recordset is assigned a value from the member data of the Customer object.

Control returns to the Save method. Here the Update method on the recordset is called. This saves the current recordset row changes to the database.

If the value of m_id is zero, you must retrieve the value from the id column in the recordset. This is because the value for the id column is automatically generated by the database. You want to retrieve this value so that the Customer object can continue to be used and any further updates would force an UPDATE of a Customer record and not an ADD. The return value of the function is set to True and the method exits.

Finding a Customer

To find a specific Customer object in the database, you are going to create a Find method on the Customer class. The idea is that you create a new Customer object then call the Find method, which searches the database for a specific customer. The Find method is responsible for all the logic in finding the customer data. If the customer record is found, the data is retrieved and the Find method returns True. If the customer record is not found, the Find method returns False. The Save method is responsible for saving the state of the Customer object to the database. Enter the following code in the Customer class:

Customer(Customer.cls)

```
Public Function Find(ByVal customerId As Long) As Boolean
  ClearState
  Dim sSQL As String
  sSQL = "SELECT * FROM TCustomers WHERE TCustomers.id =" & Str(customerId)

  Dim rs As New ADODB.Recordset
  rs.Open sSQL, gSession.GetConn(), adOpenStatic, adLockReadOnly

  If rs.RecordCount <= 0 Then Exit Function

  FromRs rs
  Find = True
End Function

Public Sub ClearState()
  m_id = 0
```

continues

Customer(Customer.cls)—Continued

```
    m_lastName = ""
    m_firstName = ""
    m_middleInitial = ""
    m_streetAddress = ""
    m_city = ""
    m_state = ""
    m_zip = ""
    m_telephone = ""
    m_email = ""
End Sub

Public Sub FromRs(rs As ADODB.Recordset)
    m_id = rs!id
    m_lastName = rs!lastName
    m_firstName = rs!firstName
    m_middleInitial = rs!middleInitial
    m_streetAddress = rs!streetAddress
    m_city = rs!city
    m_state = rs!state
    m_zip = rs!zip
    m_telephone = rs!telephone
    m_email = nns(rs!email)
End Sub
```

Also add the following code to the modMain module:

modMain(modMain.cls)

```
Public Function nns(v As Variant) As String
    If IsNull(v) Then nns = "" Else nns = v
End Function
```

The first line in the Find method calls the ClearState method. The ClearState method clears out all the private member variable values. This method is important so that partial values from one customer are not merged with partial values from another customer.

Next, a SQL SELECT statement is constructed to find the customer record where the ID value matches the value of the customerId parameter passed to the Find method. This SQL SELECT statement is then passed to the Recordset Open method along with a Connection object retrieved from the global DbSession object, the cursor type, and the lock type. In this case, use adOpenStatic and adLockReadOnly because you will not be editing any records in the database. Read-only access is sufficient.

After the recordset is open, a check of the RecordCount property tells you if no records were found. If no records were found, the method exits and the return value defaults to False. Otherwise, a call is made to the FromRs method of the Customer object. This method contains the reverse behavior of the ToRs method. The FromRs method retrieves the columns' values of the current row in the recordset and places the values into the private member variables of the Customer object.

Notice the call to the nns function in the FromRs method. This utility function is provided to check for a Null value of a column in a recordset. If the column is Null, a blank string is returned by the function. Otherwise it returns the column value as is.

Finally, the return value of the Find method is set to True, signifying the customer record was found and the values were retrieved into the Customer object.

Deleting a Customer

To delete a specific Customer object from the database, you are going to create a Delete method on the Customer class. After you have a valid customer object that was retrieved from the database, you can call the Delete method, which deletes the customer record. The Delete method is responsible for all the logic required to delete the Customer data.

Enter the following code in the Customer class:

Customer(Customer.cls)

```
Public Function Delete() As Boolean
  If m_id <= 0 Then Exit Function

  Dim sSQL As String
  sSQL = "DELETE FROM TCustomer WHERE TCustomers.id =" & Str(m_id)

  Dim conn As ADODB.Connection
  Set conn = gSession.GetConn
  conn.Execute sSQL
  ClearState
  Delete = True
End Function
```

The first line of this method checks to see if the Customer object has a valid value in m_id. If the value is less than zero, this signifies the object values were never retrieved from the database and the method exits. Only objects that were retrieved from the database can be deleted.

Next, a SQL DELETE statement is constructed to delete the customer record identified by matching the customer ID in the database to the value of the m_id data member. A connection object is retrieved from DbSession, and then you execute the SQL directly to the database using the Execute method on the Connection object. The state of the object is cleared and the method sets the return value to True.

16

Adding Persistence to the `Product` Class

You just added `Save`, `Find`, and `Delete` methods to the `Customer` class as well as other supporting methods. You need to add identical behavior to your `Product` class. Because the behavior is identical to the `Customer` class, you are going to list the code for the `Product` class that you need to enter. However, there is no need to redundantly describe the code here. You might want to read through the code to familiarize yourself with the additions to the `Product` class.

Saving a Product

Enter the following code to support saving a Product object:

Product(Product.cls)

```
Public Function Save() As Boolean
  If Not IsValid() Then Exit Function

  Dim sSQL As String
  If m_id <= 0 Then
    sSQL = "SELECT * FROM TProducts"
  Else
    sSQL = "SELECT * FROM TProducts WHERE TProducts.id =" & Str(m_id)
  End If

  Dim conn As ADODB.Connection
  Set conn = gSession.GetConn

  Dim rs As New ADODB.Recordset
  rs.Open sSQL, conn, adOpenKeyset, adLockOptimistic
  If m_id <= 0 Then
    rs.AddNew
  End If
  ToRs rs
  rs.Update
  If m_id <= 0 Then m_id = rs!id
  Save = True
End Function

Public Sub ToRs(rs As ADODB.Recordset)
  rs!name = m_name
  rs!author = m_author
  rs!description = m_description
  rs!productType = m_prodType
  rs!imgFile = m_imgFile
  rs!docFile = m_docFile
  rs!supplier = m_supplier
  rs!price = m_price
End Sub
```

Finding a Product

Enter the following code to support finding a Product object:

Product(Product.cls)

```
Public Function Find(ByVal productId As Long) As Boolean
  ClearState
  Dim sSQL As String
  sSQL = "SELECT * FROM TProducts WHERE TProducts.id =" & Str(productId)

  Dim rs As New ADODB.Recordset
  rs.Open sSQL, gSession.GetConn(), adOpenStatic, adLockReadOnly

  If rs.RecordCount <= 0 Then Exit Function

  FromRs rs
  Find = True
End Function

Public Sub ClearState()
  m_id = 0
  m_name = ""
  m_author = ""
  m_description = ""
  m_prodType = ""
  m_imgFile = ""
  m_docFile = ""
  m_supplier = ""
  m_price = 0
End Sub

Public Sub FromRs(rs As ADODB.Recordset)
  m_id = rs!id
  m_name = rs!name
  m_author = nns(rs!author)
  m_description = nns(rs!description)
  m_prodType = nns(rs!productType)
  m_imgFile = nns(rs!imgFile)
  m_docFile = nns(rs!docFile)
  m_supplier = nns(rs!supplier)
  m_price = rs!price
End Sub
```

Deleting a Product

Enter the following code to support deleting a Product object:

Product(Product.cls)

```
Public Function Delete() As Boolean
If m_id <= 0 Then Exit Function

  Dim sSQL As String
  sSQL = "DELETE FROM TProducts WHERE TProducts.id =" & Str(m_id)

  Dim conn As ADODB.Connection
  Set conn = gSession.GetConn
  conn.Execute sSQL
  ClearState
  Delete = True
End Function
```

Adding Persistence to the `Order`, `OrderItemColl`, and `OrderItem` Classes

The `Customer` class and `Product` class dealt with single-object persistence. The `Order` class must deal with itself and persistence for multiple aggregated objects (`OrderItem` objects). When saving and deleting orders, these objects and their relationships must be maintained in the database. It does not make sense to save and retrieve an individual OrderItem object all by itself. An OrderItem object should not exist unless it is within the context of an order. Because `OrderItems` cannot exist by themselves, you are not going to add the methods `Save`, `Find`, and `Delete` the way you did with the `Customer` and `Product` classes. In this object model, `OrderItem` objects are managed by the `OrderItemColl` objects; therefore, you are going to add methods to the `OrderItemColl` class for saving, retrieving, and deleting the `OrderItem` objects in the collection as a whole. This simplifies the management of the list of order items.

Helper Methods in the `OrderItem` Class

Let's start with the `OrderItem` class. Because you are not going to add the methods `Save`, `Find`, or `Delete` to the `OrderItem` class, this simplifies your work. You do need to add a couple methods to help in the process of saving the `OrderItem` member data, however. In the declarations section of the `OrderItem` class, enter the following code:

OrderItem(OrderItem.cls)

```
Private Const ceParentNotSet = vbObjectError + 32767
```

Enter the following code to the `OrderItem` class:

OrderItem(OrderItem.cls)

```
Public Sub FromRs(rs As ADODB.Recordset)
  ClearState
  m_id = rs!id
  m_productId = rs!productId
  m_seqNo = rs!seqNo
  m_price = rs!price
  m_discount = rs!discount
  m_qty = rs!qty
  m_total = rs!total
End Sub

Public Sub InsertInRs(orderId As Long, rs As ADODB.Recordset)
  If orderId = 0 Then
    Err.Raise ceParentNotSet, "Vbfs.OrderItem", "The parent order is not set!"
  End If

  rs.AddNew
  rs!orderId = orderId
  rs!productId = m_productId
  rs!seqNo = m_seqNo
  rs!price = m_price
  rs!discount = m_discount
  rs!qty = m_qty
  rs!total = m_total
  rs.Update
  m_id = rs!id
End Sub

Public Sub ClearState()
  m_id = 0
  m_productId = 0
  m_seqNo = 0
  m_price = 0
  m_discount = 0
  m_qty = 0
  m_total = 0
End Sub
```

The FromRs method and the InsertInRs method are provided for retrieving an OrderItem object's data from a recordset and saving an OrderItem object's data to a recordset, respectively. The purpose of these two methods are identical to the ones you created as part of the Customer and Product classes. Rather than retrieving the OrderItem properties and persisting the values into a recordset outside the OrderItem class code, these methods encapsulate the OrderItem behavior of persisting data to a recordset and retrieving data from a recordset.

16

In the `FromRs` method, a call to `ClearState` is made to clear the data member values before reading the values from the recordset. Again, this is necessary to avoid partial overwriting of member data.

The `InsertInRs` method checks the `orderid` passed to the method. If the `orderid` value is zero, this means an invalid order and the OrderItems should not be saved. In this case, an error is raised that immediately exits the method. If the `orderid` has a valid value, a new row is added to the recordset and the `OrderItem` values are put into the row. The variable named `ceParentNotSet` is defined in the declarations section of the class module. This variable is used to define an error code that can be raised.

The `ClearState` method clears the state of the `OrderItem` object on which the method is called. This method is used whenever the internal data of an `OrderItem` object needs to be cleared.

That is all the persistence code necessary for an `OrderItem` class. As you can see, the `OrderItem` does not save directly to the database but it does encapsulate saving its data to a recordset. The same goes for retrieving its values. Now let's move on to the `OrderItemColl` class.

Saving and Deleting the Collection of `OrderItem` Objects

As part of the `OrderItemColl` class you are going to add methods for saving, loading, and deleting the list of `OrderItem` objects that are related to an order. This way, the `OrderItemColl` class manages the memory management of the `OrderItem` collection as well as the database management of the collection of `OrderItem` objects. Enter the following code to the `OrderItemColl` class to save and delete a collection of `OrderItem` objects:

OrderItemColl(OrderItemColl.cls)

```
Public Sub SaveAll(ord As Order, conn As ADODB.Connection)

    DeleteAll ord, conn
    ReSequence

    Dim sSQL As String
    sSQL = "SELECT * FROM TOrderItems " & _
           "WHERE TOrderItems.orderId = " & Str(ord.id)

    Dim rs As New ADODB.Recordset
    rs.Open sSQL, conn, adOpenKeyset, adLockOptimistic

    Dim i As Long, oi As OrderItem

    For i = 1 To m_coll.Count
      Set oi = m_coll.Item(i)
      oi.InsertInRs ord.id, rs
```

```
    Next i

End Sub

Public Sub DeleteAll(ord As Order, conn As ADODB.Connection)

    Dim sSQL As String
    sSQL = "DELETE FROM TOrderItems " & _
           "WHERE TOrderItems.orderId = " & Str(ord.id)

    conn.Execute sSQL

End Sub
```

The `SaveAll` method has two parameters: an order and a database connection. The first line in the method calls the `DeleteAll` method, passing the Order object and the Connection object. The `DeleteAll` method constructs a SQL `DELETE` statement to delete all the order item records that are related to the order record as specified by the id property on the Order object. The `Execute` method of the Connection object is called to directly execute the SQL `DELETE` statement. Then the `DeleteAll` method exits and returns to the `SaveAll` method. Next, the `Resequence` method is called to ensure the OrderItems contain the correct sequence values.

After the `Resequence` call, a SQL `SELECT` statement is constructed for the purposes of adding records to the database. The SQL `SELECT` string is passed to the `Open` method of a new recordset object. This opens the recordset, which should contain zero rows because you deleted all the order item records for the order in the previous lines of code.

After the recordset is opened, the code iterates through the collection of OrderItem objects in memory and calls the `InsertInRs` method on each of the objects. Each call to `InsertInRs` causes a new row to be created in the recordset and populates the row with values from the internal data of the `OrderItem` object.

Retrieving the Collection of `OrderItem` Objects

Enter the following code to the `OrderItemColl` class for retrieving the collection of `OrderItem` objects related to an order:

OrderItemColl(OrderItemColl.cls)

```
Public Sub RetrieveAll(ord As Order)
    ClearState

    Dim sSQL As String
    sSQL = "SELECT * FROM TOrderItems " & _
           "WHERE TOrderItems.orderId = " & Str(ord.id) & _
```

continues

OrderItemColl(OrderItemColl.cls)—Continued

```
            " ORDER BY TOrderItems.seqNo"

    Dim rs As New ADODB.Recordset
    rs.Open sSQL, gSession.GetConn(), adOpenForwardOnly, adLockReadOnly

    Dim oi As OrderItem
    Do While Not rs.EOF
      Set oi = New OrderItem
      oi.FromRs rs
      m_coll.Add oi
      rs.MoveNext
    Loop

End Sub

Public Sub ClearState()
  Set m_coll = New Collection
End Sub
```

The RetrieveAll method supports the retrieval of the collection of OrderItem objects from the database. This method has one parameter, an Order object, which is the order that the order items are related to.

The first line in the method makes a call to the ClearState method. This is necessary to clear out the current internal collection of OrderItem objects if there are any. The ClearState method creates a new Collection object. Setting m_coll to a new Collection object frees the previous Collection object, and therefore frees any OrderItem objects that might have been in the collection. The ClearState method then exits and returns to the RetrieveAll method.

Next, a SQL SELECT statement is constructed to select the order item records related to the order record. The order record is specified by the ID property on the Order object passed to the RetrieveAll method. Also, notice the order item records are ordered by sequence number as instructed by the SQL SELECT statement.

A new recordset object is created, and its Open method is called by passing the constructed SQL statement. This selects the order item records in the database.

The Do...While loop statement is used to iterate through the selected records. The Do...While loop continues looping while the specified condition is True. In this case, the condition Not rs.EOF means "while the recordset is not at the end of the list." In the loop, a new OrderItem object is created and its FromRs method is called. This populates the internal data of the newly created object from the recordset. The object is then added to the internal collection within the OrderItemColl object. The MoveNext method is called to advance the position in the recordset to the next record. If the position advances past the last record, the loop ends and the method exits.

Saving an Order

Now you are ready to write the code to save an order. When saving an order, you must make sure all the order items are also saved and in the same database transaction. You have not needed to worry about this so far because you have been saving single objects. Now that you are saving multiple objects that are related to each other, you must be clear of the transactional scope. For example, if you save the Order object and then get an error while saving one of the OrderItem objects, you want to undo changes to the database regarding the OrderItem objects and the Order object. You do not want a partially saved order—it is all or nothing. Enter the following code to the Order class for supporting the saving of an order and its order items:

Order(Order.cls)

```
Public Function SaveOrder()
  RecalculateTotal

  Dim sSQL As String
  If m_id <= 0 Then
    sSQL = "SELECT * FROM TOrders"
  Else
    sSQL = "SELECT * FROM TOrders WHERE TOrders.id =" & Str(m_id)
  End If

  Dim conn As ADODB.Connection
  Set conn = gSession.GetConn()
  If conn Is Nothing Then Exit Function
  conn.BeginTrans

  Dim rs As New ADODB.Recordset
  rs.Open sSQL, conn, adOpenKeyset, adLockOptimistic

  On Error GoTo SaveOrder_Fail
  If m_id <= 0 Then rs.AddNew

  rs!customerId = m_customerId
  rs!dateEntered = m_dateEntered
  rs!dateShipped = m_dateShipped
  rs!dateBilled = m_dateBilled
  rs!datePaid = m_datePaid
  rs!prodStatus = m_prodStatus
  rs!billStatus = m_billStatus
  rs!shippingType = m_shippingType
  rs!subTotal = m_subTotal
  rs!discount = m_discount
  rs!taxPercent = m_taxPercent
  rs!shippingCharge = m_shippingCharge
```

16

continues

Order(Order.cls)—Continued

```
    rs!total = m_total
    rs!cancelled = m_cancelled
    rs.Update
    If m_id <= 0 Then m_id = rs!id

    m_orderItems.SaveAll Me, conn
    conn.CommitTrans
    SaveOrder = True
    Exit Function

SaveOrder_Fail:
  MsgBox Err.description, vbCritical, Err.description
  conn.RollbackTrans
End Function
```

In the SaveOrder method, the first line calls the Recalculate method to ensure the order is updated with the correct calculated totals. Next, a SQL SELECT statement is constructed. If the value in the m_id private data member is less than or equal to zero, the order has not been saved previously. This implies the order must be added to the database. If the m_id contains a value greater than zero, it means the order has been previously saved and implies the order needs to be updated in the database.

A new Connection object is then retrieved from the global DbSession object. If the Connection object is not valid, the method exits. Otherwise, the BeginTrans method is called on the Connection object. This instructs the database to start a transaction. All work done from this point to the call to the CommitTrans method is considered to be one unit of work. The unit of work is saved to the database as a whole. If any errors are generated before the CommitTrans method is called, the transaction is rolled back.

A new Recordset object is created and the Open method is called by passing it the constructed SQL SELECT statement and the Connection object. The adOpenKeyset cursor type is used because you need to update the recordset and retrieve any auto-generated values back from the database. After the Open method call, the On Error statement is used to set the error handling. If any errors occur in the method after the On Error statement, program execution is set to the line after the SaveOrder_Fail label.

The value in the m_id data member is again checked. If the value is less than or equal to zero, this signifies a new order record should be created. In this case, the AddNew method is called on the Recordset object to create a new row. Then, all the values of data members are put into the recordset and the Update method is called. This causes the recordset to update the database with the changes to the current row in the recordset.

Next, the autogenerated ID value is retrieved from the recordset, if necessary. The `SaveAll` method is called on the internal OrderItemColl object as defined by `m_orderItems`. The first parameter value passed to the method is `Me`. `Me` always represents the current object and in this case represents the current Order object because you are in a method of an order. The second parameter is `conn`, which is the database connection object. The `SaveAll` method, once again, saves all the `OrderItem` objects related to this Order object.

The transaction is then committed using the `CommitTrans` method on the Connection object. The return value of the method is set to True and the method exits.

If for any reason an error is generated, the lines after the `SaveOrder_Fail` label display a message box to the user and the transaction is rolled back. This undoes the entire unit of work.

When you first created the `Order` class in Chapter 14, the following methods contained a commented line of code: `OrdCancel`, `OrdShip`, `OrdBill`, `OrdPaid`. These methods need to call the `SaveOrder` method after an order status is changed. At the time you created these methods, the `SaveOrder` method did not exist. Now that you have a `SaveOrder` method defined, update the methods by uncommenting the `SaveOrder` lines so that they look like the following:

Order(Order.cls)

```
Public Function OrdCancel()
  If m_prodStatus = psShipped Or _
     m_billStatus = bsBilled Or _
     m_billStatus = bsPaid Then
     Exit Function
  End If

  m_cancelled = True
  SaveOrder
  OrdCancel = True
End Function

Public Function OrdShip(ByVal dateShipped As Date)
  m_prodStatus = psShipped
  m_dateShipped = dateShipped
  SaveOrder
  OrdShip = True
End Function

Public Function OrdBill(ByVal dateBilled As Date)
  m_billStatus = bsBilled
  m_dateBilled = dateBilled
  SaveOrder
```

continues

16

Order(Order.cls)—Continued

```
    OrdBill = True
End Function

Public Function OrdPaid(ByVal datePaid As Date)
  m_billStatus = bsPaid
  m_datePaid = datePaid
  SaveOrder
  OrdPaid = True
End Function
```

Finding an Order

Assuming an order exists within the database, you need a way to retrieve it. You need a Find method just like the ones you created in the Customer and Product classes. Enter the following code to support the retrieval of an order from the database:

Order(Order.cls)

```
Public Function Find(ByVal orderId As Long)
  ClearState

  Dim sSQL As String
  sSQL = "SELECT * FROM TOrders WHERE TOrders.id =" & Str(orderId)

  Dim rs As New ADODB.Recordset
  rs.Open sSQL, gSession.GetConn(), adOpenStatic, adLockReadOnly

  If rs.RecordCount <= 0 Then Exit Function

  FromRs rs
  Find = True
End Function

Public Sub ClearState()
  m_id = 0
  m_customerId = 0
  m_dateEntered = 0
  m_dateShipped = 0
  m_dateBilled = 0
  m_datePaid = 0
  m_prodStatus = psInvalid
  m_billStatus = bsInvalid
  m_shippingType = stInvalid
  m_subTotal = 0
  m_discount = 0
  m_taxPercent = 0
  m_shippingCharge = 0
  m_total = 0
```

```
    m_cancelled = False
    Set m_orderItems = New OrderItemColl
End Sub

Public Function FromRs(rs As ADODB.Recordset)
    m_id = rs!id
    m_customerId = rs!customerId
    m_dateEntered = rs!dateEntered
    m_dateShipped = rs!dateShipped
    m_dateBilled = rs!dateBilled
    m_datePaid = rs!datePaid
    m_prodStatus = rs!prodStatus
    m_billStatus = rs!billStatus
    m_shippingType = rs!shippingType
    m_subTotal = rs!subTotal
    m_discount = rs!discount
    m_taxPercent = rs!taxPercent
    m_shippingCharge = rs!shippingCharge
    m_total = rs!total
    m_cancelled = rs!cancelled
    m_orderItems.RetrieveAll Me
End Function
```

In the `Find` method, the first line calls the `ClearState` method of the Order object. This clears the values in the data members of the Order object. A SQL `SELECT` statement is constructed for finding an order as specified by the `orderId` parameter passed to the method.

This SQL statement is passed to a new Recordset object as part of calling the `Open` method. The database connection is retrieved from the global `DbSession` object and passed directly to the second parameter of the Recordset `Open` method. If the resulting record count is zero or less, the method exits. If a record is found, the `FromRs` method is called to copy the values from the recordset to the internal data members of the Order object. Also notice the call to the `RetrieveAll` method of the `m_orderItems` data member. You defined this method earlier to retrieve the OrderItems for the Order passed to the `RetrieveAll` method. In this case, the value of `Me` is passed to the `RetrieveAll` method, which represents the current order object.

After the `FromRs` function returns control back to the `Find` method, the return value is set to True and the `Find` method exits.

Next Steps

In this chapter, you added persistence to your `Customer` and `Product` classes for saving, finding, and deleting customer and product objects, respectively.

You also added persistence to the Order, OrderItemColl, and OrderItem classes for saving orders to the database. This involved saving objects and related objects within a transaction to support saving the Order and OrderItems as one unit of work. We did not include support for deleting orders because we want to discourage deleting order records from the database.

In Chapter 17, "Finalizing the Classes in the Project," you complete the addition of object persistence by adding methods on the DbSession class for getting the lists of customers, products, and orders from the database.

You also need the capability to get a list of orders created by a customer. To support this, you will add a GetOrders method to the Customer class.

Finally, in the next chapter you will add a CheckLogin method to the DbSession class for supporting the Login dialog window. You will replace the current version of CheckLogin with this new method that uses the database to validate user information.

Chapter 17

In this chapter

- *Add Database Support to Validate the User*
- *Adding Class Events*

Finalizing the Classes in the Project

This chapter focuses on completing the classes. Recall the first dialog box you created as part of this application (the Login dialog). When you implemented this form, you created a public function named CheckLogin in the main code module. This function was created for the purpose of validating the user before entering the application. The function did not actually validate the user. Instead, it just returned True. Now that we have database support as part of our application you are going to create a working CheckLogin function.

You also created classes that have relationships between them. Specifically, you have created classes that contain objects of other classes. The approach taken to implementing the order and order items has a limitation. If OrderItems are added to an OrderItemColl object, the order that contains the OrderItemColl has no knowledge of this event. Therefore, the order total does not change and reflects the total as specified before the OrderItem was added. It is the responsibility of the code that added the OrderItem to call the RecalculateTotal method on the order to update the total. It would be better if the order automatically updated its total whenever an OrderItem was added or deleted. In this chapter, we implement a solution for this and it relies on using class events.

Add Database Support to Validate the User

You are now going to provide database access in the process of validating a user when logging in to the application. The simplest approach is to just fill in the current CheckLogin function with code that accesses the database. This approach, however, leads you down a path of adding database logic in many places within your application. The goal should be to encapsulate the database as much as possible to minimize the amount of code dependency on the database. This means that the more places in your application that need to know the structure of the database, the more you are confined to this structure. Changing the structure at a later point could require you to make significant changes to your code.

So instead of adding database code to the CheckLogin function, you are going to add a method in the DbSession class for validating the user. You are doing this because the DbSession already encapsulates the database connection. Therefore, extending this class to provide utility database functions makes perfect sense.

In developing the CheckLogin function, you are making a distinction between utility functions and object functions. The classes you added in the previous chapters also encapsulate database access routines. However, the database logic that is encapsulated pertains to the object itself. For example, a customer class does not have code to read product information. The customer class knows only how to refer to customer information within the database.

Add the following code to the DbSession class:

DbSession(DbSession.cls)

```
Public Function CheckLogin(ByVal userId As String, _
                           ByVal password As String) As Boolean
    Dim conn As ADODB.Connection
    Set conn = GetConn()
    If conn Is Nothing Then Exit Function

    Dim sSQL As String
    sSQL = "SELECT * FROM Tusers WHERE Tusers.userId = '" & userId & "'"

    Dim rs As New ADODB.Recordset
    rs.Open sSQL, conn, adOpenStatic, adLockReadOnly

    If rs.RecordCount <= 0 Then Exit Function
    If password <> rs!password Then Exit Function
    CheckLogin = True
End Function
```

This method gets the connection by calling the GetConn method of the current object. To call a method on an object, you would normally be required to specify an object variable along with the method using the following format:

```
Object.Method
```

Because the CheckLogin method is part of the DbSession class, other methods of the DbSession class can be invoked directly without having to specify an object variable.

The current object instance is the object variable by default. If you want to be explicit, you can use the well-know object variable named Me. The variable Me refers to the current object and can be used only within methods of a class. Here is an example of explicitly calling the GetConn method using the variable Me:

```
Set conn = Me.GetConn()
```

Once again, if you do not specify the variable Me, the current object instance is used by default when calling other methods in the class.

After getting the connection, the connection is checked to make sure you got one. If the connection object is nothing (meaning you did not get a connection) the CheckLogin function exits with a default return value of False.

If the connection object is valid, the code then creates a SQL string for selecting the one specific user record within the database as specified by the userId parameter to the CheckLogin function. This approach is more efficient than creating a SQL SELECT statement to retrieve all user records and then iterating through the results, comparing the userId with the value of the userId parameter passed to the CheckLogin function. This SQL string is passed to the Open method of a Recordset object along with the connection object. After the Open method executes and returns to your method, the recordset contains either one or zero records. If the count of records is zero, the function exits and the return value defaults to False.

If you have not exited the method at this point, this means you got a connection and retrieved the one user record from the database. The recordset is currently positioned on the first record. The value in the password field of the recordset is compared to the value of the password parameter passed to the CheckLogin function. If the password matches, the return value is set to True. Otherwise, the method returns False, indicating that the user does not have login rights.

Adding Class Events

In the previous chapters, you developed the Order, OrderItemColl, and OrderItem classes. Although these classes are integrated and work together to represent an overall order, something is missing. Figure 17.1 represents an instance diagram of an order. Here you can see an Order object has one OrderItemColl object. The OrderItemColl object has two OrderItem objects. The total in the Order object is $20 based on the sum of the amount in each of the OrderItem objects. In this case, both OrderItem objects contain an amount of $10.

Figure 17.2 shows how you would add a new OrderItem object to the Order. They way you implemented the classes, you add OrderItem objects to the OrderItemColl object directly.

Figure 17.1

A sample instance diagram for an order.

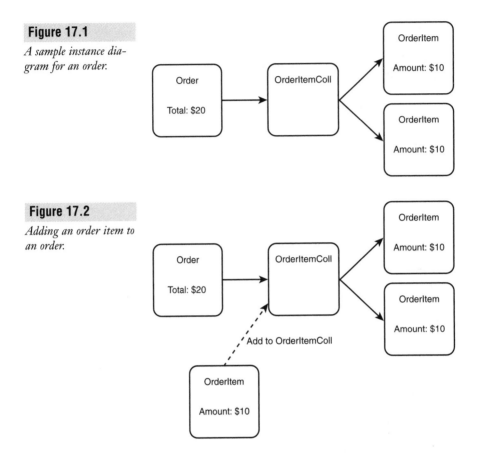

Figure 17.2

Adding an order item to an order.

Figure 17.3 shows the newly added OrderItem object added to the order. Now if you add another OrderItem object to the order, how does the total get automatically updated? The current answer is the order total is not automatically updated. The RecalculateTotal method must be called if the total is to reflect the additional OrderItem.

We could have chosen to add the OrderItem object to the Order object, and then the Order object would in turn add the object to the OrderItemColl, as shown in Figure 17.4. In this case, because the OrderItem would be added to the Order object, the Order could then automatically recalculate the total after the OrderItem object was added to the OrderItemColl object.

If you did this, you would make the OrderItemColl private to the Order class. This would require you to create another method on the Order class to add an OrderItem. Essentially, this leads you down a path of creating public methods on the Order class to manipulate the OrderItemColl object that is internal to the Order class. This approach is commonly referred to as *delegation*. In this example, the Order class delegates the adding of OrderItem objects to the OrderItemColl object. This is a legitimate approach but requires developing more methods on the Order class to manage the OrderItemColl object. If the OrderItemColl object was private to the Order, all the current methods on the OrderItemColl would need to be exposed by the Order class using delegation.

Figure 17.3

An order with a newly added order item.

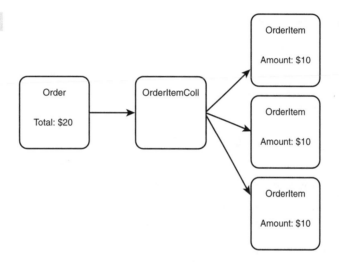

Figure 17.4

Another approach to adding an order item to an order.

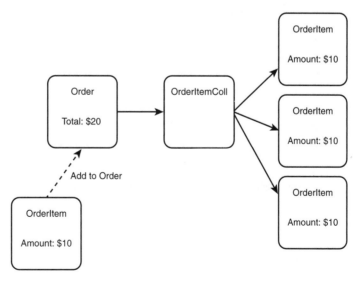

Another approach to addressing this whole problem involves using events. After the OrderItem object is added to the OrderItemColl object, the OrderItemColl object could send an event that the collection was updated. An event handler could be created to respond to the event. In this case, the Order class could respond to an event from the OrderItemColl and automatically recalculate the total. Let's take a look at how this works.

The first step you need to take is to declare an event within the OrderItemColl class. To do this, enter the following code in the declarations section of the OrderItemColl class:

OrderItemColl(OrderItemColl.cls)

```
Public Event ItemsChanged()
```

This code declares an event named `ItemsChanged`. Any number of events can be declared as part of a class. After the event is declared, it can be sent or raised, as necessary, within the code. After an event is raised, it can be caught or trapped by writing more Visual Basic code. Before we show how to catch and respond to an event, let's go through the OrderItemColl class and raise the `ItemsChanged` event where necessary.

Modify the `AddOrderItem` method of the OrderItemColl class so that it looks like this:

OrderItemColl(OrderItemColl.cls)

```
Public Sub AddOrderItem(oi As OrderItem)
  oi.seqNo = m_coll.Count + 1
  m_coll.Add oi
  RaiseEvent ItemsChanged
End Sub
```

Notice the new line before exiting the method. This line illustrates how to raise or send an event from within a class. We put this line of code here so that after the OrderItem object is added to the collection, an event is raised notifying other objects (as long as they catch the error) to facilitate any necessary processing. Specifically, the Order object containing the OrderItemColl object will now be able to catch the `ItemsChanged` event and recalculate the total whenever the event is raised.

The `AddOrderItem` method is not the only method that modifies the collection of OrderItems. Because you want to send an event whenever the collection is modified, you also must update each of the following methods:

- `RemoveOrderItem`
- `RetrieveAll`
- `SaveAll`
- `Resequence`
- `ClearState`

The modification to each of these methods is to put the following line of code as the last line before exiting the method:

```
RaiseEvent ItemsChanged
```

The resulting methods in the OrderItemColl class should look like this:

OrderItemColl(OrderItemColl.cls)

```
Public Sub RemoveOrderItem(ByVal seqNo As Long)
  Dim oi As OrderItem, i As Long

  For i = 1 To m_coll.Count
    Set oi = m_coll.Item(i)
    If oi.seqNo = seqNo Then
      m_coll.Remove i
      Exit For
    End If
  Next i
  ReSequence

  RaiseEvent ItemsChanged
End Sub

Public Sub RetrieveAll(ord As Order)
  ClearState

  Dim sSQL As String
  sSQL = "SELECT * FROM TOrderItems " & _
         "WHERE TOrderItems.orderId = " & Str(ord.id) & _
         " ORDER BY TOrderItems.seqNo"

  Dim rs As New ADODB.Recordset
  rs.Open sSQL, gSession.GetConn(), adOpenForwardOnly, adLockReadOnly

  Dim oi As OrderItem
  Do While Not rs.EOF
    Set oi = New OrderItem
    oi.FromRs rs
    m_coll.Add oi
    rs.MoveNext
  Loop

  RaiseEvent ItemsChanged
End Sub

Public Sub SaveAll(ord As Order, conn As ADODB.Connection)

  DeleteAll ord, conn
  ReSequence
```

continues

continued

```
    Dim sSQL As String
    sSQL = "SELECT * FROM TOrderItems " & _
           "WHERE TOrderItems.orderId = " & Str(ord.id)

    Dim rs As New ADODB.Recordset
    rs.Open sSQL, conn, adOpenKeyset, adLockOptimistic

    Dim i As Long, oi As OrderItem

    For i = 1 To m_coll.Count
      Set oi = m_coll.Item(i)
      oi.InsertInRs ord.id, rs
    Next i

    RaiseEvent ItemsChanged
  End Sub

Public Sub ReSequence()
  Dim i As Long, oi As OrderItem

  For i = 1 To m_coll.Count
    Set oi = m_coll.Item(i)
    oi.seqNo = i
  Next i

  RaiseEvent ItemsChanged
End Sub

Public Sub ClearState()
  Set m_coll = New Collection
  RaiseEvent ItemsChanged
End Sub
```

At this point, you have declared an event as part of the OrderItemColl class and have raised the event in every method in which the collection of OrderItems is modified. So how is the event caught and responded to? Let's move on to the Order class to answer the question. Currently, the OrderItemColl object within the Order class is declared as shown by this line of code:

Order(Order.cls)

```
Private m_orderItems As OrderItemColl
```

For the Order class to catch any events generated by the OrderItemColl object as represented by the m_orderItems variable, you must change the declaration by adding the WithEvents keyword as shown here:

Order(Order.cls)

```
Private WithEvents m_orderItems As OrderItemColl
```

The `WithEvents` keyword tells Visual Basic that you want to catch the events generated by the object referenced by the `m_orderItems` variable. The way in which you catch the event is quite simple after you have specified the `WithEvents` keyword. You must create an event procedure just like you have previously done for responding to a click event generated by a command button.

Now create an event procedure the easy way. Double-click the `Order` class in the Project Explorer. This displays the code for the `Order` class in the code window. At the top of the code window are two combo boxes. The combo box at the top left enables you to select general elements, class elements, and object elements within the class. Select `m_orderItems` from this combo box, as shown in Figure 17.5.

Figure 17.5

Creating an event procedure.

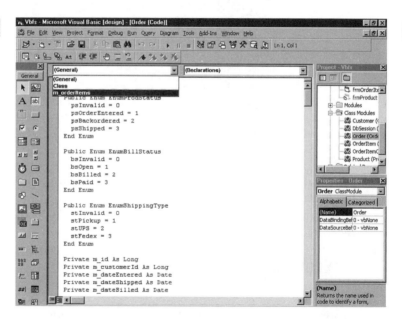

The combo box at the top right of the code window is displayed with options based on your selection in the top-left combo box. Because you selected `m_orderItems`, the combo box at the top right now displays a list of events that are generated by the `m_orderItems` object. Currently, only one event is defined, so the combo box contains one item. Notice that when you selected `m_orderItems` from the top-left combo box, the single event in the top-right combo box was highlighted, and an event procedure was automatically generated (see Figure 17.6). Within the event procedure, add the call to `RecalculateTotal` so that the procedure looks like this:

Order(Order.cls)

```
Private Sub m_orderItems_ItemsChanged()
   RecalculateTotal
End Sub
```

Figure 17.6

The event generated by m_orderItems.

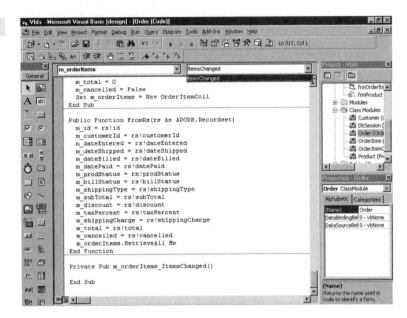

After you create an event procedure, the corresponding event in the top-right combo box of the code window shows up in bold text. This way you can display all the events using the combo box and quickly scan which ones you have defined event procedures for and which ones you have not.

EXCURSION
Handling Events

Events are very useful for immediately indicating that something happened within an application. Without events, developers are left to write code that periodically checks for predefined conditions even though nothing might have changed within the application. This is called *polling* and can result in wasteful computer processing.

To trap an event, a variable must be defined using the WithEvents keyword. After a variable is defined this way, you can trap an event by creating a procedure that follows a specific naming convention for the procedure name. The procedure name is comprised of two elements: the name of the variable declared using WithEvents and the name of the desired event to trap. The variable name and event name are separated with an underscore character. Using the combo boxes at the top of the code window automatically generates event procedures for you. Your only responsibility is to write the code within the procedure that is invoked in response to an event.

It is important to note that when defining an object variable using WithEvents, you must specify the class name. You cannot use events with variables declared as type Object. You cannot declare variables using WithEvents in standard modules, and you cannot use WithEvents when declaring arrays.

You cannot use the New keyword along with the WithEvents keyword when declaring a variable. This forces you to define the variable and set the variable to a new object at some later time. After the variable is set to a valid object reference, events can be trapped for the object. To turn off event trapping for the variable, you can set the contents of the variable to Nothing.

This event procedure follows a specific naming convention. The convention is based on using the object variable name and the event name. In this case, the first part of the procedure name uses m_orderItems and the second part of the procedure name uses ItemsChanged. The two parts of the procedure name are separated using the underscore (_) character. Based on the naming convention, Visual Basic knows to call this procedure when the ItemsChanged event is generated by the object referred to by the m_orderItems variable.

The body of the procedure calls the Recalculate method of the current Order object. Therefore, this procedure is called when the event is raised and in turn recalculates the total of the order. Also keep in mind that this event procedure is just like any other method on the Order class. This implies two things. One, the event procedure acts on a specific instance of the Order class, and it can call other methods of the Order class. This is shown by the call to RecalculateTotal, which is another method of the Order class. In addition, the event procedure acts just like any other method in that it can be called directly by other methods if you choose to.

Unfortunately, you cannot use the WithEvents keyword when declaring an array variable. This feature would be very useful if you needed to maintain an array and wanted to know whether any object in the array generated an error. Because Visual Basic does not support this, you are limited to using WithEvents with single object variables.

Figure 17.7 shows what happens now when a new OrderItem object is added to the OrderItemColl object. The OrderItemColl object adds the OrderItem to the collection of OrderItem objects. Then the OrderItemColl object sends the ItemsChanged event. The Order is defined to respond to these events when they occur. When the Order receives the event, the Order recalculates the total order amount. In this example, the total amount changes from $20 to $30.

Figure 17.7

The event sequence of adding an order item to an order.

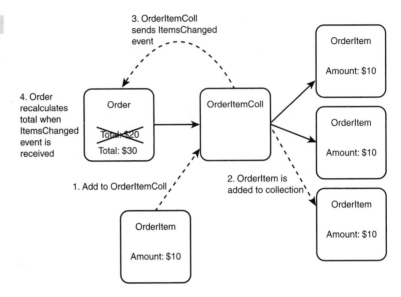

Next Steps

In this chapter you added a method to the DbSession class for the purposes of validating user information based on the login form. You then modified the code of the login form to make a call to this new method. After modifying the code of the form, the login form is completed and now validates user information against valid users defined in the database.

Also, you finished your persistent objects in this chapter by adding event support to the Order class and the OrderItemColl class.

Now, it is time to start using these persistent objects throughout the application. In Chapter 18, "Saving and Retrieving Data," you do exactly that by updating the Customer form, Product form, and Order form to use objects that access a database.

Part IV

Integrate the Subsystems: Finalizing the Application

In this chapter

- *Adding Persistence to the Customer Form*
- *Adding Persistence to the Product Form*
- *Adding Persistence to the Order Item Form*
- *Adding Persistence to the Order Form*

Chapter 18

Saving and Retrieving Data

In this chapter, you will start integrating the persistent classes you developed in the previous chapters with the user interface forms and controls you designed in the second part of the book. You will start with the customer data entry form.

We also introduce the concept of multitiered (layered) application development using Microsoft's Distributed Component Object Model (DCOM).

The complete code for this chapter can be found in the Chapter18 folder of the main VBFS folder on the CD that accompanies this book.

Adding Persistence to the Customer Form

Persistence is a property of a data element that enables that element to transcend time and space; that is, to exist even after the application that generated (or acquired it) is no longer running. *Persisting data* is the process of storing data so that it is available for later use by the same or other users. Data in this case is defined as user input values or application-computed (or otherwise acquired) data values. The place the data is stored is generically known as *persistent storage*, and it can be a relational database, a file (or system of files), or any other device that can retain information for long periods of time.

In simple terms, you must get the data the user is entering using the user interface forms and control and save it to the database so that the data is available later to the same or other users. You can achieve this by using the persistent classes you developed earlier. These classes have the logic of how to save, retrieve, and erase data from persistent storage. You use the classes by creating instances of these classes (that is, objects), then set or get the properties of these objects and call the appropriate methods to save, retrieve, or delete data from the database.

Introduction to Three-Tiered Software Topology

The *topology* of a software system is the way the components of that system are distributed, and the interactions between these components. It is also known as the *architecture* of the system.

Start with your customer form and class. You must integrate the functionality of the `Customer` class into the code for the `frmCustomer` form. To perform the persistent operations required, associate one `Customer` object with each customer form. This object performs all the operations for you. For example, to create a new customer, transfer the data from the customer form (actually from the controls on the form) to the object and then save the object (see Figure 18.1).

Figure 18.1

Persisting a new object.

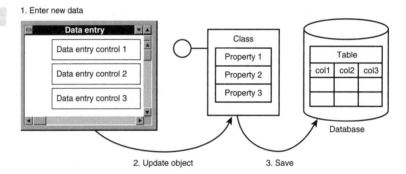

To modify an existing customer, you retrieve an object and transfer the data from the object's properties into the form controls. Then, after the user has finished changing it, transfer it back to the object (validating it in the process), and save the object. See Figure 18.2 for an illustration of this process.

Figure 18.2

Modifying and persisting an existing object.

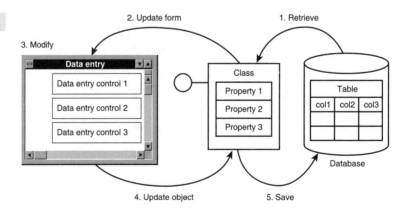

From both Figure 18.1 and Figure 18.2, you can see that the application is divided into three logical layers: the user interface or *presentation layer* (responsible for presenting data to the user and collecting user input), the *middle layer* (responsible for processing and persisting data), and the *persistence layer* (the database, responsible for safe-keeping persistent data). You might wonder why you need a middle layer, when you could write the data directly from the user interface to the database. Indeed, many older applications used to operate under this paradigm (and some of them still do). This topology (using the client accessing directly the database) is known as *client/server*. The fact that it has a monolithic structure (that is, hard to maintain, any changes to code are expensive to implement, and error prone), and that it does not scale very well (if the number of users of a given server increases over a certain limit, the application performance degrades severely) are both major drawbacks.

In a three-tiered topology, each logical layer is implemented by one or more physical components. Each component consists of a set of classes, exposing one or more interfaces. Objects (class instances) from different components interact with each other using the public interfaces. There are several reasons to use a three-tiered, component-based topology:

- Scalability—If required, the components can run on different physical computers to increase performance.
- Encapsulation—Each component is used only through its interface, the implementation details are hidden.
- Maintainability—Due to layer and component encapsulation, each component becomes easier to maintain (that is, fix errors and add new features).

You explore this type of software architecture in more detail in Chapter 26, "Distributed Components: The Way of the Future."

Modify the Customer Form to Make It Persistent

Start by adding some code to the frmCustomer form. Open the code editor for the customer form. At the top of the form module, just under the Option Explicit statement, add the following line of code:

```
Private m_customer As Customer
```

Declare a variable of type Customer (that is, a reference to an instance of the Customer class) to be a private member of the frmCustomer form class. Note that we do not use the New keyword, which means the variable will start by being Nothing when the form is initialized.

This variable holds the object used to persist data. You need to add procedures to transfer the data from the object to the form controls and back to the object. First, add a private procedure to get the data from the object into the controls on the form. Let's call this procedure OtoF, shortcut for Object-to-Form. Enter this code in the frmCustomer form module:

```
Private Sub OtoF()
  Me.txtFirstName = m_customer.firstName
  Me.txtMiddleInitial = m_customer.middleInitial
  Me.txtLastName = m_customer.lastName
  Me.txtStreetAddress = m_customer.streetAddress
  Me.txtCity = m_customer.city
  Me.txtState = m_customer.state
  Me.txtZip = m_customer.zip
  If Len(m_customer.telephone) > 0 Then
    Me.txtTelephone = m_customer.telephone
  End If
  Me.txtEmail = m_customer.email
End Sub
```

The code is setting the values of all the TextBox controls on the form to the values of the corresponding m_customer object properties. In the case of the txtTelephone (which is a MaskedEditBox control), you must check to be sure you do not assign an empty string to it because this causes an error (hence the guarding if statement).

Let's enter the code for the reverse procedure that reads the data from the controls on the form and assigns it to the properties of the object. Call this procedure FtoO (standing for Form-to-Object). Enter this code:

```
Private Sub FtoO()
  m_customer.firstName = Me.txtFirstName
  m_customer.middleInitial = Me.txtMiddleInitial
  m_customer.lastName = Me.txtLastName
  m_customer.streetAddress = Me.txtStreetAddress
  m_customer.city = Me.txtCity
  m_customer.state = Me.txtState
  m_customer.zip = Me.txtZip
  m_customer.telephone = Me.txtTelephone
  m_customer.email = Me.txtEmail
End Sub
```

This procedure also is straightforward, assigning the text contained in the TextBox and MaskedEditBox controls to the corresponding property of the m_customer object. Note that you do not explicitly use the .Text notation for each control because Text is the default property of both TextBox and MaskedEditBox controls.

Now you need a way to pass the object reference to the form. Use a public method for this. Enter the following procedure in the frmCustomer form module:

```
Public Sub SetData(cust As Customer)
  Set m_customer = cust
  OtoF
End Sub
```

The SetData method saves the object reference that was passed in the cust argument into the private data member m_customer. Then it calls the OtoF procedure to update the controls on the form with the data from the object passed in. If the object is empty (that is, a new customer), the text in all controls on the form will be reset to the default value (empty).

You now must save the object when the user clicks the cmdSave button. Let's modify the code in the cmdSave_Click event procedure to do this. Enter the lines of code shown here in bold type:

```
Private Sub cmdSave_Click()
  If Len(txtFirstName) <= 0 Then
    MsgBox "First name is required to save changes!", vbExclamation
    txtFirstName.SetFocus
    Exit Sub
  End If
  If Len(txtLastName) <= 0 Then
    MsgBox "Last name is required to save changes!", vbExclamation
    txtLastName.SetFocus
    Exit Sub
  End If

  FtoO
  If Not m_customer.Save() Then Exit Sub
  Unload Me
End Sub
```

After validating that the first and last name of the customer are entered, transfer the data from the controls to the object (using the FtoO procedure). Now attempt to save the customer. Invoke the Save() method of the Customer class. This method returns a Boolean value indicating whether it succeeded. If the method failed, you do not want to close this form, so exit the procedure, bypassing the Unload Me statement. The reason for proceeding this way is so the user gets a chance to fix the problem, maybe by entering valid data.

The last thing you need to add to this form is the code that releases the object reference held by m_customer when the form is unloaded. That ensures that the object is deleted when no longer needed (that is, when no other reference to it exists). It is a good practice to release all form-level object references when the form is unloaded. The best place to do this is the Unload event of the form. Locate the Form_Unload event procedure and enter the line of code shown in bold type:

```
Private Sub Form_Unload(Cancel As Integer)
  frmMain.SbrMessage ""
  Set m_customer = Nothing
End Sub
```

Setting an object reference to the intrinsic value Nothing releases the reference this form holds on the object.

The customer form is now complete; you need to modify the code in the main form to call the form correctly.

Open the code editor for the frmMain form module. Find the mnuFileNewCustomer_Click event handler and change the code to look like the code shown here:

```
Private Sub mnuFileNewCustomer_Click()
  Dim f As New frmCustomer, obj As New Customer
  f.Show
  f.SetData obj
End Sub
```

Declare both the form and the Customer object as new objects, then after showing the form, call the SetData method (which you implemented previously). At this point, the customer form is visible and the user can make changes to the data. Note that when this procedure exits, the reference to the obj Customer object is released. However, the opened form has a reference to the object. When the form is unloaded, the last reference to the object you created is released and the object will be removed from memory.

You can now test your code and try to add a customer. Save your code and run the application. Select New Customer from the File, New menu. Enter some valid data and click the Save button. If the data you provided was okay, the object is saved and the form is unloaded. Check the database (the TCustomer table) to make sure the customer is really there. If anything was wrong, you will get an error message stating the problem.

Next, integrate the product data entry form with the Product class you implemented in the previous chapters.

Adding Persistence to the Product Form

You will use a similar approach as for the customer form done previously. You will create a private variable that will hold a Product object reference, two procedures to transfer data between the form and the object, and then use the object to persist the data.

Open the code editor for the frmProduct form. Add the private declaration for the object reference variable at the top of the form module, just under the Option Explicit statement.

```
Private m_product As Product
```

Now add the two private procedures to transfer data between the object and the form. You will use the same names as we did for the customer form (OtoF and FtoO). Enter the following code:

```
Public Sub OtoF()
  Me.txtName = m_product.name
  Me.txtAuthor = m_product.author
  Me.txtDescription = m_product.description
  Me.cmbProductType = m_product.prodType
  Me.txtImgFile = m_product.imgFile
  Me.txtDocFile = m_product.docFile
  Me.txtSupplier = m_product.supplier
  Me.txtPrice = m_product.price
End Sub
```

The code sets the values of all the controls on the form to the values of the Product object properties. Enter the FtoO procedure as show here:

```
Public Sub FtoO()
  m_product.name = Me.txtName
  m_product.author = Me.txtAuthor
  m_product.description = Me.txtDescription
  m_product.prodType = Me.cmbProductType
  m_product.imgFile = Me.txtImgFile
  m_product.docFile = Me.txtDocFile
  m_product.supplier = Me.txtSupplier
  m_product.price = Me.txtPrice
End Sub
```

The procedure transfers the data from the form to the object after the user has finished making changes.

Now you need to add the public method to initialize the object reference. Use the same procedure as used for the frmCustomer. Enter this code:

```
Public Sub SetData(prod As Product)
  Set m_product = prod
  OtoF
End Sub
```

The SetData method stores the object reference passed in the argument into the private data member then it calls the OtoF procedure to update the controls on the form with the data from the object passed in.

Now alter the cmdSave_Click event procedure to save the changes. Enter the lines of code shown here in bold type:

```
Private Sub cmdSave_Click()
  If Len(txtName) <= 0 Then
    MsgBox "Product name is required to save changes!", vbExclamation
    txtName.SetFocus
```

18

```
    Exit Sub
  End If

  FtoO
  If Not m_product.Save() Then Exit Sub
  Unload Me
End Sub
```

The code added transfers data back to the object and attempts to save the object. If the save succeeds (that is, the `Save()` method returns True), this instance of the form is unloaded. Otherwise the procedure exits, allowing the user to make changes as required.

You must release the object reference when the form is unloaded. Add the code shown in bold type to the `Form_Unload` event procedure:

```
Private Sub Form_Unload(Cancel As Integer)
  frmMain.SbrMessage ""
  Set m_product = Nothing
End Sub
```

Modify the code in the main form to open the form correctly. Open the code editor for the `frmMain` form module. Find the `mnuFileNewProduct_Click` event handler and change the code to look like this:

```
Private Sub mnuFileNewProduct_Click()
  Dim f As New frmProduct, obj As New Product
  f.Show
  f.SetData obj
End Sub
```

The code is similar to the one you used for the Customer form and object. Create a new form and object, then open the form and pass the object reference to the form.

You can now test your code and try to add a product. Save your code and run the application. Select New Product from the File, New menu. Enter some valid data and click the Save button. If the data you provided was okay, the object is saved and the form is unloaded. Check the database (the TProduct table) to make sure the object was saved correctly.

Adding Persistence to the Order Item Form

Throughout the rest of this chapter, you will add code to persist the order and its aggregated order item objects. You will start by adding code to the `frmOrderItem` form.

The first task is to populate the `cmbProducts` ComboBox control with the current products in the database. You will start by retrieving a list of all the products in the database in a private module-level variable, then you will populate the `cmbProducts` control from the list.

To retrieve a list of all the products in the database, add a new method to the class `DbSession`. The new method retrieves the list of products, creates a Product object for each record retrieved, and adds the object to a Collection object. It then returns the Collection object to the caller.

Retrieving a List of Products from the Database

Open the `DbSession` class module. Add the method `GetProductsList` as shown in this code:

```
Public Function GetProductsList(Optional whereClause As String = "", _
                                Optional orderBy As String = "") As Collection
  Dim conn As ADODB.Connection
  Set conn = GetConn()
  If conn Is Nothing Then Exit Function

  Dim sSQL As String
  sSQL = "SELECT * FROM TProducts "

  If Len(whereClause) > 0 Then
    sSQL = sSQL & "WHERE " & whereClause
  End If
  If Len(orderBy) > 0 Then
    sSQL = sSQL & " ORDER BY " & orderBy
  Else
    sSQL = sSQL & " ORDER BY TProducts.name"
  End If

  Dim rs As New ADODB.Recordset
  rs.Open sSQL, conn, adOpenStatic, adLockReadOnly

  Dim coll As New Collection, prod As Product
  Do While Not rs.EOF
    Set prod = New Product
    prod.FromRs rs
    coll.Add prod, LTrim(Str(prod.id))
    rs.MoveNext
  Loop
  Set GetProductsList = coll
End Function
```

The method has two optional String arguments: `whereClause` and `orderBy`. The `whereClause` argument specifies the subset of records to be retrieved from the database. If it is empty (the default), all the records will be retrieved. The `orderBy` argument specifies how the retrieved records are sorted. If it is empty, the records will be sorted by product name. The return value of the procedure is a Collection object that contains all the objects created from the rows retrieved.

The procedure starts by declaring a variable of type Connection (ADO). Next open the connection to the database using the `GetConn()` method of this class.

Following this, the SQL statement is built. Start with the SELECT FROM part and add the WHERE clause (if one is provided). Then add the ORDER BY clause passed in, or the default (sort by name) if the `orderBy` argument is empty.

EXCURSION

Different Ways to Retrieve Items

In a real-world application, you would not use the `whereClause` and the `orderBy` strings as you do here. The reason is that their usage requires the developer of the user interface (you, in this case) to have knowledge of the database structure and how the `Products` class is mapped to the TProducts table. For example, to retrieve only products that have a specific author, the developer must supply the `whereClause` as `"author = 'Aristotle'"`. This implies that the developer knows that the `author` property of the class `Product` is mapped to the `author` column of the table TProducts. We have actually broken the encapsulation of the `Product` class, as the only one knowing how to persist data from the TProducts table. There are mechanisms to avoid this pitfall but they involve advanced techniques beyond the scope of this book. For example, you might use metadata and mapping information and pass the `where` and `order by` clauses in terms of class attributes instead of table columns.

The next step is to create and open the `Recordset` variable that contains the records that match your criteria. Pass the `sSQL` string and the `conn` variables to the `Open` method of the recordset. Use a static, read-only recordset because you will make no changes to the data retrieved.

In the final part of the procedure, create a new Collection object that holds the Product objects and the object variable that you use in the loop. Iterate through each record in the recordset. For each record retrieved from the database, construct a new Product object, populate it from the current record (using the `FromRs` method), and then add it to the Collection object. Use the product ID as a key to the collection, after you transform it to a string (using the `LTrim` and `Str` intrinsic functions). The `MoveNext` method advances to the next record in the `Recordset` variable. If there are no more records, the `EOF` property will return True and you exit the loop.

The last line of code in the method sets the return value of the method to the Collection object you have created and which now contains all the Product objects you constructed from the retrieved records. Note the use of the `Set` operator to assign the Collection object to the return value of the function. You must use `Set`, in this case, because the return value is of object type.

Populating the Products Combo Box

You now have all the elements required to populate the products combo box. Open the code editor for the frmOrderItem form module. Let's declare a module-level variable of type collection to hold the products list. Add this code to the top of the module:

```
Dim m_prods As Collection
```

Note As you have probably guessed, keeping a collection of all the products in the database for each instance of this form is not the most efficient way to achieve your scope because we are wasting a lot of memory (to hold the objects) and processing time (to retrieve the object in the collection every time the form is opened). Normally, you would have a global Collection object, shared between forms, that retrieves data on request and creates the objects as needed. However, this method involves concurrency and synchronization issues that are beyond the scope of this book.

Next, add a private procedure for retrieving products collection and populating the ComboBox control. Add the following code to the frmOrderItem:

```
Private Sub RefreshProductsList()
  Dim o As Product, i As Long
  Set m_prods = gSession.GetProductsList()
  cmbProducts.Clear
  For i = 1 To m_prods.Count
    Set o = m_prods.Item(i)
    cmbProducts.AddItem o.name
    cmbProducts.ItemData(cmbProducts.ListCount - 1) = o.id
  Next i
End Sub
```

The code retrieves the Collection of Product objects, using the GetProductsList method of the global object gSession. Note that you do not use any of the optional arguments because you need all products and you want them sorted by name. Assign the returned collection to the m_prods module-level variable.

Next, use the Clear method of the ComboBox control to remove any items from the control. The Clear method is used to empty the content of the List property of the ComboBox and ListBox controls. You need to take this measure of precaution in case this procedure is called more than once.

In the following For loop, iterate through each object in the m_prods collection. You get a reference to the object at index i and use the AddItem method of the control to add the product name to the list. When the user selects a product from the list, you

18

must be able to determine which product was selected. You can achieve this by storing the product ID into the ItemData indexed property of the control. The ItemData property is an array of Long values with the same size as the List property array. Each string in the list has a corresponding Long value in the ItemData array at the same index. Assign the product ID to the ItemData value at (ListCount - 1) index. This is the last string in the list, that is, the one you just added.

Next, you need to call the procedure you implemented previously to refresh the products ComboBox control. The best place to place the call to RefreshProductsList() is in the Form_Load procedure. Select the Load event for the Form object and enter this code:

```
Private Sub Form_Load()
  RefreshProductsList
End Sub
```

You also need to release the reference to the Collection variable when the form is unloaded. Select the Unload event for the form and enter the following code:

```
Private Sub Form_Unload(Cancel As Integer)
  Set m_prods = Nothing
End Sub
```

Now you are ready to add the OrderItem object variable that will hold the persistent information for this order item. This time you will not persist the data when you save the changes because this is an order item and must be saved with the order that contains it. You will store the changes the user does to the order item into the collection of order items of the order object, and when the order is saved the order items also will be saved. Add the following line of code at the top of the module, under the Option Explicit statement:

```
Dim m_oi As OrderItem
```

The next step is to implement a public method for this form so that this variable can be initialized. Enter the code as follows:

```
Public Sub SetData(oi As OrderItem)
  Set m_oi = oi

  If m_oi.productId <= 0 Then Exit Sub ' new item

  Dim i As Long, p As Product
  For i = 0 To cmbProducts.ListCount - 1
    If cmbProducts.ItemData(i) = m_oi.productId Then
      cmbProducts.ListIndex = i
      Exit For
    End If
  Next i
End Sub
```

The code is initializing the m_oi variable to refer to the OrderItem object passed in. Then if it is a new object (that is, the productId property is not set), it exits the sub. Otherwise, you must position the cmbProducts ComboBox to show the correct product. You can achieve this by setting the ListIndex property to the correct index. To determine this index, iterate through all items in the list and compare the productId property of the m_oi object with the value of the ItemData property at the current index. You set the ItemData values to the product ID for each product when you populated to the ComboBox control in the RefreshProductsList. If product IDs match, you found the product. You set the ListIndex to be the current index and exit the For loop. Setting the ListIndex makes the product the current selection in the ComboBox and displays it on the form.

Refreshing the Controls on the Form

You still must populate the other controls on the form. Do this in a private method also used to calculate the total field. Enter the method as shown here:

```
Private Sub RecalculateTotal()
  If cmbProducts.ListIndex < 0 Then Exit Sub

  Dim id As Long, p As Product
  id = cmbProducts.ItemData(cmbProducts.ListIndex)
  Set p = m_prods.Item(LTrim(Str(id)))
  txtPrice = p.price
  txtTotal = m_oi.CalcTotal(p, Val(txtDiscount), Val(txtQty))
End Sub
```

The first thing in the procedure is to determine whether a product has been selected. If no product has been selected, the ListIndex property of the ComboBox will be set to –1. If this is true, you cannot proceed with the calculation (you need a price), so you exit the procedure.

Next, retrieve the ID of the product currently selected in the cmbProducts control from its ItemData property. Then, get a reference to the Product object stored in the m_prods collection. Use the Item method of the Collection class, passing in the product ID in string format. You set this to be the key for each object when you populated the Collection.

Now that you have the product, set the value of the txtPrice control. After this, you set the value of the txtTotal control using the CalcTotal method of the OrderItem object. Remember that CalcTotal does not change the state of the object (that is, it does not alter the values of any properties). It simply calculates the total based on a product, discount, and quantity. Notice that you rely on the object (middle layer) to provide you with this value; you do not implement the calculation in the form (user interface layer). In this way, you implement the separation between layers.

18

Now you can add the call to RecalculateTotal to the SetData procedure, so that the price and total control are also set. Modify the SetData procedure by adding the code in bold type, as shown here:

```
Public Sub SetData(oi As OrderItem)
  Set m_oi = oi

  If m_oi.productId <= 0 Then Exit Sub ' new item

  Dim i As Long, p As Product
  For i = 0 To cmbProducts.ListCount - 1
    If cmbProducts.ItemData(i) = m_oi.productId Then
      cmbProducts.ListIndex = i
      Exit For
    End If
  Next I
  txtDiscount = m_oi.discount
  txtQty = m_oi.qty
  RecalculateTotal
End Sub
```

The next step is to ensure that the values in the price and total controls are updated when the user selects another product, enters a discount, or changes the quantity of the ordered item. Select the Click event of the cmbProducts ComboBox and enter the code as shown here:

```
Private Sub cmbProducts_Click()
  RecalculateTotal
End Sub
```

You call RecalculateTotal every time the user selects another product. In a similar fashion, enter the code for the Change event of the txtDiscount and txtQty TextBox controls. Enter the code as shown here:

```
Private Sub txtDiscount_Change()
  RecalculateTotal
End Sub
Private Sub txtQty_Change()
  RecalculateTotal
End Sub
```

Saving Changes and Returning a Flag

Next, implement the Click events of the two CommandButton controls cmdCancel and cmdOk. If the user clicks on the Cancel button, you want to close the form and let the client of the form (the frmOrder in this case) know that the user has cancelled the changes. In the case of the OK button, you want to transfer the changes the user has made into the m_oi OrderItem object and let the client know that the user has made changes to the object. In both cases, you must pass a flag to the client indicating if the operation was canceled. You can use the Tag property of the form as a flag.

The Tag property is a String property of all forms and most controls that is used as a placeholder. The developer can place any data in the Tag property; Visual Basic does not use or change it in any way. This property is normally used to associate an application-defined value to a form or control. In this case, you will use it to pass a True or False value to the client of this dialog form, indicating whether the object passed in the SetData method was modified (that is, it will be true if the object is modified).

 Note   Some custom controls (most notably the controls in the Windows Common Controls component) have a Tag property of type Variant, which enables objects to be attached to the control. For example, you might want to attach an object to each Node object in a TreeView control.

The code for cmdCancel is straightforward:

```
Private Sub cmdCancel_Click()
  Me.Tag = False
  Me.Hide
End Sub
```

Set the Tag property to False and then call the Hide method of this form. The Hide method sets the Visible property of the form to False, hiding the form. Because this form is a modal dialog, the execution control returns to the line of code following the Show method that was used to display this instance of the form. For example, a client would use this dialog box in this way:

```
Dim oi As New OrderItem, f As New frmOrderItem, r As Boolean
Load f
f.SetData oi
f.Show vbModal, frmMain
r = CBool(f.Tag)
If r Then
  ' do something with the changed oi
Else
  ' do something else, oi is not changed
End If
Unload f
```

First, the client code creates a new OrderItem object and a new instance of the frmOrderItem form. Then it calls the intrinsic method Load, to load the form. This brings the form into memory, but it is not visible yet. Next, the SetData is invoked to pass the object reference oi to the form. Then the Show method is called, requesting that the form be shown as modal. At this point the form becomes visible and the user can make changes to the data. When the user clicks the Cancel button, the form Tag property is set to False and the form is hidden. At this point, the preceding code snippet continues with the statement after the Show; that is, with the assignment to

18

the Boolean r variable. The variable gets the value of the Tag property of the form after being converted to Boolean. Note the use of the conversion intrinsic function CBool, which attempts to convert any value to a Boolean (in this case from the String type Tag property to Boolean).

Note that you do not use the Unload method in the cmdCancel_Click, because the Unload causes the form object and its Tag value to be released from memory. This causes any code that refers to the form to fail with an error. In this particular case, the f.Tag would fail.

Let's implement the Click event procedure for the OK button. Enter the code as shown here:

```
Private Sub cmdOK_Click()
  If cmbProducts.ListIndex < 0 Then
    MsgBox "A product must be selected", vbExclamation, "Order Item"
    cmbProducts.SetFocus
    Exit Sub
  End If

  Dim id As Long, p As Product
  id = cmbProducts.ItemData(cmbProducts.ListIndex)
  Set p = m_prods.Item(LTrim(Str(id)))
  m_oi.SetItem p, Val(txtDiscount), Val(txtQty)

  Me.Tag = True
  Me.Hide
End Sub
```

This procedure validates that a product was selected (otherwise it would be an invalid order item). If none was selected, the user is informed using the MsgBox, the focus is transferred to the list of products in cmbProducts, and the Exit Sub is executed.

If you have a valid product, you must identify it. You get its ID using the ItemData value at the current value of the ListIndex property of the ComboBox. Then you get a reference to the object in the m_prods collection, using the ID (converted to string). Then you call the SetItem method of the m_oi OrderItem object, which changes the data in the object to reflect the changes made by the user.

The last two lines of code in the procedure set the Tag property of the form to True (to indicate that there are changes) and then hide the form, so that control is passed back to the client of this form (similar to the Cancel button above, only the Tag value is now True).

You must add one line of code to the Unload event of the form to release the reference to the OrderItem object. Add the code shown in bold type to the Form_Unload procedure:

```
Private Sub Form_Unload(Cancel As Integer)
  Set m_oi = Nothing
  Set m_prods = Nothing
End Sub
```

Handling the Form Close User Action

There is one more procedure you need to add to this form to cover the case when the user unloads the form by clicking on the Close (X) button of the form. This action triggers an `Unload` event, the form is unloaded, and the client code that expects it to be there crashes with an error (see the sample client code shown previously). This means you need to prevent the form from being unloaded when the user clicks the Close button. You can do this by handling the `QueryUnload` event of the form. The `QueryUnload` is triggered before the `Unload` event and allows the developer to cancel the unload of the form, if required. Select the `QueryUnload` event from the Form drop-down list of events, and then enter the following code:

```
Private Sub Form_QueryUnload(Cancel As Integer, UnloadMode As Integer)
  If UnloadMode <> vbFormControlMenu Then Exit Sub
  Cancel = True
  Me.Tag = False
  Me.Hide
End Sub
```

The `QueryUnload` event procedure has two `ByRef` arguments: `Cancel` and `UnloadMode`. The `Cancel` argument defaults to False and is used to tell Visual Basic if this form cancels the unload operation. Setting it to True cancels the unload operation; leaving it alone tells VB to continue unloading this form. The `UnloadMode` argument indicates what is causing the unload operation to take place. It can be one of the following intrinsic constants:

Value	Description
vbFormControlMenu	User selects the close button or Close command of the form menu
vbFormCode	The `Unload` statement was invoked from your code
vbAppWindows	The current Windows session is ending
vbTaskManager	The Windows Task Manager requested the application to terminate
vbMDIForm	An MDI child is closing because its parent (the MDIForm) is closing
vbFormOwner	The owner of the form is closing and requests all its children to close

18

In this case you are interested in the case when the user is closing the form, vbFormControlMenu. Hence, the first line of code in the procedure checks to see whether the UnloadMode is vbFormControlMenu. If it is not, it exits the procedure.

 Note   It is not recommended that you cancel the unload of a form when the system requests it (that is, vbAppWindows or vbTaskManager). The only thing you can do in this case is to save any unsaved changes (or use a modal dialog box to prompt the user to save the changes). Canceling an unload while the system is shutting down might cause the system to force your application to terminate, ignoring your request, which might lead to corrupted data (for example if you have any open files or databases).

If the user is closing the form, you will cancel the unload and instead set the Tag property of the form to False and invoke Hide to make the form invisible. This is the same effect as if the user clicked the Cancel button.

This concludes the implementation of the methods and procedures for the frmOrderItem form. In the next section, you will integrate it with the frmOrder form and the Order persistent object.

Adding Persistence to the Order Form

Start by adding code to populate the list of customers on the form, using the ComboBox control cmbCustomers. You use a similar approach you used for the products list on the frmOrderItem shown previously. You will implement a method on the DbSession class to retrieve a collection of Customer objects from the database. Then, you will use this collection to populate the cmbCustomers control from it.

Populating the Customer List

Start by adding the GetCustomersList public method on the DbSession class. Open the DbSession class module and enter the following code:

```
Public Function GetCustomersList(Optional whereClause As String = "", _
                                 Optional orderBy As String = "") As Collection
  Dim conn As ADODB.Connection
  Set conn = GetConn()
  If conn Is Nothing Then Exit Function

  Dim sSQL As String
  sSQL = "SELECT * FROM TCustomers "

  If Len(whereClause) > 0 Then
    sSQL = sSQL & "WHERE " & whereClause
```

```
      End If
      If Len(orderBy) > 0 Then
        sSQL = sSQL & " ORDER BY " & orderBy
      Else
        sSQL = sSQL & " ORDER BY TCustomers.lastName"
      End If

      Dim rs As New ADODB.Recordset
      rs.Open sSQL, conn, adOpenStatic, adLockReadOnly

      Dim coll As New Collection, cust As Customer
      Do While Not rs.EOF
        Set cust = New Customer
        cust.FromRs rs
        coll.Add cust
        rs.MoveNext
      Loop
      Set GetCustomersList = coll
    End Function
```

The code is similar to the GetProductsList method implemented previously. You create and open an ADO Connection object then you build the SQL statement that will be used to open the recordset. You use the optional arguments whereClause and orderBy, if they are given, to construct the SQL statement. Then, you create and open the recordset, using the SQL string, the connection object, and the static and read-only flags. You then create a Collection object, and for each record in the recordset you create a new customer from the record (using the FromRs method of the Customer class). You add the object to the collection, and then move to the next record in the recordset (using the MoveNext method).

Now you can implement a private procedure in the frmOrder form module to refresh the list of customers contained in the ComboBox control. Open the form module for the frmOrder form, and enter this code:

```
Private Sub RefreshCustomersList()
  Dim custList As Collection, c As Customer, i As Long
  Set custList = gSession.GetCustomersList()

  cmbCustomers.Clear
  For i = 1 To custList.Count
    Set c = custList.Item(i)
    cmbCustomers.AddItem c.name
    cmbCustomers.ItemData(cmbCustomers.ListCount - 1) = c.id
  Next i
End Sub
```

The first line of code declares the variables used in this procedure. Note that you use a local variable of type Collection this time because you do not use it in the rest of the code. You get the collection of all customers from the database, using the

GetCustomersList method of the global DbSession object gSession. You need all the customers in the database, so you do not use either of the optional arguments of the method.

Following this, you invoke the Clear method of the ComboBox to make sure you do not end up with duplicate customers in the list. Next, you iterate through the collection of Customer objects and for each object in the collection you add one item to the ComboBox (for example, the name of the customer). You also assign the customer ID to the parallel ItemData array value, at the current index. Note that when the procedure ends the local collection variable custList will be released, and in turn all the objects it contains are released.

Now you can call this method from the Load event procedure of the form. Locate the Form_Load procedure and add the code in bold type as shown here:

```
Private Sub Form_Load()
  RefreshCustomersList
  grd.Rows = 1
  grd.ColWidth(0) = 720
  grd.ColWidth(1) = 2500
  grd.ColWidth(2) = 720
  grd.ColWidth(3) = 720
  grd.ColWidth(4) = 720
  grd.ColWidth(5) = 720
  grd.Row = 0
  grd.Col = 0: grd.Text = "Seq."
  grd.Col = 1: grd.Text = "Product"
  grd.Col = 2: grd.Text = "Price"
  grd.Col = 3: grd.Text = "Disc."
  grd.Col = 4: grd.Text = "Qty."
  grd.Col = 5: grd.Text = "Total"
End Sub
```

Integrating with the Persistent Order Object

Now, add an object variable of type Order as a private variable to the form. Also add a Boolean flag that indicates whether the object was saved. You use this flag to determine whether you need to prompt the user to save the changes if he closes the form without saving changes first. Add the following two lines of code at the top of the frmOrder form module:

```
Private m_order As Order
Private m_saved As Boolean
```

Add code to release the Order object when the form is unloaded. Select the Unload event for the Form object, and enter the code as shown here:

```
Private Sub Form_Unload(Cancel As Integer)
  Set m_order = Nothing
End Sub
```

Now you need a utility function to retrieve the shipping type (pick-up, UPS, or FedEx) from the controls on the form (in this case the optShipType OptionButtons control array). The function should return the shipping type as the enumerated type used by the Order class (the EnumShipType enumeration). Implement this function as a custom property of the form. Enter the code as shown here:

```
Property Get shipType() As EnumShippingType
  If optShipType(0).Value Then shipType = stPickup: Exit Property
  If optShipType(1).Value Then shipType = stUPS: Exit Property
  If optShipType(2).Value Then shipType = stFedex: Exit Property
  shipType = stInvalid
End Property
```

The Property Get procedure checks the value of each control in the optShipType control array, and returns the corresponding value from the EnumShipType enumeration. Note the return type of the property as being of the EnumShipType enumerated type. Also note the use of the Exit Property statement, performing a similar action to the Exit Sub and Exit Function statements.

You will take a different approach for the Order object associated with this form. You can create the object inside the form and release it when you are finished. The reason for this is that this form is used only to enter new orders, and not to modify existing orders, while both the frmCustomer and frmProduct forms are used to add new and modify existing customers and products, respectively. This means that the object is used only from inside this form, therefore it makes sense to keep it private. Modify the Load event procedure of the form to create the Order object. Locate the Form_Load procedure in the form module for the frmOrder form, and enter the code shown in bold type:

```
Private Sub Form_Load()
  RefreshCustomersList

  grd.Rows = 1
  grd.ColWidth(0) = 720
  grd.ColWidth(1) = 2500
  grd.ColWidth(2) = 720
  grd.ColWidth(3) = 720
  grd.ColWidth(4) = 720
  grd.ColWidth(5) = 720
  grd.Row = 0
  grd.Col = 0: grd.Text = "Seq."
  grd.Col = 1: grd.Text = "Product"
  grd.Col = 2: grd.Text = "Price"
  grd.Col = 3: grd.Text = "Disc."
  grd.Col = 4: grd.Text = "Qty."
  grd.Col = 5: grd.Text = "Total"
```

```
Set m_order = New Order
    m_order.InitOIList
End Sub
```

You create a new Order object and then invoke its InitOIList method, which initializes the collection of OrderItem objects contained inside the Order object.

You need a procedure that calculates the subtotal and total values for this order. This procedure is called when the user makes a change to the order, for example, when order items are added, modified, or removed, or when the discount and tax fields are changed. Add the following code:

```
Private Sub RefreshTotal()
  If m_order Is Nothing Then Exit Sub
    m_order.RecalculateTotal Val(Me.txtDiscount), _
                             Val(Me.txtTax), _
                             Val(Me.txtShippingCharge)
  txtSubtotal = m_order.subTotal
  txtTotal = m_order.total
End Sub
```

The procedure is declared as Private because it is used only in this module. First, make sure the order object was created, if not, there is nothing to calculate, so exit the procedure. Next, use the RecalculateTotal method of the Order object to update its subtotal and total properties. Then assign the values of this properties to the txtSubtotal and txtTotal controls.

Now you need a procedure to populate the grid control from the list of order items in this order. Enter this code:

```
Private Sub RefreshGrid()
  grd.Rows = 1

  If m_order Is Nothing Then Exit Sub

  Dim oi As OrderItem, oic As OrderItemColl, i As Long, sRow As String
  Set oic = m_order.orderItems
  For i = 1 To oic.Count
    Set oi = oic.Item(i)
    sRow = LTrim(Str(oi.seqNo)) & vbTab
    sRow = sRow & oi.productName & vbTab
    sRow = sRow & Format(oi.price) & vbTab
    sRow = sRow & LTrim(Str(oi.discount)) & vbTab
    sRow = sRow & LTrim(Str(oi.qty)) & vbTab
    sRow = sRow & Format(oi.total)
    grd.AddItem sRow
  Next i
  RefreshTotal
End Sub
```

This procedure is also Private, for the same reason as the RefreshTotal procedure used previously—it is used only inside this module. The first line of code sets the number of rows in the grid control to 1, using its Rows property. This clears the grid contents but keeps the first row (the column headers you added in the Form_Load). Next, check whether the Order object was initialized, if not, there is nothing to add to the grid, so exit the procedure. Next, iterate through all objects in the list and for each object, add a row to the grid control. You get a reference to the list from the m_order variable, using its orderItems property. Then you get a reference to each OrderItem object in the list and build a string that will be used to add a row to the grid. Use the AddItem method of the MSFlexGrid control to add one row of data. The AddItem method takes one argument of type String containing the data for all the cells in the row, delimited by Tab characters. Note the use of the VB intrinsic constant vbTab, in conjunction with the String concatenation operator & to build the string containing the row data. After you have added the data for all order items to the grid, call the RefreshTotal procedure to recalculate the subtotal and total values for this order.

Next, you must add code for the CommandButton controls that add, modify, and remove order items from this order. Let's start by implementing the Click event for the Add CommandButton. Enter the code as shown here:

```
Private Sub cmdAdd_Click()
  Dim oi As OrderItem, oic As OrderItemColl
  Set oic = m_order.orderItems
  Set oi = oic.NewOrderItem

  Dim f As New frmOrderItem, r As Boolean
  Load f
  f.SetData oi
  f.Show vbModal, frmMain
  r = CBool(f.Tag)
  If Not r Then Exit Sub

  oic.AddOrderItem oi
  RefreshGrid
End Sub
```

First get a reference to the list of order items from the Order object. You create a new OrderItem object using the NewOrderItem method of the OrderItemColl class. This method creates a new OrderItem, assigns its parent Order, and returns the OrderItem reference to you. Next, create a new OrderItem edit form (frmOrderItem). Load it and call its SetData method to pass the order item object to it then show it as a modal dialog. At this point, the user will make changes of the OrderItem object and will either confirm or cancel the changes. The value of the Tag property of the dialog tells you whether the item was changed. Note the use of the

CBool intrinsic function to convert from String (the type of the Tag property) to Boolean. If the user cancelled the changes, exit the procedure. Otherwise, add the new item to the list of items for this order, and call RefreshGrid to update the grid and the calculated subtotal and total values.

You can use a similar approach to modify an existing item from the list. Enter the following code:

```
Private Sub cmdEdit_Click()
    Dim r As Long, i As Long
    r = grd.Row
    If r <= 0 Then Exit Sub
    grd.Col = 0
    i = Val(grd.Text)

    Dim oi As OrderItem, oic As OrderItemColl
    Set oic = m_order.orderItems
    Set oi = oic.GetItem(i)

    Dim f As New frmOrderItem, retVal As Boolean
    Load f
    f.SetData oi
    f.Show vbModal, frmMain
    retVal = CBool(f.Tag)
    If Not retVal Then Exit Sub

    RefreshGrid
End Sub
```

This time you need to identify the item, based on the currently selected row in the grid control. You get the current row using the Row property of the grid. If the row value is less than zero (no row selected) or zero (the column headers are selected), then you have no current item to edit, so exit the procedure. Otherwise, set the grid column to 0, so that it points to the cell containing the sequence number of the order item. You store this value into the i variable. You then get the list of order items from the Order object, and from the list you retrieve the OrderItem object reference with the sequence number equal to i. You then repeat the code from the cmdAdd_Click used previously that loads the dialog, sets the object reference to it, and then returns True if there are changes to the item. If no changes were made, exit the procedure, otherwise update the grid contents.

In the cmdDelete_Click procedure, you will identify the currently select order item from the grid and then remove it from the list. Enter the code as shown here:

```
Private Sub cmdDelete_Click()
    Dim r As Long, i As Long
    r = grd.Row
    If r <= 0 Then Exit Sub
```

```
    grd.Col = 0
    i = Val(grd.Text)

    Dim oic As OrderItemColl
    Set oic = m_order.orderItems
    oic.RemoveOrderItem i
    RefreshGrid
End Sub
```

Use the same code as in the cmdEdit_Click to identify the current order item. After
you found it, remove it from the list, calling the RemoveOrderItem method of the
OrderItemColl class. This method takes the item's sequence number as an argument,
and removes the item from the internal Collection object. Now refresh the grid.
Note that the code

```
Dim oic As OrderItemColl
Set oic = m_order.orderItems
oic.RemoveOrderItem i
```

is equivalent to the more condensed version:

```
m_order.orderItems.RemoveOrderItem i
```

Now you implement the Click event handler of the cmdSave, which is going to persist the Order object. Enter this code:

```
Private Sub cmdSave_Click()
  If cmbCustomers.ListIndex < 0 Then
    Beep
    MsgBox "A customer must be selected!"
    cmbCustomers.SetFocus
    Exit Sub
  End If

  Dim cust As New Customer, id As Long
  id = cmbCustomers.ItemData(cmbCustomers.ListIndex)
  If Not cust.Find(id) Then
    Beep
    MsgBox "Invalid customer!"
    RefreshCustomersList
    cmbCustomers.SetFocus
    Exit Sub
  End If

  m_order.OrdEnter cust, Now, Me.shipType, Val(Me.txtDiscount), _
                   Val(Me.txtTax), Val(Me.txtShippingCharge)

  If Not m_order.SaveOrder() Then Exit Sub
  m_saved = True
  Unload Me
End Sub
```

The first thing you must check is to see whether a customer was selected. If no customer is selected (the ListIndex of the cmbCustomers control is less than 0), you warn the user, set focus to the control, and exit. Note the use of the Beep intrinsic function, which is used to have the computer emit the default beep sound.

If a customer was selected from the list, you will need a reference to it. Retrieve the customer ID from the ItemData property of the cmbCustomers control (at ListIndex). Then use the Find method of the Customer class to retrieve the customer from the database. If the customer is not found, it means another user has deleted the customer you were looking for from the database after you have loaded the list of customers. That means our list of customers is "dirty"; that is, no longer matches the database table contents. You must refresh it and allow the user to reselect the customer (or cancel the order). That is why you call RefreshCustomerList, in addition to showing the message box and setting the focus back to the control.

Next, set the data of the Order object to reflect the values on the form, using its OrdEnter method. Now attempt to save the order. If the SaveOrder method is successful, set the m_saved variable to True and unload this form. If the order could not be saved, exit the procedure, leaving the m_saved to be False and without unloading the form.

The cmdCancel_Click procedure is quite simple—you just unload this instance of the form, discarding changes:

```
Private Sub cmdCancel_Click()
  Unload Me
End Sub
```

To protect the changes the user made in case of an accidental closing of the form, implement the QueryUnload event handler to be sure that if the order was not saved, the user really wants to lose the changes. Enter the code as shown here:

```
Private Sub Form_QueryUnload(Cancel As Integer, UnloadMode As Integer)
  If UnloadMode <> vbFormControlMenu Then Exit Sub
  If m_saved Then Exit Sub

  Dim i As VbMsgBoxResult

  i = MsgBox("Order has changed, save it now?", _
            vbQuestion + vbYesNoCancel, "Save changes")
  If i = vbCancel Then
    Cancel = True
  ElseIf i = vbYes Then
    cmdSave_Click
    If Not m_saved Then Cancel = True
  End If
End Sub:
```

First, check that it is the user that is closing the form by using the `UnloadMode` argument. If it is not the user, you have no choice but to exit. If the order was already saved, you have nothing to do but exit and allow the `Unload` event to continue. Otherwise, inform the user that the order was not saved, and ask the user if you should save it now. The user has three choices: Yes (save the order), No (don't save the order), or Cancel (the closing of the form).

If the return value of the `MsgBox` intrinsic function is `vbCancel`, you set the `Cancel` argument to True. If the return value is `vbYes`, you attempt to save the object (using a call to the `cmbSave_Click` procedure you implemented previously). If this call fails (the `m_saved` is still False), then cancel the unload for the form. If the return value is `vbNo`, then exit the sub (none of the branches of the `If` statement will be executed).

You must add a call to `RefreshTotal` to the procedure that handles the `Click` event for the Shipping Type option buttons. Add the line shown here in bold type to the `optShipType_Click`:

```
Private Sub optShipType_Click(Index As Integer)
  Dim i As Long
  For i = 0 To 2
    If Index = i Then
      optShipType(i).Value = True
    Else
      optShipType(i).Value = False
    End If
  Next i

  If Index = 0 Then
    txtShippingCharge = ""
    txtShippingCharge.Enabled = False
  Else
    txtShippingCharge.Enabled = True
    txtShippingCharge = IIf(Index = 1, "4.50", "12.50")
  End If
  RefreshTotal
End Sub
```

You also need to add the call to `RefreshTotal` to the `Change` events for the TextBox controls that affect the total amount of the order: txtDiscount, txtShippingCharge, and txtTax. Enter the code as shown here:

```
Private Sub txtDiscount_Change()
  RefreshTotal
End Sub

Private Sub txtShippingCharge_Change()
  RefreshTotal
End Sub
```

18

```
Private Sub txtTax_Change()
  RefreshTotal
End Sub
```

This concludes the implementation for the `frmOrder` and `frmOrderItem` forms. Save the project, then run the application. You should be able to add a new order, add items to the order, change the total, and so on. Figure 18.3 shows the order form with a order item dialog box open.

Figure 18.3

Entering an order.

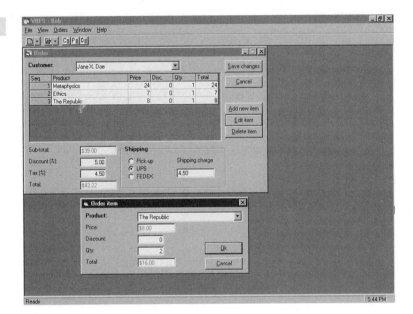

Next Steps

In this chapter, you have added persistence to your data entry forms, using the classes you implemented in Part III. You have explored a few techniques of persisting data, including handling of aggregated objects and using collection classes. You also have explored more advanced events and properties of the forms and some controls.

In the next chapter, we will continue the journey by adding a few new forms that deal with searching and editing existing objects.

Chapter 19

In this chapter

- *Adding a Search Form for the Customer*
- *Implementing Code for the Customer Find Form*

Retrieving and Editing Objects from the Database

In the previous chapter, you explored what is involved in persisting a new object (Customer, Product, and Order). You will continue your journey by adding new functionality required to find an existing object, allowing the user to edit the data, and then saving the changes to the database.

You will explore new controls and new properties, methods, and events of some of the controls you have already used.

The complete code for this chapter can be found in the Chapter19 folder of the main VBFS folder on the CD that accompanies this book.

Adding a Search Form for the Customer

The first step is to add to our project a new form that will allow the user to search for an existing customer and edit it. The user should have the capability to search by customer ID, or alternatively, by customer name and city. If multiple customers match the search criteria, the user should have the capability to select the customer to be edited from a list of all customers that were matched.

Designing the Form

Begin by adding a new form to the project. Change the Name of the form to frmDlgFindCustomer, the BorderStyle to 3 - Fixed Dialog, the Caption to Find Customer, and the StartupPosition to 1 - CenterOwner.

Continue by adding controls to the form. Use the finished form as illustrated in Figure 19.1 as a guide to the size and position of the controls.

Figure 19.1

The Find Customer form.

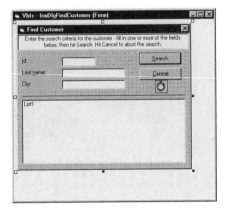

First, let's add a Label control to give the user some indication of how to use this search form. Add a new Label control at the top of the form. Change its name to lblDescription, its Alignment property to 2 - Center, and its BorderStyle to 1 - Fixed Single. Recall that the Alignment property indicates the way the text is shown in the control: aligned to the left, right, or centered. The BorderStyle property for controls is slightly different than for forms. It is used to confer the control the 3D shape when set to vbFixedSingle (1), rather than the flat look it would have if the BorderStyle would be set to vbBSNone (0).

 **Note**   For Line and Shape controls, the BorderStyle property has a different set of possible settings.

Use the color drop-down list to set the BackColor to white. Set the ForeColor to blue. The BackColor and ForeColor are used to set the background and text color, respectively. You can pick any other colors that are different from the regular form colors. For example, if your default background color is white, you might want to select another color for the background of this label so it is easily readable. Change the caption of the label to match the one shown in Figure 19.1.

Next, add the regular labels and text boxes that will get the user input, that is, the search criteria. Add a new label, underneath the existing one. Change its caption to Id:. Add a new text box for the customer id to the right of the Label. Change its Text to be empty, and its Name to txtId.

Repeat the preceding steps twice, once for the Last &name: label and txtLastName text box, and then for the City: label and txtCity text box.

Now, add a Line control to delimit between the upper part of the form and the lower part. Select the Line control in the toolbox and draw a Line control on the form as shown in Figure 19.1. The Line control is a simple graphical control that appears as a line on the form. The most important properties of the Line control are BorderStyle, BorderWidth, and the coordinates (X1, Y1, X2, Y2). The BorderStyle property indicates the line style and can be one of the following enumerated properties:

Value	Description
vbTransparent	Transparent line
vbBSSolid	Solid line (default)
vbBSDash	Dashed line
vbBSDot	Dotted line
vbDashDot	Succession of dash-dot pairs
vbDashDotDot	Succession of dash-dot-dot triplet
vbInsideSolid	Similar to solid

The BorderWidth is a numeric property that indicates how thick the line is. If the BorderWidth is greater than 1, the line will show as solid, no matter what the BorderStyle is. The X1, Y1, X2, and Y2 properties are used to indicate the position of the line on the form. The coordinates are dependent on the ScaleMode and the other scale properties of the container object.

19

 Note The Line control is one of the few visible controls that have position (Top, Left) and size (Width, Height) properties.

Now add a List control under the line, as shown in Figure 19.1. The List control is similar to the drop-down part of a combo box. They share a number of properties, for example: List, ListCount, ListIndex, ItemData, and more. They also share some methods, like Clear and AddItem, and most events. The ComboBox is a superset of the List control, in terms of properties, methods and events.

Change the List control's name to lst. Note that lst is the recommended prefix for this type of control. Change the IntegralHeight to False. The IntegralHeight property indicates whether the control adjusts its size to fit an integral (integer) number of rows (based on the height of each row, as determined by the Font property). That is, if you set a height that would fit 5.5 rows of text, the control will resize itself slightly to fit five rows. This behavior makes arranging the control into the form slightly more difficult; that is why it is set to False.

Add the two CommandButtons, one for Search (set its name to `cmdSearch`) and one for Cancel (set its name to `cmdCancel`).

If a search returns more than one customer that matches the criteria, you would like to indicate this to the user. One way to do this is to have a label with flashing text (alternating the ForeColor property). That means you need some event that is fired on a regular basis, so that you can toggle the ForeColor property. A Timer control helps achieve this.

Add a Timer control anywhere on the form. Change its name to `tmr` (which is the recommended prefix for this kind of control). The Timer control is used to generate an event at regular intervals. The event name is also `Timer`. The interval length is determined by the value of the Interval property, in milliseconds. The Enabled property indicates whether the control is active (that is, is generating the `Timer` event every Interval milliseconds) or inactive (not doing anything). The maximum value for the Interval property is 65535 milliseconds. Set the Interval property to 500 milliseconds, and the Enabled property to False.

You are now finished with the graphical design. Make sure you save your project. Next, you will add code to implement the functionality of this form.

Implementing Code for the Customer Find Form

You will use this form to retrieve an existing customer from the database, based on the data entered by the user. The best way to achieve this is to add a public method on this form that receives a Customer object reference, then shows the form as a modal form (dialog). The user enters the search criteria, then you will search for the customer. If you find the data in the database, you create a Customer object and return the object reference to the procedure that has called the public method.

You will need two form-level variables to hold the Customer object reference and a Collection variable that will hold a list of customers, in case the search will return more that one match. Open the form module for the `frmDlgFindCustomer`, and add the following code at the top of the form module:

```
Private m_customer As Customer
Private m_custList As Collection
```

Next, add the public function that opens the form and sets the Customer object reference to the object retrieved. Enter the following code:

```
Public Function DoModal(obj As Customer, owner As Form) As Boolean
  Dim retVal As Boolean

  Me.Show vbModal, owner
  retVal = CBool(Me.Tag)
  If Not retVal Then
    Unload Me
    Exit Function
  End If
  Set obj = m_customer
  Unload Me
  DoModal = True
End Function
```

The function takes two arguments: the `obj` (customer) and the `owner` (form). The `obj` contains the reference to the customer found (if any). The `owner` is used as an argument to the `Show` method, so that the dialog box is centered properly. The function returns a Boolean that indicates whether the search was successful. The first thing the function does is open this form as a modal form, passing in the `owner` argument. At this point, the control is transferred to the form and does not return until the form is closed, that is, the user has found a customer or has canceled the search. Now check the Tag property of the form. As you have seen before, you will use the Tag property of the form to indicate whether the search was successful. If the search failed, the `retVal` local variable will be set to False. The only thing you need to do in this case is unload this form from memory (using the `Unload Me` statement) and return from the function. If the search was successful, set the `obj` argument to refer to the `m_customer` data member (which at this point is the Customer object found), unload this form and set the return value of the function to True.

Continue by implementing the `Load` event of the form. Enter the following code:

```
Private Sub Form_Load()
  Me.Height = Line1.Y1 + Me.Height - Me.ScaleHeight
  lst.Visible = False
End Sub
```

The first line of code resizes the form so that only the controls above the `Line1` control are visible. You use the Line control's Y1 property to determine the height of the client area of the form, to which you add the height of the nonclient area of the form (calculated as the difference between the Height and the ScaleHeight property of the form). As you have seen before, the client area of a form is the area in which you can draw and place controls. The nonclient area is the borders and the caption bar of the form.

Note that although the List control will not be visible on the form (due to the size of the form), its Visible property is still set to True, meaning that it might receive focus. That can be disconcerting for someone using the Tab key to navigate between controls because it will seem as if the focus has disappeared. It is good practice to set the Visible property of controls that are able to receive focus that are not visually accessible to False, to prevent them from getting focus. That is the reason set the Visible property of the lst List control to False.

In the Unload event of the form you want to release the two form-level object references. Enter the following code:

```
Private Sub Form_Unload(Cancel As Integer)
  Set m_customer = Nothing
  Set m_custList = Nothing
End Sub
```

The next step is to handle the QueryUnload event in the case the user closes the form using the Close button. Enter this code:

```
Private Sub Form_QueryUnload(Cancel As Integer, UnloadMode As Integer)
  If UnloadMode <> vbFormControlMenu Then Exit Sub
  Cancel = True
  Me.Tag = False
  Me.Hide
End Sub
```

You must intercept the Unload event in this case and change it to a call to the Hide method. At the same time, set the Tag property to False.

Next, implement code that enables the user to enter either the customer ID or the customer name and city, but not both. If there is any text in the txtId, you want to clear the txtLastName and txtCity and disable them. If there is any text in the txtLastName or txtCity, you want to empty and disable the txtId. You can achieve this by implementing the Change event of the three text boxes. Let's start with the txtId. Enter the following code:

```
Private Sub txtId_Change()
  If Len(txtId) <= 0 Then
    txtLastName.Enabled = True
    txtCity.Enabled = True
  Else
    txtLastName = ""
    txtLastName.Enabled = False
    txtCity = ""
    txtCity.Enabled = False
  End If
End Sub
```

You receive the Change event every time the Text property of the control is changed, that is, the user enters or deletes data or the Text property is set from code. Use the intrinsic Len function to check whether there is any text in the control. If there is none, enable the other two TextBox controls. If there is text in this control, empty the `txtLastName` and `txtCity` (by assigning the empty string "") and disable them (by setting the Disabled property to True).

In a similar fashion implement the `Change` event for the `txtLastName`. Enter this code:

```
Private Sub txtLastName_Change()
  If Len(txtLastName) <= 0 And Len(txtCity) <= 0 Then
    txtId.Enabled = True
  Else
    txtId = ""
    txtId.Enabled = False
  End If
End Sub
```

For the `txtCity` control, enter the following code:

```
Private Sub txtCity_Change()
  If Len(txtLastName) <= 0 And Len(txtCity) <= 0 Then
    txtId.Enabled = True
  Else
    txtId = ""
    txtId.Enabled = False
  End If
End Sub
```

The code in both procedures checks to determine if there is any text in either `txtLastName` and `txtCity`. If there is no text in both, it will enable the `txtId`. Otherwise it will empty and disable the `txtId` control. The code for these previous two procedures is identical; you can create a separate private method and call it from both event procedures. You might want to try this as an exercise.

Next, implement the methods that do the search in the database. You have two cases to deal with:

- The user entered the customer ID
- The user entered the last name and/or city

Implement one method for each case. Let's start with the user entered customer ID. Enter the following code:

```
Private Sub FindById()
  Dim c As New Customer
  If Not c.Find(Val(txtId)) Then
    MsgBox "Customer with id" & Str(txtId) & _
           " was not found!", vbExclamation
    Exit Sub
  End If

  Set m_customer = c
  Me.Tag = True
```

19

```
  Me.Hide
End Sub
```

First, you created a new Customer object, then used its Find function to attempt to retrieve it from the database. If the customer is not found, the function returns False. In this case, display a message box indicating the fact to the user and exit the function. If a customer is found, the object will be populated with the data retrieved from the database. Save the reference from the object into the m_customer form-level variable, set the form Tag to True, and hide this form. Control returns to the DoModal function you implemented previously. The search was successful.

The second case, when the search criteria is customer last name and/or city, is a bit more involved. In this case, the search also might return more than one customer. If this is the case, you would like to allow the user to select which one is to be set as the result of the search. Enter the following code:

```
Private Sub FindByNameCity()
  Dim sWhere As String

  If Len(txtLastName) > 0 Then
    sWhere = "lastName LIKE '" & txtLastName & "%'"
  End If
  If Len(txtCity) > 0 Then
    If Len(sWhere) > 0 Then sWhere = sWhere & " AND "
    sWhere = sWhere & "city LIKE '" & txtCity & "%'"
  End If

  Dim coll As Collection
  Set coll = gSession.GetCustomersList(sWhere)
  If coll.Count <= 0 Then
    MsgBox "No customers match the criteria you entered", _
           vbExclamation
    Exit Sub
  End If

  If coll.Count = 1 Then
    Set m_customer = coll.Item(1)
    Me.Tag = True
    Me.Hide
    Exit Sub
  End If

  ' more than one match, allow the user to select
  If Not lst.Visible Then
    Me.Height = Me.Height * 2
    lst.Visible = True
  Else
    lst.Clear
  End If
```

```
  Dim c As Customer, i As Long
  For i = 1 To coll.Count
    Set c = coll.Item(i)
    lst.AddItem c.lastName & ", " & c.firstName & ": " & _
                c.streetAddress & ", " & c.telephone
  Next i
  Set m_custList = coll

  lblDescription.Caption = _
    "The search returned more than one match for the " & _
    "criteria you entered, please choose one customer " & _
    "from the list - double-click on the row"
  tmr.Enabled = True
  lst.SetFocus
End Sub
```

You will attempt to get a list of customers, using the criteria entered by the user (in txtLastName and/or txtCity). To get the list of customers, use the GetCustomersList method of the DbSession class, passing in a SQL WHERE clause.

The first part of the procedure constructs the SQL statement that you will send to the function that gets the list. The local variable sWhere contains the final SQL WHERE clause. If there is any text in the txtLastName, a first LIKE statement is added to the string. Note how the string is constructed so that the single quotes are placed around the actual value. Also note the wildcard % added at the end of the text. It is meant to retrieve all customers who have a last name starting with the text entered by the user.

If the txtCity is not empty, a second LIKE statement is added to the string. Note the inline If statement that checks if sWhere is empty, and if is not the " AND " string is concatenated to sWhere, before the LIKE statement for the city. At this point, you have the WHERE clause ready.

You declare a local variable of type Collection, then call the GetCustomersList method of the global object gSession. This returns a list of all customers that match the criteria. If the Count value of the collection is less than or equal to 0, you have no customers that match the criteria. Inform the user about this using a message box and then exit the procedure.

If the Count is 1, you have found exactly one object. Set the m_customer form-level variable to the one object in the collection, then set the Tag of the form to True and use the Hide method to make this form invisible. At this point the code in DOModal continues; the search has succeeded.

If the count is greater than 1, it means you have multiple customers that match. The first thing you must do is make sure the lst list is visible. If it is not, the form is in its shrunken size (as you loaded it originally). Set the height to the original value

19

(which in this case is twice the height when the list is not visible), and set the Visible property of the lst list to True. If the list was already visible, use the Clear method to remove all items in the List.

Next, add all the customers returned by the GetCustomersList method to the List control. You loop through the collection and for each Customer object in the collection you add an item to the list. The item is a string composed of the most important attributes of the customer, so the user can decide which one to choose. When you are finished with the loop, set the form-level variable m_custList to refer to the local collection represented by coll. In this way, you keep a reference to the collection of customers. You will need it when the user decides which customer to pick.

The last lines of code are used to change the caption of the lblDescription label. Inform the user what choices are available, then the Timer control is enabled. From this point on, it sends Timer events to the form. You will see shortly what you use them for. Finally, set focus to the List control.

Now you will implement the Timer event for the Timer control. As you have seen previously, this event is fired regularly every Interval milliseconds. Note that the event is fired only if the program is not busy executing some other procedure in your code. Enter the code as shown here:

```
Private Sub tmr_Timer()
  If lblDescription.ForeColor <> RGB(255, 0, 0) Then
    lblDescription.ForeColor = RGB(255, 0, 0)
  Else
    lblDescription.ForeColor = RGB(0, 0, 255)
  End If
End Sub
```

The procedure is quite simple. If the ForeColor property of the lblDescription label is red (RGB(255, 0, 0)), it is toggled to blue (RGB(0, 0, 255)), and vice versa. This means the color alternates between red and blue, which is what you wanted. The RGB intrinsic function takes three arguments that correspond to the intensities of the three basic colors, red, green, and blue, and returns the Windows color that consists of the three values combined. As you have seen before, the values of each argument can be between 0 (minimum) and 255 (maximum). For example, RGB(255, 0, 0) returns bright red, whereas RGB(0, 0, 255) returns bright blue.

 Note A timer control can be used whenever the application must perform a (normally brief) task at regular time intervals. Examples include animation and other advanced graphic functions, cache and state refresh functions, and others.

You must implement the DblClick event for the lst List control. The DblClick event occurs when the user double-clicks the list. If an item in the list was double-clicked, the ListIndex property is set to point to that item. Enter the following code:

```
Private Sub lst_DblClick()
  If lst.ListIndex < 0 Then Beep: Exit Sub
  Set m_customer = m_custList.Item(lst.ListIndex + 1)
  Me.Tag = True
  Me.Hide
End Sub
```

The code is straightforward: if an item in the list is clicked, the m_customer variable is set to the corresponding Customer object from the m_custList collection. Then the form Tag is set to True and the form is hidden, which means the search succeeded.

The final two procedures you need for this form to be fully functional are shown here (cmdSearch_Click and cmdCancel_Click):

```
Private Sub cmdSearch_Click()
  If Len(txtId) > 0 Then
    FindById
  Else
    FindByNameCity
  End If
End Sub
```

The Click event of the cmdSearch button calls one of the two private Find procedures. If the Text of the txtId is set, the FindById is called; otherwise, FindByNameCity is called. These two routines are dealing with the actual find, as you have seen previously.

```
Private Sub cmdCancel_Click()
  Me.Tag = False
  Me.Hide
End Sub
```

cmdCancel_Click is, as usual, quite simple. Set the Tag to False and hide the form. The user has canceled the search, and False is returned to the DoModal function.

The last thing you need to do is hook this form and its code with the rest of the project. You will add code to open this form from the main form. Open the main form and select from the menu bar File, Open, Customer. Enter the code as shown here:

```
Private Sub mnuFileOpenCustomer_Click()
  Dim d As New frmDlgFindCustomer, obj As Customer
  If Not d.DoModal(obj, Me) Then Exit Sub

  Dim f As New frmCustomer
  f.Show
  f.SetData obj
End Sub
```

19

The code creates a new `frmDlgFindCustomer` and calls its `DoModal` method, passing the `obj` customer local variable. If the method returns False (that is, the user has canceled the search), leave the procedure. Otherwise, create a new `frmCustomer` form and pass the retrieved object to this form to be modified as required.

Save your project. You can run the application now and try to find customers using different combinations of name and city.

The next logical step in the project is to implement a similar form for the products. However, the code is similar to the code in this form, so we leave this as an exercise for you. You can use the finalized form from the code folder on the CD (in Chapter19) as a guide.

Next Steps

In this chapter, you have implemented a Find form for the customer. You used a new control (the Timer control). You explored new properties, methods, and events of some known controls. You also implemented some advanced UI features (like dynamically sizing a dialog box and displaying a flashing label).

In the next chapter, you add a new form that displays a sortable list of customers. It will also allow the user to add, modify, and delete the customers in the list. We explore, in detail, the error-handling mechanism in VB and learn some useful coding techniques.

In this chapter

- *Adding a Tabular Data Form for the Customer*
- *Adding Code to the Customer List Form*
- *Error Handling and Reporting in Detail*

Chapter 20

Error Handling and Reporting

You will continue your journey by implementing a tabular data form; that is, a form listing the customers from the database. You also will explore the Visual Basic error handling mechanism. You will learn programming techniques that deal with error handling, reporting, and logging.

The complete code for this chapter can be found in the Chapter20 folder of the main VBFS folder on the CD that accompanies this book.

Adding a Tabular Data Form for the Customer

You would like to offer the user the capability to view the list of the customers in the database in a tabular format (in a grid). You also want the user to be able to sort this list, add new customers, modify existing customers, delete customers from the list, and view a list of all the orders for any customer in the list.

Designing the Form

Start by adding a new form to the project. Change the Name of the new form to frmCustomerList, the Caption to Customer List, and the MDIChild property to True. Also, set the ScaleMode to 3 - Pixels; you will need it when resizing the form.

Add a Frame control to the top of the form. You can use Figure 20.1, which illustrates the completed form, as a guide for the size and position of the controls. Change the Name of the Frame control to fraSettings and its Caption to an empty string.

Figure 20.1

The Customer List form.

Next, add a Label control in the upper-left corner of the frame. Change its Caption to Sort by:

Now add three OptionButton controls as a control array. Start by adding one OptionButton just underneath the label. Set its Name to optSortBy, its Caption to &Name, and its index to 0. Copy it and paste it in the frame (make sure the frame is selected when you paste). Position it underneath the other OptionButton controls. Change its Caption to &State/City/Address. Paste another copy in the frame, underneath the previous OptionButton control. Change its Caption to &Zip code. Note the use of mnemonics to enable the user to select a sort option by pressing the appropriate key combination. Select the first OptionButton by clicking on it and set its Value property to True.

Continue by adding the CommandButton controls that will permit the user to perform the refresh, add, modify, delete, and show order functions.

Add a new CommandButton to the form. Change its size and position to match Figure 20.1. Change its Name to cmdRefresh and its Caption to Refresh. You will add an icon for this button to make it more intuitive for the user. Select the Picture property in the Properties window. Click on the ellipsis button (labeled ...) that appears to the right of the value for the Picture property. A dialog box is shown, allowing you to select a picture for the button. Select the icon file named customer.ico from the Program/Res resources folder on the CD, and then click the OK button. The value of the Picture property is updated to show (icon). You also need to change the Style property of the CommandButton to 1 - Graphical. The Style property indicates whether the control is a standard button (the picture property will be ignored) or a graphical button (both the Caption and the Picture properties are composed to create the button face).

Note that the .ico extension might not be visible, depending on the settings in the Windows Explorer for your machine. In the Windows Explorer the View, Options menu opens an Options dialog box. If the Hide File Extensions for Known File

Types check box is checked, the .ico extension will not be visible when you select icons.

Select and copy this control, then paste it into the frame to the right of the first control. Visual Basic asks you if you want to create a control array; select the No button. Change the Name of the pasted control to cmdAddNew and its Caption to Add New.

Repeat the paste operation. Change the Name of the pasted control to cmdEdit and its Caption to &Edit. Repeat the operation for the Delete button. Set its Name to cmdDelete and its Caption to &Delete.

Repeat the paste one more time for the Show Orders button. Set its Name to cmdOrders and its Caption to Show &Orders. Select the Picture property in the Properties window. Select a different icon for this button. Click the ellipsis button and select the icon file order.ico from the Program/Res resources folder on the CD.

The last control you need to add on this form is the grid that holds the list of customers. Select the MSFlexGrid control from the toolbox, and then add it to the form as shown in Figure 20.1. Change its name to grd, and the Cols property to 8 (you need eight columns, one for each attribute of the Customer class that you display in the list).

You are finished with the graphical design of this Customer list form. Next, you will add code to implement the miscellaneous functions you need here.

Adding Code to the Customer List Form

You want this form to be used in two different modes:

- As a list of all the customers in the database
- As a filtered list of customers, showing only a subset of the customers in the database

In the first case, you will implement the whole functionality, that is, sort, add, and so on. The second case will be a read-only list, for example, to show all the customers who ordered a specific product. In the latter case, you do not need the capability to sort, add, modify, or delete customers, so you will have to disable these functions.

Use a module-level Boolean variable to distinguish between the two modes in which this form operates. Open the code editor for the form and enter the following module-level declarations—frmCustomerList(CustomerList.frm)—at the top of the form module, just under the Option Explicit statement:

```
Private m_filtered As Boolean
Private m_custList As Collection
```

The `m_filtered` variable is the Boolean flag described previously. You also need a Collection object reference to the list of Customer objects that this list contains (the `m_custList` variable).

Now you need to set the column headers and widths of the grid control. You do this once when the form is loaded. Select the `Load` event for the form and enter the following code, `frmCustomerList(CustomerList.frm)`:

```
Private Sub Form_Load()
  grd.Rows = 1
  grd.ColWidth(0) = 360
  grd.ColWidth(1) = 2160
  grd.ColWidth(2) = 2160
  grd.ColWidth(3) = 1080
  grd.ColWidth(4) = 540
  grd.ColWidth(5) = 720
  grd.ColWidth(6) = 1440
  grd.ColWidth(7) = 1440
  grd.Row = 0
  grd.Col = 0: grd.Text = "Id"
  grd.Col = 1: grd.Text = "Name"
  grd.Col = 2: grd.Text = "Address"
  grd.Col = 3: grd.Text = "City"
  grd.Col = 4: grd.Text = "State"
  grd.Col = 5: grd.Text = "Zip"
  grd.Col = 6: grd.Text = "Phone"
  grd.Col = 7: grd.Text = "EMail"
End Sub
```

Set the number of rows in the grid control (grd) to 1 using the Rows property; that is, only the column headers are visible when the form is loaded. Then, set the width (in twips) of each column, using the ColWidth indexed property. Next, set the column headers for row 0, using the Col and Text properties of grd.

Next, you need to handle the `Resize` event of the form in order to adjust the size and position of the controls when the user resizes the form. Note that the `Resize` event is rarely used if the form BorderStyle property is set to a setting that does not allow the user to resize the form, like `vbFixedSingle` or `vbFixedDouble` (dialog). Enter the following code—frmCustomerList(CustomerList.frm)—in the `Resize` event procedure for the form:

```
Private Sub Form_Resize()
  If Me.WindowState = vbMinimized Then Exit Sub

  Const m = 5

  Dim w As Single, h As Single, t As Single
```

```
    w = Me.ScaleWidth - 2 * m
    If w <= 0 Then Exit Sub
    If m_filtered Then
      fraSettings.Visible = False
      h = Me.ScaleHeight - 2 * m
      If h <= 0 Then Exit Sub
      grd.Move m, m, w, h
    Else
      fraSettings.Visible = True
      fraSettings.Move m, m, w
      t = fraSettings.Top + fraSettings.Height + m
      h = Me.ScaleHeight - m - t
      If h <= 0 Then Exit Sub
      grd.Move m, t, w, h
    End If
End Sub
```

You can ensure that the form is not minimized (iconic) by checking its WindowState property. If it is, you have nothing to resize so exit the procedure.

Note the declaration of the constant m (set to 5 pixels). You will use it in the calculations that follow as the size of the border (margin) between the frame/grid controls and the form. You also declare three variables of Single type also used later.

Compute the width of the grid and frame controls by subtracting two margins, m (left and right), from the current ScaleWidth of the form and assigning it to variable w. If the width is 0 or negative, leave the procedure (you cannot set the width of any control to a negative value).

The next step is to use the m_filtered flag to distinguish between the two modes under which this form operates. If m_filtered is True then you are displaying a read-only list (the Then branch of the If statement). Hide the fraSettings Frame control by setting its Visible property to False. In this way, you hide all the controls that the Frame control contains. Then, you compute the height of the grid control that now fills the entire form, minus the two margins (top and bottom). If h is 0 or negative, you cannot resize the control, so exit the procedure. Otherwise move the grid control to the upper-left corner of the form (leaving m margins), at the same time resizing it to w width and h height (using the Move method).

If m_filtered is False, you have both the frame and grid visible. First, move the frame to the upper-left corner of the form (leaving the margins) and adjust its width to w. Note that you did not change the height of the frame by omitting the last optional argument of the Move method. We then calculate the top coordinate of the grid control and place the resulting value into the local t variable. The top coordinate of the grid should be just under the frame, leaving m pixels between them. Hence, it is the Top + the Height of the frame + m. The Height of the grid must now be the rest of the form. Compute it as the difference between the form's ScaleHeight and the t coordinate, also leaving a margin m at the bottom. If the value of h is 0 or negative, you cannot resize the grid, therefore exit the procedure. Otherwise, move the grid control to its new position and size using the MoveMethod.

You must release the module-level object reference you hold to the list of customers. Do this in the Unload event of the form. Enter the following code— frmCustomerList(CustomerList.frm):

```
Private Sub Form_Unload(Cancel As Integer)
  Set m_custList = Nothing
End Sub
```

You now need to add a public method that sets the *modus operandi* for this form, as well as passes in a reference to the collection object containing the subset of customers to display (if operating as a filtered list). Add the following code— frmCustomerList(CustomerList.frm):

```
Public Sub SetData(Optional coll As Collection)
  If Not coll Is Nothing Then
    m_filtered = True
    Set m_custList = coll
  End If
  RefreshGrid
  Form_Resize
End Sub
```

The public procedure enables the callers to pass in the collection reference, which can be Nothing. Note the use of the operator Is in conjunction with the Nothing keyword to determine whether an object reference variable holds a valid object or is empty (holds nothing).

If the coll argument is set to a valid collection, set m_filtered to True and save the coll reference into the module-level variable m_custList. We then refresh the grid (using a procedure that you will implement next) and directly calls the Form_Resize event procedure.

 Note Note that the form and control event procedures can normally be called directly (that is, without the actual event to happen, in this case, the size of the form did not change). However, this is not recommended practice because some event procedures might assume that the environment (Visual Basic runtime) is in a specific state. If that is not the case when you call the function directly, you might crash Visual Basic or your application.

Next, add a procedure to refresh the contents of the grid control. Add the following code—frmCustomerList(CustomerList.frm):

```
Private Sub RefreshGrid()
  Dim sOrd As String

  If Not m_filtered Then
    If optSortBy(1).Value Then
      sOrd = "state, city, streetAddress"
    ElseIf optSortBy(2).Value Then
      sOrd = "zip"
    Else
      sOrd = "lastName, firstName, middleInitial"
    End If
    Set m_custList = gSession.GetCustomersList("", sOrd)
  End If

  Dim o As Customer, i As Long, sRow As String

  grd.Rows = 1
  For i = 1 To m_custList.Count
    Set o = m_custList.Item(i)
    sRow = LTrim(Str(o.id)) & vbTab
    sRow = sRow & o.fullName & vbTab
    sRow = sRow & o.streetAddress & vbTab
    sRow = sRow & o.city & vbTab
    sRow = sRow & o.state & vbTab
    sRow = sRow & o.zip & vbTab
    sRow = sRow & o.telephone & vbTab
    sRow = sRow & o.email
    grd.AddItem sRow
  Next i
End Sub
```

The procedure is divided into two logical parts: first you retrieve the list of customers from the database (if m_filtered is False only), then you populate the grid from the collection of Customer objects in m_custList (either from the database or passed in using the SetData method).

If m_filtered is False, in the first part of the procedure, you determine the sort criteria for the list. You achieve this by checking the Value property of the three OptionButton controls in the optSortBy control array. Depending on this value, you set the sOrd local variable String to the appropriate value for the three cases. Note that the control array is 0-based, which means the Else part of the If statement corresponds to the first button, functioning also as a default. Then you get the list using the GetCustomersList method of the gSession global object.

In the second part of the procedure, you populate the grid control using the same method you used for the grid on the frmOrder. For each Customer object in the

20

collection you construct a string by concatenating all the attributes for that customer, using the tab character to delimit each value. Then, use the `AddItem` method of the grid control to add the whole row at once.

In the Edit, Delete, and ShowOrder procedures, you need to find out the Customer object corresponding to the currently selected row in the grid (the one that the user intends to edit, delete, or see orders for). To add a private function to implement this functionality, add the following code—frmCustomerList(`CustomerList.frm`):

```
Private Function GetCurrentCustomer() As Customer
  Dim r As Long
  r = grd.Row
  If r <= 0 Then Beep: Exit Function

  Set GetCurrentCustomer = m_custList.Item(r)
End Function
```

The function returns a Customer object if the grid is positioned on a valid row, or `Nothing` if not. First, you get the value of the Row property of the grid. If it is negative or zero, it means no row or the column headers row is selected, respectively. Exit the function, returning Nothing in this case (because no current customer is selected). Otherwise, use the `Set` operator to return a reference to the corresponding Customer object in the module-level collection variable.

You can now add code to handle the Click events for the command buttons on the form. Let's start with the Refresh button. Add this code—frmCustomerList(`CustomerList.frm`):

```
Private Sub cmdRefresh_Click()
  RefreshGrid
End Sub
```

The single line of code in this procedure calls the RefreshGrid procedure you implemented previously. Continue with the Add New button. Enter the code as shown here—frmCustomerList(`CustomerList.frm`):

```
Private Sub cmdAddNew_Click()
  Dim f As New frmCustomer, obj As New Customer
  f.Show
  f.SetData obj
End Sub
```

This code is identical to the similar procedure in the main form. It creates a new `frmCustomer` form and a new Customer object, then opens the form and sets its data.

The `cmdEdit` Click event procedure is quite simple: retrieve the current Customer object. If `Nothing` is returned, exit the procedure. Otherwise, create and open a new customer form and pass the object to it.

Enter this code—frmCustomerList(CustomerList.frm):

```
Private Sub cmdEdit_Click()
  Dim obj As Customer
  Set obj = GetCurrentCustomer()
  If obj Is Nothing Then Exit Sub
  Dim f As New frmCustomer
  f.Show
  f.SetData obj
End Sub
```

The code for cmdDelete_Click is shown here—
frmCustomerList(CustomerList.frm):

```
Private Sub cmdDelete_Click()
  Dim obj As Customer
  Set obj = GetCurrentCustomer()
  If obj Is Nothing Then Exit Sub

  On Error GoTo cmdDelete_Fail
  If obj.Delete() Then
    RefreshGrid
  End If
  Exit Sub
cmdDelete_Fail:
  MsgBox Err.description, vbInformation, Err.Source
End Sub
```

First, you fetch the object to be deleted from the list. If there is none, then you exit. Otherwise, you attempt to delete it. The delete method might fail (for example, if a customer has active orders, the database engine will reject the delete operation, stating that the relational integrity of the database would be violated. At this point, the Delete method fails and an error is raised. If you do not handle this error, the application will crash as we have seen briefly before. You can handle this error by installing an error handler. This is exactly what the On Error GoTo <label> statement does. It tells Visual Basic that if an error occurs between the line following this statement and the end of the procedure, it should transfer execution control to the statement following the <label> (in this example cmdDelete_Fail). In this case, the first statement after the label displays a message box that lets the user know what happened, and then the procedure ends.

In Visual Basic, the global object named Err represents the last error that occurred. This object has properties and methods as any other object, but only one instance of it exists in your application. The Description property is a string associated with the error, which describes what happened. The Source property normally indicates what module the error comes from. We will discuss error handling and reporting in detail later in this chapter.

20

If the `Delete` method is successful, the grid is refreshed to show the changes. Note the `Exit sub` statement just above the `cmbDelete_Click` label: this statement avoids displaying an error message when no error happened.

Next, you need to add code for the `cmdOrders_Click` event procedure. This procedure is supposed to show a list of orders for this customer. You need to add a method to retrieve a list of orders from the database, similar to the `GetCustomersList` method of the `DbSession` class. You also will add it on the `DbSession`. Open the `DbSession` class module and add the code as shown here—`DbSession(DbSession.cls)`. A discussion of the code follows.

```
Public Function GetOrdersList(Optional whereClause As String = "", _
                              Optional orderBy As String = "" _
                              ) As Collection
  On Error GoTo GetOrdersList_Fail

  Dim conn As ADODB.Connection
  Set conn = GetConn()
  If conn Is Nothing Then Exit Function

  Dim sSQL As String
  sSQL = "SELECT * FROM TOrders "

  If Len(whereClause) > 0 Then
    sSQL = sSQL & "WHERE " & whereClause
  End If
  If Len(orderBy) > 0 Then
    sSQL = sSQL & " ORDER BY " & orderBy
  Else
    sSQL = sSQL & " ORDER BY TOrders.dateEntered"
  End If

  Dim rs As New ADODB.Recordset
  rs.Open sSQL, conn, adOpenStatic, adLockReadOnly

  Dim coll As New Collection, obj As Order
  Do While Not rs.EOF
    Set obj = New Order
    obj.FromRs rs
    coll.Add obj, LTrim(Str(obj.id))
    rs.MoveNext
  Loop
  Set GetOrdersList = coll
GetOrdersList_Exit:
  Exit Function

GetOrdersList_Fail:
  If MsgBox(Err.description, vbCritical + vbRetryCancel, _
            Err.Source) = vbRetry Then
    Resume
```

```
    End If
    Resume GetOrdersList_Exit
End Function
```

The method is similar to the GetCustomersList and GetProductsList you implemented previously. The difference is that you added more involved error handling code. Let's start by analyzing what the procedure does first, we will talk about the error handling code later.

The method takes two optional arguments of type String that represent the WHERE and ORDER BY clauses of the SQL statement you will build.

First, open a connection to the database. If no connection could be established, exit the procedure. Continue by constructing the SQL statement that will be used to fetch the records from the database. Start with the SELECT and FROM clauses, then add the WHERE and ORDER BY clauses if they are present. At this point, you have built the complete SQL statement.

Create a new ADO recordset and open it using the connection and SQL string. Open the recordset as static and read-only because you are fetching data only. Then, create a new Collection object to store the retrieved Customer objects. You iterate through the recordset and for each row you construct a new Customer object, populate it from the recordset, and add it to the Collection object. Then, set the return value of the function to refer to the coll object and exit the function.

This is how the procedure operates under normal conditions. Let's see what happens when an error occurs.

Error Handling and Reporting in Detail

An *error* is an abnormal condition that can occur when running an application. Many things can cause an error to occur: invalid user input, invalid data in a file or database, resources exceeded (database connections, memory, disk space, and so on), programming deficiency, and many others. If an error occurs while the user runs the application and is not caught by the application code, the operating system (OS) will display a brief and cryptic message and will terminate the application. This is not what the users are expecting from a well-written application. The correct way to deal with errors is to catch them, display a meaningful error message so that the user understands what caused the error, and if possible correct it. Eventually, you must log the error, especially if the application runs in unattended mode (that is, no users). If the error is recoverable, attempt to recover, or ignore it. If it is unrecoverable; that is, a critical function of the application has failed, attempt to exit gracefully, closing down database connections, closing any open files, and so on.

Error handling is also known as error trapping or catching.

As you have seen previously in Visual Basic, the last error is represented by the Err global and unique object. The VB runtime will set the properties for this object when an error occurs. Then it will look for an active error handler. An error handler is a statement that tells VB what to do if an error occurs in a portion of code. We have seen the On Error GoTo and On Error Resume Next error-handler statements. The first one tells VB that in case of an error, the execution of the program should continue with the statement immediately following the label specified. On Error Resume Next specifies that in case of an error the next statement should be executed (that is, in effect ignoring any errors while this statement is active). An error handler is active starting with the statement immediately following and ends when one of the following conditions occur:

- The function, sub, or property is exited (either through the Exit ? or the End ? statements
- Another error handler is encountered
- The On Error GoTo 0 statement is encountered

The On Error GoTo 0 statement is used to disable any error handling. It also clears the Err object, resetting all its properties to blank (empty) values. If another error handler is encountered, that handler becomes the active handler. If any of the Exit Sub, Exit Function, Exit Property, End Sub, End Function, or End Property statements occurs, the error handler is deactivated (by being out of scope) and the Err object is cleared.

It is important to understand that error handling is hierarchical. That means that if a procedure X that has an active error handler calls another procedure Y that does not have an error handler, and if an error occurs, the error will be caught in the error handler of procedure X, although it has occurred in procedure Y.

This means that in case of an error, VB looks for an active handler first by searching for an active handler in the current procedure. If one is present it will use it. If none is present it will search the procedure that has called the current procedure. If this one has an error handler it will use it, otherwise it will go on searching the procedure that called that procedure until it finds an error handler or it reaches the top level procedure (normally an event procedure on a form). At this point, if the error was not handled it will display a message box stating the error number and description and it will halt execution.

The error-handling code (in this case the code following the GetOrdersList_Fail label) usually displays an error message and then it can proceed in one of three ways:

- Use a `Resume` statement to re-execute the statement that caused the error
- Use a `Resume Next` statement to continue with the next statement after the one that caused the error
- Do something else, for example clean up and exit the procedure

In this case, you offer the user the chance to retry the statement that caused the error or to cancel the operation and exit the procedure. The retry (using the `Resume` statement) is useful in cases when a database connection failed or a table is locked by someone else. The user can wait a few minutes and try again or cancel and exit.

It is important to understand the way `Resume` and `Resume Next` work in the case where the active handler is not in the same procedure as the statement that caused the error. Consider the following example:

```
Private Sub X()
  On Error GoTo X_Fail
  Dim i As Long
  Y i
  Exit Sub

X_Fail:
  If MsgBox(Err.Description, vbRetryCancel) = vbRetry Then
     Resume
  End If
End Sub

Private Sub Y(i As Long)
  Dim j As Long

  i = i + 1
  i = i / j  ' will fail, j = 0
End Sub
```

The procedure X has an error handler that directs Visual Basic to, in case of an error, branch control to the `If` statement following the X_Fail label. Procedure X declares a Long variable i and passes in by reference to procedure Y. Y increments the value of i by one and then divides it by j. Because j is 0, it generates a Division by zero error. At this point, Visual Basic searches for an error handler in Y. Not finding one, it continues to search the caller of Y, that is, X, for an event handler. It finds the `On Error GoTo X_Fail` and continues by executing the `If` statement after the label. The Retry-Cancel message box is displayed next. If the user selects Retry, the `Resume` statement will be executed. The execution will not resume with the actual statement that caused the error (`i = i / j`) but rather with the call to the procedure that caused the error, that is with the `Y i` line of code, in the same procedure. It is important to understand that the error appears to have taken place on the line of code that called the procedure that contains the statement that caused the error, and not on the actual statement that caused the error to be raised.

An important method of the Error object is the `Raise` method that allows you to generate your own custom errors. The `Raise` method takes five arguments described here:

Name	Description
Number	The error number, between 0 and 65535. Range 0–512 is reserved by VB.
Source	Source of the error (string formatted as project.module)
Description	Description of the error (string)
Helpfile	Name of a help file that contains more help regarding this error (string)
Helpcontext	Context ID in the above help file (Long)

Except for `Number`, all other arguments are optional. Invoking `Err.Raise` is equivalent to generating an error, which will be treated as any normal error by VB: it will search for a handler, if none is found, the application will be halted. If you use the `Raise` method in class modules, you must set the `Number` argument using the intrinsic constant `vbObjectError` as a base (for example, to Raise error with number 1000, use

```
Err.Raise vbObjectError + 1000, "My description for error 1000"
```

Continue by implementing a method to get all the orders for one customer in the `Customer` class. Open the class module `Customer` and add the following code—`Customer(Customer.cls)`:

```
Public Function GetOrders() As Collection
  Dim sWhere As String
  sWhere = "customerId =" & Str(m_id)
  Set GetOrders = gSession.GetOrdersList(sWhere)
End Function
```

The method uses the `m_id` private data member to construct the SQL `WHERE` clause then returns the collection returned by the `GetOrdersList` method of the global `gSession` object.

Now you can implement the `Click` event handler for the `cmdOrders` button. Enter the following code—`frmCustomerList(CustomerList.frm)`:

```
Private Sub cmdOrders_Click()
  Dim obj As Customer
  Set obj = GetCurrentCustomer()
  If obj Is Nothing Then Exit Sub
```

```
   Dim c As Collection
   Set c = obj.GetOrders

   'Dim f As New frmOrderList
   'f.Show
   'f.SetData c
End Sub
```

You get the current customer first. If there is none, you exit the procedure. Then, you get a Collection object with all the orders for this Customer object using the method that you implemented previously of the Customer class. Next, open the form that shows the list of all orders, but because you did not implement it, comment the code out.

You have concluded the development of this form, for now. You will return and uncomment the snippet of code that opens the Orders List form, after you implement that form.

The final thing you must do is to add code to the frmMain to open this form when the menu item is clicked.

Open the form module for the main form in the code editor and add the following code—frmMain(Main.frm):

```
Private Sub mnuViewCustList_Click()
  Dim f As New frmCustomerList
  f.Show
  f.SetData
End Sub
```

Save your project and try the new form you added to your project.

Next Steps

In this chapter, you have seen how to create a tabular data form used to show multiple objects as rows in a grid. You have also explored in detail the error handling and reporting mechanism of Visual Basic. You also have studied the properties and methods of the Err built-in object.

In the next chapter, you will learn how to print from Visual Basic. You will implement a dialog box that enables the user to select a printer and set its properties, then you will implement the code required to print an order.

In this chapter

- *Adding a Custom Printer Selection Dialog Box*
- *Printing an Order*

Chapter 21

Printing

You will continue your journey by adding printing capabilities to your project. You will design and implement a modal form (dialog) that will enable the user to select a printer and set some of its properties. Then you will add code to print an order.

The complete code for this chapter can be found in the Chapter21 folder of the main VBFS folder on the CD that accompanies this book.

Adding a Custom Printer Selection Dialog Box

In Visual Basic, the currently selected printer is represented by a global object named Printer. You cannot create new instances of this object, but you can change its properties and invoke its methods. Also, Visual Basic offers a list of all printers available on the machine where the application is executed in the form of a global collection object named Printers. You cannot add or remove Printer objects from this collection, but you can set the current printer to be any Printer object in the collection, as you will see later on.

You will need the capability to let the user choose the physical printer to which the print output is going, and also to select some print settings for that printer. You will achieve this by designing and implementing a new dialog box for printer selection.

 Note

You can use the Common Dialog control to display the Windows standard Printer Selection dialog box. The usage is similar to the File Open dialog box you saw in Chapter 11. In this example you will build a custom dialog box to illustrate some of the properties of the built-in Printer object.

Designing the Form

Begin by adding a new form to the project. Change the Name of the new form to `frmDlgSelectPrinter`, the Caption to Select Printer, the BorderStyle property to 3 - Fixed Dialog, and the StartUpPosition property to 1 - CenterOwner.

Add a List control in the upper-left corner of the form. You can use Figure 21.1, which illustrates the completed form, as a guide for the size and position of the controls. Change the Name of the List control to `lst`. It is better to change its IntegralHeight property to False, so that you can align it better, but that's up to you.

Figure 21.1

The Select Printer dialog box.

Add a Label control to the right of the list. Change its Caption to Copies:. Next to it add a TextBox control. Change its Text property to 1 (you will print one copy by default), set its name to `txtCopies`, its Alignment to right justified, and its MaxLength property to 2. The maximum number of copies is limited to 99, so setting the MaxLength to 2 prevents the user from entering a larger number causing an error.

Add a CheckBox control underneath the list. Change its Caption to Use color if available, its Name to `chkColors`, and its Value property to Checked.

Underneath the CheckBox add a small Frame control for the page orientation. Change its Caption to Page Orientation.

In this Frame control, add an OptionButton control. Set its Name to `optPageOrientation`, its Caption to Portrait, and its Index to 0 (to avoid being asked by VB if you want to create a control array). Now copy this control, and then select the frame and paste a copy of it into the frame. Change the Caption of the pasted control to Landscape. Now select the OptionButton labeled Portrait and set its Value property to True (which in this way becomes the default).

Add another Frame control to the right of this one. Change its Caption to Print Quality. Add a new OptionButton control into this frame. Change the OptionButton's Name to `optPrintQuality`, its Caption to Draft, and its Index to 0.

Copy it and paste a copy of it three times in the same frame as the original. Position them as shown in Figure 21.1, and then change their Captions to Low, Medium, and High.

Add a CommandButton to the form in the upper-right corner. Change its Caption to &Print, its Name to cmdPrint, and its Default property to True.

Add a new CommandButton control just underneath the cmdPrint. Set its Caption to &Cancel, its Name to cmdCancel, and its Cancel property to False.

Now you have finished designing your dialog box. Next, you will add code to populate the list of printers, set the print properties, and handle events from the controls on this form.

Adding Code to the Select Printer Dialog Box

Start by populating the list of available printers using the Printers collection global object. The best place to do that is when the form is loaded; that is, in the Form_Load event procedure. Open the form module code editor window and enter the code as shown here (frmDlgSelectPrinter(DlgSelectPrinter.frm)):

```
Private Sub Form_Load()
  Dim i As Long, p As Printer
  For i = 0 To Printers.Count - 1
    Set p = Printers(i)
    lst.AddItem p.DeviceName & " [" & p.DriverName & "]"
  Next
End Sub
```

First, declare two local variables: one (i) of Long type for the loop counter and the other (p) of Printer type. Note that the Printers collection is 0-based (unlike the regular Collection objects). For each Printer object in the collection, you get a reference to it and add it to the lst List control. You use the AddItem method to add (for each printer) a string composed of the printer name and its driver name (in square brackets). The DeviceName property of a Printer object returns the name as set in the Windows Control Panel under the Printers dialog box. The DriverName property returns the name of the actual driver that will be used for that printer (it is usually a DLL name).

Next, implement the QueryUnload event (as you did for all dialog boxes) to prevent the code that uses this dialog box from crashing if the user is closing the dialog box using the Close button rather than using the Cancel button provided. Enter the code as here (frmDlgSelectPrinter(DlgSelectPrinter.frm)):

```
Private Sub Form_QueryUnload(Cancel As Integer, UnloadMode As Integer)
  If UnloadMode <> vbFormControlMenu Then Exit Sub
  Cancel = True
```

21

```
  Me.Tag = False
  Me.Hide
End Sub
```

You use the Tag property of the form to indicate to the code that uses this dialog box that the user has selected a printer (Tag value set to True) or has canceled the print operation (Tag value set to False). In this procedure, you set the Cancel to true (to avoid unloading the form) and set the Tag to False and hide this form, which is the equivalent of the Cancel_Click event.

Next, you need to handle the Click event of the cmdCancel control. Enter the following code (frmDlgSelectPrinter(DlgSelectPrinter.frm)):

```
Private Sub cmdCancel_Click()
  Me.Tag = False
  Me.Hide
End Sub
```

Set the Tag property of this form to False and use the Hide method of this form to make it invisible, so that the code that called this form can continue. Next, you add code for the cmdPrint (frmDlgSelectPrinter(DlgSelectPrinter.frm)).

```
Private Sub cmdPrint_Click()
  If lst.ListIndex < 0 Then Beep: Exit Sub
  If Not SetPrinter() Then Exit Sub
  Me.Tag = True
  Me.Hide
End Sub
```

First, make sure a valid item was selected from the lst list. If no current printer is selected, you just alert the user and exit. If there is a printer, you attempt to set its properties using the SetPrinter function, which you will implement shortly. If SetPrinter returns True, set the Tag property of the form to True and hide this form. Otherwise (if SetPrinter returns False), exit the procedure.

Setting Printer Properties

Now implement the SetPrinter procedure as a private member of this form. Enter the code as shown here (frmDlgSelectPrinter(DlgSelectPrinter.frm)):

```
Private Function SetPrinter() As Boolean
  Set Printer = Printers(lst.ListIndex)

  On Error GoTo SetPrinter_Fail
  Dim sFeature As String

  sFeature = "Copies"
  Printer.Copies = Val(txtCopies)

  sFeature = "ColorMode"
```

```
   If chkColor.Value = vbChecked Then
      Printer.ColorMode = vbPRCMColor
   Else
      Printer.ColorMode = vbPRCMMonochrome
   End If

   sFeature = "Orientation"
   If optPageOrientation(0).Value Then
      Printer.Orientation = vbPRORPortrait
   Else
      Printer.Orientation = vbPRORLandscape
   End If

   sFeature = "PrintQuality"
   If optPrintQuality(0).Value Then
      Printer.PrintQuality = vbPRPQDraft
   ElseIf optPrintQuality(1).Value Then
      Printer.PrintQuality = vbPRPQLow
   ElseIf optPrintQuality(2).Value Then
      Printer.PrintQuality = vbPRPQMedium
   Else
      Printer.PrintQuality = vbPRPQHigh
   End If
   SetPrinter = True
   Exit Function

SetPrinter_Fail:
   Dim retVal As VbMsgBoxResult
   retVal = MsgBox(Err.description & vbCrLf & _
                   "Feature: " & sFeature, _
                   vbAbortRetryIgnore + vbExclamation, _
                   Err.Source)
   If retVal = vbRetry Then
      Resume
   ElseIf retVal = vbIgnore Then
      Resume Next
   Else
      Exit Function
   End If
End Sub
```

First, set the Printer global object to be the printer the user selected from the list. Use the ListIndex property of the List control to retrieve the corresponding Printer reference from the collection.

Next, tell Visual Basic that, in case of an error, it should branch execution to the code following the SetPrinter_Fail label. You expect that an error will occur if the selected printer does not support a specific feature you are trying to set. Because the error message in that case is generic (that is, does not tell the user which feature is not supported), declare a local String variable (sFeature) to hold the name of each feature as you set it. If the assignment to the Printer property fails, this variable will hold the name of the feature that failed. You will use it in the code that handles the error.

Then, set the Copies property of the Printer object to the number of copies entered by the user in the txtCopies TextBox control. The value of this property indicates the number of copies the printer will print. Not all printers support this property (for example, Laser printers generally support it, while inkjets generally do not).

Next, set the value of the ColorMode property. This property is used to indicate whether the printer should use color (if available) or shades of gray to emulate color. The two constants vbPRCMColor and vbPRCMMonochrome are intrinsic VB constants. If the printer is not color, this property is not supported.

Next, set the PageOrientation property using intrinsic constants. This property can be portrait or landscape. Not all printers support both settings.

Finally, set the PrintQuality property using the VB intrinsic constants as shown previously, based on the selected control of the optPrintQuality control array. Note that you also can set this property to a value, in dots per inch (dpi). For example, to use your printer's 600 dpi resolution, set the PrintQuality to 600.

If everything is okay, return True (by setting the SetPrinter function name to True and then exiting the function). If an error occurs, you display an Abort/Retry/Ignore message box with the description of the error that occurred, concatenated with the name of the feature that caused the failure from the sFeature local variable. Depending on the action the user chooses, you will retry the statement that caused the error (using the Resume statement), ignore the offending statement (using the Resume Next statement), or leave the function (implicitly returning False).

As a convenience for the user, implement the DblCLick event for the list to enable the user to select from the list by double-clicking (instead of selecting from the list and then clicking the Print button). Add the following code (frmDlgSelectPrinter(DlgSelectPrinter.frm)):

```
Private Sub lst_DblClick()
  cmdPrint_Click
End Sub
```

In this procedure, you simply call the cmdPrint_Click event procedure.

You now are finished implementing the Select Printer dialog box. Next, you will add code to the order form to print an order after it is saved, where we will use our select printer dialog.

Printing an Order

You will make a few changes to the order entry form. You will add a Print button and remove the line of code that closes the order form when the save operation is finished.

Open the frmOrder form. Add a new CommandButton control in the lower-right corner, as shown in Figure 21.2. Change its Caption to Print Order and its Name to cmdPrint. In the Properties window, select the Picture property of this control, then use the ellipsis button to open the Add Picture dialog box. From the Program/Res resource folder on the CD, select the icon file named customer.ico. Do not set the button style to graphical. You will use this picture as a logo on the printed order.

Figure 21.2

The modified order entry form.

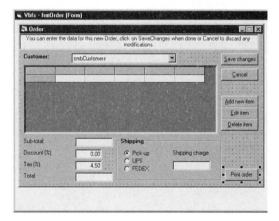

First, remove a line of code from the cmdSave_Click event procedure to prevent closing this form when the order is finished. Remove the line of code in bold type shown here (frmDlgSelectPrinter(DlgSelectPrinter.frm)):

```
Private Sub cmdSave_Click()
  If cmbCustomers.ListIndex < 0 Then
    Beep
    MsgBox "A customer must be selected!"
    cmbCustomers.SetFocus
    Exit Sub
  End If

  Dim cust As New Customer, id As Long
  id = cmbCustomers.ItemData(cmbCustomers.ListIndex)
  If Not cust.Find(id) Then
    Beep
    MsgBox "Invalid customer!"
    RefreshCustomersList
    cmbCustomers.SetFocus
```

21

```
    Exit Sub
  End If

  m_order.OrdEnter cust, Now, Me.shipType, Val(Me.txtDiscount), _
                   Val(Me.txtTax), Val(Me.txtShippingCharge)


  If Not m_order.SaveOrder() Then Exit Sub
  m_saved = True
  Unload Me
End Sub
```

Now double-click on the cmdPrint control to create the empty Click event procedure. Enter the following code (frmDlgSelectPrinter(DlgSelectPrinter.frm)):

```
Private Sub cmdPrint_Click()
  If Not m_saved Then
    MsgBox "Order must be saved first!", vbInformation, "Print order"
    cmdSave.SetFocus
    Exit Sub
  End If

  Dim f As New frmDlgSelectPrinter, r As Boolean
  f.Show vbModal, frmMain
  r = CBool(f.Tag)
  Unload f
  If Not r Then Exit Sub

  PrintOrder
End Sub
```

First, check to see that the order is saved; an unsaved order does not have an order number. If the m_saved form-level variable is False, inform the user, set focus to the Save button to give him or her a hint, and leave this procedure.

If the order is saved, you can proceed to print it. First, let the user select a printer and set its properties using the Select Printer dialog box. To achieve this, use the Show method with the modal flag set and pass the frmMain as an owner of the dialog (so that is displayed centered within the main form).

When the user has finished selecting a printer, the dialog box will be hidden and the control returned to the statement following the Show method. You assign to the local variable r the value of the Tag property of the dialog f (converted to Boolean). This value tells you whether the user has selected a printer or has cancelled the operation. In either case, you must unload the dialog box. Then, if the value was False, you exit the procedure, otherwise you print the order using the PrintOrder procedure that you will implement shortly. First, you need to add two utility functions that will pad a string with spaces up to a given length. Open the modMain module in the code editor and add the following code (modMain(Main.bas)):

```
Public Function Padr(ByVal src As String, trgLen As Long) As String
  If trgLen <= 0 Then
    Err.Raise 32767, "Vbfs.modMain", "Invalid arguments passed to Padr"
  End If
  If Len(src) >= trgLen Then
    Padr = Left(src, trgLen)
  Else
    Padr = src & String(trgLen - Len(src), " ")
  End If
End Function
```

This first method adds the required number of spaces to the src argument, so that it ends up being trgLen characters long. If trgLen is less than or equal to zero, raise an error. If the length of the src string is greater than or equal to trgLen, return the trgLen leftmost characters of src. Otherwise, you concatenate src with the required number of spaces so that it ends up trgLen characters long. In both cases, you return the string by assigning it to the Padr function name.

The second function does a similar padding, but the spaces are added to the left (beginning) of the src string. Enter the code as shown here:

```
Public Function Padl(ByVal src As String, trgLen As Long) As String
  If trgLen <= 0 Then
    Err.Raise 32767, "Vbfs.modMain", "Invalid arguments passed to Padl"
  End If
  If Len(src) >= trgLen Then
    Padl = Right(src, trgLen)
  Else
    Padl = String(trgLen - Len(src), " ") & src
  End If
End Function
```

You can now return to the frmOrder form module.

The PrintOrder procedure is a rather long routine, so to dissect it we will step through each portion of the code. Enter the code as shown here (frmDlgSelectPrinter(DlgSelectPrinter.frm)):

21

```
Private Sub PrintOrder()
  On Error Resume Next

  Printer.Font.Size = 12
```

First, tell VB that you want to ignore any error that might occur during printing. For example, if a specific printer feature is not available, you will skip the statement that uses it.

Next, set the Size property of the Font object used by the Printer to 12. Font and StdFont are VB intrinsic classes used to abstract the fonts used by miscellaneous objects in Windows. The Font objects are present as properties of the objects. You cannot create a new Font object, but you can get a reference to one and set its properties. For example, you can set the Size property of the Font object of the Printer object. The StdFont objects can be created with the New keyword and their properties can be set as required. You can then assign a StdFont object to the Font property of another object. Their properties are presented in Table 21.1.

Table 21.1 Font and StdFont Object Properties

Property	Type	Description
Bold	Boolean	Get or set the bold style of the font
Charset	Integer	Get or set the character set used by the font (0 is the standard Windows charset)
Italic	Boolean	Get or set the italic style of the font
Name	String	Get or set the font name of the object (for example, "Arial" or "Courier New")
Size	Integer	Get or set the font size in points. Maximum value 2048. Minimum value is 6.
StrikeThrough	Boolean	Get or set the strikethrough style of the font
Underline	Boolean	Get or set the underline style of the font
Weight	Integer	Get or set the font weight. The only supported values are 400 (nonbold) and 700 (bold). If you set it to a different value, VB will convert it to either 400 or 700.

You will use some of the properties in Table 21.1 as you go on implementing this procedure. Enter the code as shown here:

```
Printer.DrawWidth = 5
```

You set the DrawWidth property of the Printer object to 5. DrawWidth indicates how thick the lines drawn will be. This value is always in pixels (regardless of the ScaleMode setting) and defaults to 1. That means that the lines drawn will be 1 pixel thick. This property works in conjunction with the DrawStyle and DrawMode properties. You have previously seen the DrawStyle property. It indicates the line style (solid, dashed, and so on). The DrawMode property indicates how the line is combined with the background on which it is drawn; that is, how the line color is combined with the background color to yield the color of the line drawn. It has 16 settings, with vbCopyPen as the most common. Copy pen sets the graphical result of drawing a line (that is, the affected pixels) to be the color of the line, specified by the ForeColor property. Next add the following lines of code:

```
Printer.Line (0, 0)-(Printer.ScaleWidth, 0)
Printer.CurrentX = 0
Printer.CurrentY = 1440
```

Use the Line method of the Printer object to draw a line at the top of the current page, then reset the current x coordinate of the printer to 0. Printing in VB occurs one page at a time. You can output text and graphics to that page, using the miscellaneous methods of the Printer object. The current coordinates x and y (represented by the CurrentX and CurrentY properties) are the last location where a pixel is set on the current page. Whenever printing starts on a new page, these values are set to the upper-left corner of the page. The ScaleMode, ScaleTop, and ScaleLeft properties determine the values and units of measure. By default, the ScaleMode is twips and the ScaleTop and ScaleLeft are 0. When a Printer method is executed that has graphical or text output (for example, drawing a line) CurrentX and CurrentY are updated to point to the last pixel drawn, that is, the end of the line in this example. Most graphical and text methods use the current coordinates as a starting point by default. You can set the CurrentX and CurrentY value to point anywhere on the page, for example, to draw something at that location.

One of the most common graphical methods is the Line method. The Line method has the following syntax:

```
Line [Step] (x1, y1) - [Step] (x2, y2), [color], [B][F]
```

Optional arguments are in square brackets. The arguments are described in Table 21.2.

Table 21.2 Line Method Arguments

Argument	Type	Description
Step	-	Keyword indicating (if present) that the start coordinates (x1, y1) are relative to the current coordinates of the device, rather than absolute positions.
x1, y1	Single	x and y coordinates where the line starts. Units of measure depend on the ScaleMode setting. If not specified, the current coordinates are used.
Step	-	Keyword indicating (if present) that the end coordinates (x2, y2) are relative to the current coordinates of the device, rather than absolute positions.
x2, y2	Single	x and y coordinates where the line ends. Units of measure depend on the ScaleMode setting. Required.
color	Long	Specifies the line color, using the standard Windows colors. Optional, if not specified the ForeColor is used.
B	-	Literal that indicates that this is a box not a line, with the end coordinates representing the opposite corner of the rectangle drawn. Optional.
F	-	Literal, used only in conjunction with B to indicate that the box should be filled with the same color as the line.

21

If you are using the Line method to draw a rectangle (using the B optional argument), the box will be filled using the FillColor and FillStyle properties. The FillColor is a Windows color used to fill all shapes drawn on the device (a printer, in this case). The FillStyle represents the style used to fill the shapes and can have one of the following values:

Value	Description
vbFSSolid	Use the solid color
vbFSTransparent	No filling occurs, FillColor
vbFSHorizontalLine	See Figure 21.3
vbFSVerticalLine	See Figure 21.3
vbFSUpwardDiagonal	See Figure 21.3
vbFSDownwardDiagonal	See Figure 21.3
vbFSCross	See Figure 21.3
vbFSDiagonalCross	See Figure 21.3

Figure 21.3

Example of fill styles.

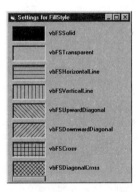

When using the BF combination the box will be filled with the same solid color as the color used to draw the line, the FillColor and FillStyle are ignored.

Returning to your code, note that you reset the current coordinates to point to one inch below the top of the page (CurrentY is 1440 twips, which is one inch), on the left margin of the printable area (CurrentX is 0). You do this to leave some room at the top of the page.

Now you can print some order information. Enter this code:

```
Printer.Font.Bold = True
Printer.Print "ORDER NO" & Str(m_order.id)
Printer.Print "DATE: " & Format(m_order.dateEntered, "Long date")
Printer.Font.Bold = False
```

Set the font to bold, and then use the Print method to output text to the page. Add two lines of code for the order number and the date the order was entered. You get the data from the m_order form-level Order reference variable. Note the use of the Str intrinsic function to convert from a number to a string. The Str function adds a space to the front of the string (if the number is positive). Also note the use of the Format intrinsic function. This function is useful when outputting data that needs formatting. The complete syntax of the Format function is

Format(expression[, format[, firstDayOfWeek[, firstWeekOfYear]]])

The first argument is the value to be formatted, the second argument is the formatting string, similar to the Format property of a MaskedEditBox control. The last two arguments are seldom used; they default to the system settings. The format string can be one of the named values, that is, derived from the local settings in the Control Panel. Examples are "short date", "long date", "short time", "currency", and so on.

The last line in this code snippet resets the font to be nonbold again. You continue your printing routine with the code shown here:

```
Dim cust As New Customer
cust.Find m_order.customerId
Printer.Print
Printer.Print "CUSTOMER:"
Printer.Print , cust.fullName
Printer.Print , cust.streetAddress
Printer.Print , cust.city; ", "; cust.state; ", "; cust.zip
Printer.Print , cust.telephone
Printer.Print
```

You want to print the customer information. You first need to retrieve the Customer object from the database using the Find method and the customerId property of the Order object. Then use Print to output the information to this page. The Print method has the following syntax:

```
Print [expressionList]
```

The expressionList is optional. If it is not supplied, an empty line is printed.

expressionList is defined as a list of expressions, separated by commas (,) or semicolons (;). An expression is defined as

```
{ Spc(x) ¦ Tab(x) ¦ expression }
```

The Spc intrinsic function inserts x spaces. The Tab intrinsic function moves the current position at the specified x column and is useful for tabular data. Note that depending on the font used for output, the position of the tabs may vary. If a proportional font (such as Arial) is used, the space taken by each character is different. For

21

example, the M character takes more space that the i character. This is not the case with fixed-spaced fonts such as Courier or Courier New. That is why the Tab function is quite useful when outputting tabular data.

A comma positions the next expression to the next tab stop on the line. Tab stops occur every eight characters. A semicolon positions the next expression immediately after the previous one.

If the expressionList does not end with a semicolon, the line is considered finished and the current position moves to the left margin, one line down. If the line does end with a semicolon, the current coordinates will point to the end of the line, after the last expression.

Note that in some of the Print lines of the preceding code the expression list starts with a comma. This means that the next expression will be positioned on the tab stop; that is, eight spaces to the right of the left margin of the printable area of the page.

Also note the use of the semicolon to separate the expressions on the line of code that prints the city, state, and zip code.

Let's continue this procedure. Enter the following code:

```
Printer.Font.name = "Courier new"
Printer.Font.Size = 10
Printer.Print "No"; Tab(6); "Name"; Tab(40); "Qty"; Tab(48); "Price"
```

Change the font by setting its Name to Courier New and its size to 10. Then print the column headers for the order detail (line) items, using the Print method. Note the use of the Tab function to space the columns properly. Print the item name at column 6, quantity at column 40, and price at column 48. Next, add a line to separate the column headers from the actual order item data. Enter the following code:

```
Printer.Line -(Printer.ScaleWidth, Printer.CurrentY)
Printer.CurrentX = 0
Printer.Print
```

Draw the line from the current position (omitted) to the right margin of the printable area of the page, keeping the y coordinate (CurrentY) the same. Then reposition the x coordinate at the left margin and print a blank line. Now you will start printing each order item, one per line. Enter the following code:

```
Dim items As OrderItemColl, Item As OrderItem
Set items = m_order.orderItems
Dim i As Long
For i = 1 To items.Count
  Set Item = items.Item(i)
  Printer.Print Item.seqNo; _
              Tab(6); Item.productName; _
```

```
                Tab(40); Padl(Str(Item.qty), 3); _
                Tab(48); Padl(Format(Item.total, "Currency"), 10)
  Next I
```

First, you get a reference to the order items collection from the m_order variable, then iterate through each item in the collection. For each item, you get a reference to it and use the Print method to output it to the page. Note the use of the same tab settings as used previously. Also note the use of the Padl function you implemented previously to have the numeric and currency values to be right aligned. Showing numbers and currency right aligned is a common convention. Next, add another line after the last item has been printed.

```
Printer.Line -(Printer.ScaleWidth, Printer.CurrentY)
Printer.CurrentX = 0
Printer.Print
```

Now print a blank line after the graphical line you drew. Next, you add a line for the subtotal, freight, discount, tax, and grand total values.

```
Printer.Print Tab(32); "Subtotal"; _
              Tab(48); Padl(Format(m_order.subTotal, "Currency"), 10)
Printer.Print

Dim sFreight As String
sFreight = "[" & m_order.shippingTypeStr & "]"
Printer.Print Tab(32); "Freight " & sFreight; _
              Tab(48); Padl(Format(m_order.shippingCharge, "Currency"), 10)
Printer.Print

If m_order.discount > 0 Then
  Printer.Print Tab(32); "Discount"; _
                Tab(48); Padl(Format(m_order.discount / 100, "#0.00%"), 10)
  Printer.Print
End If

If m_order.taxPercent > 0 Then
  Printer.Print Tab(32); "Tax"; _
                Tab(48); Padl(Format(m_order.taxPercent / 100, "#0.00%"), 10)
  Printer.Print
End If

Printer.Font.Bold = True
Printer.Print Tab(32); "Grand total"; _
              Tab(48); Padl(Format(m_order.total, "Currency"), 10)
Printer.Print
```

You use the Print method to output these values. We use the tab at column 48 for the numeric and currency values. Note the use of the special formatting for the percentage values. The % formatting character in the format strings for the discount and tax causes the Format function to multiply the value by 100 and then display it as a percentage. However, in this case you already have the values as percentages, so to avoid this side effect of the % format, divide the values by 100 before passing them to the Format function. Print the grand total line in bold.

At this point you want to print a logo image at the top of the page. The Printer object helps by providing the PaintPicture method. This method takes a Picture object reference and outputs it to the current coordinates on the page, optionally sizing and cropping it. The complete syntax of the PaintPicture method is shown as follows:

```
PaintPicture picture, x1, y1, w1, h1, x2, y2, w2, h2, opcode
```

The arguments are described in Table 21.3.

Table 21.3   PaintPicture Method Arguments

Argument	*Type*	*Description*
picture	Picture	Must be a Picture property of an object or the result of a LoadPicture function.
x1, y1	Single	The upper-left corner of the destination area where the picture will be transferred. Units of measure depend on the ScaleMode of the Printer object.
w1, h1	Single	Width and height the picture will have on the page. The picture will be stretched to fit. If omitted, no stretching will occur.
x2, y2	Single	The upper-left corner of the area of the source that is going to be transferred. If omitted, the upper-left corner of the picture is used.
w2, h2	Single	Width and height of the area of the source that will be transferred to destination. If omitted, the width and height of the picture are used.
opCode	Long	This is a flag that indicates the bitwise operation to be performed when the picture is applied to the destination background. The most commonly used values are vbSrcCopy (overwrite the destination) and vbMergeCopy (merge with source). Applies only to bitmap pictures.

You will use this method to transfer the picture from the cmdPrint CommandButton (we set it to an icon, above) to the upper-left corner of the page. Enter the code as shown here:

```
Printer.PaintPicture cmdPrint.Picture, 0, 0
```

You are now finished printing this order. You now need to tell the Printer object that this print session is concluded. Use the EndDoc method to do this. The EndDoc method submits the document to the printer. If you needed more than one page in this document, you can call the NewPage method to add a new page to the document.

If you want to cancel printing the current document, you can use the `KillDoc` method. This method of the Printer object cancels the print job.

```
  Printer.EndDoc
End Sub
```

You have finished implementing the PrintOrder procedure. You can now test it. Save your project and run the application. Create a new order, select a customer, add a few items to it, then save it. Make sure a printer is available and click the Print button. Select a printer, change its settings if required, and click Print. Your order should be printed properly.

Next Steps

In this chapter, you have looked in detail at printing. You have learned how to select a printer, set its properties, and then print text, graphics, and even images. You also have studied a few new methods and properties of the Printer object that also apply to forms, the PictureBox, and other graphical controls.

21

Part V

Final Touches: Debugging and Testing the System

Chapter 22

In this chapter

- *Finalizing the Customer Orders Form*
- *Adding an About Form*
- *Adding Help to the Application*

Finalizing the Project

You will continue by adding code to the customer orders form to populate the TreeView and ListView control. Then you will add an About box to the Help menu of the main form, explore the methods and properties of the global App object, and add help support to the application.

The complete code for this chapter can be found in the Chapter22 folder of the main VBFS folder on the CD that accompanies this book.

Finalizing the Customer Orders Form

You must add code to populate the controls on the frmCustOrders form, which you added to the project in Chapter 11, "Creating an Explorer-Style Form Using TreeView and ListView Controls." First, you will retrieve the customers list from the database and populate the TreeView control, and then you will retrieve all orders for each customer and add them as child nodes to that customer. You will implement a method to populate the ListView control with details for the selected item in the TreeView.

Start by adding the RefreshTreeView method. Open the frmCustOrders form module in the code editor and enter the following code:

frmCustOrders(CustOrders.frm)

```
Private Sub RefreshTreeView()
  tvw.Nodes.Clear

  Dim custList As Collection
  Set custList = gSession.GetCustomersList()
```

continues

continued

```
    Dim n As Node, sParentKey As String, i As Long, cust As Customer
    Dim ordList As Collection, ord As Order, j As Long, sOrdKey As String
    For i = 1 To custList.Count
      Set cust = custList.Item(i)
      sParentKey = "C" & LTrim(Str(cust.id))
      Set n = tvw.Nodes.Add(, tvwNext, sParentKey, cust.name)
      n.Image = 1

      Set ordList = cust.GetOrders
      For j = 1 To ordList.Count
        Set ord = ordList.Item(j)
        sOrdKey = "O" & LTrim(Str(ord.id))
        Set n = tvw.Nodes.Add(sParentKey, tvwChild, sOrdKey, _
                Format(ord.dateEntered, "Short Date"))
        n.Image = 2
      Next j
    Next i
End Sub
```

First, you must clear the Nodes collection of the tvw TreeView control.

You have learned that each TreeView control has a collection of Node objects. This collection is indexed by each Node object's Index property. Also each Node object can be (optionally) identified by its Key property. The Node class also has a Text property—the caption displayed in the control. Other properties of the Node object are listed in Table 22.1.

Table 22.1   Properties of the Node Class

Property	Type	Description
Bold	Boolean	Text is shown in bold type
Checked	Boolean	A check mark is displayed next to the item
Child	Node	Return a reference to the first child
Children	Integer	Number of child nodes
Expanded	Boolean	Get or set the node's children to be visible (that is, expanded) or not
ExpandedImage SelectedImage	Integer	Index in the associated ImageList for the image to be displayed when the node is expanded or selected, respectively
FirstSibling LastSibling	Node	The first and last siblings (from the parent node's children collection)
FullPath	String	The full path that leads to the node; that is, the Text of all nodes on the path, delimited by the PathDelimiter string property of the TreeView control

Property	Type	Description
Next, Previous	Node	The next and previous sibling nodes in this node's parent children collection
Parent	Node	The parent of this node, can be set or retrieved
Root	Node	The root node of the TreeView control
Selected	Boolean	Get or set the selected status of this node
Visible	Boolean	Get or set the visibility of this node (and implicitly of all its child nodes)

The Nodes is a property of the TreeView control that returns a list of all Node objects the tree holds. It can be sorted and has the regular methods of any collection: Item, Add, Remove, Count.

Next you retrieve a list of all customers in the database and store it in the custList local variable. Then for each Customer object in the collection you will add a node to the TreeView control using the Add method of the Nodes collection of the TreeView control. The Add function of the Nodes collection takes a set of arguments, as described in Table 22.2.

Table 22.2   Arguments of the Add Function of the TreeView Nodes Collection

Argument	Type	Description
relative	Variant	Index or key of the Node object to which the newly added node is related. Optional. If none specified, this is added as the last node to the top level (root node).
relationship	Enumeration	The relationship to the relative object, can be of: tvwFirst, tvwLast, tvwNext, tvwPrevious, tvwChild constants. This specifies the position of the new node to the relative Node object. Optional.
key	String	A unique key that is used to identify the new node in the Nodes collection. Optional. If not specified, the only way to identify the Node object is by index.
text	String	Text displayed as caption in the TreeView control. Required.
image	Integer	Index in the associated ImageList control that specifies the image to be displayed for this item. Optional.
selImage	Integer	Index in the associated ImageList control that specifies the image to be displayed for this item when it is selected. Optional.

22

The Add function returns a reference to the newly created Node object, which can be used to set other properties. In this case, omit the relative argument (which will default to the root of the tree). Add the new node in the next position (after the last node inserted). Set the key to the string obtained by concatenating the letter C (for Customer) with the stringified version of the customer ID (which is unique for all customers).

You cannot use only the ID as a unique key because you will also add orders to this TreeView control, and the orders have IDs too. It is possible to encounter an order with the same ID as a customer. This causes an error (duplicate key) to be raised at runtime. Therefore, you need to prefix the customer node keys with C and the order node keys with O to distinguish between them.

You also use the customer name as the text property of the Node object. Then set the Image property of the new node to 1 (the index of the customer image in the associated ImageList control you set when designing this form).

Next, retrieve all the orders for this customer using the GetOrders function of the Customer class. Then, for each order in the collection, add a child node to the customer node you added previously. Note that this time you prefix the key of the object with O (for order). In the Add method, specify the key of the parent (customer) node and specify the relationship argument as tvwChild. You want the order node to be a child of the customer node. Set its Text to be the date the order was entered using the Format intrinsic function to convert it to string. The Image property is 2 in this case (the second image in the iml12 associated control).

Finally, you need to add code to refresh the contents of the ListView control every time the selected item in the TreeView control changes. If a customer node is selected, display a list of all orders for that customer; otherwise, if an order node is selected, display a list of all the order items (details) for that order. Before you implement the RefreshListView procedure you must explain in some detail how the ListView class works.

Each ListView control has a collection of ListItem objects. This collection is indexed by each ListItem object's Index property. Also, each ListItem object can be (optionally) identified by its Key property. The ListItem class has also a Text property—the caption displayed in the control. Other properties of the ListItem object are listed in Table 22.3.

Table 22.3 Properties of the ListItem Class

Property	Type	Description
Ghosted	Boolean	The item appears dimmed, indicating that it is unavailable
Icon, SmallIcon	Integer	Index in the associated ImageList to the icon or small icon to be displayed in the respective views
Selected	Boolean	Get or set the selected status of this ListItem

Property	Type	Description
SubItems	String	Array of strings that are used in the report view as details. They correspond to the ColumnHeaders of the ListView (the Text is at index 0, the SubItems start at index 1)
ToolTipText	String	The ToolTip that is displayed when the mouse hovers above this item for a few seconds

The ListItems is a property of the ListView control that returns a list of all ListItem objects in the list. It can be sorted and has the regular methods of any collection: Item, Add, Remove, and Count.

Enter the following code:

frmCustOrders(CustOrders.frm)

```
Private Sub RefreshListView()
  lvw.ListItems.Clear
  lvw.ColumnHeaders.Clear

  Dim n As Node, li As ListItem
  Set n = tvw.SelectedItem
  If n Is Nothing Then Exit Sub

  Dim sKey As String
  sKey = n.Key
  If Left(sKey, 1) = "C" Then
    ' it is a customer, show orders
    lvw.ColumnHeaders.Add , , "Ordered on"
    lvw.ColumnHeaders.Add , , "Prod. status"
    lvw.ColumnHeaders.Add , , "Bill status"
    lvw.ColumnHeaders.Add , , "Total"

    Dim cust As New Customer
    If Not cust.Find(Val(Mid(sKey, 2))) Then Exit Sub

    Dim ordList As Collection, ord As Order, j As Long, sOrdKey As String
    Set ordList = cust.GetOrders
    For j = 1 To ordList.Count
      Set ord = ordList.Item(j)
      sOrdKey = "O" & LTrim(Str(ord.id))
      Set li = lvw.ListItems.Add(, sOrdKey, _
              Format(ord.dateEntered, "Short Date"))
      li.Icon = 2
      li.SmallIcon = 2
      li.SubItems(1) = ord.prodStatusStr
      li.SubItems(2) = ord.billStatusStr
      li.SubItems(3) = Format(ord.total, "$#,##0.00")
    Next j
```

22

continues

continued

```
Else
   ' it is an order, show order items
   lvw.ColumnHeaders.Add , , "Name"
   lvw.ColumnHeaders.Add , , "Qty"
   lvw.ColumnHeaders.Add , , "Price"
   lvw.ColumnHeaders.Add , , "Total"

   Dim ordr As New Order
   If Not ordr.Find(Val(Mid(sKey, 2))) Then Exit Sub

   Dim oiList As OrderItemColl, oi As OrderItem, i As Long, sOIKey As String
   Set oiList = ordr.orderItems
   For i = 1 To oiList.Count
      Set oi = oiList.Item(i)
      sOIKey = "I" & LTrim(Str(oi.id))
      Set li = lvw.ListItems.Add(, sOIKey, oi.productName)
      li.Icon = 3
      li.SmallIcon = 3
      li.SubItems(1) = LTrim(Str(oi.qty))
      li.SubItems(2) = Format(oi.price, "$#,##0.00")
      li.SubItems(3) = Format(oi.total, "$#,##0.00")
   Next i

   End If
End Sub
```

First, clear the collection of ListItems and ColumnHeaders of the `lvw` ListView control. Then, you determine the selected node object of the TreeView object. If no node is selected, you exit. Otherwise you get the key of the selected node object. Based on the first letter of the key you distinguish two cases: a customer node and an order node. The rest of the procedure is split in two parts, each dealing with one of these two cases.

If you have a customer node, set the ColumnHeaders of the ListView to the name of the properties that you will display for the orders of this customer. Use the `Add` method of the ColumnHeaders collection. This method has the following syntax:

```
Add(index, key, text, width, alignment, icon)
```

The `index`, `key`, and `text` have the same meaning as for the ListItem or Node objects. The `width` is the width of the column (in twips). The `alignment` can be right-aligned, left-aligned, or centered. The `icon` is an index into the associated ImageList for the column header icons.

Then get all the orders for these customers as a collection of Order objects. For each object in this collection, create a unique key, using the same principle as used previously. Then add it to the ListItems collection using the Add function of this collection object. The syntax of this function is

```
Add(index, key, text, icon, smallIcon)
```

All arguments are the same as the ListItem properties with the same name. All of the arguments are optional. The function returns a reference to the newly added ListItem.

We set the Icon, SmallIcon, and the SubItems properties of the returned ListItem object.

 Note You could have used the icon and smallIcon arguments of the Add function to set the Icon and SmallIcon properties (which would have been a better implementation). We did it this way to illustrate that it can be done either way.

Note the use of the ?Str properties of the Order class to get a description of the enumerated properties prodStatus and billStatus.

In the second case, (an Order is selected in the TreeView control) you proceed in a similar fashion. You set the ColumnHeaders, which this time will reflect the labels of the order item properties. Next, you get the order from the database, then get the OrderItem objects for that order (using the OrderItemColl object). For each item in this collection, you add a ListItem to the lvw ListView control. You then set the Icon, SmallIcon, and required SubItems of the new ListItem.

Now you must add the appropriate calls for these methods. First, modify the Form_Load event procedure. Enter the following line of code that is in bold type:

frmCustOrders(CustOrders.frm)

```
Private Sub Form_Load()
  m_ratio = 0.33

  RefreshTreeView
End Sub
```

Next, implement the event procedure for the mnuLvwRefresh menu item (from the pop-up menu). Enter the following code:

frmCustOrders(CustOrders.frm)

```
Private Sub mnuLvwRefresh_Click()
  RefreshListView
End Sub
```

Now implement the `NodeClick` event of the `tvw` TreeView control to refresh the ListView every time a new node becomes selected. Add the following code:

frmCustOrders(CustOrders.frm)

```
Private Sub tvw_NodeClick(ByVal Node As MSComctlLib.Node)
  RefreshListView
End Sub
```

These are the final touches you needed for this form. Save your changes and run the project. Open the customer orders form and make sure it works properly.

Adding an About Form

In the rest of this chapter you will learn a few things about how to add help features to your application. The simplest feature many Windows applications have is an About box. This dialog box lists the application name and version, as well as license information and company information.

Add a new form to the project. Change its Name to `frmAbout`, its Caption to About MyApp, its BorderStyle to 3 - Fixed Dialog, and its StartUpPosition to 1 - Center Owner.

Add a Label control to the form. Use the form as depicted in Figure 22.1 as a guide for the final size and position of the controls on the form. Change the Label control's name to lblTitle and its Caption to Application title.

Figure 22.1

The About dialog box.

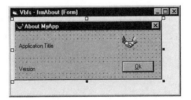

Add a second Label control. Change its Name to `lblVersion` and its Caption to Version.

Add a CommandButton as shown in Figure 22.1. Change its Name to `cmdOk`, its Caption to &Ok, its Default property value to `True`, and its Cancel property value to `True`.

Optionally add an image control and set its Picture property to an icon or bitmap of your choice.

Now let's write some code for this form. In the `Form_Load` event procedure, enter this code:

frmAbout(About.frm)

```
Private Sub Form_Load()
  Me.Caption = "About " & App.Title
  lblVersion.Caption = "Version " & App.Major & "." & _
                       App.Minor & "." & App.Revision
  lblTitle.Caption = App.Comments
End Sub
```

You are using the App global object to set the properties for this form. The App object is one of the global objects that VB provides to help your development task. It falls in the same category as the Err, Printer, Screen, and (as you will see later) the Debug object. No other instances of this class can be created (using the New operator or otherwise). The properties of this object are listed in Table 22.4.

Table 22.4   Properties of the App Object

Property	Type	Description
Comments	String	Get the comments about the application (as entered in the project settings).
CompanyName	String	Get the company name (as entered in the project settings).
EXEName	String	Get the name of the executable file without the extension. If running from VB itself, returns the name of the project.
FileDescription	String	Get the file description from the project settings.
HelpFile	String	Name of the helpfile (.hlp) associated with this application.
hInstance	Long	Application instance handle (HINSTANCE). It is used in some WIN32 API function calls.
LegalCopyright LegalTrademarks	String	The legal copyright and trademark information as entered in the project settings.
LogMode	Enumerated	Get the current log mode (used when the `LogEvent` method is invoked). Can be a combination of one or more of the following VB intrinsic constants:
		`vbLogAuto` Automatic (file or NT log)
		`vbLogOff` No logging
		`vbLogToFile` Log to the file specified in LogPath
		`vbLogToNT` Log to the NT event log
		`vbLogOverwrite` Clear the log (if to file)
		`vbLogThreadID` Log the calling thread ID
LogPath	String	Name of the file to be used for logging messages.

continues

Table 22.4   continued

Property	Type	Description
Major, Minor, Revision	Long	Numbers identifying the version of the product (Major.Minor.Revision). They are set at design time and have values between 0–9999.
Path	String	The full pathname of the running application, not including the application name and the terminal \.
PrevInstance	Boolean	Return True if another instance of this application is running. Useful if you want to prevent multiple instances of the application running at the same time.
ProductName	String	The name of the product as defined in the project settings.
Title	String	The title of the application as defined in the project settings.

Some advanced properties related to ActiveX/COM servers and DLLs were omitted.

You have used the Title, Comments, Major, Minor, and Revision properties to expose some information to the users.

You also must implement the cmdOk_Click event procedure. Enter this code:

frmAbout(About.frm)

```
Private Sub cmdOK_Click()
  Unload Me
End Sub
```

You just unloaded the dialog box. This concludes the implementation of the About dialog box. Now let's add code to show this form when the user clicks on the Help, About menu item. Open the code editor for the main form, and add the following code:

frmMain(Main.frm)

```
Private Sub mnuHelpAbout_Click()
  Dim f As New frmAbout
  f.Show vbModal, Me
End Sub
```

Save your project. Before running it you must set the information that will be displayed at runtime in the About dialog box. From the Project menu, select the item labeled VBFS Properties. The Project Properties dialog box will be opened as illustrated in Figure 22.2.

Figure 22.2

The Project Properties dialog box—General tab.

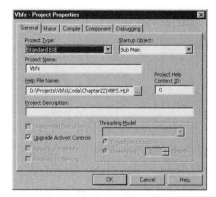

 Note If you are working with the Visual Basic Working Model Edition, the Make tag is not available. You can skip this step and the program will still work.

Now you will concentrate on the second tab, labeled Make. Click on the Make tab. It should be similar to the one illustrated in Figure 22.3. Change the Title to VBFS - Chapter 22. In the Version frame, select Comments from the list, then enter These are comments in the Value text box to the right of the list.

Figure 22.3

The Project Properties dialog box—Make tab.

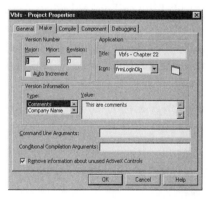

Now if you run the application and select the Help, About menu item from the main form you should see a dialog box like the one illustrated in Figure 22.4.

Figure 22.4

The About dialog at runtime.

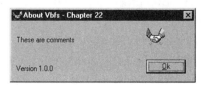

Adding Help to the Application

The task of adding help to the application is quite important. The users of your application will appreciate the additional information provided at runtime by the help system. Help is normally provided by one or more help files (.hlp). Usually, adding help to a project consists of two different tasks: Write the actual text that goes into the help files and link those files to the project. We will not go into details on how to create the help files because this has little to do with programming. We will explore in more detail the second task; that is, creating the link between the application and the help files.

The Windows help system consists of one or more help files. Each help file consists of many help topics. Each topic has a unique identifier known as a topic ID or help context ID. The topics can be organized in a table of contents and can be indexed for easier searching. The user can jump from one topic to the another or display smaller topics in pop-up windows. From the programming point of view, the help context IDs are the link between the application and the help file.

We have developed the help file that will be used with your project. You can find the code on the CD that accompanies this book in the Help folder under Vbfs/CodeChapter22. It consists of a rich text format (RTF) document. You can look at it with any text editor that supports RTF format (Microsoft Word, for example). It also consists of a help project file (.hpj) and the compiled help file (Vbfs.hlp).

The compiled help file is built from the RTF file, the help project file, and any additional files, using the Help compiler. The compiler is provided as an add-on with some of Microsoft's development tools. For further information on this topic see the documentation for the help compiler.

A help context ID can be translated as a constant numeric (Long) value. This help file contains the following help context IDs:

```
IDH_CONTENTS      1
IDH_CUSTOMER      101
IDH_PRODUCT       102
IDH_ORDER         103
IDH_PRODUCTTYPE      1004
```

Add the help file to your project. Copy the help file (Vbfs.hlp) from the Help folder on the CD to your project folder, and then open the Project Properties dialog box (from the Project menu, select VBFS properties). In the Help File Name select the file you have copied, and click OK.

The next step is to link the help topics with forms and controls of the project. In VB, each form and control has a HelpContextID property that indicates the value of the help context ID from the help file of the project. If the user presses the F1 key (the universal help key), VB will look at the HelpContextID of the active control. If this is set (that is, nonzero), it will search the help file for that context ID. If it is found, it will display it. If the active control has no valid HelpContextID, it will try the same with its container's HelpContextID, up to the form level. If the form has a valid context ID, it will display that help topic. In this way if you set the HelpContextID of a form, it will be displayed (when the user hits F1) for any control on that form that does not have its own HelpContextID.

Open `frmCustomer`. Set its HelpContextID property to 101. Repeat the operation with `frmProduct` and `frmOrder`—use 102 and 103, respectively. On `frmProduct`, select the `cmbProductType` combo box and set its HelpContextID to 1001. The numbers come from the topic IDs, defined previously.

This concludes the implementation of our support for help files. Save your project. Now you can try the new Help feature. Run the project. Select the New Product menu item or the toolbar button, and press F1. The help screen for the Product Form should be displayed. Select the ProductType combo box and press F1 again. The Product Type help screen is now displayed.

Next Steps

In this chapter, you have finalized the customer orders form, learning some new methods and properties of the TreeView and ListView controls. You added an About box to the Help menu of the main form. You looked at the properties and methods of the global App object and also added a help file and help support to your project.

In the next chapter, you learn about application settings; in particular, you discover how to read and write these settings. You also look at the use of conditional compilation.

22

Chapter 23

Application and Project Settings

In this chapter, you will learn more about project and application settings. You will also learn about the preprocessor directives and their usage.

The complete code for this chapter can be found in the Chapter23 folder of the main VBFS folder on the CD that accompanies this book.

Application Settings

We will start by exploring the application settings. To further enhance the usability of the user interface part of your application, it would be nice if the application could somehow remember the customized settings for each user; for example, if it could remember the last position of the main form or some other settings (like size, position, search, and filter options for different forms, and so on).

VB offers this functionality using the Windows Registry as storage media. The Registry is a persistent hierarchical storage system. It is organized like a file system: it has keys (the equivalent of folders in a file system), which can hold other keys or named values. A named value is a name-value pair. For example, you can store a value that has the name Maximized and the actual value True. The Registry contains a set of top-level keys (the rough equivalent of drives in a file system). Among these keys, the one of interest to us is HKEY_CURRENT_USER, where settings for the currently logged-in user are stored.

 Note You can view Registry settings using a tool named REGEDIT.EXE. This tools comes on both Windows NT and Windows 95/98. The tool enables you to both view and edit Registry keys. It is recommended that you do not modify any values for Registry keys manually, unless you know exactly what you are doing.

The GetSetting and SaveSetting intrinsic functions are used to access the information stored in the Registry and to store this information in the Registry, respectively. The information is saved under the current user key. The full name of the key is

```
HKEY_CURRENT_USER\Software\VB and VBA Program Settings\<AppName>
```

where the <AppName> is your application name. That also is where the GetSetting function looks for the requested values.

You will use the GetSetting and SaveSetting functions to get and save the last position of the main form of your application. Of course, the methods can be used to store and retrieve any other user options for any form in your project.

Open the main form module in the code editor. Change the code in the MDIForm_Load event procedure by adding the lines shown here in bold type:

frmMain(Main.frm)

```
Private Sub MDIForm_Load()
  Me.Caption = "VBFS - " & m_userName
  SbrMessage "Ready"
  Me.Left = GetSetting(App.Title, "Settings", "frmMain_Left", 1440)
  Me.Top = GetSetting(App.Title, "Settings", "frmMain_Top", 1440)
  Me.Width = GetSetting(App.Title, "Settings", "frmMain_Width", 1440 * 8)
  Me.Height = GetSetting(App.Title, "Settings", "frmMain_Height", 1440 * 6)
End Sub
```

As you can see, you are setting the position and size of the main form using the data returned by the GetSetting function, which retrieved it from the Registry. The syntax of the GetSetting function is

```
GetSetting(appName, section, key, default)
```

The appName is the name under which the settings for this application have been saved in the Registry. Usually this is the application title, which is what is used here (through the Title property of the App object).

The section argument identifies a subkey (section) of the application Registry key that contains the particular setting you are looking for. You can choose to have multiple sections divided by functionality or one section for each form in the project. In this example, you have only one section named Settings, which contains all values.

The key argument is the name of the named value that you are looking for. If the named value is found, its value is returned. Otherwise, if the value is not present, the value specified by the default argument is returned.

Default the Top and Left properties to 1 inch from the margins, the width to 8 inches, and the height to 6 inches. (Remember that you are using screen measure units, which are always twips, 1440 twips/1 inch).

The next thing you must do is save the last known position of the main form when this form is unloaded. Add the lines of code as shown in the following code, to the MDIForm_Unload event procedure:

frmMain(Main.frm)

```
Private Sub MDIForm_Unload(Cancel As Integer)
  If Me.WindowState <> vbMinimized Then
    SaveSetting App.Title, "Settings", "frmMain_Left", Me.Left
    SaveSetting App.Title, "Settings", "frmMain_Top", Me.Top
    SaveSetting App.Title, "Settings", "frmMain_Width", Me.Width
    SaveSetting App.Title, "Settings", "frmMain_Height", Me.Height
  End If
End Sub
```

You will save this position only if the form is not minimized. Use the SaveSetting function to write the values to the Registry. The syntax of the SaveSetting function is shown here:

```
SaveSetting(appName, section, key, value)
```

The first three arguments have the same meanings as those of the GetSetting function. The value argument is the value that will be written. If the key with that name exists, it will be overwritten; otherwise a new key will be created and its value set to the value argument.

There are two more useful functions related to application settings: DeleteSetting and GetAllSettings. Their syntax and behavior are discussed next.

```
DeleteSetting(appName, section[, key])
```

The DeleteSetting method removes a key or entire section from the Registry. The arguments have the same meaning as those of the GetSetting and SaveSetting functions. If you try to delete a nonexistent section or key, a runtime error is raised.

```
GetAllSettings(appName, section)
```

The GetAllSettings function returns a list of all keys under that section. If the section does not exist or there are no keys, an empty Variant is returned.

You can now try your changes. Save your project. Run it and change the size and position of the main form. Close the project and run it again. This time the main form should show up in the same position and be the same size as when you closed it.

23

Project Settings

In a few places, you have used the Project Properties dialog box to alter some settings for the project. Now we will explore these settings in a little more detail.

Open the Project Properties dialog box from the Project menu. The first tab of the dialog box, labeled General, contains a few global settings for the project. The project type is one of the possible VB project types; normally it is set when you start a new project. The startup object indicates what form will be opened first when the project starts. It can be either a form (any normal or MDI form) or a special public procedure named Sub Main. Chapter 22 told you what the help file name is. The project help context ID is normally the help ID of the Contents help topic. Change this setting to 1 (your context ID for the help contents topic). The project description is going to be the description of the binary executable for the application. The Upgrade ActiveX Controls check box indicates whether VB will automatically upgrade the project to use a newer version of the ActiveX controls in the project (if one is available). If you uncheck this option, VB will ask for confirmation before upgrading to a new version of any ActiveX control. The other settings are specific to other types of projects (ActiveX DLL and EXE projects). The General tab of the project settings dialog box is illustrated in Figure 23.1.

Figure 23.1

The General tab of the Project Properties dialog box.

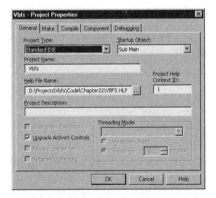

 Note   If you are working with the Visual Basic Working Model Edition, only the General Tab is available. You can skip this step and the program will still work.

Click the Make tab of the dialog box. This tab enables you to set information about the version of the application, as well as other settings such as Comments, Company name, and so on. These settings will be reflected at runtime through the App global object. You have the option to have the revision part of the version number incremented automatically by VB every time you build the project. To enable this feature, you must check the AutoIncrement check box.

The Make tab of the Project Properties dialog box is illustrated in Figure 23.2.

Figure 23.2

The Make tab of the Project Properties dialog box.

The command line arguments enable you to pass some arguments to your application while testing it from the development environment.

EXCURSION

Command-line arguments to VB programs

The command-line arguments represent the additional information passed to your application when it starts. These arguments can be passed by starting the application from a command prompt and following the application name with the arguments. For example, let's consider a simple application that deletes a file. The code is in the SafeDel folder under the Chapter23 subdirectory on the CD that came with this book. The application name is SafeDel and the code is shown here. It has only one procedure (Sub Main) and no forms or classes.

```
Sub Main()
  Dim sFile As String
  sFile = Trim(Command)

  If Len(sFile) <= 0 Then
    MsgBox "No file specified"
    Exit Sub
  End If

  If MsgBox("Confirm deletion of file " & sFile, _
          vbQuestion + vbOKCancel) <> vbOK Then
    Exit Sub
  End If

  Kill sFile
End Sub
```

23

The application deletes a file passed as argument, after asking for confirmation from the user. Use the keyword `Command` to retrieve the arguments passed to the application at run-time. When running from the VB environment, you get the text you enter in the command-line argument's TextBox in the project settings. To use the application from the command prompt, build the executable, and then open a command prompt window and change directories to the SafeDel folder. You can now run the application by entering the following command:

```
SafeDel MyUselessFile.txt
```

This command activates your application, passes in the argument MyUselessFile.txt and the SafeDel application deletes the file after asking for your confirmation. Figure 23.3 illustrates the SafeDel application running.

Figure 23.3

The SafeDel sample running.

The conditional compilation arguments TextBox enables you to define one or more preprocessor constants used in conditional compilation when the project is built. We will look in detail at the preprocessor usage later on, in this chapter.

Finally, the check box labeled Remove Information About Unused ActiveX Controls tells Visual Basic to delete any reference to unused controls from the project when building the project. This option should be left checked because it reduces the number of controls your project depends on to the minimum required. For example, if you add a MaskedEditBox control to the project but do not use it, having this option checked will remove the reference to the control. This means the machine on which your application is running does not have to have the MaskedEditBox control installed. If the option is not checked, your application will not run without the MaskedEditBox control installed, although it is not using it.

The Compile tab of the dialog box (illustrated in Figure 23.4) enables you to set compiler options. When the binary executable is generated, VB will use these settings to compile and optimize your application. The most commonly selected settings are the Optimize for Fast Code button and Favor PentiumPro check box.

Figure 23.4

The Compile tab of the Project Properties dialog box.

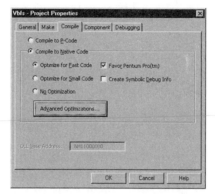

The Advanced Optimizations button displays a dialog box (illustrated in Figure 23.5) that enables you to set advanced optimizations that will increase the speed of the application. Because most of these optimizations are not safe (can cause side effects), it is better to leave them unchecked.

Figure 23.5

The Advanced Optimizations dialog box.

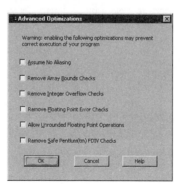

Both the Component and Debugging tabs of the dialog box are used exclusively by the ActiveX DLL or executable project types, so they will be grayed (disabled) for a standard application like yours.

Conditional Compilation and Preprocessor Usage

Conditional compilation means that you can have portions of code compiled and linked into the application only if a specific condition (or set of conditions) are met.

Visual Basic achieves this by using a set of preprocessor directives. The preprocessor is the first step in the build process, and it precedes compilation. The preprocessor can include or exclude a portion of code from the build process.

The preprocessor directives are #const and #If. The #const directive declares a constant value that can be used by the #If directive. The syntax is

```
#const name = value
```

where name is the name of the preprocessor constant and value is its value. The #const declaration is always private in the module in which it was declared. To declare public preprocessor constants, you must use the Make Tab on the Project Properties dialog box as discussed previously. For example, to declare a private preprocessor constant named DDEBUG that has the value True, use the following syntax:

```
#const DDEBUG = True
```

To create a public (global) preprocessor constant with the same name, you would enter the following into the Conditional Compilation Arguments text box on the Make tab of the Project Properties dialog box:

```
DDEBUG = True
```

 Note Note that you cannot use this constant in code. The only place it can be used is the #If directive or to construct other preprocessor constants.

The #If directive is used to determine whether a portion of code is included in the build. The syntax is

```
#If expression Then
   statements
[#ElseIf expression2 Then
   statements]
[#Else
   statements]
#End If
```

The #If can optionally contain an #ElseIf or an #Else part. The expression and expression2 must consist of preprocessor constants and literals, and they must evaluate to True or False. If expression is True, the statements following the #If will be included in compilation. If expression is False, the statements will be omitted from compilation as if they did not exist.

For example:

```
#If DDEBUG Then
  Debug.Print "MyValue = "; myValue
#End If
```

The application includes this code only if the DDEBUG constant is True. This technique can be used to eliminate from the final executable portions of code used to test the application. Simply bracket these portions of code with an #If directive and define a constant (like DDEBUG) to be True. When you are ready to build the final release of the application, change the value of DDEBUG to False and build the project. That can save you a lot of time (to go through code and comment out the portions that need not be part of the final release).

The conditional compilation can also be useful when the application is meant to run on different target platforms and there are portions of code specific to each platform (for example Macintosh, Windows 9x and Windows NT). In these cases, you would use an #If directive to bracket the code that is specific to each platform, then define a global constant that reflects the target OS and rebuild the application once for each platform.

Next Steps

In this chapter, you learned more about the project and application settings. You also learned about the preprocessor directives and their usage.

In the next chapter, you learn about debugging applications. You explore how to prepare for a debugging session as well as learn debugging techniques and gain an understanding of event tracing and logging.

23

In this chapter

- *Introduction to Debugging*
- *Debugging Techniques*
- *Testing the Application*

Chapter 24

Debugging and Testing the Application

In this chapter, you learn how to debug and test a Visual Basic application. You also study the components of the debugger built in the Visual Basic environment.

The complete code for this chapter can be found in the Chapter24 folder of the main VBFS folder on the CD that accompanies this book and in the DebugTest subfolder of that folder.

Introduction to Debugging

You have previously learned what errors are in VB and how to handle them. You will use that knowledge in this chapter, which deals with ways to eliminate errors from the final release of your application.

Errors also are known as *bugs* in programming jargon. Hence, the process of detecting errors in an application is called *debugging*. The errors can be classified within the following categories:

- Compile-time errors
- Exceptions
- Runtime errors

Compile-Time Errors

Compile-time errors are the easiest type to deal with. They are caught by the compiler when you either start the application with full compile (Ctrl+F5) or when you build the application. If the compiler encounters an error, it will halt compilation, open the module that contains the invalid statement, and let you correct the problem. Examples of compile errors are calling a function with an invalid number of arguments or with an argument of an invalid type, missing loop or conditional end-statements (such as Loop, Next, End If, and so on), or improper syntax.

If you start the application without a full compile (by pressing F5, for example), VB will compile each function and procedure as it is called (loaded). This procedure saves the time required to compile the project up front, but has the disadvantage that some compile-time errors are not caught until you reach the subroutine that contains the invalid code. So you might get compile errors while the application is running, but the error is still a compile-time error. To avoid this type of error, start the application with a full compile (Ctrl+F5 instead of F5).

Related to this type of error are syntactical errors. Syntactical errors are normally errors that violate the syntax of the language (for example omitting the Then at the end of an If statement line). By default, Visual Basic lets you know if you made a syntactical error by using a message box and changes the color of the line in question to red (the color might differ depending on the color schema used on your machine). You must fix all syntactical errors before running the application, regardless of whether or not you start with full compile.

Exceptions

Runtime exceptions are serious and unexpected problems that arise in the environment while the application is running. Examples include disk or other hardware failures, database disconnects, network problems, and so on. The application has no control over an exception, and normally the only solution is to inform the user and attempt to exit gracefully. By exiting gracefully, we mean closing any open files and any connection and, optionally, attempting to log any meaningful information that is available about the exception. This information might be helpful to the application developers in locating the source of the exception. In some circumstances, the application can continue after an exception. Even in these cases it is recommended that a message about the exception be logged.

 Note   VB represents both errors and exceptions using the same mechanism: the Err global object, as you have learned previously.

The global App object has two methods that are used to log errors and exceptions. The StartLogging method (see the following syntax) is used to initialize the log target:

```
StartLogging logTarget, logMode
```

The `logTarget` argument specifies the name and path of the text file that will be used to log events. This argument is optional, depending on the value of the `logMode` argument (that is, required only if the log target is a file). The `logMode` argument indicates the type of logging that will be used, and is one of the constants described in Table 22.3 for the LogMode property of the `App` object.

The `LogEvent` method is used to write messages to the log. The syntax for the `LogEvent` method is

```
LogEvent logBuffer, eventType
```

The `logBuffer` is a string containing the message to log. The `eventType` argument indicates whether the event is an error (or exception), a warning, or just an informational message. The values used are one of the built-in VB constants: `vbLogEventTypeError`, `vbLogEventTypeWarning`, or `vbLogEventTypeInformation`.

Runtime Errors

Runtime errors are the most common defects facing a VB developer. They can be also subclassified into two categories: *programming errors* (errors raised as a result of coding problems) and *logical errors* (no physical error occurs, but the application does not behave as expected). An example of a programming error is shown here:

```
Dim c As New Collection, i As Long
c.Add "Test1"
For i = 0 To c.Count
  Debug.Print c(i)
Next i
```

This code snippet creates a new `Collection` object, adds one item to it, and then loops from 0 to the last item in the collection c and outputs the item to the immediate window. This code will compile, but at runtime you will get an error (`Subscript out of range`) indicating that the collection c has no item at 0 (because collections are 1-based).

An example of a logical error is to have correct code that collects data from a form into an object, but then neglects to call Save on the object to persist the data. No error will be raised, but the changes made by the user do not make it to the database, which is hardly what the user expects.

Debugging Techniques

The VB development environment helps you in many ways to find both (programming and logical) types of runtime errors. We will investigate each one of them in this section.

24

Monitoring Variable and Expression Values at Runtime

When an error is raised and no error handler is installed, VB will display a message box with the error number and description, and execution of the program is halted. If you choose the Debug button, VB will switch from *run* mode to *debug* mode. The line of code that caused the exception to be raised is highlighted. In debug mode, the execution of the program is temporarily suspended so that you can see what went wrong. The first and most often used technique to determine what is wrong is to look at the values of the variable (or variables) that caused the error.

For nonobject type variables you can do this by placing the mouse cursor above the variable name (which can be any variable in the currently executing procedure) and letting it rest a few seconds so the ToolTip displays. In the previous example, you could let the mouse hover above the variable i, the ToolTip would indicate that the value is 0, which would point out what the problem is. See Figure 24.1 for an illustration.

Figure 24.1

Investigating the value of a variable at runtime.

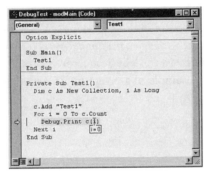

For object variables, you can use the Watches window to look at the attributes of the object. To do this, select the object variable you want to inspect (in this case c) and then select Quick Watch from the Debug menu (or press Shift+F9). A dialog box is displayed asking you to confirm that this is the expression you want to watch (see Figure 24.2).

Note the Context field of the dialog box. It specifies the location of that variable within the project and the module. The reason for this is so that you can distinguish between variables with the same name from different procedures or even different modules. Select Add. The Watches window will be displayed with the c object shown as in Figure 24.3.

The variables and expressions in the Watches window can have a + box next to them, indicating that their view can be expanded to show their attributes. Each item in this view also has the type and the execution context displayed. You can resize the width

Figure 24.2

Adding an expression to the Watches window.

Figure 24.3

The Watches window.

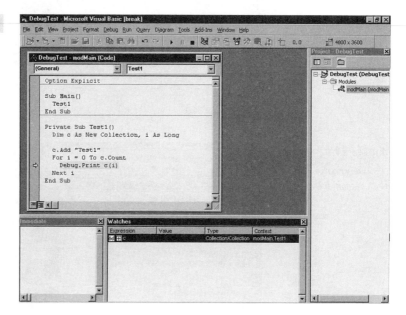

of the columns displayed, if necessary, to view the column data nontruncated. Figure 24.4 illustrates viewing the attributes of the collection c.

You can view values only for the variables and constants that are either global (Public scope) or local to the function currently being executed (that is, in context). If you have in the Watches window variables that are local to other subroutines, their values will be shown as <Out of context>.

Expressions also can be added to the Watches window. For example, the expression c(i) can be added to the Watches window using the same procedure as described previously for c. If the expression evaluation raises an error, the error description is shown as a value in the Watches window (see Figure 24.5).

24

Figure 24.4

The Watches window details.

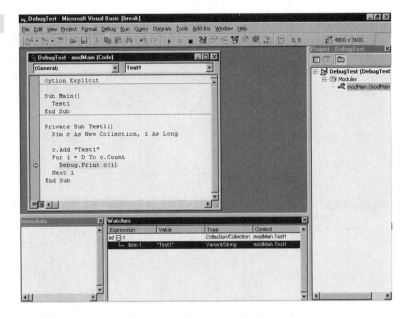

Figure 24.5

An expression in the Watches window.

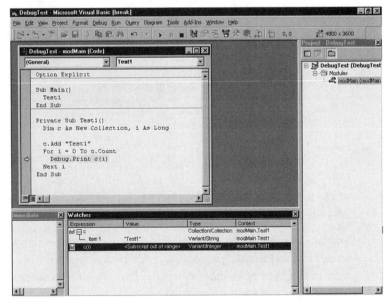

Another way to view the value of a variable or expression within the current context is to use the Immediate window. You can display the value using the ? operator followed by the variable name or expression to view. VB displays the result on the next line (or lines if necessary). See Figure 24.6 for an illustration.

Figure 24.6

A variable in the Immediate window.

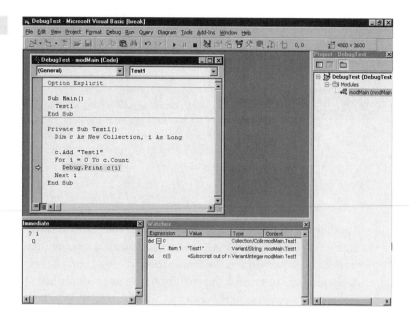

The expressions evaluated with the ? operator can be totally unrelated to the variables of your program and can use any valid function (VB intrinsic or yours). For example, Figure 24.7 illustrates the use of the Hex function to display the hex value of the decimal 1000.

Figure 24.7

An expression in the Immediate window.

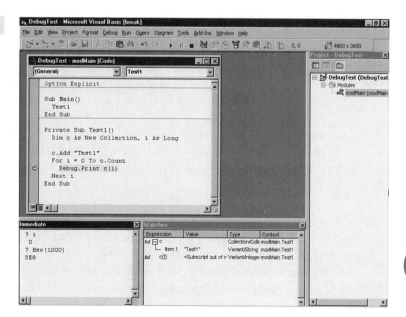

24

The difference between the two modes to inspect the value of an expression (the Watches and the Immediate windows) is that the values shown in the Watches window change as you step through your program, as you will see shortly.

Note You can remove watch expressions from the Watches window by right-clicking on them and selecting the Delete Watch menu item. If you do not delete them and stop the program, the next time you run it, the watch expressions will still be there (provided you didn't exit VB in the mean time). The same holds true for the Immediate window: Its contents can be emptied by selecting all text and pressing the Delete key.

Another way to list the value of a variable or an expression at runtime is to use the built-in global Debug object. This object has only two methods: Print (to output the value of an expression to the Immediate window) and Assert. Assert is used as a debugging aid to test for the validity of an expression while the program is executing. If the expression passed to Assert evaluates to false, program execution is halted and you are positioned on the failed Assert statement. For example, placing the following line of code in the previous For loop will prevent the error:

```
Dim c As New Collection, i As Long
c.Add "Test1"
For i = 0 To c.Count
  Debug.Assert i > 0
  Debug.Print c(i)
Next i
```

Note As you probably guessed, the preceding code is provided to illustrate the use of the Assert method, not as a working example.

An older method to achieve the same results as the Assert method, from the times when the Debug object was not available, is using a Stop statement, combined with an If statement, as shown here:

```
If i <= 0 Then Stop
```

The Stop statement causes VB to break while debugging an application. However, when executing the compiled application it functions as an End statement, causing the application to terminate. That means you must manually remove all calls to the Stop statement before compiling the application for release. In contrast, the calls to the Assert method are automatically removed when compiling the application. That is a good reason to use Assert and not Stop.

Changing the Value of Variables While Debugging

Another important debugging feature of Visual Basic is that it enables you to change the value of a variable while in debug mode. For example, you might realize what went wrong and want to continue the program. In this case, you need to set the value variable i to a legal value, that is, 1. You can do this using the Immediate window.

In the Immediate window, you can assign 1 to i using the = operator and pressing Enter. Then you can let the program complete properly. Figure 24.8 illustrates this.

Figure 24.8

Error-trapping options.

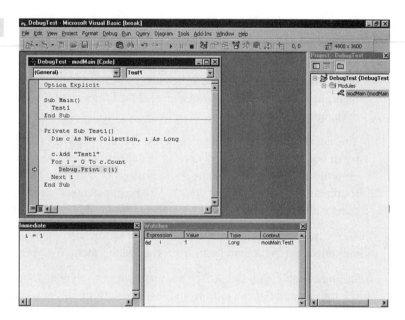

As you can see, after executing the line i = 1 in the Immediate window the value of i (shown in the Watches window) is 1. For objects, you can create new objects and use the Set operator to assign them to variables in context.

Changing the Code While Debugging

Visual Basic lets you change the code while debugging an application. In most cases, you can continue the debugging session without the need to restart. In some instances (for example, when changing the type of a variable or adding a new variable declaration), you might not be able to continue. In that case, Visual Basic offers you the choice to cancel your code changes or stop the debugging session.

24

Note Code changes can be made only while in debug mode and will not be saved to corresponding disk files. If Visual Basic crashes before you exit the debug session and save the files, your changes are lost. Note that code changing while debugging is a feature useful to correct minor problems, not to develop the application.

You can, in your example, change the lower bound of the For loop from 0 to 1. This fixes your problem.

Changing the Next Statement to Be Executed

You also have the option to reposition the *next statement*. The next statement is highlighted in yellow in debug mode (if you use the default color settings). This is the next statement that Visual Basic attempts to execute and can be any executable statement, including the End, Next, Loop, and Exit statements, but not including variable declarations (Dim, Redim).

You can set the next statement to be executed, with some restrictions. This is useful when you need to skip a few lines of code (for example, to avoid a known error), or even more useful to re-execute some portion of code (for example, to trace the source of a specific value or error). The next statement must be in the same procedure as the current statement, and normally should be outside loops.

To set the next statement, place the cursor on the statement you want to execute next and select Set Next Statement from the Debug menu (or press Ctrl+F9).

In this example, you can set the next statement to the For loop line after you change the lower bound of the loop from 0 to 1. You can then let the program run normally.

Note To set the next statement to a different procedure on the stack (that called the current procedure directly or indirectly) you can set the next statement of the current procedure to the End Sub (or End Function/End Property) statement and step out of the current procedure. Repeat these steps until you are in the procedure you want to set the next statement. Now you can set the next statement.

Note that this is an advanced feature and in some cases may produce unexpected results.

Error Handling Considerations When Debugging

If error handling is enabled, Visual Basic will not break on the line that caused the error; instead, it will pass the error to the handler. This is all fine when the application is in its final release form at the user site. However, it is a problem when debugging the application because you seldom can determine what line caused the error. There are two solutions to this problem.

The first solution involves using the Immediate window and the keyword `Resume`. Normally, if a handler is installed, you are displaying a message box with the error description. You can break after the error message is displayed, using Ctrl+Break. This places you on the line following the MsgBox call. At this point you can use the keyword `Resume`, typed in the Immediate window (without the preceding ?) to resume execution to the line that caused the error to be raised. The drawback of this method is that if the error is not raised in the method that has the error handler, you will not be positioned on the line that raised the error, but rather on the call to the method, function, or property from which that the error was raised.

The second method is simpler and more efficient. From the Tools menu, select Options. The Options dialog box opens. Select the General tab. The frame labeled Error Trapping has three options available, as illustrated by Figure 24.9. Selecting Break on All Errors causes Visual Basic to ignore the error handlers and break on each error as it is raised.

 Note   The Break in Class Modules option (default) has VB break for any unhandled error in a class module. This is useful for debugging ActiveX controls. The Break on Unhandled Errors has VB break on any error for which there is no error handler.

Figure 24.9

Error-trapping options.

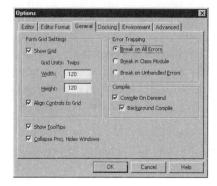

24

These options are preserved between sessions, so you might want to disable Break on All Errors when you test your error handlers.

Using Breakpoints and Stepping Through Code

Sometimes catching the exact cause of an error is harder than just stopping on the line that raises an error. This is especially true in real-life programs, where there are a lot of nested procedures, or when error handling is enabled, as you have seen previously.

For these cases, Visual Basic offers the capability to halt the program execution at any point in code (valid executable statement). These points are called breakpoints, and you can set a breakpoint in design or debug mode by positioning the cursor on the statement and selecting Toggle Break Point from the Debug menu, pressing F9, or clicking in the left margin of the code window next to the statement.

The line of code is highlighted in red and a breakpoint indicator is shown on the left margin of the code window as a red dot, as illustrated by Figure 24.10.

Figure 24.10

Setting a breakpoint.

A breakpoint instructs Visual Basic to stop there unconditionally. At this point you can inspect or change values of variables or allow the program to continue. If you need to step through each instruction as it is executed, you can use Debug, Step Into from the menu (or, even easier, use the F8 key). This executes the current statement, updates the variables, and sets the next statement according to the program logic. If the statement executed was a method or function call of one of your objects, pressing F8 will step into that method or function, hence the name Step Into.

If you know what a routine does and you do not want to step into it, but would rather execute it and step to the next statement in the current routine, you can use Debug, Step Over from the menu (or press Shift+F8).

If you inadvertently stepped into a procedure that you are not interested in, you can use Debug, Step Out from the menu (Ctrl+Shift+F8). This completes the current routine normally and breaks to the next statement in the code that called the first routine.

Yet another useful navigation function is to execute code up to a specific statement in which you are interested. You can do this without setting a breakpoint by using Debug, Run To Cursor from the menu (Ctrl+F8). This executes the code from the current statement to the first statement on the line where the cursor is in text.

Try these techniques in the sample program provided.

Using Conditional Breakpoints

The unconditional breakpoints are useful, but they do not cover all cases you encounter while debugging. Consider the following case: Procedure A calls function B from within a long loop (say a few hundred times). Function B crashes somewhere in the middle because of a Null value, and you must set a breakpoint in B to determine the cause. If you set the regular breakpoint, you will have the application stop a lot of times before you actually get the condition that caused the error. This can be a major waste of time.

This is where a conditional breakpoint (watch) comes in handy. In Visual Basic, you can set a watch on an expression that will cause a break when a certain condition becomes true or when the expression changes. For example, in this case you can set a conditional watch for the expression $c(i)$. Select the expression in code and select Debug, Add Watch from the menu. A dialog box similar to the one in Figure 24.11 is presented.

As you will notice, at the bottom of the dialog box there is a frame labeled Watch Type. This enables you to select the regular watch or one of two available break-watch combinations. The first break-watch type breaks when the expression evaluates to True, the second breaks when the value of the expression changes. The expression in this case is editable; you can use regular Visual Basic operators and functions as well as your own functions and object properties. For example, you could enter as a "break when true" expression:

```
i = 1 And c(i) = "Test1"
```

24

Figure 24.11

Setting a conditional breakpoint and watch.

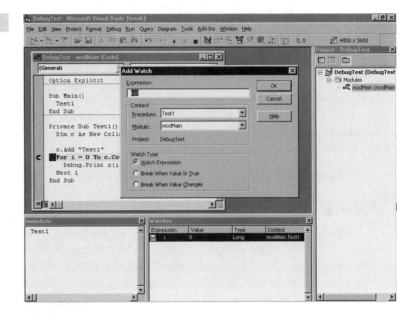

Testing the Application

After coding is completed for the application, you need to test the application for bugs. Testing applications is as important as developing them. It is important to catch as many problems as possible before releasing the application to the users.

We have left the implementation of the last forms that need to be added to this project (frmOrderList, frmOrderItems, and frmProductList) as an exercise for you, because they are similar to frmCustomerList. If you want to skip this step, copy the .frm and the .frx files from the Chapter24 folder on the CD to your development folder and add them to your project. Then, you must enable the menu items and toolbar buttons that open them from frmMain.

The testing process normally involves a few distinct steps:

- Unit testing
- System integration testing
- Quality control testing

Unit testing is mandatory for all applications and is the responsibility of the developer. It involves testing the functionality of the application as extensively as possible.

This is usually achieved by using a series of test cases, or scenarios that emulate what the user goes through while using the application.

In this case, you have done some testing as you developed each form. Now that the project is complete, you need to test the whole functionality: add, modify, and delete a customer; browse the customers list; add, modify, and delete a product; browse products list; create an order; and add items. Change the order status, browse the orders list, try the image and document view forms for the product, try all the menus and toolbars, and try the help system.

This is considered the unit test for this application.

The system integration testing and quality control testing are generally used in software development shops and are performed by specialized personnel (quality control engineers) using special tools and systems. These testing methods are beyond the scope of this book.

Next Steps

In this chapter, you learned about debugging and testing applications. You have classified the types of errors an application can run into. You have explored most debugging techniques offered by Visual Basic, including the Debug object, and you have learned some useful tips on how to efficiently remove bugs from your programs.

The next chapter summarizes the steps you went through to build this project.

24

In this chapter

- *Analysis*
- *Design*
- *Implementation*
- *Documentation and Testing*

Chapter 25

Revisiting the Process

This chapter summarizes what you have learned so far. We will start by revisiting the development life cycle of an application. As we go through the various phases of the development cycle, we will review the most important Visual Basic programming concepts you have learned.

During the course of this book we have walked through most of the steps required in developing an application, although not always in order. The following paragraphs will summarize these steps.

Analysis

It is said that the analysis must provide an answer to the question "What?". The first important step in the development of an application is the analysis phase. This phase consists of collecting and analyzing the information that will determine what the application is supposed to do. This information normally comes from the users of the application. It can be informal (simply discussing with the users what they want) or formal (a document outlining the user requirements).

The scope of this phase is to understand exactly who the users of the application are and what needs this application is going to solve for them. This means that you need to have a global understanding of the functionality of the application you are planning to develop.

EXCURSION

Analysis and Use Case Scenarios

For large systems, the analysis phase is very important. Understanding what the system is going to do once developed is of utmost importance. In these cases, the output of the analysis phase is normally a set of formal documents that outline the results of the analysis. The content and the detail level of these documents is highly dependent on the type of application and the methodology employed in the analysis phase. For example, if a variation of use-case methodology is used, then the output is a set of use-case scenarios and diagrams.

A *use case* consists of a sequence of operations the system will perform in response to a request from a user. The users of a system, as well as any other entities that interact with the system, are known as *actors* in the context of this methodology.

We did not emphasize the analysis phase in this book because the main goal was to learn Visual Basic programming.

In this case, we wanted to build a simple order entry application for a small business. Users of the application would be the sales staff of the business. The functions that the system must provide were the capability to add and maintain information about customers and products, to enter orders, and so on.

Design

The next phase in developing an application is to design the application. Again, the exact definition of what this phase is supposed to accomplish is dependent on the type and size of the application developed, and on the development methodology. It can be as simple as a few diagrams sketched on paper or as detailed as design documents incorporating hundreds or even thousands of diagrams of various types.

It is generally agreed that the design phase is providing the answer to the question "How?" When this phase is completed, the developer should have an idea of how to implement the functionality specified by the analysis phase. The design phase can consist of a few steps: global design, proof of concept (or prototype), and detail design. Again, each of these steps can mean different things in different development methodologies and development shops.

A special step in designing an application is modeling the data on which the system will operate. This step often consists of modeling a persistent data storage system, usually a relational database. We have seen briefly what the output of this step is in the previous chapters.

Although we did have a design in mind while building our application, we did not dedicate a lot of time explaining it. The reasons behind this decision were twofold: Understanding the design would require special knowledge, and it is not really part of the scope of this book.

EXCURSION
Analysis and Design Tools

The analysis and design of an application require knowledge of a modeling language, normally the Unified Modeling Language (UML), and the use of one of the design tools available. One of the most commonly used tools for analysis and design is Rational Rose. The Visual Basic 6 Enterprise Edition comes with Visual Modeler, which is a limited version of Rational Rose.

These tools enable the user to create a model of the application. The model consists of classes and objects and the relationships between them. Each class has properties and methods. Normally the entities in a model are shown using several kinds of diagrams. The best known are class diagrams, collaboration diagrams, sequence diagrams, and state diagrams.

When a model is finalized, it is presented to the developers who are going to implement it. Sometimes the original design is not complete, and might change a few times during the development process (for example, as a result of finding a better solution or to avoid a problem discovered during implementation). This approach is called iterative development and is relatively new.

Implementation

We illustrated the implementation phase in this book. This phase consists of writing the code that will, in the end, be the application itself or one of its components. The code is normally based on the design specifications from the previous phase. Depending on the type of application being developed, the implementation strategies can differ quite a bit. We will focus on user interface (UI) applications, which are the type of applications to which Visual Basic is targeted.

Graphical Design of the UI

The first phase of implementing a UI application is to design the main forms of the application.

 Note   By *design* in this context, we mean *graphical* design of the user interface, which is not the same as the design phase for the application as mentioned previously.

It is important to design these forms with the user in mind. There are a few concepts to remember when designing forms in Visual Basic:

- Keep the forms simple and intuitive. Do not add too many controls on one form—it can get confusing.
- Do not add controls on the same form that perform totally unrelated functions.
- Select the controls that best fit the function they are meant to do.
- Group together controls that are related by functionality. Use Frame controls or other container controls to group controls together.
- Set the TabIndex properties correctly, according to the order in which you expect the user to access them.
- Provide alternate ways to execute the same operations, that is, menus and tool-bar buttons, command buttons and shortcut keys, pop-up menus, and so on. Different users have different preferences in the methods they use to access a specific function of your system.
- Saving user preferences (like form positions, items open, and so on) between sessions can be a highly appreciated feature.
- Align and size the controls properly. Remember that different users might use different screen resolutions.
- Use the standard color schema as much as possible. Hard-coding colors can render a beautifully designed form unreadable, if the user has a nonstandard color schema.
- Use resizable forms for displaying items that can potentially be larger than would fit in the form (for example, grids, trees, lists, images, and so on).

After the forms are designed, the next step is to implement navigation. This is done by implementing the event procedures for the menus, buttons, mouse, and similar controls. It is important to plan and correctly implement form- and application-level navigation. For example, make sure you ask for confirmation before closing a form that contains data that was changed, and also handle the QueryUnload event to hide a dialog box rather than close it if another part of code waits for some data from that dialog box.

Adding Objects

The next step normally involves implementing the objects that access the data the application is using or provide the logic behind the program. We cannot stress enough the importance of separating the logic of an application (that is, the business rules) from the UI forms; hence, the need to create the business objects the UI is using to implement its functionality.

These objects are normally class modules that encapsulate the data manipulated by the application and the methods associated with that data. A few tips and ideas on how to implement this type of objects follows:

- Do not use public data members. It breaks the fundamental principle of encapsulation.

- Provide public accessor (Get) properties for all data members that need to be exposed. Provide update properties (Set/Let) only for the properties that can be changed by the clients of the class.

- Make sure to release all object reference data members in the Class_Terminate procedure.

- Use friendly names for classes and methods. Even within a programmer-friendly environment like Visual Basic, a method named DC does not mean a lot to the clients of the class. A better name would be DeleteCustomer.

- Make sure you trap the errors correctly. Use assertions to guard against programming errors during the development time.

- Implement collection classes to handle lists of objects correctly.

- Be careful in handling object references—avoid circular references.

- Do not add redundant functionality: if you have a property Set/Let for a data member, adding another method to set the value of that member is not only useless, but confusing.

After the business objects for the application are implemented, you can proceed to the next step, which is to integrate their functionality with the user interface forms and controls.

Integrating the System

Adding the functionality behind the forms using the business objects is the most complex part of programming we have seen so far. It involves knowledge of both the user interface and of the business objects. Quite often this step consists of a few iterations. The following are some general ideas on how to proceed:

- Try to keep the UI code clean—use the functionality provided by the business objects to implement business rules, the UI code to deal with displaying and gathering of data.

- Make sure you release the object references when you are finished with them.

- Do not keep instantiated objects around longer than necessary.

- Limit the number of objects that are used by each form; do not load large lists of objects in one form.

- If more forms share the same object, pass a reference to it rather than create a new instance.
- Trap the errors and display meaningful error messages to the user. Allow them to retry the failed operation, if applicable.
- Any data conversions, calculations (non-UI), and validation should be done by the objects and not by the form.

When this step is completed you can say that you have a working application. The final steps involve documenting and testing the application.

Documentation and Testing

Every application must have some form of help, to assist the user in day-to-day work with the system. It can be as simple as ToolTips and a document explaining what the most important functions of the application are, and how to use them. Or it can be an involved online help, with references and examples.

Testing is the last phase before delivering the application. As you have briefly seen in the previous chapter, this is also an important step. The developer is supposed to test every function of the system, ideally in more than one set of conditions. This ensures that all bugs in the system are caught before the user runs into them.

This concludes the summary of the phases involved in developing an application.

Next Steps

In this chapter, we summarized the steps involved in creating a new application as you have learned them during the course of this book.

In the next chapter, you learn about components and distributing your application. You create an ActiveX component DLL and place all the classes in this DLL.

Chapter 26

Distributed Components: The Way of the Future

Introduction

Throughout this book, you have developed a complete application using one Visual Basic project. This was intentional to focus on the development of the application and the use of the Visual Basic language. We did not want to make the learning process more complicated than what was required. Now that you have finished the application, we need talk about an alternative approach to constructing the application.

As the application stands right now, you have one project named VBFS that creates a VBFS.EXE executable file. This VBFS.EXE file contains all the code you developed throughout the book. In this chapter, you are going to create another Visual Basic project and split some of the code you already developed into the current project and the new project.

 Note The code within VBFS.EXE is actually compiled code and is not readable like the code you can see in the Code window.

If you used the Visual Basic Working Model Edition as you developed the application in the book, you will not be able to use it to follow along with this chapter. This is because you cannot create DLL projects with that version.

A *Dynamic Link Library (DLL)* contains compiled code that can be called from an application executable or from another DLL. DLLs are useful for placing commonly used code in one place. This allows many applications to use the same code without having to actually link the code directly into the applications executable file. Windows supports placing common code and services in DLLs for many applications to benefit from. If there needs to be a change to the code in the DLL, the change can be made in one place, and all users of the DLL benefit from the change. Without DLLs, changes would need to be made to each application.

The topics discussed in this chapter are commonly used in developing Visual Basic applications. Now that you are almost finished with this book and have a much better understanding of how to build applications in Visual Basic, you might want to get a copy of Visual Basic that enables you to create DLLs.

Advantages of Distributed Components

If the application is complete and works, why would you want to split up the code? In the simplest case, you could call the application complete and distribute the application as it is—just one executable file. However, let's talk about some advantages to splitting it up first.

The prevailing theme in modern application development is developing multiple logical tiers. The term *tier* is meant to describe a logical layer of application logic. Each logical layer has distinct responsibilities in relation to other logical tiers within an application. The idea is that the first tier talks to the second tier, the second tier talks to the third tier, and so on. Each tier performs its defined role and responsibilities. Figure 26.1 shows a three-tiered application.

Figure 26.1

A three-tiered application.

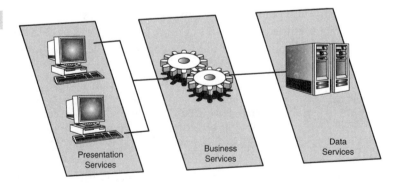

Presentation Services

Business Services

Data Services

The first tier is comprised of the Presentation Services, which is also commonly referred to as the User Interface (UI). The Presentation Services communicates with

26

the second tier to get information to display to the user and to send back the user's input.

The second tier is comprised of the Business Services. The word *Business* is used here to describe the type of logic that exists at this layer. This logic generally revolves around some business processing or workflow and is specific to the business requirements of the application. We also want to point out that the code in this tier has the potential to change frequently. This code must change as the business requirements of the application change.

The third tier is made up of the Data Services. The code in this layer is responsible for providing access to the necessary data for the Business Services layer. Ideally, this layer totally encapsulates the storage of data so that the second tier does not need to know anything about where the data lives.

As you can see, each tier has a defined role it plays in an overall application. Microsoft has also recognized this and now has a term that defines its vision of the application development model for multitiered applications: Windows DNA.

 Windows DNA stands for Microsoft Windows Distributed interNet Applications Architecture. Basically, Windows DNA is the roadmap for developing n-tiered applications using Microsoft technologies. Windows DNA defines three logical tiers: Presentation, Business Logic, and Data.

EXCURSION

Windows DNA

Windows DNA is a multitiered distributed applications model. Within this model, Microsoft presents three logical tiers: Presentation, Business Logic, and Data. Based on these three tiers, Microsoft also presents technologies that can be used in each of these tiers to develop applications that solve business problems.

In the Presentation tier, you can develop Web pages using HTML to present Web content to users. A variety of tools today help with the development of professional-looking Web pages. The advantages of using HTML in the Presentation tier includes browser independence and a thin client. Browser independence is important so that you are not requiring your users to use a specific browser to view your Web pages. A thin client is important to reduce the complexity and resources involved with using your application. If you must require your users to install software on their computers in order to use the application you develop, your user base will be limited and require more work when it comes time to upgrade the application. Not all Presentation tiers are HTML based today; there remains the need for developing this tier as an executable. This can be accomplished using a tool such as Visual Basic.

The Business Logic tier begins to get more interesting with a more extensive set of available technologies. Available technologies for this tier include IIS, MTS, MSMQ, and COM+.

Microsoft Internet Information Server (IIS) makes it easy to serve Web pages to requesting Web browsers. IIS also supports Active Server Pages (ASP). ASP is essentially scripting support added to HTML pages. With ASP, you are able to inject scripting of components into your HTML pages. This enables you to work with COM components written in VB, C++, or Java directly within your HTML page. Because the process of ASP scripts is performed on the server and not the client, the COM components scripted by ASP need to exist only on the Business Logic tier. This retains browser independence.

Microsoft Transaction Server (MTS) supports the development of transactional COM components. As part of the Business Logic tier, this enables you to develop components that perform business logic with a simplified component transactional model. MTS simplifies the starting and committing of transactions including thread management, security, database connection pooling, and component administration.

Microsoft Message Queueing (MSMQ) supports a message-based architecture. MSMQ supports the submittal of a message into a queue for later delivery. The message sender can then move on to do other tasks while MSMQ takes responsibility for delivering the message.

COM+ is the result of combining COM services with MTS services and will be introduced as part of the Windows 2000 operating system.

The Data tier is where the data resides. Microsoft's strategy for this tier is Universal Data Access (UDA). As it is defined today, UDA has two parts, OLE DB and ADO. OLE DB is a defined set of interfaces that encapsulates a wide variety of data stores, including relational and nonrelational databases. ADO is a high-level programming interface that simplifies the process of writing database code.

The goal of developing an application based on logical tiers is to support componentized development. By componentized, I mean the development of code that is grouped into separate areas of functionality. When an application is developed this way, it is possible to entirely change the user interface without affecting the code that deals with business processing and data storage. If the business processing changes (not the interface), you can modify the business logic without affecting the user interface and data storage. Also, if the structure of the database changes, you can modify the code at the data services layer without affecting the user interface or business processing.

In fairness, there are changes that occur at each of these layers that could require changes in the other layers. This implies that the interfaces between the layers require changing. To minimize these changes, you must have a well-thought-out design of your application and pay close attention to the interfaces between the layers. You want to design interfaces specific to your application that also support a broader use. A well-thought-out design based on multiple tiers pays off in the end.

A multitiered application also provides options when it comes time to deploy the application. Depending on the expected number of users, you can deploy components on several servers to meet the demand. As the demand increases or decreases, you can manage this without affecting the application logic. You now have the ability to create a deployment strategy for your application to meet the demand without requiring software changes.

If you are using Visual Basic in the development of mulitiered applications, the first tier (UI) is built using forms and UI controls. The second and third tiers are built by creating VB classes as part of a DLL. After building the DLLs, the classes are exposed as COM components. This enables you to create objects, based on your classes, within other Visual Basic projects. We will see exactly how this happens later in this chapter.

Exposing your classes as COM components enables you to deploy your application on multiple computers. Essentially, you can have the user interface running on one computer, business-related COM components running on another computer, and data-related COM components running on yet another computer. There are many considerations for determining exactly how you deploy your application components, which we will not get into here. The point is that creating Visual Basic classes in a DLL project gives you the capability to deploy them as you choose.

Splitting the Projects

You might be thinking that all this multitiered stuff might be a little too much for this beginner-level Visual Basic book. The intention is to give a broader picture of the types of applications being developed today and where VB fits into that picture. Throughout this book you are shielded from this big picture on purpose so you could focus on learning Visual Basic. Because DLLs are an important aspect of Visual Basic programming and software development, let's go through the development of a Visual Basic DLL project.

Let's start splitting the code into two projects so that you can see how this is done. The goal here is to create another VB project, named VBFSDLL, and move all the class modules from the VBFS project to the new VBFSDLL project.

The first step is to remove all the class modules from the VBFS project. To do this, right-click on each class module in the Project Explorer window and select Remove on the menu that appears. If you right-click on the Customer class module, you will see a menu item with the caption Remove Customer.cls. The caption changes for each class module on which you right-click. Doing this does not delete the actual file. It only removes it from the project. After all the class modules are removed from the VBFS project, save the project.

Next, you must create another VB project. Click on the File, New Project menu item.

After selecting this menu item, a dialog box appears similar to the one shown in Figure 26.2. Click the ActiveX DLL icon to create a DLL project that supports the development of COM components. Once again, you will need a version of Visual Basic besides the Working Model Edition to create an ActiveX DLL project.

Figure 26.2

Create an ActiveX DLL project.

This creates a new project with a new class module named Class1. Delete the Class1 class module by right-clicking it in the Project Explorer window and selecting the Remove Class1 menu item. A dialog box then appears asking you if you want to save the class module. Click No. Change the name of the project by first selecting the project in the Project Explorer, then modifying the name property in the Properties window. Change the name to VBFSDLL. Now save the project using the File, Save Project menu item and save the VBFSDLL.vbp file in the same directory as the VBFS project.

Now, you need to add the class modules that you developed as part of the VBFS project. Click on the Project, Add Class Module menu item to add class modules. A dialog box appears that is similar to the one shown in Figure 26.3.

Figure 26.3

The Add Class Module dialog box.

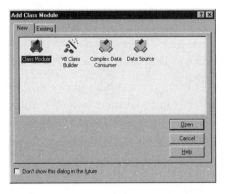

Select the Existing tab to add existing class modules to the current project. Browse your directories to find the existing class files you have already developed. If you created the VBFSDLL project in the same directory as the VBFS project, the class modules should already be showing on the Existing tab window. This window does not allow for multiple selection. Therefore, you must use the Project, Add Class Module menu item for each class module. When you are finished adding all six of the class modules (Customer, DbSession, Order, OrderItem, OrderItemColl, and Product), save the project.

Now you need to set the Instancing property on each of these classes. This property is now available to set because the class modules are within an ActiveX DLL. Table 26.1 lists the valid values of the Instancing property.

Table 26.1   Instancing Property Values

Value	*Description*
1 - Private	The default setting that enables you to only create objects of this type within the current project. Other applications are not allowed to create objects of this type.
2 - PublicNotCreatable	Other applications are not allowed to create objects of this class but they can use the objects if they were created within this project first.
3 - SingleUse	This setting allows other applications to create objects of this class but forces a new instance of your project to be started. This setting is not allowed in ActiveX DLL projects.
4 - GlobalSingleUse	Just like SingleUse, plus the properties and methods of the class can be invoked just as if they were regular global functions. This setting is not allowed in ActiveX DLL projects.
5 - MultiUse	Other applications are allowed to create objects of this class. One instance of the project can create any number of these objects.
6-GlobalMultiUse	Just like MultiUse, plus the properties and methods of the class can be invoked just as if they were regular global functions.

For the Customer, Order, OrderItem, and Product class modules, set the Instancing property to MultiUse. This allows the VBFS application project to instantiate these types of objects.

Because the Order creates the OrderItemColl object within it and the VBFS application does not, set the Instancing property on the OrderItemColl class to PublicNotCreateable.

Also, the DbSession class has methods that you want to call directly from the VBFS application. To support this, set the Instancing property to GlobalMultiUse. You will see how this is used later in this chapter.

If you try to build the VBFSDLL project at this point, you will get a compile error because the implementation of the classes relies on a couple of functions in the modMain module within the VBFS application and the global DbSession variable.

To resolve the global variable reference problem, create a new code module in the VBFSDLL project and name it dllMain, and then save it. Enter the following code into the dllMain code module:

dllMain(dllMain.cls)

```
Public gSession As New DbSession
```

Now the VBFSDLL project has its own global DbSession object to use.

The last problems to solve are the functions nns and EnsureMaxLength. Both projects, VBFS and VBFSDLL, use these functions. One approach is to just duplicate the functions in the VBFSDLL project. This involves copying the functions from the modMain module of the VBFS project to the dllMain module of the VBFSDLL project. Although this would work, duplicating code is not a good idea. The solution here is to put the functions into the VBFSDLL project and modify the VBFS project to use the functions defined in the VBFSDLL project. That way, both projects are reusing the same code.

To do this, you are going to create another class in the VBFSDLL project and put the two functions in this class. Then you are going to set the instancing property of the class to GlobalMultiUse. This enables the main VBFS project to call the functions nns and EnsureMaxLength directly without having to specify an object variable name. This means you do not need to change the way the functions are called within the VBFS project.

Create a new class module and name it Utility. Then enter this code in the class module:

Utility(Utility.cls)

```
Public Function nns(v As Variant) As String
  If IsNull(v) Then nns = "" Else nns = v
End Function

Public Sub EnsureMaxLength(s As String, ByVal maxLen As Long)
  If Len(s) > maxLen Then s = Left(s, maxLen)
End Sub
```

Within the VBFSDLL project, these functions are now within a class module. The instancing property value of GlobalMultiUse is treated as MultiUse from within the project. This means that within the VBFSDLL project you cannot directly call the EnsureMaxLength function as in the following sample code:

Customer(Customer.cls)

```
Public Property Let lastName(x As String)
  EnsureMaxLength x, 32
  m_lastName = x
End Property
```

You must create a Utility object and call the EnsureMaxLength method of that object. To do this, first add the following code to the dllMain code module:

dllMain(dllMain.cls)

```
Public gUtility As New Utility
```

This creates a global Utility object within the VBFSDLL project. Next, replace all calls to EnsureMaxLength and nns with gUtility.EnsureMaxLength and gUtility.nns, respectively. For example, the updated code would look like this:

Customer(Customer.cls)

```
Public Property Let lastName(x As String)
  gUtility.EnsureMaxLength x, 32
  m_lastName = x
End Property
```

Because the VBFS project is now using the functions nns and EnsureMaxLength, which reside in the VBFSDLL project, you should now delete the nns and EnsureMaxLength functions from the VBFS project because they are no longer needed.

At this point, the VBFSDLL project contains all the necessary code. The next section deals with the project settings before you can build and run it.

Project Settings

Earlier in the book, you set the project references to include the Microsoft ActiveX Data Objects 2.0 Library because you needed the components within this library to access the database. Now that you have created another project and moved your classes to it, you need to set the project references in the VBFSDLL project to include the Microsoft ActiveX Data Objects 2.0 Library. Click the Project menu then click the References menu item to bring up the project References dialog box. This dialog box is shown in Figure 26.4. Scroll down to find the Microsoft ActiveX Data Objects 2.0 Library entry and click to select it. Then click OK to accept the changes.

The VBFSDLL project requires the Microsoft ActiveX Data Objects 2.0 Library because the classes contain all the database code for your application. Because you just moved the classes from the VBFS project to the VBFSDLL project, there is no longer any need for the VBFS project to have a reference to the Microsoft ActiveX Data Objects 2.0 Library because the remaining code in the VBFS project does not interact with a database. At this point, remove the reference to the Microsoft ActiveX Data Objects 2.0 Library from the VBFS project. If you do not remove the reference, the project still works but you will need to include the ADO library as part of the installation program you create to distribute your application. This would be additional unnecessary overhead because the ADO library is not used for the VBFS project.

Figure 26.4

The VBFSDLL project References dialog box.

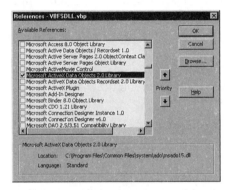

Now build the project by clicking the File menu and then clicking the Make VBFS-DLL.dll menu item. A dialog box appears with the default filename of VBFSDLL.dll. Leave this name as is and click OK to build the DLL. The DLL should now be built and ready to use.

You now need to go back to the VBFS project, clean up some code, and include the reference to the VBFSDLL project in order to use it. Open the VBFS project (if it is not already open), and click the Project-References menu item to bring up the dialog box to include a reference to VBFSDLL. Scroll down until you see VBFSDLL and click it to select it, then click OK to accept the changes. Figure 26.5 shows the project References dialog box and the selected reference to VBFSDLL.

In the VBFS project, you defined a global variable named gSession in the modMain code module. This variable stores the global DbSession object that is used by the classes and the application. Because you moved the global variable to the dllMain code module within the VBFSDLL project, you must comment out the line here because you do not need it. Change the line declaring the global gSession variable to look like this:

Figure 26.5

The VBFS project References dialog box.

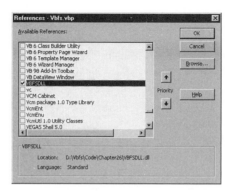

26

modMain(modMain.cls)

```
'Public gSession As New DbSession
```

This comments out the line so that it is not included in the compiled application. Now after you do this, any reference to the gSession variable in the VBFS project causes a compile error. Remember earlier when you set the Instancing property on the DbSession class to GlobalMultiUse? You did this so that you could call the methods on the DbSession object directly. In order to fix the compile errors you just created by commenting out the gSession variable declaration, you must modify every line of code in the VBFS project that uses gSession. The fastest way to do this is to press the Ctrl+F5 key combination that compiles the project. The first error you encounter should be on a line that references the gSession variable. Here is an example that you could run into:

frmLoginDlg(frmLoginDlg.frm)

```
Private Sub cmdLogin_Click()
  If Not gSession.CheckLogin(txtUserId, txtPassword) Then
    MsgBox "Invalid user ID or password", vbCritical, "Login failed"
    Exit Sub
  End If

  frmMain.userName = txtUserId
  frmMain.userPwd = txtPassword
  frmMain.Show
  Unload Me
End Sub
```

On the second line of code, notice the use of the gSession variable. Change the code to remove the gSession like this:

frmLoginDlg(frmLoginDlg.frm)

```
Private Sub cmdLogin_Click()
  If Not CheckLogin(txtUserId, txtPassword) Then
    MsgBox "Invalid user ID or password", vbCritical, "Login failed"
    Exit Sub
  End If

  frmMain.userName = txtUserId
  frmMain.userPwd = txtPassword
  frmMain.Show
  Unload Me
End Sub
```

You can do this because you set the Instancing property of the DbSession class module to GlobalMultiUse. This enables you to directly call a method of the DbSession class as though it were a global function. Keep using the Ctrl+F5 key combination to find and resolve the compile errors. Whenever the use of the gSession variable is the cause of the problem, modify the code as you just did in the previous code example. Now save the project.

At this point, you have completed the task of splitting the project into two projects. Build the executable file by selecting the File, Make VBFS.exe menu item, and run it.

Although we are finished, there are more project settings worth noting in the VBFS-DLL project. Open the VBFSDLL project (if it is not already opened) and select the Project, VBFSDLL Properties menu item. This brings up the dialog box shown in Figure 26.6.

Figure 26.6

The Project Properties dialog box.

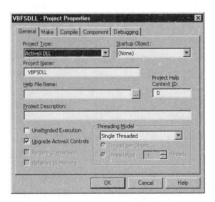

The two tabs you want to concern yourself with are the Component tab and the Debugging tab.

Click the Component tab to display the window shown in Figure 26.7.

Figure 26.7

The Component tab of the Project Properties dialog box.

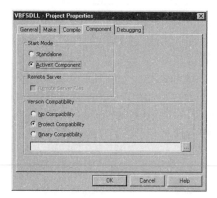

On this window, you can set the Version Compatibility of this project.

There are three types of Version Compatibility from which to choose. Before we review these types, you need to understand type library information. As mentioned a few times already, class modules in an ActiveX DLL project are the way to create COM objects using Visual Basic. Also, COM is a binary compatible standard that supports building language-neutral components. These components can then be used within several different software languages including C++, Visual Basic, and Java (using the Microsoft Java Virtual Machine). When you build COM components, you are required to provide the type library information that is used to express the definition of the components. This definition includes specific unique identifiers for the project or library, the classes, and the interfaces. Visual Basic simplifies all this for you by managing the type library information automatically. There are certain cases where you do not want Visual Basic to manage this entirely for you and you need some control. Hence, the capability to set the version compatibility on the project.

After you have built the ActiveX DLL project and include a reference to it in another project, you must be aware of what happens when you rebuild the ActiveX DLL and what the repercussions are. If you set No Compatibility, all the unique identifiers for the library, classes, and interfaces are regenerated every time the project is rebuilt (using the Make DLL option from the File menu). Using your example, assume you built the VBFSDLL project and in the VBFS project you set a reference to the VBFSDLL. If you then go back and rebuild the VBFSDLL project, all the unique identifiers are regenerated. This causes the reference in the VBFS project to be broken and requires you to clear the reference, and then re-add the reference to the VBFSDLL as part of the VBFS project.

The next option is Project Compatibility. This option retains the unique identifiers in the type library information with one exception. If the interface becomes binary incompatible to earlier versions of the component, a new unique identifier is generated for the interface. An interface becomes incompatible if you add a method to a class, remove a method from a class, or change the number or types of parameters.

The last option is Binary Compatibility. This option is identical to Project Compatibility except that if an incompatibility is detected during the building of the project, you are presented with a warning message. If you ignore the warning, all identifiers are kept intact and no identifiers are regenerated. If you do not ignore the warning, the interface identifiers are regenerated for the interfaces that have changed.

For the VBFSDLL project, set the version compatibility to Project Compatibility.

Now click on the Debugging tab to display the window shown in Figure 26.8.

Figure 26.8

The Debugging tab of the Project Properties dialog box.

On this window, you can set the application that uses this project. DLLs do not run by themselves the way applications (EXE) files do. DLLs are loaded by an application and used while the application is running. After the application exists, the DLL is unloaded from memory. So if you want to start debugging a DLL, you need an application that uses it. On this window, you have a few options to define the controlling application when you start the debugging process.

The first option is Wait for Components to Be Created. Selecting this option loads the DLL into memory and waits for an application that uses the DLL to start. Once an application that uses the DLL starts, the application connects to the DLL already running and binds to it. If there are any breakpoints defined in the DLL project, program control stops once a breakpoint is encountered.

The second option is Start Program. This option enables you to browse and select an executable file (EXE) to run when you start the debugging process. Presumably,

26

you would choose an executable file that you know uses this DLL. In this example, you could select the VBFS.EXE file to automatically start when you initiate the debugging process.

The third option is Start Browser with URL. This option enables you to run a Web browser with a given URL. This is used to support the debugging of your DLL that may be used in the context of a Web application. In this text box, specify the URL for the browser to point to. If the Use Existing Browser" check box is checked, this means the debugging session will check to see whether there is already a browser window opened. If one is opened, it is used, otherwise a new browser window is opened.

For the Debugging options, set the Start Program to VBFS.EXE. This enables you to automatically start the compiled VBFS application that uses the VBFSDLL project. You can set breakpoints and debug as you normally would. Keep in mind you cannot debug the main application this way because you started the debugging process by launching VBFS.EXE. A useful way to debug both projects using two separate instances of Visual Basic is to set the Start Program to launch Visual Basic. To do this, edit the text box to specify the location of Visual Basic and the name of the project to start. For example, on my computer I would set the Start Program option to C:\Program Files\Microsoft Visual Studio\VB98\Vb6.exe VBFS.vbp. This automatically starts another Visual Basic workspace and opens the VBFS project. After this project is opened, press the F5 key to start debugging the VBFS project. At this point, you have two projects that you are debugging.

Next Steps

In this chapter, you took the complete application you built throughout the book and split it into two VB projects. We did this to demonstrate the ability to partition an application to provide several benefits. These include reusable components, the capability to change code at each layer without affecting the entire application, and the capability to have deployable units of software based on specific application layers. Today's software applications are built by combining several components into one user experience.

We chose to move all the class modules to the second VB project, which is defined as ActiveX DLL project. After the class modules are moved and the second project is built, the resulting DLL contains a set of COM components that can be used within another VB application. The COM components also can be used by other languages such as C++ and Java, if you are interested.

We also reviewed the project settings associated with ActiveX DLL projects. This includes setting the appropriate version compatibility and the debug settings.

Part VI

Appendixes

Appendix A

COM, ActiveX, and Automation

This appendix summarizes the basic principles of the Component Object Model (COM). We will also explain some related terms, such as ActiveX and Automation.

COM is a standard (originally developed by Microsoft) that defines the mechanisms that enable *software components* to interact with each other as binary objects. Software components consist of data and the associated methods to access and manipulate this data. These components are known as COM classes. The methods a component exposes are grouped within *interfaces*. An interface can be viewed as a group of methods exposed by the *server component* (the component that exposes the interface) and the *client* (the software that is using the component interface). After an interface is defined, it becomes a fixed contract between the client and the server.

The client component is guaranteed that a published interface will not change, and it will behave in a consistent manner, no matter what server is exposing it. The client uses an instance of the server component as a binary object; it does not have access or knowledge about how the server component is implementing the interface.

Because this is a binary standard, the server component can be developed in any language and on any operating system that supports COM. It can be used from the same process as the client or from a different process, on the same machine or on a remote machine.

It is important to understand that COM is a standard and not a language for building distributed applications. It does not specify any implementation details. These depend on the language and operating system in which the implementation takes place. However, COM does specify the requirements the components must satisfy in order to interact with each other and with the client, regardless of the programming language used to implement them.

Implementing COM Interfaces

COM defines a set of base interfaces that can be used by a component. It also defines a small set of global utility functions.

A COM class is said to *implement an interface* if it provides an implementation (code) that matches the definition for that interface. An interface can *inherit* from another interface, which means it has all the methods of the interface from which it is inheriting. In Object-Oriented (OO) terminology it is said that, if interface B inherits from interface A, B *extends* A, B *specializes* A, or B is *derived* from A.

> In Visual Basic, this is accomplished by using the `implements` statement in a class module followed by the name of the interface you want to implement. There are some restrictions on the types of interfaces that can be implemented in VB classes.

A COM class can implement multiple interfaces, which means it must provide code for all methods of each interface it implements.

All COM classes must implement one base predefined interface, named `IUnknown`. This can be done by directly implementing `IUnknown` or implementing an interface that is derived from `IUnknown`. All interfaces (both the ones specified by COM and the ones you create) must inherit from the `IUnknown`.

The `IUnknown` interface has three methods: `QueryInterface`, `AddRef`, and `Release`. That means that each COM component supports these three methods. The `AddRef` and `Release` methods control the lifetime of the object by maintaining an internal reference count. The `AddRef` increments the count by one, while `Release` decrements the count by one. If an object's reference count reaches 0, the object is deallocated (deleted). The `QueryInterface` method determines whether an object supports a specific interface, passed in as an argument. If it does, it will return a reference to that interface, which the client can use to access methods defined by that interface.

> In Visual Basic you do not have to worry about this interface because all COM objects you create have them. The Visual Basic runtime is handling these methods automatically for you.

COM provides mechanisms to reuse components developed by others, and to extend their functionality to match your needs. This reusability is one of the basic concepts of object-oriented development. COM offers two mechanisms to implement reusability: *containment/delegation* and *aggregation*. It does not support inheritance at the class level.

Containment/delegation consists of a class (known as the container or the outer class) that extends the functionality and contains a reference to the extended class (known as the inner class). When the outer class needs to access the inner class methods, it uses this reference. The outer and inner classes do not necessarily implement the same interfaces.

Aggregation is similar to containment/delegation, but the outer class exposes the methods of the inner class directly, as they would be part of outer class itself.

 Aggregation is not supported in VB, as of version 6.

Microsoft COM-Based Technologies

COM is used in multiple ways in software development. A few COM-based technologies are worth mentioning:

- OLE (Object Linking and Embedding)—These technologies deal with compound documents (for example document files that contain embedded spreadsheets and images).
- ActiveX—This technology includes development of visual components known as controls. These controls use a lot of other COM derived objects, such as compound documents, property pages, and so on.

 ActiveX controls are the controls that we used during the project; for example TreeView, MaskedEditBox, and so on.

- Automation—This is defined as the capability of an application to programmatically control another application (known as an automation server). For example, from Visual Basic you can control the way Word displays and prints a document.

Appendix B

Visual Basic Controls

This appendix summarizes the standard properties, methods, and events common to all VB controls. Next, we will discuss the most significant properties, methods, and events for the intrinsic VB controls.

Standard Properties, Methods, and Events

A set of properties, methods, and events is common to all or most controls (both intrinsic and custom). They are summarized in Tables B.1 through B.3. The [All] tag indicates that call controls support this property, method, or event. The [Some] flag indicates that only some controls support it (potentially most controls).

Table B.1   Standard Properties

Property	Type	Description
Name	String	The name of the control [All]
Index	Integer	The index of the control in a control array [All].
Container	Object	The object on which the control is placed [All].
Parent	Object	The form, object, or collection that contains the control [All].
Tag	String	A user-defined value attached to each control. For some controls this is a Variant (that is, can be an object) [All].
Appearance	Integer	Indicates whether the control is shown flat or using a 3D enhanced frame [Some].
BackColor, ForeColor	Color	The background and foreground colors used by the control [Some].

continues

Table B.1 continued

Property	Type	Description
DragIcon, DragMode		Properties used while a control is being dragged [Some].
Enabled	Boolean	Indicates whether the control is enabled or disabled [Some].
Font	Font	The font used by the control [Some].
FontBold, FontItalic, FontStrikeThru, FontUnderline, FontSize, FontName		Properties of the font used [Some].
Top, Left, Height, Width	Single	Coordinates of the upper-left corner and size of the control (in scale units of the container) [Some].
HelpContextId	Long	ID of the help topic associated with this control [Some]
HWnd	Long	Handle to the control window, a WIN32 HWND handle [Some]
MouseIcon, MousePointer		The type of the mouse cursor to use when the mouse is positioned above the control, and if custom mouse cursor, the graphic to use. [Some].
OLEDragMode, OLEDropMode		Support for OLE drag-and-drop operation [Some].
TabIndex	Integer	The position in tab order of this control [Some].
TabStop	Boolean	True is the control is a tab stop [Some].
ToolTipText	String	The string that will be displayed as a ToolTip for the control [Some].
Visible	Boolean	True if the control is visible [Some].
WhatsThisHelpID		ID of the help topic for the "What is this" help mode [Some].

Table B.2 Standard Methods

Method	Description
Drag	Begins, ends, or cancels a drag operation [Some]
Move	Changes the control position or size [Some]
OLEDrag	Begins an OLE drag operation [Some]
Refresh	Causes the contents of the object to be repainted [Some]
SetFocus	Activates (set focus to) a control [Some]
ShowWhatsThis	Shows a "What's this?" help topic [Some]
ZOrder	Changes an object's position in the z-order (that is, brings it to the top or sends it to the back) [Some]

Table B.3   Standard Events

Event	Description
Change	The contents of the control have changed [Some]
Click	The user clicked with the mouse or selected the control using a mnemonic, a shortcut key, or the Enter key [Some]
DblClick	The user double-clicked on the control
DragDrop, DragOver	The user drags over the control or drops something on the control
GotFocus, LostFocus	The control received or lost focus [Some]
KeyDown, KeyUp	The user pressed or released a key [Some]
KeyPress	The user hit a key (press and release) [Some]
MouseDown, MouseMove, MouseUp	The user executed the corresponding action over the control [Some]
OLECompleteDrag, OLEDragDrop, OLEDragOver, OLEGiveFeedback, OLESetData, OLEStartDrag	Miscellaneous events during an OLE drag-and-drop operation [some]

Intrinsic VB Controls

Intrinsic controls are the controls that are built into Visual Basic. They look and feel similar to the ActiveX controls, but they are not part of an external component library (OCX or DLL).

CheckBox

This control can be used to represent a True/False or Yes/No value. The Caption property represents text displayed next to the check box, the Value property represents the state of the check box (vbChecked or vbUnchecked). You can use the Alignment property to indicate on which side of the check box the caption shows (vbLeftJustify, vbRightJustify).

The Click event is normally used to detect when the value changes (the user has clicked on the control).

ComboBox

This control consists of a combination of a TextBox with a ListBox, and it is used to present the user with a set of choices (the ListBox) for a text entry (the TextBox part). Depending on the style of the control, the user might be forced to select an entry from the list (vbDropDownList), in which case the Text property of the control becomes read-only.

You can use the List, ListIndex, and ListCount properties to navigate the list. It also has an ItemData indexed property that can hold an associated long value for each string item in the List. The list can be maintained using the AddItem, RemoveItem, and Clear methods. The Sort property indicates whether the list items are sorted. The NewIndex property returns the index of the most recently added item.

The Change event indicates that the Text property has changed. The Click event occurs when the user selects an item in the list (using the mouse or keyboard).

CommandButton

This control is normally used to enable the user to execute an action. It has a Caption property, which is the text shown on the button. It also has a Style property that (in conjunction with the Picture property) allows for graphical buttons to be designed.

The Default property indicates that this is the button that will get a Click event if the user presses Enter while the form this control is on is active. The Cancel property is similar, except the Esc key will trigger the Click event.

The Click event indicates that the button was pressed. This is normally the event used for CommandButtons.

Data

The Data control is used as a data source for the controls on the form it is on. It manipulates a set of rows from a specified database, and the controls on the same forms can be bound to individual columns in the rowset it maintains.

This control is used mostly in client/server applications but less in object-oriented applications because it requires the presentation layer to have knowledge of the database structure.

DirListBox, DriveListBox, and FileListBox

These controls allow you customized access to the file system. They provide access to the drives, folders, and files on the computer where your application is running.

Note that most of the functionality required from the file system has to do with opening and saving files, which can be easily achieved using a CommonDialog control. As a result, these controls are used only for specialized tasks.

Frame

This control is used as a labeled container for other controls. Its Caption property is the text displayed at the top of the frame. The Frame control is normally used to group OptionButton controls.

HScrollBar and VScrollBar

The horizontal and vertical custom scrollbar controls are used to represent a bounded set of values (represented by their Min and Max Integer properties). The user can change the position of the thumb using the mouse and the keyboard. The current position of the thumb is represented by the Value property (a value between Min and Max).

The LargeChange and SmallChange properties indicate the amount by which the Value is incremented or decremented when the user scrolls up or down. If he uses the arrows at the end of the scrollbar or the arrow keys, a SmallChange is added or subtracted from Value. If he uses the PageUp or PageDown key or clicks the area between the thumb and the end arrows, a LargeChange amount is added or subtracted from the current value and the position of the thumb is adjusted properly.

Image

This control is used to display a graphics image. The image can be in any of these formats: bitmap, icon, metafile, enhanced metafile, JPEG, or GIF.

You can set the Picture property at design time (by selecting an image) or at runtime using the `LoadPicture` or `LoadResPicture` intrinsic functions.

The Stretch property allows resizing of the graphic displayed. The Image control supports the `Click` and `DblClick` events (along with other standard VB events).

Label

One of the most used controls in any VB application, the Label control provides the user with additional information about other controls. Its Caption property represents the text that is displayed in the label.

Line

This control is used to enhance the UI forms with lines. The DrawWidth property indicates the line width. The DrawStyle represents the type of line used. The coordinate properties (X1, Y1, X2, and Y2) represent the starting point and ending point of the line in container coordinates.

ListBox

This control is used to present the user with a set of choices, of which the user can choose one or more. The selection method is dependent on the Style property (normal or check box style).

You can use the List, ListIndex, and ListCount properties to navigate the list. It also has an ItemData indexed property that can hold an associated long value for each string item in the List. The list can be maintained using the AddItem, RemoveItem, and Clear methods. The Sort property indicates whether the list items are sorted. The NewIndex property returns the index of the most recently added item. The Selected and SelCount property are used to determine whether a particular item is selected and the total number of selected items, respectively.

The Click event occurs when the user selects an item in the list (using the mouse or keyboard). The ItemCheck event occurs when the user selects an item of a check box style list.

Menu

This is the control used for building form or pop-up menus. It can be a top-level menu, a submenu, or a separator. The Caption property is the text displayed. The Checked property indicates whether a check mark is displayed next to the text (useful to provide a choice among a set of options). The Enabled property indicates whether the control is enabled or disabled (grayed). The Shortcut property represents the shortcut key associated with the control.

OptionButton

Option buttons are normally used as groups of controls, used to give the user the chance to choose among multiple choices. The Caption property represents the text displayed near the actual graphic button. The Value indicates whether the control is the chosen one from the group.

PictureBox

The PictureBox control is similar to the Image control, but with a much larger set of properties and methods. It can act as a container for other controls, and it provides drawing methods for displaying customized graphics.

Because its methods and properties are similar to the Printer object, it is often used in print preview forms.

Shape

This control is used in a similar fashion as the Line control to enhance the UI of Visual Basic forms. It can display a rectangle, rounded rectangle, ellipsis, or circle. It has drawing and filling properties, as well as a Shape property that indicates what style the control will have (one of the above-mentioned shapes).

TextBox

This control is used to gather data from the user. Its Text property can be set by the programmer (design- or runtime) and changed by the user at runtime. It allows the user to select portions of text (represented by the SelStart and SelLength properties) and to cut, copy, and paste text (if the control is enabled).

The Alignment property indicates how the text is displayed in the control. The Locked property restricts user input to the control. The MaxLength property limits the number of characters the user can enter.

The MultiLine property permits multiple lines of text to be entered. The ScrollBars property (for multiline controls only) allows the user to scroll the text up/down and left/right.

The Change event occurs every time the user changes the text of the control.

Timer

This is an invisible control. It is used to generate Timer events. The Interval property represents the time interval between two such events. The Enabled property indicates whether the control is active (that is firing Timer events).

B

m, adding,

r keys, 16
ructured
anguage
pport, 248

es, ActiveX
Objects (ADOs),
63
tions section,
rd modules, 55
sal Data (UDA),

method values,

andling,
24
event
tions with
ivate events,
ct forms,
56
of in form life
108

activating pop-up
  menus from code,
  182-185
Active Server Pages
  (ASP), 432
ActiveX projects, 23
ActiveX controls, 449.
  See also RichTextBox
  control
ActiveX Data Objects
  (ADOs), 262-263, 266
actors, 424
adAsyncConnect value,
  273
Add function, 385-386,
  389
Add method, 239, 388
AddIn project, 23
adding
  applications, 423-428
  buttons
    drop-down, 126-129
    Order Entry forms,
    193
    ToolBar, 125
  classes
    Customer, 212-218
    DbSession, 270-272
    OrderItem, 236-242

code
  cancel buttons, 76-77
  Customer List forms,
    349-357
  login forms, 62-64
  Order Entry and
    Order Item forms,
    196-200
  Product forms,
    148-163
  Splitter forms,
    174-181
  ToolBar control events,
    129-130
colors, custom, 121
constants, public,
  173-174
controls, 46
  arrays to store menu
    items, 100-101
  Customer forms,
    133-138
  ImageList, 119-122,
    172-173
  label, 191-193
  ListView, 169-172
  MaskedEdit, 136-137
  Product forms,
    146-148
  StatusBar, 113-118
  ToolBar, 123-131
  TreeView, 166-169
  Windows Common,
    112-113
data source names
  (DSNs), 256-258
database support for
  validating users,
  293-295
datatypes, Declarations
  section, 56

dialog boxes
  Order Item, 193-195
  Select Printer dialog
    box, 363-368
events
  classes, 295, 298-304
  command button pro-
    cedures, 76-77
  menu click, 101-102
executables, 85, 87-89
files, custom resources,
  173-174
forms
  About, 390-393
  custom properties and
    methods, 105-109
  Find Customer,
    335-338
  Multiple Document
    Interface (MDI),
    93-95, 102-105
  New Customer Orders
    View, 165-166
  Order Entry,
    187-193
  Product, 145-148,
    156-162
  tabular data, 347-349
functions
  CheckLogin, 57-61
  login forms, 53-54
  private, 354
grids, Order Entry
  forms, 189-191
help links, 394-395
images, 122
labels, 46-50
lists, 148-155
menu bars, 95-101

menus
  child, 97-99
  right-click pop-up,
    182-185
  submenus, 97-99
messages, MsgBox, 66
methods
  DbSession class, 294
  Delete, 279-285
  Find, 277-281,
    290-291
  Helper, 282-284
  public, 352
  RefreshTreeView,
    383-384
  Retrieve, 285-286
  Save, 274-277, 280,
    284-290
modules, 57-61,
  434-435
objects
  global DbSession, 273
  user interface (UI)
    applications,
    426-427
  Utility, 437
order items, 242-245
panels, StatusBar con-
  trol, 115-117
persistence
  Customer class,
    273-279
  Customer forms,
    307-312
  encapsulating data-
    bases, 269-273
  Order classes,
    282-291
  Order forms, 324-334
  Order Item forms,
    314-324

Product class, *280-282*

Product forms, *312-314*

procedures
  login forms, 53-54
  to display status bar *messages, 118*

projects
  from scratch, 43-44
  login forms, 45-51

properties
  Customer class, *212-213*
  Visual Basic classes, *209*

submenus, 97-99

text boxes, 49-50

variables for holding arrays, 31

AddItem method, **454-456**

AddRef method, 448

AddressOf operator, 34

adjusting. *See* changing

adLock values, 276

administrative services, defining requirements, **41-42**

administrators, database **(DBA), 247**

ADO. *See* **ActiveX Data** **Objects**

adOpen values, 276

Advanced Optimization **tab, Project Properties** **dialog box, 403**

aggregation, 188, 449

Align menu, 48-49

Align property, 114

Align to Grid option, 49

aligning controls, 45, **48-49**

alignment grids, 45

Alignment property, **116, 457**

AllowBigSelection prop- **erty, FlexGrid control,** **190**

AllowColumnReorder **property, ListView** **control, 171**

AllowCustomize **Boolean property, 124**

AllowUserResizing **property, FlexGrid** **control, 190**

analysis phase, applica- **tion development,** **423-424**

And operator, 34

App object, 391-392, **408**

Appearance enumerated **property, 124**

Appearance property, **73, 451**

applications
  adding help links to, 394-395
  analysis and design, 425
  components, 447
  creating executables, 85-89
  defining requirements, 39-41
  development phases, 423-428
  errors. *See* errors
  event-driven, 77-81
  multitiered, advantages of, 430-433

Rational Rose, 425

setting to use specific projects, 442-443

settings, 397-399

testing, 85, 420-421

three-tiered topology, 308-309

user interface (UI), 425-427

Visual Modeler, 425

See also projects

appName argument, **398**

architecture. *See* **topol-** **ogy**

arguments
  Add function, 385
  App object, 409
  command-line, 401-402
  Line method, 373
  MouseMove event, 177
  Move method, 175
  PrintPicture method, 378
  Raise method, 360
  UnloadMode, 323
  See also specific argu- ments

Arrange enumerated **property, ListView** **control, 171**

Arrange method, values, **105**

arrays
  control, 100-101, 134
  described, 31-33
  See also specific arrays; values

Asc() function, 65

ASP. *See* **Active Server** **Pages**

Assert method, 414
attributes, 204
Auto Increment check
 box, 86
Auto Syntax Check
 option, 24
Automation, 449
AutoSize property, 116

B

B argument, 373
BackColor property, 74,
 451
Basic file type, exten-
 sion for, 23
Bevel property, 116
Binary Compatibility
 option, 442
body, methods, 214
Bold property, 372, 384
Boolean datatype, sup-
 ported values, 29
Boolean properties,
 ToolBar control, 124
Boolean values, expres-
 sions, 62
BorderStyle property,
 124, 133, 337
BorderWidth property,
 337
Bottom property, 114
Bottoms control align-
 ment option, 48
Break in Class Modules
 option, 417
breakpoints, 418-419
bugs, 407

building Dynamic Link
 Library (DLL) files
 and projects, 438
built-in controls,
 Customer form prop-
 erties, 138-141
built-in datatypes, 29-30
Business Services, 431
Button argument,
 MouseMove event,
 177
ButtonClick events,
 implementing,
 129-130
buttons
 cancel, adding code to,
  76-77
 command
  *adding, Order Entry
   forms, 193*
  events, 76-81, 198
  properties, 71-76
 minimize, enabling,
  134
buttons parameter,
 65-68
Buttons tab, adding
 ToolBar buttons, 125
By keywords, 59-60
Byte datatype, sup-
 ported values, 29
ByVal s As String para-
 meter, 229

C

CalcTotal function, 238
calculated property val-
 ues, implementing,
 232-233

Cancel argument, 323
cancel buttons, adding
 code to, 76-77
Cancel Click event,
 handling, 153-155
Cancel command but-
 ton, handling Click
 events, 198
Cancel property, 72-74
canceling form unloads,
 324
Caption property,
 455-456
 changing, 47
 described, 74
carriage return charac-
 ter, 65
Case statement, 131
catching. *See* errors,
 handling
CausesValidation prop-
 erty, 74
cd1OFN values, 152
Centers control align-
 ment option, 48
Change event, 340-341,
 453-454, 457
changes, saving for
 Order Item forms,
 320-323
changing
 code
  lines of, 439-440
  *while debugging,
   415-416*
 controls
  *font properties,
   135-136*
  position of, 350-351
  size of, 158, 350-351
  spacing between, 49

forms
  Customer, 309-312
  icons and titles, 45
  sizes of, 158
menu items, 96
mouse shape, Splitter
  forms, 176-178
next statement, 416
objects, databases,
  335-346
properties
  Cancel, 72
  Caption, 47
  font, 135-136
records, 264
variable values while
  debugging, 415
characters, 65
Charset property, 372
check boxes
  Hide File Extensions
  for Known File
  Types, making .ico
  extension visible, 348
  Remove Information
  About Unused
  ActiveX Controls,
  402
CheckBox control, 453
Checkboxes property
  ListView control, 171
  TreeView control, 169
Checked property, 384,
  456
checking project set-
  tings for compiles, 85,
  88
CheckLogin function,
  adding to login forms,
  57-61
child class, 208

child forms, Multiple
  Document Interface
  (MDI), 102-105
child menus, creating
  for main forms, 97-99
Child property, 384
Children property, 384
choosing
  form icons, 45
  controls
    multiple, 47
    Windows Common,
    112
  records, 264
Class file type, exten-
  sion for, 23
Class Initialize event,
  211
class modules
  accessibility, public
  variables, 209
  adding to projects, 212,
  434-435
  described, 37, 54
  removing from pro-
  jects, 433
  See also objects
Class Terminate event,
  211
classes
  adding
    persistence, 269-291
    to projects, 212-221
  described, 37, 204-206
  finalizing, 293-304
  properties, 209-211
  Visual Basic, 208-209
  See also specific classes
Clear method, 454-456
ClearState method, 278,
  284

Click event, 345,
  453-456
  adding to forms,
  101-102
  described, 80
  handling, Customer
  forms, 142-143
client components, 447
client/server topology,
  309
Clip properties, 138
close user actions, han-
  dling, 323-324
cmdDelete Click event,
  355
cmdEdit Click event,
  354
cmdLogin Click proce-
  dure, 62
cmdOrders Click event,
  356-357
code
  activating pop-up
  menus from, 182-185
  adding
    cancel buttons, 76-77
    Customer List forms,
    349-357
    login forms, 62, 64
    Product forms,
    148-155, 159-163
    Select Printer dialog
    box, 365-366
    Splitter forms,
    174-181
    ToolBar control events,
    129-130
  changing
    lines of, 439-440
    while debugging,
    415-416

extending StatusBar control functionality with, 118

handling errors in, 152-153

implementing, Find Customer form, 338-346

modules, accessibility to public variables, 209

native and P, 84

stepping through, 418-419

Code window, 19-20

Collection objects, properties and methods, 239

collections, Order Items, 234-245

color argument, 373

color selection dialog box, Palette and System tabs, 121

Color tab, Property Pages dialog box, 191

colors, creating custom, 121

Cols property, FlexGrid control, 189

columns

databases, 250

headers, setting

storing strings exceeding size of, 138

width, setting, 196, 350

See also databases; primary keys; foreign keys

ColWidth property, setting values, 196

combining values, 68

combo boxes

adding, Order Item dialog box, 194-195

products, populating, 317-319

ComboBox controls, 146-148, 454

command buttons

adding, Order Entry forms, 193

events, 76-81, 198

properties, 71-76

Command keyword, 402

Command object, 263

command-line arguments, 401-402

CommandButton control, 454

commands, Structured Query Language (SQL), 253-256. *See also* operators

Comments property, 391

Common Dialog controls, 148-152

CommonDialog class, Filter property, 151

CompanyName property, 391

Comparison operator, 34

compilation, conditional, 403-405

compile error message boxes, 89

Compile tab

described, 87

Project Properties dialog box, 403

Compile to settings, 88

compile-time errors, 407-408

compiled languages, 83

compiling applications, verifying project settings, 85, 88

Component Object Model (COM), 447

implementing interfaces, 448-449

technologies, 449

Component tab, setting Version Compatibility, 441-442

componentized development, 432

components, 429-433, 447

client, 447

conditional breakpoints, 419

conditional compilation, 403-405

Connection class, Open method, 273

Connection object, 263

connection strings, defining, 267

connections, opening in databases, 263

ConnectionStr parameter, 273

connectivity, Open Database (ODBC)

creating data source names (DSNs), 256-258

described, 265, 271-272

constants

declaring, 33

defining, 34

public, creating,
173-174
Unload Mode argu-
ment, 323
when to use, 56
See also specific con-
stants; values
Container property, 451
**containers, Scale Mode
property, 166**
**containment/delegation,
449**
**context ID, help files,
394**
**context parameter, 65,
68**
**control arrays, 100-101,
134**
**control events, adding
code to handle,
129-130**
**control of source code,
22**
controls
adding
*to forms, 46,
113-138, 146-148
forms, 156-162*
images, 122
aligning, 45, 48-49
built-in, Customer
form properties,
138-141
changing
*font properties,
Customer forms,
135-136
positions of, 350-351
sizes of, 158, 350-351
spacing between, 49*
described, 46
handling Click events,
197

integrating object func-
tionality with,
427-428
label, Order Entry
forms, 191-193
locking, 50
opening files with,
149-152
refreshing
*forms, 319-320
grids, 353*
resizing, Splitter forms,
175-181
selecting multiple, 47
sizing and positioning,
47, 50
See also specific con-
trols
**coordinate properties,
456**
Count property, 239
**Create New Folder
icon, 21**
creating
applications, 423-428
buttons
*drop-down, 126-129
Order Entry forms,
193
ToolBar, 125*
classes
*Customer, 212-218
DbSession, 270-272
OrderItem, 236-242*
code
*cancel buttons, 76-77
Customer List forms,
349-357
login forms, 62-64
Order Entry and
Order Item forms,
196-200*

*Product forms,
148-163
Splitter forms,
174-181
ToolBar control events,
129-130*
colors, custom, 121
constants, public,
173-174
controls, 46
*arrays to store menu
items, 100-101
Customer forms,
133-138
ImageList, 119-122,
172-173
label, 191-193
ListView, 169-172
MaskedEdit, 136-137
Product forms,
146-148
StatusBar, 113-118
ToolBar, 123-131
TreeView, 166-169
Windows Common,
112-113*
data source names
(DSNs), 256-258
database support for
validating users,
293-295
datatypes, Declarations
section, 56
dialog boxes
*Order Item, 193-195
Select Printer dialog
box, 363-368*
events
*classes, 295, 298-304
command button
procedures, 76-77
menu click, 101-102*

executables, 85, 87-89

files, custom resources, 173-174

forms
About, 390-393
custom properties and methods, 105-109
Find Customer, 335-338
Multiple Document Interface (MDI), 93-95, 102-105
New Customer Orders View, 165-166
Order Entry, 187-193
Product, 145-148, 156-162
tabular data, 347-349

functions
CheckLogin, 57-61
login forms, 53-54
private, 354

grids, Order Entry forms, 189-191

help links, 394-395

images, 122

labels, 46-50

lists, 148-155

menu bars, 95-101

menus
child, 97-99
right-click pop-up, 182-185
submenus, 97-99

messages, MsgBox, 66

methods
DbSession class, 294
Delete, 279-285
Find, 277-281, 290-291

Helper, 282-284
public, 352
RefreshTreeView, 383-384
Retrieve, 285-286
Save, 274-277, 280, 284-290

modules, 57-61, 434-435

objects
global DbSession, 273
user interface (UI) applications, 426-427
Utility, 437

order items, 242-245

panels, StatusBar control, 115-117

persistence
Customer class, 273-279
Customer forms, 307-312
encapsulating databases, 269-273
Order classes, 282-291
Order forms, 324-334
Order Item forms, 314-324
Product class, 280-282
Product forms, 312-314

procedures
login forms, 53-54
to display status bar messages, 118

projects
from scratch, 43-44
login forms, 45-51

properties
Customer class, 212-213
Visual Basic classes, 209

submenus, 97-99

text boxes, 49-50

variables for holding arrays, 31

Currency datatype, supported values, 29

cursors, mouse, 173-174

CursorType parameter, 276

cust parameter, 244

custom colors, creating, 121

custom dialog boxes, Select Printer, 363-368

custom properties
adding to forms, 105-109
StatusBar control, 114-116

custom resources files, adding to projects, 173-174

Customer class
adding to projects, 212-218
persistence, 273-279

Customer Find form, implementing code, 338-346

Customer forms
adding controls, 133-138
handling events, 141-143
persistence, 307-312

Customer List forms, adding code, 349-357

customer lists, populat-ing, 324-326

Customer Orders form, finalizing, 383-390

customer services, defining requirements, 42-43

customizing Visual Basic environment, 24-25

D

data

persistence, 307-334

integrity, 253

members

m_id private, 275

private, 223

Data control, 454

Data Definition Language (DDL), 249-253

Data Project, 23

Data Services, 431-432

data source names (DSNs), 271-272

creating, 256-258

defining connection strings, 267

databases

access, ActiveX Data Objects (ADOs), 262-263

adding support to vali-date users, 293-295

concepts, 249-253

connections, opening, 263

described, 247-248

encapsulating, 269-273

Object Linking and Embedding (OLE DB), 265-266

relational, 248

retrieving

editing objects and, 335-346

product lists from, 315-316

tables, 251-253

See also columns; records; rows

datatypes, 29-31, 56. *See also* specific datatypes; variables

Date datatype, sup-ported values, 29

Database Administrator (DBA), 247

dateEnt parameter, 244

DBA. *See* Database Administrator

DblClick event, 345, 453, 455

DbSession class

adding methods, 294

creating, 270-272

DDL. *See* Data Definition Language

Deactivate event

interactions with Activate events, Product forms, 155-156

order of in form life time, 108

debug mode, 410, 416

debugging applications, 407-421

Debugging tab, setting applications using spe-cific projects, 442-443

Declarations section, standard modules, 55-56

declaring

constants, 33

events within OrderItemColl class, 298

variables, Declaration section, 55

default display, MsgBox, 35

default location, saving project files, 21

Default property, 74, 454

defining

constants, 34

datatypes, Declarations section, standard modules, 30-31, 56

expanding Order class to contain Order Items collections, 234-245

interfaces, 227-245

projects, 39-43

schema, 259-262

See also choosing

delegation, 297

DELETE command, Structured Query Language (SQL), 255

Delete method, 279-285

DeleteSetting function, 399

deleting

class modules, 433

expressions, Watches window, 414

images, 122
records, 264
deploying components, 432
Described argument, 360
design phase, 424-425
Designer file type, extension for, 24
designing
forms, 426
Find Customer, 335-338
tabular data, 347-349
Select Printer dialog box, 363-368
DHTML Application project, 23
dialog boxes
color selection, Palette and System tabs, 121
Load Icon, choosing form icons, 45
Make Project, 88
New Project, 12
Options, 24
Order Item, 193-195, 198-199
Printer Selection, displaying, 363
Project Properties, 85-88, 400-401
Property Pages
Color tab, 191
Font and Picture tabs, 169
opening, ImageList control, 122
Select Printer, adding, 363-368
Dialog controls, 148-152

Dictionary objects, 241
Dim keyword, declaring variables, 31
Dim statement
declaring variables, 55
purpose of, 28
directives, #const and #If, 404
directories, saving projects to, 21-22
DirListBox control, 454
DisabledPicture property, 74
disabling
alignment grid, 45
event trapping, variables, 303
discount property, 237
discPercent parameter, 244
displaying
custom properties, StatusBar control, 114
documents, 160-162
file properties window, 87
forms, 100-101
images, 156-159
ListView controls, right-click pop-up menus, 182-185
Printer Selection dialog box, 363
Product forms, 159
Registry settings, 397
status bar messages, 118
version numbers of projects, 87
DISTINCT keyword, 255

distributed components, 429-443
DNA. *See* **Windows Distributed interNet Applications Architecture**
documentation, applications, 428
documents
described, 94
viewing, 160-162
See also files
dot notations
described, 30
Get, Let, and Set properties, 107
Double datatypem supported values, 29
DownPicture property, 74
Drag events, 453
Drag method, 452
DragDrop event, 80
DragIcon property, 74, 452
DragMode property, 75, 452
DragOver event, 80
DrawStyle property, 455
DrawWidth property, 372, 455
DriveListBox control, 454
drop-down buttons, adding, 126-129
Dropdown formats, 147
DSN. *See* **data source names**
dynamic arrays, 33
Dynamic Link Library (DLL)
building files, 438
described, 430

E

editing
  code
    lines of, *439-440*
    while debugging,
      415-416
  controls
    font properties,
      135-136
    position of, *350-351*
    size of, *158, 350-351*
    spacing between, *49*
  forms
    Customer, *309-312*
    icons and titles, *45*
    sizes of, *158*
  menu items, *96*
  mouse shape, Splitter
    forms, *176-178*
  next statement, *416*
  objects, databases,
    335-346
  properties
    Cancel, *72*
    Caption, *47*
    font, *135-136*
  records, *264*
  variable values while
    debugging, *415*
**Editor tab window,
  24-25**
editors, 96
ellipses, 16
**Enabled property, 75,
  124, 452, 456**
**enabling minimize but-
  ton, 134**
encapsulation
  databases, *269-273*
  described, *207*

EndDoc method, 378
**EnsureMaxLength func-
  tion, 436-437**
Enum keyword, 222
**enumerated properties,
  ToolBar control, 124**
**enumerations, order
  status properties,
  221-225**
Eqv operator, 34
erasing
  class modules, *433*
  expressions, Watches
    window, *414*
  images, *122*
  records, *264*
Error object, 263
errors
  compile, message
    boxes, *89*
  compile-time, *407-408*
  described, *152*
  handling, *152-153,
    349-361, 417-418*
  logical, *409*
  programming, *409*
  reporting, *349-361*
  runtime, *409*
event handlers, 78
**event order, form life
  time, 108**
**event procedures, creat-
  ing for command but-
  tons, 76-77**
**event-driven program-
  ming, 77-81**
events
  adding
    classes, *295, 298-304*
    code to handles,
      129-130

  command buttons,
    78-81
  declaring within
    OrderItemColl class,
    298
  handling, *302-303*
    from controls on
      Customer forms,
      141-143
    OptionButton controls,
      197
    Save and Cancel
      Click, *153-155*
    Save and Cancel com-
      mand buttons, *198*
  interactions between,
    forms, *155-156*
  triggering, *101*
  See also specific events
**exceptions, runtime,
  408-409**
**executables, creating,
  85, 87-89**
**Execute method,
  264-265**
**executing, multiple
  statements on same
  line, 64**
**EXEName property,
  391**
Exit Function line, 272
Exit Sub statement, 63
**Expanded properties,
  384**
expanding
  names array, *33*
  Order class to contain
    Order Items collec-
    tions, *234-245*
Explorer. *See* **Windows
  Explorer**

expressions
Boolean values, 62
Case statement, 131
Immediate window, 412, 414
values, monitoring at runtime, 410-411, 414
Watches window, 410-411, 414
extending StatusBar control functionality with code, 118

F

F argument, 373
Field object, 263
fields, subtotal, 191-193
file properties window, viewing, 87
FileDescribed property, 391
FileListBox control, 454
FileName property, 151
files
opening with Common Dialog control, 149-152
Visual Basic environment, types of, 23-24
See also documents; specific file types
Fill properties, 374
Filter properties, 151
filtered out, 119
finalizing
classes, 293-304
Customer Orders form, 383-390

Find Customer form, adding, 335-338
Find method, 277-281, 290-291
FirstSibling property, 384
Fixed properties, 189
flags
m_filtered, 351
returning, Order Item forms, 320-323
Flags property, values, 152
FlatScrollBar property, ListView control, 171
flex values, 190
FlexGrid control, 189-191
focus, moving between controls, 141-142
FocusRect property, FlexGrid control, 190
Font object, 372
Font properties, 452
changing, controls, 135-136
described, 75
ForeColor property, 451
foreign keys, databases, 252-253
Form file type, extension for, 23
form icons, changing, 45
Form Layout window, 19
Form Load event procedure, 389
form modules, 54
form titles, changing, 45
Format menu, 47-49

Format property, 137
formats, ComboBox control, 147
forms
controls
adding, 46
refreshing, 319-320
aligning, 45
custom properties and methods, 105-109
described, 35
designing, 426
implementing menu click events, 101-102
integrating object functionality with, 427-428
labels, 46-50
positioning, 19, 50
shortcut keys, 51
sizing, 50, 158
tab stops, 50-51
text boxes, 49-50
unloads, 323-324
viewing, 100-101
See also specific forms
Forms window, 18
Frame control, 455
FROM keyword, 255
FromRs method, 284
FullPath property, 168, 384
FullRowSelect property
ListView control, 171
TreeView control, 169
functionality
objects, forms and controls, 427-428
StatusBar control, extending with code, 118

functions
adding, login forms,
53-54
described, 35-36
MsgBox as, 68-69
signatures, 179
See also methods; spe-
cific functions; values

G

General tab
custom properties,
StatusBar control,
115
Project Properties dia-
log box, 400
Get keyword, 214
Get property, 107
GetAllSettings function,
399
GetSetting function,
398
Ghosted property, 386
global DbSession
objects, creating, 273
Global statement,
declaring variables, 56
global variable
references, trou-
bleshooting, 436
GlobalSingleUse value,
435
GotFocus control, han-
dling events, 141-142
GotFocus event, 80, 453
grayed text, 16
grid controls
refreshing, 353
setting Rows property,
196-197

GridLines properties
FlexGrid control, 191
ListView control, 171
grids
adding, Order Entry
forms, 189-191
aligning, 45
Group values, 66-67
GROUP BY keyword,
255
growing names array, 33

H

h arguments, 378
handlers, event, 78
handling
close user actions,
323-324
errors
Customer List forms,
349-357
considerations while
debugging, 417-418
described, 357-361
in code, 152-153
tabular data forms,
347-349
events, 302-303
Click, 197-198
control, adding code
for, 129-130
from controls on
Customer forms,
141-143
Save and Cancel
Click, 153-155
mouse, Splitter forms,
178-181
HAVING keyword, 255

headers, columns, 350
Height property, 76
help links, adding to
applications, 394-395
Helpcontext argument,
360
HelpContextID prop-
erty, 75, 394, 452
Helper method,
OrderItem class,
282-284
Helpfile argument, 360
helpfile parameter, 65,
68
HelpFile property, 391
Hide File Extensions for
Known File Types
check box, making .ico
extension visible, 348
Hide properties,
169-171
Highlight property,
FlexGrid control, 190
hInstance property, 391
holding arrays of names,
creating variables for,
31
Horizontal Spacing
submenu, adjusting
spacing between
controls, 49
HotImageList property,
124
HotTracking property
ListView control, 171
TreeView control, 169
HoverSelection prop-
erty, ListView control,
172
HScrollBar control, 455
HTML. *See* Hypertext
Markup Language

HWnd property, 452
Hypertext Markup
  Language (HTML),
  advantages of using in
  Presentation tier, 431

I

Icon, SmallIcon prop-
  erty, 386
icons
  Create New Folder, 21
  described, 16
  forms, changing, 45
  opening, 12
ID
  as unique key, 386
  context, help files, 394
id property, 237
If statement, 414
If...Then statements,
  64-65
IIS Application project,
  23
IIS. *See* Internet
  Information Server
image argument, 385
Image control, 156-159,
  455
ImageList control,
  adding to forms,
  119-122, 172-173
ImageList property,
  123, 168
images, adding and
  removing, 122
Immediate window, 412,
  414, 417
Imp operator, 34

implementation phase,
  application develop-
  ment, 425-428
implementing
  code, Find Customer
    form, 338-346
  Component Object
    Model (COM) inter-
    faces, 448-449
  described, 206
  events
    Button, 129-131
    menu click, 101-102
  navigation, 426
  objects, 427
  property procedures,
    106-109
  values, 232-234
  user interface (UI)
    applications, 425-426
implements statement,
  448
Indentation property,
  TreeView control, 168
Index property, 451
  arrays, 134
  described, 76, 115
indexes, databases, 253
Informix, Structured
  Query Language
  (SQL) support, 248
inheritance
  described, 207-208
  Scale Mode property
    from containers, 166
Initialize event, order of
  in form life time, 108
INSERT command,
  Structured Query
  Language (SQL),
  253-254
inserting records, 263

InsertInRs method, 284
InstallShield, 85
instances. *See* objects
Instancing property,
  setting, 435-436
Integer datatype, sup-
  ported values, 29
integrating
  forms with persistent
    order objects,
    326-334
  object functionality,
    427-428
integrity, data and referential, 252-253
interactions in forms,
  Activate and
  Deactivate events,
  155-156
interfaces
  administrative, defining
    requirements, 41-42
  Component Object
    Model (COM),
    implementing,
    448-449
  customer, defining
    requirements, 42-43
  defining, 227-245
  described, 447
  public, 37
  user. *See* presentation
    layer
Internet Information
  Server (IIS), 432
interpreted languages,
  83-85
intrinsic controls,
  453-456
invisible controls, 119
Is operator, 34
IsMissing() function, 61
IsValid method, 274

Italic property, 372
Item function, 241
Item method, 239-240
ItemCheck event, 456
items
order, adding, 242-245
retrieving from data-
bases, 315-316
iterative development,
425
IUnknown interface,
448

K

key argument, 385, 398
Key events, 453
Key property, 116
Key events, 80
keys
accelerator, 16
foreign, 252-253. *See
also* columns
primary, 251. *See also*
columns
shortcut, 16, 51, 99
unique, ID as, 386
KeyUp event, 80
keywords. *See* specific
keywords
KillDoc method, 379

L

Label controls, 134-135,
191-193, 455
LabelEdit property
ListView control, 171
TreeView control, 168

labels
adding
*Order Item dialog
box*, 194-195
to forms, 46-50
example of, 272
LabelWrap property,
ListView control, 171
languages
compiled, 83
Data Definition
(DDL), 249-253
Hypertext Markup
(HTML), advantages
of using in
Presentation tier, 431
interpreted, 83-85
Structured Query
(SQL), 248, 271
LargeChange property,
455
LastSibling property,
384
launching Visual Basic,
12
layers, 309
Left property, 76, 114
Lefts control alignment
option, 48
Legal properties, 391
Len function, changing
focus, 143
length
message strings, 65
variable names, 38
Let keyword, 215
Let property, 107
libraries, Dynamic Link
(DLL), 430, 438
life time, forms, 108
Like operator, 34

Line control, 455
Line method, 373-374
linefeed character, 65
LineStyle property,
TreeView control, 168
lining up. *See* aligning
links, help, 394-395
List properties, 454, 456
ListBox, 456
ListItem class, 386-387
lists
customer, 324-326
populating, Product
forms, 148-155
products, retrieving
from databases,
315-316
ListView controls,
169-172, 182-185
Load event, 108, 339
Load Icon dialog box,
choosing form icons,
45
LoadResPicture func-
tion, 180
Locked property, 457
locking controls, 50
LockType parameter,
276
logBuffer argument,
409
LogEvent method, 409
logical errors, 409
logical operators, 229
login forms
adding
*code, 62-64, 76-77
procedures and func-
tions, 53-54
standard modules,
57-61*

creating, 45, 47-51

running, 51-52

setting command button properties, 71-73

Log properties, 391

logTarget argument, 409

Long datatype, supported values, 29

LostFocus control, handling events, 141-142

LostFocus event, 80, 453

M

m_filtered flag, 351

m_id private data member, 275

main forms, adding controls, 112-131

Major, Minor, Revision property, 392

Make Project dialog box, 88

Make Same Size menu, sizing controls, 47

Make tab, 86-88, 400

Mask property, 138

MaskColor property, 74, 119-121

MaskedEdit controls, Customer forms, 136-137

MaskedEditBox control, 402

master-detail forms, 187-200

MaxLength property, 138-139, 457

MDI. *See* **Multiple Document Interface forms**

MDIChild forms, StartupPosition property, 194

Me keyword, 64

menu bars

adding to main forms, 95-101

Visual Basic environment, 14-17

menu click events, implementing, 101-102

Menu control, 456

Menu Editor, editing menu items, 96

menu items. *See* submenus

menus

Align, 48-49

child, creating, 97-99

creating control arrays to store items in, 100-101

Format, order of selecting controls, 48

right-click pop-up, 182-185

Visual Basic environment, 14-17

MergeCells property, FlexGrid control, 191

message strings, length of, 65

messages

creating, MsgBox, 66

status bar, adding procedures to display messages, 118

methods

App object, 408

Collection objects, 239

custom, adding to forms, 105-109

described, 204-206

IUnknown interface, 448

Visual Basic classes, 211

See also functions; procedures; specific methods

Microsoft Access, Structured Query Language (SQL) support, 248

Microsoft Message Queuing (MSMQ), 432

Microsoft SQL Server, Structured Query Language (SQL) support, 248

Microsoft Transaction Server (MTS), 432

middle layer, 309

Middles control alignment option, 48

minimize button, enabling, 134

MinWidth property, 116

mnemonics. *See* accelerator keys

Mod operator, 34

modal and modeless windows, 67

models, Component Object (COM), 447-449

modes. *See specific modes*

modifying
code
lines of, 439-440
while debugging,
415-416
controls
font properties,
135-136
position of, 350-351
size of, 158, 350-351
spacing between, 49
forms
Customer, 309-312
icons and titles, 45
sizes of, 158
menu items, 96
mouse shape, Splitter
forms, 176-178
next statement, 416
objects, databases,
335-346
properties
Cancel, 72
Caption, 47
font, 135-136
records, 264
variable values while
debugging, 415
module-level object ref-
erences, releasing, 352
modules
class
accessibility, public
variables, 209
adding to projects,
212, 434-435
described, 37
removing from
projects, 433
code, 209
described, 36, 54-55

standard, login forms,
57-61
See also specific mod-
ules
monitoring variable and
expression values at
runtime, 410-414
mouse cursors, creating
public constants,
173-174
Mouse events, 178-181,
453
Mouse properties, 452
mouse shapes, Splitter
forms, 176-178
Mouse events, 81, 177
MouseIcon property, 75
MousePointer property,
75, 180
Move method, 175, 452
moving
controls, 47, 50
focus between controls,
141-142
forms, 50
next statement, 416
MsgBox
as procedure or func-
tion, 68-69
default display, 35
parameters, 65-68
MSMQ. *See* **Microsoft**
Message Queuing
MTS. *See* **Microsoft**
Transaction Server
multidimensional
arrays, 32
MultiLine property, 457
multiple controls,
selecting, 47
Multiple Document
Interface (MDI) forms,
93-95

multiple statements,
executing on same
line, 64
MultiSelect property,
ListView control, 171
multitiered applications,
advantages of, 430-433
MultiUse value, 435
m_ prefix, 106

N

Name property, 73, 372,
451
names
creating variables for
holding arrays of, 31
data source (DSN),
271-272
creating, 256-258
defining connection
strings, 267
names array, growing
and resizing, 33
naming
project files, 21
naming conventions
variables, 37-38
native code, 84
navigation, implement-
ing, 426
New Customer Orders
View form, 165-173
new directories, saving
projects to, 21-22
New keyword, 303
New operator, 103
New Project dialog box,
12

NewIndex property, 454, 456

next statement, changing, 416

Next, Previous property, 385

nns function, 436-437

No Compatibility option, 441

No Optimization setting, 88

Node class, properties, 384-385

NodeClick event, 390

nodes, 166

nonobject variable. *See* normal variable

nonprinted characters, 65

normal text, 16

normal variable, 37

Not operator, 34

notations, dot
described, 30
Get, Let, and Set properties, 107

Number argument, 360

0

obj argument, 339

Object datatype, supported values, 29

Object Linking and Embedding (OLE), 449

Object Linking and Embedding Databases (OLE DB), 265-266

object references. *See* references

object-oriented concepts, 204-208

objects
adding user interface (UI) applications, 426-427
described, 37, 204-206
implementing, 427
integrating functionality, forms and controls, 427-428
module-level references, releasing, 352
retrieving and editing, databases, 335-346
See also class modules; specific objects

ODBC. *See* Open Database Connectivity

OLE DB. *See* Object Linking and Embedding Databases

OLE events, 453

OLE. *See* Object Linking and Embedding

OLEDrag method, 452

OLEDragMode property, 452

OLEDropMode property, 75, 452

one-dimensional arrays, 31

opCode arguments, 378

Open Database Connectivity (ODBC)
creating data source names (DSNs), 256-258
described, 265, 271-272

Open method, 273

opening
Code Window, 19
database connections, 263
files, Common Dialog control, 149-152
icons, 12
Order Item dialog box, 198-199
Project Properties dialog box, 85
Property Pages dialog box, ImageList control, 122
Visual Basic, 12

operators
described, 34
logical, 229
See also commands; specific operators

Optimize settings, 88

Option Base statement, 31

Optional keyword, 60

OptionButton controls, 197, 456

options, aligning controls, 48. *See also* specific options

Options dialog box, 24

Or operator, 34

Oracle, Structured Query Language (SQL) support, 248

OrdBill method, 245

OrdCancel method, 245

orders, 187

ORDER BY keyword, 255

Order class, 218-225, 282-291

Order Entry forms, 187-200

Order forms, adding persistence, 324-334
Order Item Dialog box, 193-195
Order Item forms
  adding code, 196-200
  adding persistence, 314-324
order items, 242-245
Order Items collection, expanding Order class to contain, 234-245
Order object, integrating forms with, 326-334
order of events, form life time, 108
order status properties, enumerations, 221-225
orderId property, 237
OrderItem class
  adding persistence, 282-291
  creating, 236-238
OrderItemColl class
  adding persistence, 282-291
  creating, 238-242
  declaring events within, 298
orders, printing, 369-379
Ord methods, 245
owner argument, 339

P

P-Code, 84
Package and Deployment Wizard, 85

pages. *See* tabs
Palette tab, color selection dialog box, 120
panels, adding with StatusBar control, 115-117
Panels tab, 115-116
Parameter object, 263
parameters
  ByVal s As String, 229
  MsgBox, 65-68
  Open method, 273
  s As String, 229
  setting order information, 244
  See also specific parameters
parent class, 208
Parent property, 385, 451
Password parameter, 273
Path property, 392
PathSeparator property, TreeView control, 168
persistence
  adding
    classes, 269-291
    forms, 307-334
  described, 307
persistence layer, 309
persistent order objects, integrating forms with, 326-334
persistent storage, 307
persisting data, 307
picture argument, 378
Picture property, 74, 116, 455
PictureBox control, 456
polling, 302
polymorphism, 208

pop-up menus, 182-185
populating
  lists
    customer, 324-326
    Product forms, 148-155
  products combo box, 317-319
positioning
  controls, 47, 50, 350-351
  forms, 19, 50
prefixes
  in variable names, 38
  m_, 106
preprocessors, 403-405
presentation layer, 309
Presentation Services, 430-431
PrevInstance property, 392
price property, 237
primary keys, databases, 251. *See also* columns
Print method, 375-377
Printer Selection dialog box, displaying, 363
printing
  adding Select Printer dialog box, 363-366, 368
  orders, 369-379
PrintPicture method, 378
Private constants, 57
private data members, 223
private function, adding, 354
Private keyword, 214-215, 222
Private procedure, 57

Private property, 107
Private statement,
  declaring variables, 55
Private value, 435
procedures
  adding
    login forms, 53-54
    to display status bar
      messages, 118
  cmdLogin Click, 62
  event, creating, 76-77
  MsgBox as, 68-69
  properties, Visual Basic
    classes, 210-211
  Property, 106-109,
    214-218
  Public and Private, 57
  signatures, 179
  See also methods
Product class
  adding to projects,
    218-221
  persistence, 280-282
Product forms
  adding, 145-148
    code, 148-155
    persistence, 312-314
    to display images,
      156-159
    to view documents,
      160-162
  interactions, Activate
    and Deactivate
    events, 155-156
product lists, retrieving
  from databases,
  315-316
productId property, 237
ProductName property,
  392
products combo box,
  populating, 317-319

programs
  adding help links to,
    394-395
  analysis and design,
    425
  components, 447
  creating executables,
    85-89
  defining requirements,
    39-41
  development phases,
    423-428
  errors. *See* errors
  event-driven, 77-81
  multitiered, advantages
    of, 430-433
  Rational Rose, 425
  setting to use specific
    projects, 442-443
  settings, 397-399
  testing, 85, 420-421
  three-tiered topology,
    308-309
  user interface (UI),
    425-427
  Visual Modeler, 425
  See also projects
Project Compatibility
  option, 442
Project Explorer win-
  dow, 17-18
Project Properties
  dialog box, 85-88,
  400-401
projects
  adding
    Customer classes,
      212-218
    forms, Multiple
      Document Interface
      (MDI), 93-95,
      102-105

  Product and Order
    classes, 218-221
  creating, 433, 438
    from scratch, 43-44
    login forms, 45,
      47-51
  debugging, 443
  defining, 39-43
  forms, 95-102
  naming files, 21
  running login forms,
    51-52
  saving, 21-22, 434
  setting
    applications to use,
      442-443
    properties, Multiple
      Document Interface
      (MDI) forms, 94
  settings, 400-403
    distributed compo-
      nents, 437-443
    verifying for compiles,
      85, 88
  splitting, distributed
    components, 433,
    435-437
  viewing version num-
    bers, 87
  Visual Basic environ-
    ment, types of, 23
  See also specific project
    types, 23
prompt parameter, 65
properties
  adding
    Customer class,
      212-213
    Visual Basic classes,
      209

built-in controls,
Customer forms,
138-141
changing, 47
Collection objects, 239
command buttons,
71-76
controlling tab order,
51
described, 204-206
FlexGrid control,
189-191
Font object, 372
ImageList control,
119-121
implementing values,
232-234
ListItem class, 386-387
ListView control,
170-172
Node class, 384-385
OrderItem class, 237
setting
*Multiple Document
Interface (MDI)
forms, 94*
printers, 366-368
StatusBar control,
114-116
StdFont object, 372
ToolBar control,
123-124
translating data mem-
bers into, 223
TreeView control,
168-169
validating values,
228-232
viewing, StatusBar
control, 114

Visual Basic classes,
209-211
See also specific properties
**Properties window,
Visual Basic environ-
ment, 18**
**Property Get proce-
dure, 214-215**
Property keyword, 215
**Property Let procedure,
215-216**
Property object, 263
**Property page file type,
extension for, 24**
**Property Pages dialog
box**
Color tab, 191
Font and Picture tabs,
169
opening, ImageList
control, 122
**property procedures,
implementing,
106-109**
**Property Set procedure,
216-218**
Public constants, 57
**public constants, creat-
ing, mouse cursors,
173-174**
public interfaces, 37
**Public keyword,
214-215, 222**
**public method, adding,
352**
Public procedure, 57
Public property, 107
**Public statement,
declaring variables, 56**
**Public Type, End Type
statement, defining
datatypes, 30-31**

**public variables, accessi-
bility, 209**
**PublicNotCreatable
value, 435**

Q

qty property, 237
**QueryInterface method,
448**
**QueryUnload event,
108, 323, 340**

R

Raise method, 360
Rational Rose, 425
**RecalculateTotal
method, 244**
records, 251, 263-264.
See also databases
records. *See* rows, 251
Recordset object, 263
ReDim keyword
growing names array,
33
resizing names array,
33
references
described, 37
module-level object,
releasing, 352
referential integrity, 252
Refresh method, 452
refreshing
controls, forms,
319-320
grid controls, 353

Refresh TreeView method, 383-384

Registry, viewing settings, 397

relational databases, 248

relationship argument, 385

relationships, 248

relative argument, 385

Release method, 448

releasing module-level object references, 352

RemoteItem method, 456

Remove Information About Unused ActiveX Controls check box, 402

Remove method, 239

RemoveItem method, 454

removing

  class modules, 433

  expressions, Watches window, 414

  images, 122

  records, 264

reporting errors, 347-361

repositioning

  controls, 47, 50

  focus between controls, 141-142

  forms, 50

  next statement, 416

Require Variable Declaration option, 25

required property values, implementing, 233-234

requirements, defining for projects, 39-43

resizing

  controls, 50, 175-181

  forms, 50

  names array, 33

  Product, adding code for, 160-163

  Splitter, with code, 174-179, 181

resolving reference and function problems, 436-437

Resource file type, extension for, 23

Resume keyword, 417

Retrieve method, OrderItem class, 285-286

retrieving

  data, 307-334

  objects, 335-346

  product lists, 315-316

  records, 264

return values, MsgBox, 68-69

returning flags, Order Item forms, 320-323

RichTextBox control, 160-162. *See also* **ActiveX controls**

right-click pop-up menus, adding to projects, 182-185

Rights control alignment option, 48

RightToLeft property, 75

Root property, 385

RowHeightMin property, FlexGrid control, 191

rows, 250. *See also* databases

Rows property

  FlexGrid control, 189

  setting, grid control, 196-197

run mode, 410

running

  login forms, 51-52

  Visual Basic, 12

runtime, 408-411, 414

S

s As String parameter, 229

Save command button, handling Click events, 198

Save event, handling, 153-155

Save method

  Customer class, 274-277

  OrderItem class, 284-285, 287-290

  Product class, 280

SaveSetting function, 398

saving

  data, adding persistence, 307-334

  projects, 21-22, 434

Scale properties, 373

ScaleMode property, inheritance from containers, 166

schema

  defining, 259-262

  databases, 249

scope, Get and Let
properties, 107
Scroll property,
TreeView control, 169
ScrollBars property,
190, 457
SDK. *See* software
development kit
section argument, 398
SelCount property, 456
Select Case statement,
129, 131
SELECT command,
Structured Query
Language (SQL),
255-256
Select Printer dialog
box, adding, 363-368
Selected property,
385-386, 456
SelectedImage property,
384
selecting
form icons, 45
controls
multiple, 47
Windows Common,
112
records, 264
SelectionMode prop-
erty, FlexGrid control,
190
selImage argument, 385
seqNo property, 237
servers
components, 447
Internet Information
(IIS) and Microsoft
Transaction (MTS),
432
services, 41-43, 430-432

Set property, dot nota-
tions, 107
SetFocus method, 143,
452
setting
applications to use spe-
cific projects, 442-443
column headers and
widths, 350
forms
positions of, 19
shortcut keys, 50
tab stops, 50-51
Instancing property,
435-436
next statement, 416
order information,
parameters, 244
projects, distributed
components, 437-443
properties
command button,
login forms, 71-73
Multiple Document
Interface (MDI)
forms, 94
printers, 366, 368
Rows, grid controls,
196-197
values, ColWidth
property, 196
Version Compatibility,
441-442
settings
applications, 397-399
projects, 400-403
See also specific settings
Shape control, 457
shapes of mouse, chang-
ing in Splitter forms,
176-178

Shift argument,
MouseMove event,
177
ship parameters, 244
shortcut keys, 99
described, 16
setting on forms, 51
Shortcut property, 456
Show method
arguments, Multiple
Document Interface
(MDI) child forms,
103
described, 101
showing
custom properties,
StatusBar control,
114
documents, 160-162
file properties window,
87
forms, 100-101
images, 156-159
ListView controls,
right-click pop-up
menus, 182-185
Printer Selection
dialog box, 363
Product forms, 159
Registry settings, 397
status bar messages,
118
version numbers of
projects, 87
ShowWhatsThis
method
signatures, 179
Simple Combo format,
147
SimpleText property,
115

Single datatype, supported values, 29
SingleSel property, TreeView control, 169
SingleUse value, 435
Size property, 372
sizing
columns, 138
controls, 47, 50, 158, 175-181, 350-351
forms, 50, 158
names array, 33
Product forms, adding code for, 160-163
Splitter forms with code, 174-181
SmallChange property, 455
software
adding help links to, 394-395
analysis and design, 425
components, 447
creating executables, 85-89
defining requirements, 39-41
development phases, 423-428
errors. *See* errors
event-driven, 77-81
multitiered, advantages of, 430-433
Rational Rose, 425
setting to use specific projects, 442-443
settings, 397-399
testing, 85, 420-421
three-tiered topology, 308-309

user interface (UI), 425-427
Visual Modeler, 425
See also projects
software development kit (SDK), 271
Sort property, 456
Sorted property, TreeView control, 169
Source argument, 360
source code control, 22
spacing between controls, adjusting, 49
Spc function, 375
Splitter forms, 174-181
splitting projects, distributed components, 433-437
SQL Server, Structured Query Language (SQL) support, 248
SQL. *See* Structured Query Language, 248, 271
Standard EXE projects
described, 23
creating, 43-51
running login forms, 51-52
standard modules, 54-61
Standard toolbar, 17
Start Browser with URL option, 443
Start Program option, 442
Start Program to VBFS.EXE option, 443
starting Visual Basic, 12
StartLogging method, 408

StartupPosition enumerated property, values, 194
statements
Dim, 28
If...Then, 64-65
See also specific statements; subroutines
static arrays, 33
status bar, adding procedures to display messages, 118
StatusBar controls, 113-118
StdFont object, 372
Step argument, 373
stepping through code, 418-419
Stop statement, 414
storage, persistent, 307
storing strings exceeding column sizes, 138
Stretch property, 455
StrikeThrough property, 372
String datatype, supported values, 29
String properties, 137-138
strings
connection, 267
exceeding column sizes, storing, 138
message, length of, 65
Structured Query Language (SQL), 271
commands, 253-256
relational database support, 248
Style enumerated property, 124-125

Style property
  described, 74, 115-116
  TreeView control, 168
SubItems property, 387
submenus
  adding to forms, 97-99
  editing, 96
  Horizontal Spacing, 49
  Make Same Size, 47
  Project Properties,
    85-88
  Vertical Spacing, 49
subroutines, 35. *See also*
  statements
subtotal field, adding
  label control, 191-193
support for databases
  adding to validate
    users, 293-295
  Structured Query
    Language (SQL), 248
Sybase, Structured
  Query Language
  (SQL) support, 248
syntax
  #const directive, 404
  #If directive, 404
  Add function, 389
  Add method, 240, 388
  Change event, 340-341
  Click event, 345
  DblClick event, 345
  defining connections
    strings, 267
  DELETE command,
    255
  Form Load event pro-
    cedure, 389
  GetSetting function,
    398
  INSERT command,
    253

Item method, 240
Line method, 373
Load event, 339
NodeClick event, 390
Open method, 273
Print method, 375
QueryUnload event,
  340
Remove method, 240
SELECT command,
  255
Timer event, 344
Unload event, 340
UPDATE command,
  254
System tab, color selec-
  tion dialog box, 121

T

Tab function, 375
tab order, properties, 51
tab stops, setting on
  forms, 50-51
TabIndex property, 51,
  75, 139-140, 452
tables, 249-253,
  259-262. *See also* **data-**
  bases
tabs
  Advanced
    Optimization, 403
  Buttons, 125
  Color, 191
  Compile, 87, 403
  Component, 441-442
  Debugging, 442-443
  Font, 169

General
  Project Properties dia-
    log box, 400
  StatusBar control,
    115
Make
  Project Properties dia-
    log box, 400
  setting executable
    information, 86
  settings, 88
Palette, 120
Panels, 115-116
Picture, 169
System, 121
TabStop property, 51,
  75, 140, 452
tabular data forms,
  adding, 347-349
Tag property, 76, 116,
  321, 451
taxPercent parameter,
  244
TCustomers table, 259
technologies,
  Component Object
  Model (COM), 449
Terminate event, order
  of in form life time,
  108
testing
  applications, 85,
    420-421, 428
  Customer forms, 140
text, grayed and normal,
  16
text argument, 385
text boxes, adding to
  forms, 49-50
Text property, 115
TextAlignment enumer-
  ated property, 124

TextBox, 402

TextBox controls, 134, 457

TextStyle properties, 191

three-tiered software topology, 308-309

tiers, 430

Timer control, 457

Timer event, 344

title bar, 14

title parameter, 65, 68

Title property, 392

titles of forms, changing, 45

To Grid control alignment option, 48

ToolBar controls, 123-131

toolbars, 17. *See also specific toolbars*

Toolbox, 19-20

tools

  adding help links to, 394-395

  analysis and design, 425

  components, 447

  creating executables, 85-89

  defining requirements, 39-41

  development phases, 423-428

  errors. *See* errors

  event-driven, 77-81

  multitiered, advantages of, 430-433

  Rational Rose, 425

  setting to use specific projects, 442-443

settings, 397-399

testing, 85, 420-421

three-tiered topology, 308-309

user interface (UI), 425-427

Visual Modeler, 425

  See also projects

ToolTip, 17, 410

ToolTipText property, 76, 115, 387, 452

Top property, 76

Top, Left, Height, Width property, 452

top-level menu items, adding, 97

topology

  client/server, 309

  three-tiered software, 308-309

  Windows Distributed interNet Applications Architecture (Windows DNA), 431-432

Tops control alignment option, 48

TOrder tables, 261-262

total property, 237, 242

tour of Visual Basic environment, 12-22

TProducts table, 260

translating data members into properties, 223

trapping. *See* errors, handling

tree control, 17

TreeView control, 166-169

triggering events, 101

troubleshooting reference and function problems, 436-437

turning off. *See* disabling

TUsers table, 260

twips, ColWidth property, 196

U

UDA. *See* Universal Data Access, 432

UI. *See* presentation layer; Presentation Services; user interfaces

Underline property, 372

underlined characters, 16

UNION keyword, 256

unique keys, ID as, 386

unit test, applications, 421

Universal Data Access (UDA), 432

Unload event, 108, 340

Unload statement, 64

UnloadMode argument, 323

unloads, forms, 323-324

UPDATE command, Structured Query Language (SQL), 254

updating records, 264

use case, 424

UseMaskColor property, 74, 120

user actions, close, 323-324

user interfaces (UI)
   adding objects,
      426-427
   defining requirements
      for, 41-43
   implementing, 425-426
   See also presentation
      layer; Presentation
      Services
**User-defined control
file type, extension for,
24**
UserId parameter, 273
utilities
   adding help links to,
      394-395
   analysis and design,
      425
   components, 447
   creating executables,
      85-89
   defining requirements,
      39-41
   development phases,
      423-428
   errors. *See* errors
   event-driven, 77-81
   multitiered, advantages
      of, 430-433
   Rational Rose, 425
   setting to use specific
      projects, 442-443
   settings, 397-399
   testing, 85, 420-421
   three-tiered topology,
      308-309
   user interface (UI),
      425-427
   Visual Modeler, 425
   See also projects
**Utility objects, creating,
437**

V

validating
   property values,
      228-232
   users, adding database
      support to, 293-295
Value property, 456
values
   Arrange enumerated
      property, 171
   Arrange method, 105
   buttons parameter, 66
   calculated property,
      232-233
   combining, 68
   CursorType parameter,
      276
   expressions, 62
   Flags property, 152
   FocusRect enumerated
      property, 190
   Format property, 137
   Highlight enumerated
      property, 190
   Instancing property,
      435
   Line method, 374
   LockType parameter,
      276
   MaxLength property,
      139
   property, 228-232
   required property,
      233-234
   return, MsgBox, 68-69
   setting, ColWidth
      property, 196
   StartupPosition enu-
      merated property, 194
   supported, 29

variables, 410-415
   View enumerated
      property, 170
   See also arrays; con-
      stants; functions; spe-
      cific values
variables
   creating for holding
      arrays of names, 31
   declaring, Declaration
      section, 55
   described, 28-29
   disabling event trap-
      ping, 303
   naming conventions,
      37-38
   public, accessibility,
      209
   values
      *changing while debug-
         ging, 415*
      *monitoring at run-
         time, 410-414*
   See also constants;
      datatypes
Variant datatype, 29-30
**VB App Wizard project,
23**
**VB Enterprise Edition
Controls project, 23**
**VB Wizard Manager
project, 23**
**vbAbort constants,
66-68**
**vbApplicationModal
constant, 67**
**vbAppWindows con-
stant, 323**
**vbArrangeIcons value,
105**
vbCancel constant, 68

vbCascade value, actions, 105
vbCritical constant, 66
vbDefaultButton constants, 67
vbExclamation constant, 66
vbForm constants, 323
vbFS values, 374
VBFS.MDB tables, 259-261
vbIgnore constant, 68
vbInformation constant, 66
vbMDIForm constant, 323
vbMsgBox constants, 67
vbOK constants, 66-68
vbQuestion constant, 66
vbRetry constants, 66-68
vbStartUp values, 194
vbSystemModal constant, 67
vbTaskManager constant, 323
vbTile values, actions, 105
vbYes constants, 66-68
verifying project settings for compiles, 85, 88
Version Compatibility, setting, 441-442
version numbers of projects, viewing, 87
Vertical Spacing submenu, adjusting spacing between controls, 49

View enumerated property, ListView control, 170
viewing
    custom properties, StatusBar control, 114
    documents, 160-162
    file properties window, 87
    forms, 100-101
    images, 156-159
    ListView controls, right-click pop-up menus, 182-185
    Printer Selection dialog box, 363
    Product forms, 159
    Registry settings, 397
    status bar messages, 118
    version numbers of projects, 87
Visible property, 75, 385, 452
Visual Basic Enterprise Edition, 14
Visual Basic group file type, extension for, 24
Visual Basic Learning Edition, 14
Visual Basic Professional Edition, 14
Visual Basic project file type, extension for, 24
Visual Basic Working Model Edition, 14
Visual Modeler, 425
Visual SourceSafe (VSS), 22

VScroll Bar control, 455
VSS. *See* Visual SourceSafe

W

w arguments, 378
Wait for Components to Be Created option, 442
Watches window, 410-414
Weight property, 372
WhatsThisHelpID property, 76, 452
WHERE keyword, 255
width, setting for columns, 196, 350
Width property, 76
windows
    Code, 19-20
    Editor tab, 24-25
    file properties, displaying, 87
    Form Layout, 19
    Forms, 18
    Immediate, 412-414, 417
    modal and modeless, 67
    Project Explorer, 17-18
    Properties, 18
    Watches, 410-411, 414
Windows Common controls, adding to main form, 112-113
Windows Distributed interNet Applications Architecture (Windows DNA), 431-432

Windows Explorer,
  165-173
Wise Installation, 85
WithEvents keyword,
  301-303
wizards, Package and
  Deployment, 85
WordWrap property,
  FlexGrid control, 191
Wrappable Boolean
  property, 124

X-Z

x arguments, 373, 378
X properties, 456
x, y argument,
  MouseMove event,
  177
Xor operator, 34
y arguments, 373, 378
Y properties, 456
Zorder method, 452

Get **FREE** books and more...when you register this book online for our Personal Bookshelf Program

http://register.quecorp.com/

Register online and you can sign up for our *FREE Personal Bookshelf Program...*unlimited access to the electronic version of more than 200 complete computer books—immediately! That means you'll have 100,000 pages of valuable information onscreen, at your fingertips!

Plus, you can access product support, including complimentary downloads, technical support files, book-focused links, companion Web sites, author sites, and more!

And you'll be automatically registered to receive a *FREE subscription to a weekly email newsletter* to help you stay current with news, announcements, sample book chapters, and special events, including sweepstakes, contests, and various product giveaways!

We value your comments! Best of all, the entire registration process takes only a few minutes to complete, so go online and get the greatest value going—absolutely FREE!

Don't Miss Out On This Great Opportunity!

QUE® is a brand of Macmillan Computer Publishing USA.

For more information, please visit *www.mcp.com*

CD-ROM Installation

Windows 95 Installation Instructions

1. Insert the CD-ROM disc into your CD-ROM drive.
2. From the Windows 95 desktop, double-click the My Computer icon.
3. Double-click the icon representing your CD-ROM drive.
4. Double-click the icon titled START.EXE to run the CD-ROM interface.

 Note If Windows 95 is installed on your computer and you have the AutoPlay feature enabled, the START.EXE program starts automatically whenever you insert the disc into your CD-ROM drive.

Windows NT Installation Instructions

1. Insert the CD-ROM disc into your CD-ROM drive.
2. From File Manager or Program Manager, choose Run from the File menu.
3. Type <drive>\START.EXE and press Enter, where <drive> corresponds to the drive letter of your CD-ROM. For example, if your CD-ROM is drive D:, type D:\START.EXE and press Enter. This will run the CD-ROM interface.